JACOB GREEN'S REVOLUTION

# Jacob Green's Revolution

## RADICAL RELIGION AND REFORM IN A REVOLUTIONARY AGE

S. SCOTT ROHRER

THE PENNSYLVANIA STATE UNIVERSITY PRESS
UNIVERSITY PARK, PENNSYLVANIA

Library of Congress
Cataloging-in-Publication Data

Rohrer, S. Scott, 1957– , author.
Jacob Green's revolution : radical religion and reform in a
revolutionary age / S. Scott Rohrer.
        pages   cm
Summary: "Examines the ways religion influenced reform
during the American Revolution in New Jersey. Focuses on
two pivotal figures: Jacob Green, a Presbyterian minister
who advocated revolution, and Thomas Bradbury Chandler,
an Anglican minister and a leading loyalist spokesman"—
Provided by publisher.
Includes bibliographical references and index.
ISBN 978-0-271-06421-5 (cloth : alk. paper)
ISBN 978-0-271-06422-2 (pbk. : alk. paper)
1. Green, Jacob, 1722–1790. 2. Presbyterian Church—
New Jersey—Morris County—Clergy—Biography.
3. New Jersey—History—Revolution, 1775–1783—
Biography. 4. Morris County (N.J.)—Biography.
5. New Jersey—History—Revolution, 1775–1783—
Religious aspects. 6. United States—History—
Revolution, 1775–1783—Religious aspects.
7. Calvinism—United States—History—18th century.
8. Chandler, Thomas Bradbury, 1726–1790.
I. Title.

E263.N5R64   2014
974.9'03092—dc23
[B]
2014011342

*To Jeff, David, and the Mountain Lakes gang—*
*friends from the beginning*

# Contents

# Contents

# Illustrations

# *Preface*

The journey has been a winding one—marked, as rocker Neil Young might sing, by a few devilish turns along a twisted road.

When I finished my previous book on Protestant migrations in America, I knew I wanted to return to my first love, the topic that led me to become a historian in the first place—the American Revolution. My initial idea was to study a Presbyterian community in the revolutionary era to learn what made this church such a hotbed of radicalism, and to examine how a religious community functioned during the war.

But which community? I looked no further than the place I had grown up, Morris County in northwestern New Jersey. During the Revolution, Morris was a Presbyterian-Whig stronghold that stridently backed the war and provided a safe haven to General Washington's shivering Continentals. So the initial vision was a twofer: I would return to my roots by studying a community I knew intimately, and I would probe the radicalism of Presbyterianism. And having settled on this plan, I plunged into the primary sources on revolutionary Morris County.

Jacob Green had other ideas.

As I studied the county, this remarkable man from Hanover, the largest township in Morris at the time, jumped off the pages of the sources I was exploring. A Presbyterian minister, miller, farmer, physician, teacher, bestselling author, and reformer—Jacob Green was everywhere in the primary and secondary sources. Discussions of slavery in Morris County? Green was trying to abolish this most pernicious practice. Should New Jersey declare independence in 1776? Green was arguing for it in an influential tract that sold widely. Who should represent Morris in the pivotal Provincial Congress that decided whether the colony would secede from the British Empire? Green was elected by his peers to head to Burlington. And yet there was no modern biography of this ardent revolutionary.

Biographies of the era focus mostly on the leading founders. Books on Thomas Jefferson and Patrick Henry, to name but two, could fill an entire library, and the output shows no signs of abating. Understandably, Americans are endlessly fascinated with the leading revolutionaries; these were talented and brilliant men who richly deserve the acclaim they receive. Less understood and known among the general public, however, are the Jacob Greens of the independence movement—those revolutionaries who occupied the backrooms of the founding pantheon. And once again, Green told me why someone like him is worth studying. He was all about reforming society. Fifty-four in 1776, Green had the energy of someone half his age. While other New Jerseyans were reluctant—scared, even—to take on the British, he welcomed it and was confident the Americans could win the war. Green saw the Revolution as his great chance to change society, and he offered up one of the most wide-ranging reform programs of any revolutionary, including Jefferson.

The source of this revolutionary energy was especially intriguing. It drew not from the well of the political radicalism of British intellectuals like John Trenchard and Thomas Gordon, or the Enlightenment philosophy of John Locke (although Green admired Locke and cited him in his writings). The wellspring of Green's revolutionary energy was stodgy old Calvinism, a once-dominant religious movement that was slipping into irrelevance by 1776.

*Jacob Green's Revolution: Radical Religion and Reform in a Revolutionary Age*, as a result, is about several things. On the simplest level, it is the biography of one revolutionary and his experiences before, during, and after the war. On a deeper level, the book is a microhistory that seeks to understand how religion contributed to reform during the founding years. *Jacob Green's Revolution* is a microhistory in the sense that it trains a telescope on a distant figure in the American past to illuminate how a backwoods reformer thought and acted during a time of revolutionary possibility in U.S. history. *Jacob Green's Revolution*, in other words, isn't a willy-nilly accounting of one man's life but a foray into the world of religion and revolution in early America.[1]

On a third level, *Jacob Green's Revolution* is an experiment. Traditional biographies, of course, focus on one individual. This book tries something different by mixing in a brief, alternative biography between the main chapters. The primary reason for including this second story is thematic. Religion's impact on reform during the Revolution was not uniform. Calvinism produced a reformer like Jacob Green; High Church Anglicanism produced something quite different. To demonstrate the latter and further illuminate the former, the second story sketches the life of a colorful character who was the opposite of the Presbyterian minister from Hanover. Thomas Bradbury Chandler, a conservative Anglican minister, lived a few townships over from Green and was his peer in many ways. Like Green, he was a talented writer and a deeply devout man. But unlike Green, Chandler drew quite different conclusions about reform and society from his study of God. He opposed revolution and feared democracy, and his main reform cause sought to strengthen authority. Thus, in the pages of *Jacob Green's Revolution*, two tales emerge that are meant to both entertain and enlighten readers about the revolutionary experience.

In writing this book, I am indebted to a number of people. Foremost is historian Mark A. Noll of the University of Notre Dame. Noll is the dean of American religious history, a one-man writing mill who is churning out tomes on religion and American society with stunning regularity (more than twenty-five books by last count). He also is an authority on Green's life and the Edwardseanism that undergirded it, and I am indebted to his insights throughout. Beyond all that, Noll encouraged me to write this book and gave me valuable feedback throughout the long process of producing it.

I also thank John Fea, the garrulous blogger and historian who is writing a book on Presbyterians in the American Revolution. In person and by e-mail, Fea offered a number of helpful suggestions, especially regarding the introduction and the larger questions of how to structure the book. In addition, I thank Kathryn Yahner, my editor at Penn State University Press, who was so supportive of this project and who offered excellent guidance throughout. Her critique of an earlier draft was especially telling and helpful. And I thank Craig Atwood, who helped put me in touch with Yahner when I was looking for a publishing home.

Numerous friends played a role in the book's completion. Marilyn Marks and her family provided me with a place to stay during research trips to Princeton University, where the Green family papers are stored. Despite a punishing work schedule, Steve Manson, a childhood friend from Morris County, found time to do the drawings of the Green church and parsonage, as well as one of the maps. Sally Ratigan, another childhood friend, and her family also provided lodging—and beer—during research trips to Morris County. Peter Bell, a colleague at *National Journal*, did the second map.

I thank the many libraries and archives that made their holdings available to me: the staff of the rare books and manuscripts department at Princeton University Library; Mary Robison of the Christoph Keller, Jr., Library at the General Theological Seminary in New York City; Diana Yount of the Franklin Trask Library, Andover Newton Theological School; the Library of Congress; the Morris County Public Library; Harvard University Library; the New England Historic Genealogical Society; and the Historical Society of Pennsylvania.

Last but not least, I thank the two pillars in my life—my wife, Anne, and son, Josh, who have inspired me in so many ways. The book is dedicated to my two brothers, Jeff and David, who have been so supportive of me through the years, as well as to several lifelong friends from Mountain Lakes in Morris County—Steve and Janet Manson, and Sally and Kenneth Ratigan.

Friends, all.

# Introduction

When it came to war on April 19, 1775, the fighting at Lexington Green and Concord was a clarion call for the dreamers and the reformers. At last the temporizing was ending, and committed revolutionaries saw their chance to fight for the changes in American society they believed the times demanded. Their ranks were diverse. At the top were the Whig intellectuals steeped in classical thought and the writings of British radicals like John Wilkes, men who dreamed of ending monarchical government and replacing it with a republican society populated by the virtuous. For them, the American Revolution was about self-rule and the chance to create independent governments, free of British meddling, that would solidify the elites' wealth and power. At the bottom were the masses—the seamen, the laborers, the farmers, the African Americans, the "unruly"—who saw the war as a people's revolution, a chance to establish democratic rights and create a more just society that would overthrow outdated institutions and redistribute political and economic power. For these legions of people, the Revolution was about creating a better, more prosperous life.[1]

The sources of revolutionary energy were thus quite broad, and they were fed by streams flowing from vertiginous places. One such stream was from a particularly out-of-the-way place. In the Watchung Mountains of northwestern New Jersey, a backwoods reformer pursued a revolutionary program as ambitious as anything Thomas Paine could dream up. Yet he hardly fit the image of a revolutionary. He was unassuming and shy, and fairly old by the standards of revolution—fifty-three in 1775. Home was not the august halls of Williamsburg or the smoky parlor of a Boston tavern but a modest parish house in Hanover, New Jersey. He was not an erudite lawyer or an angry rioter but a quiet man of the cloth who preached discipline and obedience to God. Even after spending years in the pulpit as a Presbyterian minister, he was uncomfortable appearing before crowds of people and was an uninspiring public speaker. Bad nerves and bouts of melancholia undermined his health.

His pen, however, hinted at no such weakness, and this revolutionary brought to his task the penetrating eye of a critic who questioned not only British but American society. To an official in London reading his influential 1776 tract advocating independence, he was a troublemaker and a radical. To a slave owner in the Mid-Atlantic perusing his letters on liberty advocating a just society and denouncing slavery, he was a menace to good order. Jacob Green, a radical? He would have denied such a thing. When elected to the New Jersey Provincial Congress in May 1776, he went reluctantly and resigned his post within six weeks, as soon as decorum allowed. He scurried home to Hanover, to his library and his pulpit.

Jacob Green's concerns were wider than taxation and representation (although, as a good Whig, he was concerned with both those things). Green wanted the rebelling Americans to abolish slavery, broaden democratic rights, reform the currency, and establish a fairer, almost communistic economic system that would give the downtrodden a fighting chance to succeed against the wellborn. Most ambitiously, he wanted a society that would be defined not by materialism and self-interest but by devotion to God and the common good. And he saw the American Revolution as his chance to achieve these ambitious goals, despite the numerous failings of the American people that he perceived and publicly lamented. In pursuing such a broad and idealistic reform agenda, Jacob Green was hardly alone; the American Revolution, as is well-known, produced its share of dreamers throughout the thirteen colonies.[2]

The particularly interesting fact about Green's reform drive, as this book will fully explore, was its source: it stemmed not from Whig philosophy or Lockean principles—the famous "contagion of liberty" that inspired so many colonists to revolt—but from his religious beliefs, specifically his Calvinism and the tenets he derived from the complex thought of Jonathan Edwards.[3] Under assault from many quarters (including Enlightenment scientists and rationalists), Calvinism was a tired and harried religious movement by 1776, with many contemporaries seeing it as a barrier to reform and the improvement of society. Founded in the sixteenth century by John Calvin (1509–1564) during the early days of the Protestant Reformation, Calvinism dominated the intellectual thought of western Europe for the next three centuries, a domination resting on the simplest of premises—God preordained who was saved and who was not. In their rejection of Catholic conceptions of good works, indulgences, and purgatory, Calvin's predestinarian teachings built on the insights of Augustine and Luther. Protestant reformers of the sixteenth century maintained that humans were incapable of lifting themselves up from their fallen states through acts of charity and good works. They especially rejected the idea that someone could "buy" salvation through timely gifts to the church. The definitive statement on this heretical notion came from the great Protestant reformer Martin Luther: under his justification by faith, God grants salvation to those who believe. Calvin's followers then pushed the implication of Luther's theory to its logical extreme: God alone does the granting—good behavior cannot earn someone salvation; a person cannot "work" his or her way to eternal bliss. Moreover, in this Calvinistic schemata, an all-powerful God can see far into the future and know ahead of time what will happen because he has preordained the course of events, including who will be saved and who will be damned.[4]

From the beginning, Calvin's teachings on predestination had their critics, who recoiled against the doctrine's inherent cruelty: *God decides ahead of time who will* not *be saved, and there's nothing a person can do to keep from spending eternity in hell?* One such critic was Henry VIII, the philandering English king who broke away from Rome in the late 1530s and anointed himself head of his country's church. Under Calvinism, Henry wondered, where was the incentive to do good—to pursue reforms that would benefit society? Why should anyone behave morally and justly if good behavior did not matter? If bad behavior were preordained? While Henry agreed with Luther and Calvin that the Catholic Church had become a corrupt institution and that indulgences were wrong, he felt the reformers had gone too far in the other direction by seemingly dismissing all acts of charity. In Henry's mind, salvation would be determined only after a final accounting at the Day of Judgment when a person dies.[5]

Richard Hooker (1554–1600), the renowned English theologian during Queen Elizabeth's reign, expounded on Henry's critique: telling someone that her fate was determined before she was born and that she must follow the path laid out by God dampened the motivation for individuals to act morally. Hooker argued, instead, that reason was a gift of God, as was free will. It was up to individuals whether they wanted to do good, or bad—whether they wanted to spend their time in taverns or helping to feed and clothe the hungry and the homeless. Like Henry VIII, Hooker believed that good works played an important role in human society, and he constructed a comprehensive theological system built on reason and order that allowed for a far larger scope of human choice and action than Calvinism supposedly allowed.[6]

These challenges, which in essence called into question whether Calvinism could be an agent for the reform of individuals and ultimately society, were only the beginning. Scientists during the Enlightenment were chipping away at Calvinism from another direction by slowly unraveling the mysteries of nature and the cosmos, thanks to, among other things, the invention of the microscope and the telescope. Scientists' discoveries were raising uncomfortable questions about both the Bible and God's powers. *Was the Bible really an accurate accounting of human history? How do you explain its inconsistencies? Did God really control all? Or was free will paramount? Was God's divine power behind the workings of nature, or were other forces responsible?* The spirit of scientific inquiry brought a new, Baconian way of thinking that challenged researchers to analyze phenomena—and the Bible—based on evidence and observation, not on blind faith. The resulting skepticism brought renewed scrutiny to a sixteenth-century religious coda resting on the doctrine of predestination, and this skepticism produced what Peter J. Thuesen, a historian of Jonathan Edwards's thought, terms Enlightenment latitude—"a new skepticism [after 1725] about rigid orthodoxies and a growing indifference toward old doctrinal confidence." One result of this Enlightenment latitude was "a growing confidence in human ability and [it] entailed a strong interest in natural religion." Deists exemplified the new skepticism most forcefully: God created the universe, they said, but he then sat back and watched his handiwork unfold. It was up to man to act, and it was man who was responsible for his actions—not his creator.[7]

Thus, to its contemporary critics, Calvinism was a dour philosophy that stifled human initiative and ultimately dampened the reform drive in human society. Some modern historians looking at the religious underpinnings of the American Revolution have seen Calvinism in the same light. In Bernard Bailyn's telling, enlightened Whig thinkers "felt that it was precisely the heavy crust of custom that was weighing down the spirit of man; they sought to throw it off [during the American Revolution] and to create by the unfettered power of reason a framework of institutions superior to the accidental inheritance of the past." At the opposite end of these forward-looking, enlightened Whigs of the 1770s were "covenant theologians"—Calvinists and Puritans—who "contin[ued] to assume the ultimate inability of man to improve his condition by his own powers." For Nathan O. Hatch, the great energy unleashed by the Revolution came from evangelical upstarts like the Baptists and the Methodists; ministers who "clung to an undiluted Edwardsean theology, the authority of ordained clergymen, and the necessity of church discipline" were out of step with the emerging democratic ethos. Calvinism, in other words, was an intellectual shackle that kept its practitioners from embracing both the scientific advances of the age and the revolutionary opportunities afforded by the crisis with Great Britain.[8]

Adherents of Calvinism mounted a vigorous defense through the years, and this counteroffensive began with Calvin himself. While conceding that predestination could be seen as cruel and uncaring, he asserted that the doctrine was nevertheless indisputable because of God's unlimited power and majesty. "No one can deny," Calvin wrote, "that God foreknew the future final fate of man before He created him, and that He foreknew it because it was appointed by His own decree." God was sovereign, Calvin reminded his followers, and man was utterly and completely dependent on him. The "elect" could look forward to salvation; the "reprobates" to eternal flames. Such an answer certainly did not quiet Calvin's critics, and legions of theologians took up the task of defending Calvinism's conception of God's power. One of the most prolix was English writer William Prynne, who reiterated in 1629 "that God from eternity hath freely of his own accord, chosen out of mankinde a certaine select number of men, which can neither be augmented nor diminished; whom he doth effectually call, save, and bring to glory."[9]

More ambitiously, others denied that Calvinism ignored good works and reform. One English sermon delivered in 1592 maintained "that whether a man be predestinate or no, yet he should live so much as may be in a holy obedience . . . for he that hath that hope that he is one of God's sons doth purify himself, and being a vessel of honor must keep himself fair and clear for the use of his Master, being sanctified and prepared unto every good work." A 1579 catechism that was included with the English version of the Geneva Bible provided an even clearer answer to the question of why, under predestination, anyone should do good: "Good work is a testimony of the spirit of God, which is given to the elect only." In other words, performing good works was a way to show the world that you were not a reprobate, that you were, indeed, one of the chosen. This insight became a key tenet of faith for generations of Calvinists—from parliamentarians in 1620s England to Congregationalists in 1740s Massachusetts. Calvinism, they insisted, did not dampen moral behavior; it encouraged it.[10]

Defenders of Calvinism in the eighteenth century, however, had an even tougher task than did their sixteenth-century predecessors. The Enlightenment was a mature movement by the 1750s, and Richard Hooker's assertion that reason and free will were gifts of God had gained a wide following. Calvinists of Jonathan Edwards's generation had to reconcile reason and religion, free will and God's omnipotence. One who took up this daunting challenge was English theologian Isaac Watts. "Man is an intellectual and sociable Being," he asserted in a 1747 tract. "Human Reason is the first Ground and Spring to all human Religion. Man is obliged to Religion because he is a reasonable Creature. Reason directs and obliges us not only to search out and practice the Will of God, as far as natural Conscience will lead us, but also to examine, receive, and obey, all the Revelations which come from God."[11]

Like Watts, the brilliant American theologian Jonathan Edwards (1703–1758) did not deny the power of reason or the importance of science. True free will, he agreed, meant the ability to do what one chose to do. But while popular conceptions of free will were nebulous, even incoherent, Edwards carefully defined the term—people acted within the confines that God laid out for them. In other words, a wise and beneficent creator granted individuals a range of actions. That argument, in turn, rested on a deeper insight that undergirded Edwards's defense of Calvinism. Critics like Henry VIII said predestination was a cruel doctrine; Edwards countered that God was not cruel—he was not capricious or petty or vindictive. He was loving and good and kind, a benevolent deity who wielded his immense power wisely. Edwards's God was also clever. To explain the existence of evil and to account for the scientific advances of the age, Edwards posited that God governed the universe through multiple means: he established laws of nature for inanimate things—the laws that scientists were uncovering during the Enlightenment. But for humans, God governed with a somewhat looser hand, endowing his most important creation with reason and implanting within them free will and something called moral necessity: people were responsible for their actions. In his greatness, God allowed individuals the power to choose within the limits that God decreed. Thus, for Edwards, Calvinism did not undercut moral agency. It actually heightened it because of God's loving greatness and human free will—God gave the elect good hearts, and these chosen ones *wanted* to do good for the glory of God. They wanted, in other words, to live godly lives, to improve themselves and society. That was their Christian mandate as God's elect.[12]

Jacob Green was fascinated by this debate and followed it closely. In the early 1740s, as a farm boy soaking up the heady intellectual atmosphere of college life in Cambridge, Massachusetts, he began questioning his faith as he struggled to understand all the ramifications of Calvinism. Raised in New England in a Congregationalist household, Green at first accepted Calvinism without questioning it. Then he was intellectually whipsawed by several events: the historic revivals of 1740–41 during the Great Awakening helped lead to his rebirth and a recommitment to Calvinism, before exposure to the Enlightenment during his classwork at Harvard College had him again questioning his predestinarian beliefs. As he readied to leave Cambridge in 1744 after graduating, Green confessed to a classmate that he was thoroughly confused about Calvinism and did not know how to reconcile all its paradoxes. Not surprisingly, Green was easily unmoored from his Calvinistic beliefs by ministers with "Arminian" leanings when he arrived in New Jersey in 1745. Still unsure what to think as he settled into the ministry, Green retreated to his study to explore the writings of Isaac Watts and Jonathan Edwards and to ponder the great questions that were so frustrating him.[13]

Green's subsequent journey into the thicket of Calvinism and Arminianism (the doctrine asserting that salvation is open to all) was telling and fascinating, for it helps us to see how contemporaries grappled with the conundrum that King Henry raised back in the 1540s: how could Calvinism spur men and women to act morally, to do good for themselves and for society?

The answer to this question is the central concern of *Jacob Green's Revolution: Radical Religion and Reform in a Revolutionary Age*, albeit with an American twist: how did Calvinism (and specifically an Edwardsean version of it) produce such a strong reform drive during the American Revolution? The book's main subject is a reformer, theologian, and writer who was thrust into New Jersey revolutionary politics in spring 1776 when he published an influential tract called *Observations on the Reconciliation of Great-Britain* that urged wavering colonists to declare independence. The tract was so well received in the middle colonies that it led to Green's election to the Provincial Congress that cast New Jersey's lot with the rebelling colonists; it also led to his selection as the chairman of the committee that wrote New Jersey's first constitution as an independent state.[14]

Green was born in Malden, Massachusetts, near Boston, in 1722, the son of a struggling farmer who died a year after Jacob's birth. His mother and uncles who raised Green tried to teach him a trade or to steer him to farming, but this serious youth with a love of books had other ideas. Despite limited financial resources, Green managed to enroll in Harvard, where his great intellectual journey began and where he was exposed to not only books of the Enlightenment but also the evangelical world of George Whitefield and Gilbert Tennent. About a year after graduation, when a job offer from Whitefield fell through, Green found himself in New Jersey, where he became a minister for the Presbyterian congregation in Hanover, a farming community about twenty-six miles west of New York City. Despite his feelings of inadequacy, Green's talents and energies quickly began to emerge, as he aggressively led the Presbyterian congregation and worked as a farmer, miller, teacher, and physician. His intellectual prowess, as well as his connections in New Jersey Presbyterianism, secured him a seat on the College of New Jersey's board of trustees, and he served briefly as college president after the death of his mentor, Jonathan Edwards.[15]

From a variety of sources, including a thorough examination of biblical history and Edwards's *Freedom of the Will*, Green in the 1750s developed his ideas on Calvinism, free will, reason, and the church that, when mixed in with his Lockean understanding of politics and the cauldron that was the American Revolution, undergirded his ambitious reform efforts. For Green, the central concern in his sermons and various writings was, why act morally? Why should anyone—saved or unsaved—perform good works? In painstaking detail over four decades, Green laid out his answers.

The key issue for him—one that was fraught with political implications for the governing of society—was the need to create stronger and purer churches. While some reformers trying to smooth out Calvinism's rough edges were arguing that the church should become more inclusive by allowing more people, even the reprobate, to join, Green was taking an opposite tack. Churches, he maintained, should be *raising* standards, permitting only the elect to be full members and to partake in the sacraments. And to become full members, Green explained, applicants needed to show they were among the saved; they needed to show they were performing good works and living exemplary lives. Thus Green's most important crusade in the years before the Revolution was to purify the church. From this core interest flowed, magma-like, his broader causes—to improve religiosity, he needed to improve the behavior of individuals and society.

Green's reform regime emerged in stages over three decades. In the late 1760s, he first wrote a series of tracts for a learned audience, primarily theologians, that argued his case for creating a pure church and why it was so important to religion and society. In 1770, he took his cause to the general public, publishing a best-selling pamphlet called *A Vision of Hell* that lampooned the materialism and selfishness of contemporary society. Using illustrations by Paul Revere of Boston fame, *A Vision of Hell* was a brilliant satire that poked fun at a wide-ranging group of targets—from less-than-devout ministers to sybaritic merchants and Sabbath-ignoring farmers who cared more about the state of their crops than the state of their souls.[16]

The revolutionary crisis of the 1770s presented Pastor Green with a new set of opportunities and headaches. This Calvinist saw the arrival of war as preordained and a God-given opportunity to achieve the changes in society Green believed were needed. The crisis of war would force Americans to work harder and to put the good of society ahead of their selfish private interests, he reasoned. And the ethos of liberty had the potential to sweep away another dark cloud hovering over the landscape—the holding of Africans in slavery. However, the Revolution's emphasis on liberty and freedom of choice presented a special challenge for Green and other American Calvinists. *How do you reconcile liberty with divine control? How much freedom does God give a person? Just how controlling is he?* Moreover, *how do you maintain Christian order and improve religiosity in an era of freedom and liberty?*[17]

Green's answer was sophisticated and, at first blush, paradoxical. In the late 1770s and early 1780s, he began to preach the virtues of voluntarism and the need for granting more rights to laymen. Yet, at the same time, he also preached the need for greater discipline and for maintaining high standards in church and among the devout. Green resolved this inherent paradox— greater discipline during an era of greater freedom—by giving people a choice. They could work hard, show they were of the elect, and commit to the church—or not. It was up to them whether to act righteously or sinfully, but when they decided to join, they had to truly commit to the high standards Jacob Green was demanding.

The doctrine of the covenant helped Green reconcile his political and religious views. God, he reasoned, entered into a covenantal relationship with chosen individuals (the predestined "elect"), and it was up to these individuals to respond to his offer of salvation. No one could be coerced into grace; it could only be freely offered by God and freely accepted by man. Melding his knowledge of Lockean political philosophy with his Edwardsean thought (which stressed free choice within the bounds set by God), Green in the 1770s increasingly viewed the laity as constituting the real church—the moral authority of the congregation rested on individual believers. When one was of the elect, he or she was on an equal footing with the church's minister. Such equality gave the laity a great say in the running of their congregation. Equally important was the covenant's contribution to his conceptions of liberty. Green increasingly believed in voluntary associations of like-minded believers who joined of their own free accord. By 1780, liberty for him had come to mean the liberty to choose—within the dictates of God's mandate to act morally. He not only opposed any kind of religious establishment, he also argued that "every man . . . [should] be encouraged to think and judge for himself in matters of religion." No one, in other words, should be forced to join a church or to partake in the sacraments.[18]

In the 1770s, Green grasped the direction that American society was heading, and he was an early proponent of laymen's rights and of Jeffersonian democracy before it even existed. In the late 1770s, he wrote two letters on liberty that extolled independent yeomen and tradesmen as the bedrocks of a democratic society. Green disdained the rich and decried their excessive influence on the body politic. During the war, he broadened his rebellion against the king to the American Presbyterian Church because he saw the Synod of New York and Philadelphia as high-handed and imperious. Green opposed the centralizing trend in the church and wanted power to rest with individual congregations and their laymen. This belief led him in 1779 to secede from the Presbyterian Church—a decade *before* the American church approved a stronger, centralizing, federalist-style constitution—and to direct an independence movement resting on the creation of associated presbyteries, which were voluntary associations of like-minded churches that pursued a congregational system of Presbyterianism. Green was also out front on democratizing education. As early as 1770, he was calling for changes in how ministers were educated and ordained; Green wanted less emphasis placed on formal education and more on evangelical values—in other words, a fairer and more democratic system. He wanted the ministry opened to more people, all in an effort to create a more nimble Presbyterian Church that could meet the needs of a democratic, frontier society.

In these diverse ways, Jacob Green's attempts to reconcile Calvinism during the revolutionary era fostered an activist, democratic faith that led him to undertake an extremely ambitious reform program that had both secular and religious components. To fully understand just how radical Green's Calvinism was, *Jacob Green's Revolution* tells a *second* story. High Church Anglicanism and its values of sacramental ceremony, conformity, and obedience to the state were polar opposites of Green's Edwardsean and democratic values. Thus this second story, told as vignettes between the main chapters, focuses on another New Jersey minister, Thomas Bradbury Chandler, who lived about twenty miles from Green in Elizabeth Town.

Chandler was one of the most colorful—and hated—American members of the English church, who was despised by Presbyterians and Congregationalists because of *his* main reform cause: the effort to bring an Anglican bishop to American shores (fig. 1). Chandler's mentor was not a Calvinist like Jonathan Edwards but Samuel Johnson, the conservative theologian, royalist, and first president of King's College in New York City, and Chandler built his conservatism on the scaffolding of Johnson's High Church Anglicanism. Inferiors owed their superiors loyalty and obedience; they especially owed allegiance to their church and king. The threshold for rebellion, in Chandler's mind, was high, and the colonists had not met it. With fierce, biting sarcasm, he turned Whig arguments on their head by denouncing the Continental Congress as tyrannical and corrupt, and he warned that breaking away from Great Britain would prove suicidal for the American people.

The differences with Green went beyond crystalline ones over reform; they extended to their worldviews arising from their religious principles. Besides improving the church's administrative efficiency, Chandler believed the episcopal office was a linchpin of a properly functioning society where hierarchy and monarchy would reign. Traditional English society with its social gradations and elaborate governmental system thrilled Chandler, and he wanted it replicated in British North America. Bringing bishops to America was one way he would accomplish this goal. Jacob Green strongly disagreed with Chandler's worldview. He rejected episcopacy, believing it was unbiblical and unnecessary. Moreover, as he made clear in his 1776 tract, Green detested the British system with its hierarchical ranking of power and its multitude of offices; he derided the system as undemocratic and financially reckless—lordly offices such as the bishoprics cost money, required oppressive taxation to support, and were meddlesome in the laity's affairs. Bishops and High Church councils should *not* be running things, according to Green; the people in their congregations should. For these reasons and

*Fig. 1*   A portly man with a prickly personality, Thomas Bradbury Chandler was never one to mince words. In 1775, the Sons of Liberty drove him into exile. Yale University Art Gallery, Gift of Clarence Winthrop Bowen, B.A. 1873, M.A. 1876, Ph.D. 1882.

more, Green wanted the thirteen colonies to declare independence and establish their own nation.

Besides providing a stark contrast in the ministers' reform drives and worldviews, Chandler's story is included for two other reasons. One is to break free from the limitations of the traditional biographical format, which focuses on one individual, by employing a narrative technique commonly found in novels. That is, in telling a main story of reform and revolution, *Jacob Green's Revolution* mixes in a backstory of an Anglican loyalist whose experiences in the Revolution were 180 degrees from that of a Calvinistic patriot. Thus the dueling stories better capture the variety of revolutionary experience than would a traditional biography of one man.

The second reason for Chandler's inclusion is that the two men lived eerily parallel lives. Both were raised in the insular world of New England Congregationalism (Green, who was born in 1722, was from Massachusetts; Chandler, who was born in 1726, was from Connecticut). Green was the product of a humble family, Chandler a wealthy one. Both graduated from college (Green at Harvard, Chandler at Yale). Both arrived in New Jersey within two years of each other, settled nearby in places that reflected their personalities (Green in anodyne Hanover, Chandler in stately Elizabeth Town), and became ministers (Green reluctantly for the Presbyterian faith, Chandler enthusiastically for the Anglican) (map 1). Both were talented writers with wildly different styles (Green wrote, and spoke, in a susurration, Chandler in a shout). Both possessed wildly different personalities— Chandler was garrulous, socially outgoing, quick tempered; Green was reserved, shy, disciplined. Both died in 1790 within a few weeks of each other (Green in May, Chandler in June). Both possessed towering intellects and were shaped by Puritan culture and the Enlightenment, and both became acclaimed figures in New Jersey's revolutionary drama—Green for the rebelling colonists, Chandler for the king. It was Jacob Green in 1776 who helped persuade reluctant New Jerseyans to back independence by writing a well-regarded tract advocating separation from the king, and it was Thomas Bradbury Chandler who helped rally loyalists against the coming rebellion.[19]

And, of course, both were aggressive reformers. Green's lifelong dream was to create a stronger, purified church; Chandler's was to create a stronger *state* church. From Green's desire to create a purified church flowed a bewildering, almost vertiginous, array of causes that ranged from curbing the acquisitive impulses of Americans to outlawing slavery. Chandler's vision was narrower but powerful in its own right. Laser-like, he focused on strengthening the Church of England in the colonies, and that meant trying to bring a bishop to American shores—an unpopular cause among American Whigs suspicious of British power and intentions. No shrinking violet, Chandler fought tenaciously for an American episcopate despite violent opposition from the likes of Sam Adams, and he became the leading Anglican in

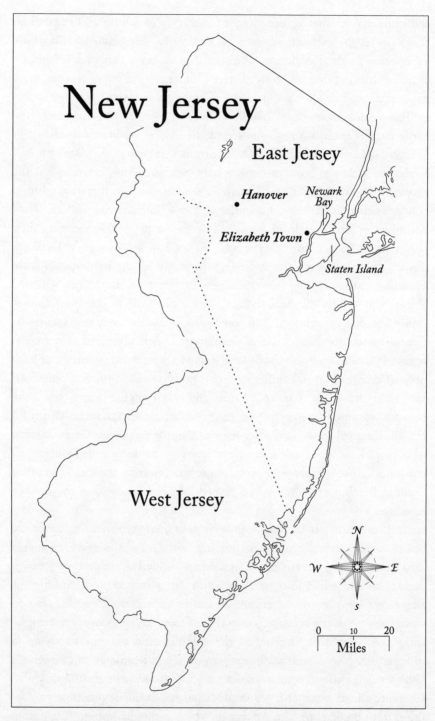

New Jersey

East Jersey

Hanover

Newark
Bay

Elizabeth Town

Staten Island

West Jersey

N

W        E

S

0     10     20
Miles

*Map 1*   Hanover and Elizabeth Town. Map by Stephen Manson.

the northern colonies as he strove to make the king's church relevant in America.[20]

The opening section of *Jacob Green's Revolution*, "The Worlds of Jacob Green and Thomas Bradbury Chandler," describes the two ministers' early lives and their intellectual development in the years leading up to the revolutionary drama. The second section, "Revolutionary Thinkers and the Trials of War," explores the drama of war and how it related to their reform regimes—Green's effort to foster revolution and shape it; Chandler's attempt to oppose it and his decision to flee to London in 1775. The final section, "Reformers on the Home Front," looks in greater depth at their reform causes during the long and frustrating war years. An epilogue tells the stories of the two men's deaths and examines their reform legacies in the new republic.

In concocting a dueling story of religion and reform during the revolutionary era, two important subthemes emerge. One is the importance of the Mid-Atlantic to Green's and Chandler's reform causes. The weakness of the English church in New Jersey and the Mid-Atlantic made Chandler obsessive about bringing a bishop to America, because he felt a strong leader was needed if the church was to successfully take on the numerous dissenting churches in the region (and for that very reason, dissenters opposed a bishop; they wanted to keep the king's church—and the king himself—weak and ineffectual in New England and the middle colonies).

For Green, geography was more complicated. He lived in Morris County, a Presbyterian–Whig stronghold that enthusiastically backed the war and became a haven for George Washington's beleaguered Continental troops during the Revolution. With the exception of the slavery issue, the county was a safe base for him that helped foster his radicalism. But New Jersey itself had a sizable population of neutrals and loyalists. The colony's reluctance to enter the fray and commit to independence in the mid-1770s forced Green to leave the safety of his pulpit and to enter politics. Then, when war arrived, New Jersey's dangerously central position in the fighting helped him to see the "glorious cause" in all its majesty and folly. The insights he gained from observing the independence movement so up close and personal informed his views and inspired him to write essays on, among other things, liberty and finance. Taken together, the experiences of Jacob Green and Thomas Bradbury Chandler tell a tale about a region that receives far less attention in the literature than does New England and the South.[21]

A second subtheme is the slippery nature of defining conservatism and radicalism during a tumultuous time in Western history, when the Enlightenment was making rapid strides in overturning traditional norms, Calvinism was struggling to remain relevant, and political revolutions were engulfing America and France. Who was a "conservative" and a "radical" may seem obvious, but the lives of Jacob Green and Thomas Bradbury Chandler show that this was not quite so. In seeking to make Calvinism a force in society after years of attack, Green was "conservative" in an important sense—he was trying to defend a traditional movement and its centuries-long view of moral agency. From the pulpit, this stern Calvinistic minister could be found railing against immoral behavior; Green decried the bibulous and the licentious in the strongest terms possible. To modern ears, Green was quite the crank and killjoy. But, of course, he was "radical" in other ways, pushing for voluntarism and democratic rights, and arguing for a fairer economic system where all could reap the rewards of hard work. Others might view Calvinism as an anachronism and a philosophy best relegated to the sixteenth century; Jacob Green did not. This "conservative" also embraced Lockean political principles and was sympathetic to the rationalism of the Enlightenment despite the huge threat it posed to his Calvinistic beliefs. Green's great tract in 1776 advocating revolution was as "radical" as anything from the pens of other American Whigs. Chandler's views were not so muddied as Green's, but he too could be hard to pigeonhole at times. Chandler was so consumed with bringing bishops to America that he was pushing for a strong state church that even Anglicans in England had rejected since the Glorious Revolution of 1688. In this sense, Chandler was more backward-looking than Green was with his defense of Calvinism. And, of course, Chandler was the epitome of a conservative in his love of traditional society, and of order and hierarchy. Thomas Bradbury Chandler did not like change, and he did not like democracy. Nor did he trust the masses; Jacob Green did. Throughout all his writings, Chandler was fighting to preserve contemporary society from an emerging liberalism. But Chandler was something of a radical in his embrace of reason and in his intuitive understanding that creating the pure church that Green envisioned was folly. He sided with power and a strong central government, two very modern notions. Thus Chandler, in this one area, was more of a realist and was more forward-looking than Green was.

The book's subtitle has its ironies as well—was Calvinism really a "radical religion"? Many would argue no, for all the reasons given above, but a number of historians of religion would answer yes. Keith L. Griffin, for instance, details in his book on *Religion and Revolution* all the ways that rebellion against a tyrannical ruler was justified under the Reformed Protestant tradition, and he maintains that Calvinism and other Reformed traditions were inherently radical. So did Alan Heimert in his famous, and hotly disputed, *Religion and the American Mind*: in complex ways, Calvinists stimulated the democratic movement that resulted in the American Revolution. To Heimert, Jonathan Edwards and his fellow Calvinists were the radicals, the liberal "rationalist" Whigs the conservatives.[22]

Another irony relating to the subtitle was Presbyterianism itself. Was the Presbyterian Church to which Green belonged radical? The British had long believed it was, because of the power the church accorded to the laity; in the 1630s and 1640s, Charles I, for one, railed against the Presbyterian system, worrying that it fostered democracy and encouraged sedition and thus posed a threat to the Crown. His counterparts in the eighteenth century were equally fearful of Presbyterianism, fuming over the church's strong support for the American rebellion. Jacob Green, ironically, would answer no—the church was not democratic enough for his tastes, and he lambasted both the church's synods and the General Assembly as dictatorial. In a final irony, the Revolution that the American Presbyterian Church backed so wholeheartedly unleashed a series of changes that by 1800 had the church looking quite unrevolutionary compared with the surging Baptists and Methodists (who were seen as pro-British during the war): it still insisted on an educated ministry, "clung" to its Calvinistic ways (to cite Nathan Hatch's phrase), sometimes downplayed emotional religion popular with evangelicals, and was slow to expand to the frontier.

In the end, the verdict on the question of radicalism should be readily apparent in *Jacob Green's Revolution*. The book takes the reader on a journey through the Enlightenment and a revolutionary age, focusing on an obscure but paradoxical man who embraced both the harshness of Calvinism and the soaring democratic hopes of the American Revolution.

# PART I

The Worlds of Jacob Green and
Thomas Bradbury Chandler

# 1

*Student*

The journey from Stoneham, Massachusetts, to Cambridge carried Jacob Green past the familiar scenes of his childhood—the farmsteads and weathered houses of Stoneham, the rocky pastures, woodlands, and hills of Malden (map 2). Spurring his horse southward in the summer heat, down the narrow lanes and rutted roads that permeated the New England countryside, he crossed the Malden and Mystic Rivers and turned west toward his destination. It was a short and easy ride in some ways, a mere nine miles over well-traveled roads that ran near Charlestown and Boston.

But, of course, in another important sense, the journey was anything but easy. Serious and hardworking—dour, even—Jacob Green remained a callow youth in 1740 as he readied to take his place among the elite of Harvard College: shy among strangers, afraid to speak in public, unsure about his plans and prospects. His father was long dead. His family was neither prominent nor rich, and his home of late was Stoneham, a hardscrabble farming community that enjoyed none of the success, prestige, or wealth of a Boston or Salem. His intellectual journey over the next four years would prove to be equally challenging; exposure to the Enlightenment and the Great Awakening had him fretting over his Calvinism in 1744, the year of his graduation.

When Jacob arrived in Cambridge on that August day in 1740, his lack of social standing became painfully evident. Harvard ranked him next to last in the thirty-three-member freshman class of 1744, one spot above James

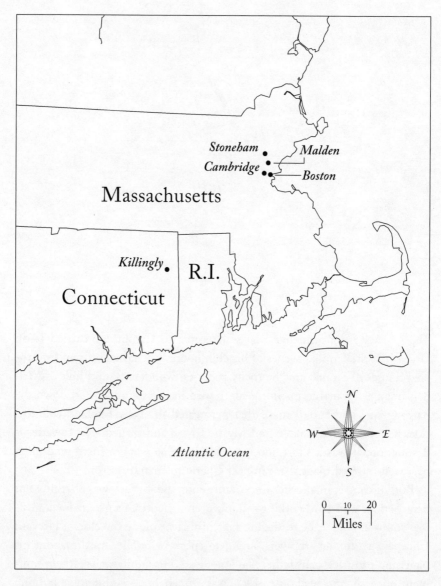

*Map 2*   Jacob Green's New England. Map by Peter Bell.

Welman of Lynn, Massachusetts, the son of a yeoman farmer who could afford Harvard only because of the beneficence of his pastor, Stephen Chase. At the top was Samuel Welles; a mere fifteen years old upon his entry to Harvard, he was the eldest son of a wealthy and respected merchant in Boston who owned a wharf and sat on the colony's Province Council. Thomas

Cushing, who went on to become a lieutenant governor of Massachusetts, was ranked fourth. His family boasted a coat of arms, a father who served as a justice of the peace, and a grandfather-merchant who built the family fortune. The Greens possessed none of these things.[1]

Jacob was a farm boy. He was born on February 2, 1722, in Malden, an agricultural village some eight miles north of Boston. He was named after a father he never got to know. In 1723, Jacob the elder died of "a nervous fever," in the son's words, when Jacob was about eighteen months old. How this loss affected Jacob is impossible to know but he surely felt his absence keenly. In his autobiography Jacob avoided the topic, keeping his description of his father to twelve words and coldly stark: "My father's name was Jacob Green, the youngest son of Henry Green."[2]

With his father dead, the task of raising Jacob fell to his mother, Dorothy Lynde Green, and a large family circle—primarily three uncles and his four older sisters. This circle of kin encompassed not only the Green clan but also the Lyndes and the Barret family, whom Dorothy married into after the death of her husband. The Lyndes and Greens were especially close; Jacob's mother was the daughter of Captain John Lynde and Elizabeth Hills, who was the widow of William Green. Dorothy's sister Martha married into the Green family a few years after Dorothy did, while years earlier Nathan Lynde had married Lydia Green.[3]

The Greens were a thoroughly conventional family of middling Puritan farmers who resided in middling Puritan towns. Jacob's grandfather Henry was descended from Thomas Green, the Puritan forebearer, who was the first in the family to arrive on America's shores. Henry had eight children; Jacob's father, who was born in 1689, was the youngest. The Green men worked as farmers and craftsmen—Henry was a weaver, and Jacob's uncles pursued an assortment of crafts. But farming was the main family occupation, and land was their most prized possession. They hoarded it and swapped it, and these farmsteads enabled them to keep their family together. Jacob's father inherited Henry's main farm, as well as a lot that was behind an uncle's house. The elder Jacob's siblings also got farms, all bordering various Greens.[4]

Malden, as a result, served as the geographical center of the Green family. Various branches clustered in the town's northwestern section, where their farms formed an arc between Ell Pond and the Reading town line. Greens, Lyndes, and Barrets could also be found in Stoneham and Leicester, as well as Killingly, Connecticut. Jacob, who primarily lived in Malden and Stoneham, was to get to know all four places during a peripatetic childhood.[5]

As modest as their economic circumstances were, the Greens did achieve some prominence in town and church affairs—Henry served as a lieutenant in the militia and held several public offices, including moderator of Malden's town meeting and a selectman in the town government. Jacob's uncle Daniel, whom Jacob lived with for a year, was a town selectman and a deacon in Stoneham's congregational church, a position of prestige and importance in Puritan communities.[6]

One reason for the vagabond existence was Dorothy's marriage to John Barret of Malden in the mid-1720s. The marital union enlarged Jacob's circle of kinship—the couple went on to have three children of their own—and presumably brought additional support from the new brood of step-siblings, aunts, uncles, and cousins. But the marriage also meant upheaval: Dorothy and John moved to Killingly in eastern Connecticut in 1729 or so, and Jacob left Malden for a time. Because the Barrets were not wealthy, Dorothy sent Jacob to live with various uncles after he turned fourteen, and he endured long absences from his mother, with one separation lasting two years.[7]

Jacob apparently was not close to his stepfather. In his autobiography, he had virtually nothing to say about John Barret. In contrast, Jacob cited his mother's influence and expressed his adoration for her. Despite the absences, it was Dorothy who instilled a love of learning in Jacob and nurtured his interest in religion. "My mother took much pains to teach me to read, and early to instil into my mind the principles of religion," he recalled. Jacob described her as a deeply devout woman who impressed upon him the importance of prayer, advice that Jacob took to heart from a young age.[8]

A pious, female-dominated household (his older sisters read religious tracts aloud to him) fused with a powerful Puritan culture to shape Jacob and steer him toward the ministry. In eighteenth-century New England, the fervor of the founding generation was gone but religion remained central in the lives of the region's inhabitants. The Sunday tableau of farmers converging on the town green for services at the congregational church was one sign of this importance; hearing the Word each Sunday remained a vital ritual of New England life. But there were many other signs as well. Bibles and religious tracts occupied a central place in the home. Religion shaped family relations, the education of children, and the organization of communities. Christianity was a source of strength and comfort in bad times and a source of wonderment during good times. Massachusetts Bay's founders were Protestant radicals who came to the New World preaching to their followers that they were a chosen people on a mission to redeem Christendom. That messianic sense, although much weakened by the fourth generation, remained in the 1720s. Communities still rested on a compact, or covenant, between God and its inhabitants, and this covenant taught that all must obey the Lord or risk bringing the wrath of God down on the entire community. Good Puritans, among other things, read the Bible, went to church, and refrained from breaking the Lord's commandments. As one historian noted, "Puritanism invited, or rather demanded, active cooperation from every member of society in the eradication of sin. It was held up as a sign of regeneration that a man should reform his friends and neighbors."[9]

Malden and Stoneham did not rebel against this congregational world. Indeed, as home to such Puritan stalwarts as Michael Wigglesworth (the best-selling author of a famous religious work) and Joseph Emerson (the stern minister of Jacob's childhood), they helped to perpetuate Puritan culture. Malden was part of Charlestown until 1638 when the colony awarded Malden's founding proprietors five-acre lots on the "Mistickside & above the Ponds." In 1722, the year of Jacob's birth, it remained a small community of several hundred people. Stoneham was both newer and poorer than Malden, its immediate neighbor to the south. Incorporated in 1725, three years after Jacob's birth, Stoneham grew only haltingly in the following years. A 1754 tax assessment ranked the town near the bottom of Middlesex County, well below Malden and the wealthy college town of Cambridge.[10]

Jacob's exposure to religion and Congregationalism was multifaceted—at home, school, church, and community. The congregational church was obviously one important source of his religious education. Occupying the pulpit during his childhood was the Reverend Emerson, who served Malden's congregational church from 1722 to 1767. Emerson graduated from Harvard and was a well-educated, scholarly man whose faith rested on Calvinism and a belief in Puritans' divine mission as a New Israel. He enforced a strict Congregationalism during his forty-five-year tenure that emphasized proper godly behavior and the need for Malden's good citizens to uphold the covenant—requirements that an adult Jacob Green wholeheartedly supported. In exhorting his flock to lead upright lives, Emerson alternately cajoled and insulted his listeners; one sermon likened the congregation's spiritual makeup to "a corrupt Fountain, a nest of Serpents, a cage of Unclean Birds, a stie of Filthiness." He decried weakness and sin, going so far as to sell his chaise because, in the words of one essayist, "of the sinful pride which it awakened in him."[11]

The community itself taught Jacob another kind of lesson. In these Puritan bastions throughout New England, all was not peace and love and harmony. Emerson found himself overseeing a devout but argumentative flock. The most troublesome issue was where to locate the meetinghouse: those who lived near it wanted it to stay there, while those farther away wanted it closer. A particularly nasty dispute occurred in 1727, and it directly affected the Greens. The secession of ten families to Reading left the Green clan isolated from Malden's religious life. In 1734, as a result, when Jacob was twelve years old, the Greens proposed that their neighborhood become part of Stoneham—such a move would reunite the family (some of whom had become Reading residents in the 1727 annexation) and bring them closer to the latter town's meetinghouse. In a petition dated June 21, 1734, the clan asked the General Court to approve the annexation. They couched their request in traditional terms, citing "their Difficulty to attend the Publick worship of God in their Towns by reason of their Remoteness from the meetinghouse there." In December, the Court granted the request, including "the land late of Jacob Green, deced."[12]

But the biggest influence on Jacob may well have come from books. New England was a literate place, and Jacob had the good fortune to grow up in a village with a direct connection to one of New England's most famed literary figures, the eccentric Michael Wigglesworth. Wigglesworth preceded Emerson as Malden minister. He was a Harvard graduate and probably outshone Emerson in dourness. As one chronicler of his life noted, "We should scarcely exaggerate, I think, if we described Michael Wigglesworth as a morbid, humorless, selfish busybody" whose passion was haranguing people to reform their ungodly ways.[13]

How many people Wigglesworth turned off to religion because of his poor people skills and dark sermons is unknown. Yet his influence as a writer on New England Puritanism is indisputable. In 1662, Wigglesworth published a 224-stanza poem called *The Day of Doom* that remained popular for more than one hundred years (indeed, it was one of the first best-selling books in the colonies) and that scared the wits out of countless generations of New England children—including Jacob Green. The poem was a favorite of his sisters, and they read it aloud to a rapt Jacob. Wigglesworth named his poem well; *The Day of Doom* was about Judgment Day, and its simple rhymes contained stark warnings about the fate that awaited "Adulterers and Whoremongers" and others:[14]

With dismal chains, and strongest reins,
Like Prisoners of Hell,
They're held in place before Christ's face,
Till He their Doom shall tell.
These void of tears, but fill'd with fears,
And dreadful expectation
Of endless pains and scalding flames,
Stand waiting for Damnation.[15]

In case anyone missed the point, the main textbook taught in the region's schools and homes, *The New-England Primer*, reproduced Wigglesworth's poem and emphasized many of its themes. Foremost was a simple one: "In *Adam's* Fall, We Sinned all." The *Primer* consisted of verses, catechisms, and religious lessons, among other things, and it stressed that "the Fall brought Mankind into an estate of Sin and Misery." Human beings were depraved, and all faced eternal damnation, even young children. Catechisms and verses warned New England's youth that death was not just for the old and the infirm: "From Death's Arrest no Age is free, Young Children too may die."[16]

Such was the religious milieu that Jacob Green lived in; along with the death of his father and the teachings of his mother and sisters, it made an exceedingly strong impression on him. *The Day of Doom* was especially important in shaping his outlook. "Before I was seven years old, I was at times much affected with the thoughts of the day of judgment, and future misery. At that age, I used with attention to hear my sisters read Mr. Wigglesworth's verses upon *The Day of Doom*," Jacob recalled. "That book used much to awaken and affect me: I have always had a peculiar regard for it." Its warnings and dark language helped to launch Jacob on a seven-year journey of exploration where he examined his "soul and future state. But my corruptions were much stronger than my convictions—In early life I discovered a nature wholly degenerate. . . . I often dreamed that the day of judgment was come."[17]

To deal with these fears, his mother, his congregational church, and *The New England Primer* taught him the importance of prayer. As the *Primer* described it, "Come unto CHRIST all ye that labour and are heavy laden, and He will give you rest." Jacob took these admonitions to heart, especially his mother's, and at eight years old he began to pray in secret. Praying brought him little comfort, however, and during these early years Jacob said he "had no religion but slavish fear, and [my] corrupt nature was all the while grow-ing stronger and stronger."[18]

Struggling in the spiritual realm, tormented by the Calvinistic thought that he was destined for hell, Jacob was not much happier in the material world either. His family expected him to do what countless generations of Greens had done—to take his rightful place as a farmer and craftsman, and young Jacob tried to fulfill their wishes. When he was fourteen years old, he went to live with his uncle Henry Green in Killingly to learn a trade, but owing to "some difficulties," according to Jacob, he failed. So Jacob then went to live with another uncle, Daniel Green, in Stoneham. There, an indenture was drawn up, binding Jacob as an apprentice until he was twenty-one. "Pecuniary difficulties," however, defeated this latest arrange-ment, and Jacob packed his bags once again to move in with yet another uncle, Thomas Lynde of Malden. This arrangement lasted only a year.[19]

It soon became apparent to his family that Jacob had little desire to learn a craft; in fact, in his autobiography, he did not even specify the trades he attempted to learn. His real passion was for books and reading, and Jacob's family and friends came to recognize his intellectual abilities. When he turned sixteen, Jacob began to think about attending college—an audacious dream, because no one in his immediate family had ever gone to college and because he lacked the money to pay for it. His half brother Bixby Barret came up with a clever plan, however: when Jacob turned twenty-one, he was to inherit land from his father's estate, and Bixby suggested selling this land immediately and using the proceeds to pay for Harvard.[20]

To execute this plan, though, Jacob would need a new guardian, who would then sell the land for him. The probate court approved the arrange-ment, and "the thing was accomplished," Jacob reported in his autobiogra-phy. He marveled at his good fortune. "I viewed it as a favorable providence, that three times I missed being bound out till I was twenty-one years old, which would doubtless have prevented a liberal education." With the money in hand, the seventeen-year-old's next challenge was to prepare for Harvard, and that involved enrolling in a grammar school, where Jacob boarded with a minister and undertook the study of Latin—standard practices at the time for those students interested in attending college.[21]

Students seeking admission to Harvard had to pass an oral exam given by the college's president and its tutors shortly before commencement was held for graduating college seniors. The exam tested whether an applicant could, in the words of the college's laws, "read, construe, and parse Tully, Virgil, or such like common classical Latin authors." The incoming freshman was also expected to be able to read Greek and be able to "decline the paradigms of Greek nouns and verbs." These entrance requirements reflected conventional notions of what constituted a classical education: scholars should be able to read the ancients. If the applicant passed the exam, he received a copy of the college laws and was required to pay all expenses for one quarter.[22]

Jacob did not record his experiences, but he likely passed the exam easily because the test focused on languages, his core strength as a student. Six weeks after taking the test, he returned to Cambridge for the fall term. He received his housing assignment and met his two "chums," or roommates. Then he braced himself for the arrival of the upper classmen, who treated freshmen like plebes in a military academy. The upper classmen made them run errands and serve as their servants. Tasks included fetching bread and beer and washing clothes. Decorum also dictated that the freshmen not wear hats at meals or "lean" at prayers or toss a ball in the yard.[23]

Harvard in 1740 was becoming a modern college, albeit slowly. Founded in 1636 in a cow pasture, the college was located in a struggling frontier town, then known as New Town, that had been abandoned earlier that year by most of its Puritan inhabitants, who migrated to the Connecticut frontier under the leadership of the Reverend Thomas Hooker. By the time of Jacob's enrollment, Harvard consisted of three main buildings grouped in a courtyard called the College Yard. The original Harvard Hall, completed in 1677, was a four-story brick building with a gambrel roof that was both imposing and practical. It was a self-contained structure, holding classrooms, library, buttery/kitchen, and living quarters for two tutors and for students. Twelve years later the college constructed the middle building, called Stoughton Hall, and in 1720 it built Massachusetts Hall. The latter faced Harvard Hall and was erected for the princely sum of 3,500 pounds, Massachusetts currency. Harvard's leading historian praised the craftsmanship of these buildings: "These 'colleges' . . . were built of the best materials and in the best style of which the colonists were capable. They contained every comfort known to the times, for the notion that college students should 'live like gentlemen' came over with our founders." Indeed, college life did carry a whiff of gentility—heady stuff for a farm boy from Stoneham. Students were trained to take their place among New England's elite, and they lived and dined in some comfort (although, like their modern counterparts, they complained incessantly about the food): the college laws specified that the tables in the "scholars' Commons," as the dining hall was known, "shall be covered with clean linen cloths of a suitable length and breadth . . . and furnished with pewter plates."[24]

In its aspirations for gentility, Harvard had an Old World feel to it. The college, however, did not forget its Puritan roots. The Harvard of 1740 still served to train Puritan ministers (as well as to prepare leaders for the colonies), and religion still dominated academic life despite the arrival of Enlightenment values. The college laws informed the class of 1744 that "all scholars shall behave themselves blamelessly, leading sober, righteous, and godly lives." All students were to "seasonably attend the worship of God in the hall morning and evening." Those late to prayers would be fined four pence per infraction. "And every scholar shall on the Lord's Day carefully apply himself to the duties of religion and piety," strictures that Michael Wigglesworth and Joseph Emerson surely would have approved.[25]

Harvard's record in living up to these lofty ideals was mixed. Out of Jacob's graduating class of thirty-three, eleven did go on to become ministers. One noteworthy example was Jonathan Mayhew, the famed Boston minister. Yet Jacob described religion at Harvard as being "at a very low ebb" during his years there, and his comment hints at just how complex the college's intellectual atmosphere was in 1740.[26]

"Liberalism" was steadily gaining a foothold on campus. A milestone of sorts had occurred in 1708, when John Leverett assumed the presidency at Harvard. Leverett was the first person to lead the college who was not a minister. Although he made few changes in the curriculum, Leverett did much to establish the college's liberal tradition, strengthening Harvard's finances and overseeing an ambitious expansion in course offerings and enrollment during his seventeen years in office: establishing the first endowed chair, the first student club, and the first student publication (*The Telltale*, which was largely secular in tone).[27]

Yet when Jacob Green took his place at Harvard, the traditional educational system remained largely intact and would have been familiar to a student of 1640. A single tutor, who served three-year terms, taught all subjects to the entire class of 1744. (It was not until January 1767, during the presidency of Edward Holyoke, that Harvard tutors specialized in a particular subject.) Jacob's first tutor was Daniel Rogers, himself a Harvard graduate, who began teaching at the college in 1732. Rogers was not particularly popular on campus or respected. His very presence at Harvard, in fact, was a symbol of his failure—after graduating, he was unable to land a job as a minister despite numerous tryouts and New England's perennial need for men of the cloth. In the 1730s, mischievous students stole his wine, beer, and silver tobacco box. A fellow tutor, meanwhile, derided Rogers as an "Ignoramus [and] Blockhead."[28]

Harvard, like Yale, based its curriculum on European models, and both colleges used virtually the same texts. Harvard's laws explained that "the Undergraduates shall be brought forward by their respective Tutors, in the knowledge of three learned Languages [Latin, Greek, and Hebrew] . . . and also in the knowledge of Rhetorick, Logick, natural Philosophy, Geography, Ethicks, Divinity, Metaphysicks, and . . . Mathematicks."[29]

To aid them in the study of the Old Testament, freshmen studied the grammar of Latin, Greek, and Hebrew. By the end of the year, their tutor expected them to be able to translate biblical passages from the original. Sophomores studied logic; juniors "natural philosophy" (basic sciences, such as physics, astronomy, and biology) and math; seniors "metaphysics" (the study of the "existence of things, their natures and causes"). Several subjects were constants for all four years: theology, ethics, oratory.[30]

The curriculum was designed to produce ministers who fully understood the Bible and possessed the ability to think and speak on their feet. To hone their skills as preachers and debaters, students delivered recitations and public disputations, culminating in the commencement exercises when the graduates delivered theses summarizing what they had learned during their time at Harvard. Yet the study of natural philosophy, math, and metaphysics also took the class of 1744 deep into the Enlightenment.

Jacob found life at Harvard demanding, even health-threatening. Part of the fault was Jacob's. "I studied too hard while I was at college—early and late, and sometimes all night, without a wink of sleep," he conceded. "I was very imprudent, and hurt myself. . . . I did not allow myself proper exercise of body, nor was I then sensible of the need of it."[31]

A typical day, according to a diary he kept during his third year, began a little after 6 a.m., when he studied the Bible for an hour. He then attended prayers in the college hall and "read part of a chapter in Hebrew, till 8 o'clock." After breakfasting, Jacob spent the rest of his day reading and studying until 7:00 p.m. He attended a religious society meeting for two hours, when, at 9:00 p.m., he supped and allowed himself the indulgence of a pipe. Jacob then prayed until bedtime, "a little before 11" (but on other nights, he stayed up as late as 1:00 a.m.).[32]

His school assignments involved examining the Bible in Greek and Hebrew, but reading also "Mr. Ray's *Consequences of the Deluge*"; papers in the

*Spectator*; "Mr. Allen's Alarm"; and John Locke and Euclid. Jacob worked hard at arithmetic. It was a thoroughly conventional schedule, typical for students of Harvard and Yale in the mid-eighteenth century.[33]

Logic was an important part of Harvard's curriculum, and the assignment of John Locke was a sign of the Enlightenment's arrival in this Puritan bastion, which revered not only Jesus Christ but Aristotle, Cicero, and other giants of the ancient world. In February 1728, Isaac Greenwood became Harvard's first Hollis professor of mathematics and natural philosophy, and he did much to introduce the college to the Enlightenment and its liberal values. Greenwood was a scientist who observed the sea and the winds, and he published papers at the Royal Society. Edward Wigglesworth, son of Michael, was the Hollis professor of divinity, and he also did a great deal to modernize the Harvard curriculum by encouraging his students to broaden their knowledge of the leading issues of the day. As one historian noted, "America's 'enlightenment' was . . . a 'moderate' and conciliatory cosmology that stressed balance, order, and religious compromise," and Harvard's students soon learned the importance of each.[34]

However, the real "liberal" advances in the curriculum came *after* Jacob graduated. As his diary shows, theology remained the most important and time-consuming subject. Jacob did not yet know whether he would become a minister after graduation, but his indecision did not really matter. At Harvard in 1740, all students were to master this most important subject. Even a "science" course had a theological twist to it: metaphysics explored nature, and its point was to glean the wisdom of God in the workings of the material world. Indeed, the Puritan philosopher William Ames stressed that metaphysics *was* a branch of theology.[35] Traditional texts from the seventeenth century and earlier remained popular, especially Ames's *Medulla Theologiae* ("The Marrow of Sacred Divinity"). Along with Johann Wollebius, Ames emphasized traditional Calvinist themes and attacked Arminianism. In doing so, both authors reinforced the covenantal teachings of Puritanism.

Students took all this religion with varying degrees of seriousness. A 1731 report on the state of Harvard lamented that "religion . . . [was] much in decay" and that "the worship of God in the Hall is scandalously neglected." Students' riotous behavior drew the condemnations of the report's authors, who complained about the students' "gross immoralities."[36]

The class of 1744 did little to improve the atmosphere. A number of them spent their four years at Harvard in nearly constant trouble. Their favorite pastime was drinking rum. Nathaniel Bourne of Marshfield, who was a year younger than Jacob, was fined for drinking it and for tempting "Several Delinquents . . . to the Breach of the Law against prohibited Liquors." Anthony Lechmere got drunk and made "indecent Noises, in the College Yard and in Town." Isaac Bowles was a bit more creative. Besides being punished for drinking rum, he was severely admonished for lying, for gambling, and for "associating Himself with Company of a loose and ill Character." Even Jonathan Mayhew, who went on to great fame as a minister and patriot, found himself in trouble for "drinking prohibited Liquors." Mayhew reacted haughtily to his being caught and, "in a very impudent manner, made an impertinent Recrimination upon some of the immediate Government of the House." In 1743, the faculty condemned the entire class for gathering to drink "prohibited Liquors" after 10:00 p.m. and for being slow to disperse after being ordered to return to their rooms.[37]

Jacob, though, avoided trouble. Even at this young age he was studious and serious. His best subjects, according to his son Ashbel, were math and languages, especially Hebrew—a notoriously difficult subject that had given generations of students fits. But not Jacob. His idea of a relaxing time was to talk Latin with his chum and to "look on the Moon through a telescope." He clearly did not approve of his classmates' antics; in a letter he wrote to Ashbel years later, Jacob condemned Harvard as a "vicious college" and stressed "the necessity of [students'] Shunning and opposing vice" while at college. Jacob practiced what he preached. He focused on his studies, winning three scholarships and becoming Scholar of the House. The latter honor was especially fitting for this stern young man—in return for being paid an annual stipend of about five pounds, Jacob policed his classmates' behavior.[38]

Jacob's main extracurricular activity was his membership in a small religious society that he joined during his first year in Cambridge. The society had a membership of about twelve and met once a week for what he characterized as "religious exercises." It was an uncomfortable experience during Jacob's freshman year. To avoid ridicule and harassment, the society was forced to meet in secret, and members were careful not to draw attention to their activities. "So contemptible and persecuted were religious and religious persons, that we dared not sing in our worship," Jacob complained.[39]

A pair of storms that swept through Harvard in the fall of 1740 and the winter of 1741 further upended the religious atmosphere on campus. The first disturbance was sparked by George Whitefield, the Anglican itinerant from England, who visited Cambridge on September 24 as part of a grueling, and wildly successful, forty-five-day tour of New England, where he delivered more than 175 sermons to crowds as large as twenty thousand. Whitefield was a mere twenty-five-years old in the fall of 1740, but he was a wizened veteran in the ways of revivalism, having conducted a successful tour of England a year earlier. Whitefield brought with him to New England a devotion to ecumenicalism, to the new birth, and to revivalism. Most of all, he brought a flair for the dramatic—he was a talented performer with a powerful voice that carried across open fields and crowded halls.[40]

Each appearance was an event. Nathan Cole, a farmer from Middletown, Connecticut, who went to hear the Great Awakener on October 23, 1740, captured the spectacle as well as anyone. Cole was working in his field when a messenger galloped by with the news that Whitefield was approaching Middletown: "I dropt my tool . . . and ran home to my wife telling her to make ready quickly to go and hear Mr. Whitfield preach at Middletown, then run to my pasture for my horse with all my might." Fearing they would arrive late, Cole and his wife hurried toward the meetinghouse where Whitefield was to preach. Cole was astounded by the scene that awaited them. As they approached, "I saw before me a Cloud or fogg rising; I first thought it came from the great River," he recalled, "but as I came nearer the Road, I heard a noise something like a low rumbling thunder . . . it was the noise of Horses feet coming down by the road." A large throng—Cole estimated the "multitude" at three or four thousand—was gathering, and all was chaos: "The land and banks over the river looked black with people and horses all along the 12 miles I saw no man at work in his field, but all seemed to be gone." Whitefield did not disappoint his hearers. Cole described him as "almost angelical; a young, Slim, slender youth before some thousands of people with a bold undaunted Countenance . . . [and] he looked as if he was Cloathed with authority from the Great God." His sermon left Cole shaken and his heart pierced: "I saw that my righteousness would not save me; then I was convinced of the doctrine of Election."[41]

The Harvard community received Whitefield cordially, with President Edward Holyoke entertaining the itinerant and students flocking to hear him speak at Cambridge's meetinghouse. Standing before the assembled students, tutors, overseers, and guests, he preached on the theme of "We are not as many, who corrupt the Word of God." Whitefield was fairly pleased with how it went: "God gave me great boldness and freedom of speech," and he returned in the afternoon to speak to a crowd of about seven thousand.

Whitefield was again satisfied with the results: "The Holy Spirit melted many hearts."[42]

Henry Flynt, who succeeded the hapless Daniel Rogers as Jacob's tutor, agreed that Whitefield's visit was a success. He found Whitefield "affecting in his delivery," a "good man [who is] sincerely desirous to doe good to the souls of Sinners." Harvard's students, Flynt reported, were tremendously moved and shaken by Whitefield: "Many Schollars appeared to be in great concern as to their souls and Eternal State."[43]

Yet, thanks to Harvard's irreligious ways, Whitefield's appearance was controversial. The Great Awakener himself thought little of Harvard. "Discipline," Whitefield confided in his journal, "is at a low ebb" at the college: "Bad books are become fashionable among the tutors and students. Tillotson and Clark are read, instead of Shepard, Stoddard, and such-like evangelical writers." When Harvard's faculty members learned of Whitefield's criticisms, they were stung. His plans to return to New England in 1744 prompted them to publish "The Testimony of the President, Professors, Tutors, and Hebrew Instructor of Harvard College, against George Whitefield." The essay condemned Whitefield on several levels—as a man (he was "an Enthusiast, a censorious, uncharitable Person, and a deluder of the People"); as a danger to organized religion ("he is presently apt to run into slander, and stigmatize them [ministers] as *Men of no religion, unconverted,* and *Opposers of the Spirit of God*"); and as an itinerant ("we apprehend this Itinerant Manner of preaching to be of the worst and most pernicious Tendency"). These critics at Harvard came to oppose the Great Awakening as a regressive and backward-looking movement, and their stance was another sign of the college's growing liberalism. It demonstrated how Harvard was becoming more latitudinarian, and more Armininian, than Yale.[44]

Jacob's position in the college's growing rift between "liberal" Arminians and "traditional" Calvinists was no mystery—he was thunderstruck by Whitefield's performance and supported him: "I heard him with wonder and affection, and approved highly of his preaching and conduct." Green at this young age wholeheartedly backed the goals of the Great Awakening—to spark a resurgence of piety—and he agreed completely with Whitefield's harsh assessment of Harvard. For Jacob, it was obvious that Harvard's staid religious scene needed shaking up.[45]

In fact, he and some other members of the Harvard community were so excited by Whitefield's preaching, and felt so strongly about what he was trying to achieve during his New England appearances, that they followed him to neighboring Massachusetts towns as he continued on his tour. Among this Harvard contingent was Daniel Rogers, the unpopular tutor of Jacob Green's who had faced ridicule from students and teachers alike.

In September 1740, Rogers still harbored dreams of preaching, and Whitefield's tour inspired him to take to the field. This, at last, was his chance to make a real difference in religion and to win a preaching position, and when the great George Whitefield himself asked Rogers to itinerate he enthusiastically concurred. The college authorities were not happy with his decision—Rogers was abandoning his students for a New Light itinerant, and they asked him to return to the classroom or to resign. Rogers did neither at first, explaining "that the blessed Spirit of God has led me out; and how far I shall proceed He only knows."[46]

Like Rogers, Green dropped what he was doing in late September and followed Whitefield as he made his way across Massachusetts. Whitefield's first stop after Cambridge was "Mr. Foxcroft's meeting-house," where the Great Awakener preached before a packed crowd. The next stop was an appearance at Roxbury before "many thousands." For Jacob, the places, and the days, must have blurred as Whitefield kept up his punishing pace: Marble Head, Salem, Ipswich on September 29; Ipswich, Newbury, and Hampton on September 30; York and Portsmouth on October 2—and on and on, into mid-October, including a stop at Malden, where Jacob had been born and lived for so many years. Green witnessed firsthand some of the most stirring appearances of the 1740 tour, including Whitefield's October 12 visit to Boston. Accompanied by the Massachusetts governor, Whitefield recounted how he preached his "farewell sermon [at the Boston Common] to near twenty thousand people,—a sight I have not seen since I left Blackheath [England],—and a sight, perhaps never seen before in America."[47]

Jacob made it as far as Leicester, which Whitefield visited on the afternoon of October 15. Green was apparently fatigued and homesick at this point—Leicester was in western Massachusetts, about six miles from Worcester, and not too far from Killingly, Connecticut, where his mother lived. She was seriously ill (indeed, she would die in December 1741), and Jacob left Whitefield to visit her. As it turned out, this was the last time he saw her.[48]

As momentous as Whitefield's tour was, the arrival of Gilbert Tennent only a few months later made an even deeper impression on Jacob. Tennent came to Cambridge in late January 1741. Uncouth, haughty, and loud, Tennent was not Whitefield's equal in speaking ability or intellect, but he stirred Jacob in ways that Whitefield did not. Part of Tennent's influence on Jacob had to do with the timing of his visit on that cold January day, and part of it with the message he delivered. Jacob had never heard of Gilbert Tennent when this controversial Presbyterian itinerant came to Harvard, and he went to hear him only out of curiosity. Tennent's sermon was on false hope. "Some of you may try to maintain your old hope, though it shakes and has no foundation, and you will flatter and deceive yourselves," Jacob recalled him saying. "But your hope must come down. I know it will be like rending soul and body asunder, but down it must come, or you must go to hell with it."[49]

These words struck Green with tremendous force. Every doubt he had long harbored about his spirituality, every fear he had long felt about his eternal fate under the Calvinistic doctrine of predestination, came washing over him as Tennent shouted his warnings from the pulpit. The sermon left Jacob deeply upset and troubled: "I saw myself fit for hell. The sinfulness of my heart and nature appeared infinitely more dreadful than ever it had done before. I had a new and dreadful sense of my wickedness." To his friends and acquaintances, Jacob was serious and hardworking, but Jacob still viewed himself as a wretched sinner. His childhood feelings of inadequacy tormented him. As a young boy raised in the Calvinistic gloom of Puritanism and the dire warnings of Michael Wigglesworth's *Day of Doom*, Jacob was convinced that he was unsaved and a sinner in the eyes of God. These doubts grew and became more specific as he got older.[50]

Before he entered Harvard, two incidents had crystallized his sense of crisis and persuaded him that he was going to hell. The first occurred at about age sixteen, when he left Leicester for the fifteen-mile ride to Killingly to see his mother. The trip entailed passing through a "gloomy wilderness" containing few houses. Jacob was unfamiliar with the trail, and he attempted to navigate it as night and rain arrived. When the path forked, Jacob took the wrong turn. Engulfed in blackness, Jacob was unable to find his way back. "What to do I knew not," he recalled. "Sometimes I moved onward, sometimes [I] stopped and considered; but generally kept moving on." Pelted by rain, tired and hungry, Jacob became scared and "my conscience fell upon me." His feelings of sinfulness resurfaced, and he prayed to God for forgiveness. "I confessed my sins and omissions," and he vowed to change if God "would deliver me out of that wilderness." Jacob also made his promise as specific as possible: "I would, within one week after I got home from that journey, begin to pray in secret evening and morning, and continue to do so for a fortnight."[51]

Appropriately bucked up, Jacob gave his horse a kick and pressed on in the rain. Almost immediately, he spied a light ahead and moved toward it. It was a house occupied by a family, who provided him with directions. They also agreed to allow a boy to help guide Jacob out of the woods. Thanks to the boy's help and the moon's emergence from behind storm clouds, Jacob finally made it to his mother's house shortly after midnight.

Jacob felt great relief at his deliverance, but he reneged on his promise to begin praying. With each passing day "I was less and less affected with a sense of my being lost in the woods, and the promise I had made." He returned to Malden feeling "careless, stupid, and insensible of my guilt." Jacob, of course, felt great guilt at his failure to keep his word to God. His guilt was so intense, it led to the second incident: on the night before he was supposed to begin praying regularly, he suffered a violent nightmare that left him even more afraid for his soul.[52]

It was the most Calvinistic of dreams. Jacob was in a large room at twilight with a group of elderly men and young boys about six years old. The room contained an open door with two pairs of stairs—the one on the right led upward, presumably to heaven; the one on the left downward, to hell. One by one the children were led to the door, where they learned their fates. In the morning, they returned unharmed, but by taking that fateful step through the door they discovered where they would spend eternity.

Jacob shook with fear as he watched the children head toward the door, and his foreboding grew as his turn approached. As the child ahead of him headed downward to hell, crying and protesting, Jacob "determined that I would not go straight out at the door, as the others did"; instead, he bolted for the stairs on the right. A strong wind, however, blocked his way and, "like a whirlpool, sucked me down the stairs." Jacob tried fighting the wind, but it was futile, and he wept bitterly "for I thought I certainly belonged to hell."

He then learned that the room contained a second door, this one on the west side: "In anguish and dreadful distress, [I] went out of this door, and there, in that yard, sat God Almighty, on a kind of throne." Jacob threw himself at God's feet and begged Him to tell Jacob why he had been condemned to hell: "He told me it was for breaking my promise made in the woods, together with the sin I had committed against light and the checks of conscience at the time of it." Jacob asked God why he could not forgive him for his sins: "'O most merciful God! Didst thou never pardon so great a sin as this!' No, said he, I never did." Jacob continued to argue with God, citing the redemption of several sinners in the Old Testament and the saving "merit of Christ," but God was adamant. Jacob awoke at dawn, trembling, when God repeated that he would not pardon Jacob for the sin he had committed.

The dream left Jacob devastated. He staggered from bed and headed to the barn, where he attempted unsuccessfully to pray: "It seemed as if [God] had turned his back upon me and heard me not." Jacob was so upset that the family he was living with asked him what was the matter. Slowly, he regained his bearings and "began to have a little hope that I might not have committed the unpardonable sin." He tried to rationalize that the dream was merely a dream, and that "dreams were not absolutely to be depended upon." But the nightmare was so vivid and spoke so convincingly to his shortcomings that Jacob concluded it must be true, "and this [realization] would cut me like a knife. After this I never lost a sense of my guilt."[53]

Jacob attempted to change nevertheless. He forced himself to pray; joined a religious society while at grammar school; attended church; and tried to lead a godly life, free of sin: "I had now some appearance of religion . . . and by degrees I obtained more and more a hope that I might obtain mercy, and that my sin was not unpardonable." It was this hope that Gilbert Tennent unwittingly shattered when he addressed the Cambridge crowd in January 1741. Jacob believed that Tennent was speaking directly to him, because the itinerant's words mocked his Arminian hopes of "working" his way to salvation.[54]

In one sense, Jacob's tale, replete with his wandering in a wilderness, was a traditional evangelical one, containing a lesson that any Calvinist could grasp: only the Lord granted salvation. Yet in another, more important sense, it was revealing of his personality, demonstrating just how much of a New Englander he was. Jacob imbibed the Puritan ethos of discipline, righteous living—and frightening insecurities about whether he was of the elect or was a "reprobate." He had been taught from an early age—by his mother, his minister, and his textbooks—that an all-powerful God saved only the chosen few, that even young children could not expect any mercy from the Lord if they were sinners in God's all-knowing eyes. Jacob's tale, right down to the parable of the wilderness, reflected these teachings. From his earliest days, he placed tremendous pressure on himself to behave and to be a virtuous Christian worthy of God's love.

Yet no matter what he did, he felt it was not enough. In his autobiography, Jacob recalled with disgust the time the minister of his grammar school invited Jacob to become a church member. The offer should have been a moment of triumph, a reward for his changed ways: the minister was impressed by Jacob's efforts at piety and believed that Jacob was worthy of church membership because of his outwardly Christian behavior. Jacob saw things differently; the offer left him "thunderstruck, for . . . I did not conceive myself to be at all qualified for it." Jacob drew two conclusions from the incident. It was "a sad instance of the minister's carelessness in admitting members to his church, and of my own presumption in consenting to his proposal." Both minister and congregant came up short in Jacob's demanding view.[55]

Jacob was extremely hard on himself in another way—he struggled to achieve a rebirth. He did not become reborn after the wilderness adventure or his terrifying dream. He did not immediately undergo a conversion even after seeing the Great Awakening up close at the hands of two of its greatest practitioners, who did so much to expose his perceived shortcomings. Instead, this momentous moment in his spiritual life finally came about two months after Jacob heard Tennent's discourse on hope. And the conversion came in the most ironic way—through study. By reading "authors on the harmony of the divine attributes," Jacob simply came to understand Jesus Christ's role in the atonement of sin, "and that God could glorify himself in pardoning a sinner through Jesus Christ." Such a simple revelation was powerful nonetheless: "When I came to see that God could be glorified and sinners saved . . . it astonished me, it filled me with raptures of admiration."[56]

Jacob's struggles, however, were not over. He spent the rest of his college years attempting to maintain the conversion he had achieved in the winter of 1741. As he put it lyrically in his autobiography, "Sometimes I would have light, joy, and comfort, for a week or two together, and then for as long a time, I would be in darkness, doubts, and fears." He also struggled to maintain his Calvinistic faith as his knowledge of the Enlightenment improved. In May 1744, Jacob confessed in a letter to a classmate just how confused he was about predestination; the classmate, Nathaniel Tucker, had taken the Arminian stance that individuals can achieve salvation on their own by embracing the gospel. Jacob wrote that he was at a loss as to how to respond, that the topic was so complicated "I cannot come to any determination of [it] in my own mind."[57]

Despite the supposed problems with backsliding and his doubts about Calvinism, Jacob's piety and intelligence were obvious to others, and, as his time at Harvard drew to a close, friends and colleagues urged him to become a minister. Jacob resisted, however. Despite his rebirth, he remained doubtful about whether he truly was of the elect. He also doubted whether he possessed the personality to be a pastor—he was shy and disliked public speaking, especially on something as personal as religion. In private, he said, "I generally had great fervour and engagedness of soul . . . but when I come to be among people, I found myself bashful and reluctant to speak." While at Harvard, Jacob admired those individuals who could "speak with freedom and earnestness to others." He wished he were one of those people.[58]

Green graduated from Harvard in July 1744, unsure about what he would do for a living. He wanted to pursue advanced studies, but he had no money left to pay for it. Unlike many of his classmates, he "had no wealthy friends to help me." Despite the entreaties of his friends and an unnamed congregation that sought to hire him, Jacob did not feel ready to for the pulpit, given his gauche ways and nagging doubt about his faith. Instead, as a stopgap, Jacob accepted a teaching position at Sutton, about fifty miles from Harvard, where Daniel Rogers was assisting the minister.[59]

When his teaching contract expired after a year, Jacob was still unsure about what to do next. It was now 1745, and a towering figure from Jacob's past was then touring New England. Learning that Green was looking for work, George Whitefield offered him the opportunity to run his orphanage in Savannah, Georgia. Jacob was delighted, calling the offer "unexpected and surprising." He accepted and agreed to meet Whitefield in New York after he settled his affairs in Massachusetts. Jacob caught up with Whitefield in Elizabeth Town, New Jersey, where he received some bad news: Whitefield had failed to raise enough money for the orphanage. Whitefield, however, volunteered to "fulfil his agreement with me for half a year, if I chose to go on with him; and that if I chose to stop, he would defray the expense I had incurred in coming thus far."[60]

Jacob's indecision now returned. He found himself in a colonial backwater, several hundred miles from home, with little money and no real job prospects. He could proceed south with the Great Awakener and hope something would materialize, or he could return home to an uncertain future. Jacob was in good company as he pondered these unappealing options—he and Whitefield's entourage were staying at the house of Jonathan Dickinson in Elizabeth Town. Dickinson was a talented Presbyterian minister who was in the process of founding the College of New Jersey (the future Princeton University), and Dickinson and his colleague, Aaron Burr, another renowned Presbyterian clergyman, suggested a third option to Green: he should become a Presbyterian minister and serve in New Jersey.[61]

Jacob was flattered, but he "viewed the ministry as a great and difficult work; I was but a poor speaker; and on the whole, I shrunk away from the work"—sentiments that he had expressed repeatedly over the past several years. Despite these protestations, Green *did* feel the pull of the ministry and what he termed "following the calls of Providence." If God wanted him to serve, this Calvinist would. He would not stand in God's way. Characteristically, though, Jacob needed reassurance from others that he was cut out for the ministry. So Green consulted with several ministers, pouring out his numerous doubts to them. They urged him to accept, warning that it was "the design of Satan to keep me out of the ministry." Jacob, however, still hesitated, and he even went so far as to put all of his objections on paper. He showed the paper to Burr, who "read it through deliberately, and then put it into the fire before my eyes, and talked to me in a very friendly and encouraging manner."[62]

Burr's confidence in him, as well as Dickinson's plans for him as an ally in the New York Presbytery, at last succeeded. Green agreed to become a minister, and he received his license to preach in September 1745. His first assignment was ministering to a struggling congregation in a Presbyterian redoubt in the mountains of northwestern New Jersey. Green had likely never heard of the place. With curiosity, and with some foreboding, he set out to see what he had gotten himself into.

---

## The Loyalist Down the Road:
### Thomas Bradbury Chandler, New Englander

The mind of America's fiercest loyalist was cultivated in the soils of republican New England.

Like Jacob Green, Thomas Bradbury Chandler was descended from good Puritan stock and was raised in a Congregational village. The gulf between the two families was wide, however, for the Chandlers possessed wealth and prestige; the Greens did not. Heirs of William and Annis Chandler, who came to the Massachusetts Bay Colony in 1637 as part of the Great Migration that brought the first Puritans to the New World, the family was talented, hardworking, pious, and rich. As leading citizens of Woodstock, Connecticut, about one hundred miles west of Malden, where Jacob Green lived, their names could be found sprinkled liberally throughout the minutes of the various town and church boards that dominated village life. Indeed, the Chandler men were all known by their titles—Deacon John, Judge John, Captain William, among others.

Captain William Chandler was the third born of the Honorable John Chandler, Esquire, who served on the town committee, represented Woodstock at the General Court, was chief justice of the Court of Common Pleas, and owned the most prestigious pew (the one next to the pulpit stairs) in the Congregational meetinghouse. Upon his death in 1743, John left behind extensive landholdings and an estate valued at nearly 8,700 pounds. The sixth child, Samuel, inherited the family seat "In Consideration of his great Prudence, Industry and Dutiful Behaviour and application in my Business." William was barely mentioned in the will. No matter. He was prosperous in his own right, the owner of a thousand-acre estate known as Chandler Hill. William's plantation hugged the town line to the east and was high enough (597 feet above sea level, according to one modern reckoning) that it afforded the Chandlers a lordly view over the surrounding countryside.

Fortune thus smiled on Thomas Bradbury Chandler, as he entered the world on April 26, 1726, when Jacob Green was four and about to embark on a vagabond existence as a fatherless child. From his father Thomas inherited the gift of command (both were physically imposing men) and from his mother his formidable intellect and piety. Jemima was a remarkable woman—she was both talented and wealthy in her own right. Her father, Thomas Bradbury of Salisbury, Massachusetts, bequeathed to her nearly his entire estate—an unusual gesture in an age when land typically went to the patriarch's sons. But it was Jemima's intellect that was most noteworthy. One family chronicler approvingly recalled her "superior natural and acquired abilities and power of mind." Jemima was literate and a strong student; she excelled at natural philosophy, geography, and, of course, religion. She was, according to a Chandler family historian, "of unaffected piety, exemplary in all her paths."

Her eldest son would disappoint neither mother nor father; at Chandler Hill, as Thomas grew into manhood, he began cultivating the mind that would thrill loyalists of the king and infuriate supporters of American independence. Thomas, it seems, was destined for big things.[63]

# 2

*Pastor*

Grand, it was not. Tucked away on nearly four acres along the Whippanong River, Hanover's Presbyterian meetinghouse looked more like a failing country store than a hieratic shrine to the Lord. A dilapidated, oblong structure built of logs, the two-story church lacked the crowning grace of a cupola or spire. Worshipers wanting to sit in the gallery had to mount stairs from the outside (fig. 2). The pulpit consisted of a carpenter's bench, the pews of crude benches. Constructed in 1718, the church was falling apart when Jacob Green arrived in late 1745, but congregation members had been unable to agree on the location for a replacement or how to pay for it. For Jacob, more discomforting than the meetinghouse's sad state was the congregation's history. The presbytery had dismissed Green's two predecessors following, in Jacob's typically understated words, "uneasiness" between the minister and his people.[1]

As dolorous as all this was, Jacob's prospects upon his arrival were not hopeless. Hanover represented the oldest and most settled township in the newly formed county of Morris, serving as the jumping-off point for the settlement of land west and north of the village. Moreover, its abundant natural resources held the promise of economic growth. The numerous rivers enticed settlers to the area and became home to forges and mills. Of greater significance to Jacob was Hanover's stature as the center of Presbyterianism in northwestern New Jersey; his congregation was the mother

*Fig. 2* The Presbyterian meetinghouse on Hanover Neck as it looked in late 1745, when Green began his pastorship. Constructed in 1718, the church was falling apart in the 1740s, but members were unable to agree on where and how to replace it until the 1750s. Drawing by Stephen Manson.

church that sired numerous offspring in the years before the American Revolution, meaning that his appointment as Hanover's interim pastor instantly made him the leader of Presbyterianism in the region.[2]

The timing of his arrival was also auspicious. The New York Synod, which oversaw Hanover, had held its first session on September 19, 1745. Led by Jonathan Dickinson and Aaron Burr, and dominated by New Siders, the synod was seeking to spread its New England brand of Presbyterianism in New Jersey and elsewhere. Dickinson and Burr viewed Jacob as an important recruit in this missionary effort. The troubles of Green's predecessor, John Nutman, presented them with the opportunity to place an ally in an important congregation in East Jersey. Jacob Green would serve as a foot soldier in the New Siders' fight for evangelism and revivalism.[3]

Jacob was flattered by the attention. Still unsure about his suitability for the ministry, he needed the encouragement from Dickinson and Burr, whom he held in "great regard." Dickinson and the young Jacob Green likely saw each other as kindred spirits; although both men supported the Great Awakening, Dickinson and Green rejected the excessive emotionalism and divisiveness that accompanied it. Dickinson, who came to Elizabeth Town in 1708, was a leading Presbyterian in the middle colonies and a moderate New Sider who sought a middle ground on the raging controversies of the day, including the dual threats of Arminianism and antinomianism.[4]

When Green arrived in Hanover, he likely found the place congenial: the township was populated by second- and third-generation Puritans-turned-Presbyterians from New England. Hanover resembled Stoneham in several ways. It was a growing agricultural community of small farms whose cultural life revolved around the meetinghouse and the family. Culturally, a New England spirit infused the place. Former Puritans from Long Island, Newark, and Elizabeth Town, whose families originally came from Massachusetts Bay, Connecticut, and elsewhere, founded the township and launched Presbyterian life in 1718 when they built the meetinghouse and began holding services. Green approvingly described these early settlers as stout Calvinists, and he strove to establish a rapport with their descendants throughout the fall of 1745. Before his formal ordination as Hanover's pastor in November 1746, Green served a one-year probation that allowed each side to get to know the other. Because the congregation's relationship with Green's two predecessors—Nathaniel Hubbard, who served until 1730, and John Nutman, who lasted until 1745—had ended badly, this was no formality. Congregants listened to Green's sermons, met with him in their houses, prayed with him in the evenings.[5]

The members obviously liked what they saw, despite the shortcomings that Jacob so candidly described about himself. During these first years in Hanover, Green remained shy and unsure of himself, even in private settings. "I could speak but poorly in publick," he lamented, "and I was bashful, backward and unapt to speak in private." One step he took to overcome his nervousness and make himself "useful" to the membership "was to give out questions in writing, and have a time appointed to meet the people and hear them answer the questions as they thought proper, and then to make my own observations upon them." The sessions could be quite freewheeling, and Green used them to become acquainted with his congregants on a personal level.[6]

Jacob's insecurities ran deeper than his personality—they extended to his religious views, which were in flux in the 1740s and 1750s and were easily swayed by the luminaries he encountered in New England and New Jersey. George Whitefield, Gilbert Tennent, and other apostles of the Great Awakening helped turn Jacob into what he termed in his autobiography a "zealous Calvinist" during his Harvard years (although this was an exaggeration). But despite his enthusiasm for John Calvin and the Reformed spirit, and despite his Puritan upbringing in Massachusetts, he departed Cambridge troubled about his Calvinistic faith and the paradoxes it presented. Across a broad front in the fields of science and religion, rationalists and advocates of the Enlightenment were questioning the theological system that had dominated western Europe for three centuries, and their attacks on predestination resonated with Jacob while he was a student at Harvard. As he confessed in the May 1744 letter to Nathaniel Tucker, he was unsure about predestination and free will and how one solved the many paradoxes they presented. Still, in 1744, his New England upbringing held firm, and he thought of himself as a Calvinist, believing that God controlled all and that "unregenerate men have now no power to embrace the offers of the Gospil."[7]

Such certainty did not survive his first encounters with Dickinson and Burr in Elizabeth Town in 1745. The two Presbyterian leaders easily brought him around to their views on Presbyterianism and on a looser church membership. Abandoning Congregationalism for Presbyterianism was not a difficult step for Green; the two faiths arose out of the same Reformed tradition and had much in common, including a commitment to Calvinism and to a biblical-based church. The reversal on membership, however, *was* a dramatic repudiation of Jacob's Puritan beliefs, which rested on the notion that only the elect could be full church members and participate in the sacraments. Dickinson and Burr, Green succinctly noted in his autobiography, "induced me to embrace Stoddard's sentiments, which before I had thought were not right." The reference was to the grandfather of Jonathan Edwards, the influential Solomon Stoddard, who as pastor of Northampton, Massachusetts, pressed for looser standards in an effort to win more converts to Christ. Jacob's bow to Stoddardean standards induced him to take an even more heretical stance: he began to accept "some notions that were Arminian, or that bordered upon Arminianism; especially as to the power of the creature, the freedom of the will, the origin of action."[8]

Despite these vicissitudes—or more accurately because of them—Green never stopped studying after he left Harvard. He read widely and thought deeply in the late 1740s and 1750s, as he worked out the views that allowed him to soften Calvinism's hard edges and pursue a purer church and society in the 1760s and later; this study also undergirded his political views of the 1770s. His most intense period of study took place over seven months, from November 1754 to May 1755. Several times a week he retreated to his study to write in two daybooks. The first daybook covered more than 160 pages and was a wide-ranging exploration of divinity and what Jacob termed "the coda of systems." In tightly packed pages that combined standard English with a system of shorthand developed by James Weston in the mid-eighteenth century, Jacob ranged over the centuries, beginning with the ancient philosophers (figs. 3 and 4). His central concerns were basic but profound: does God exist? Is the Bible accurate? What is free will? That Jacob even asked such questions was evidence of the turmoil he continued to experience in the mid-1750s. As a graduate of Harvard, he was well aware of developments in Western thought since the seventeenth century and the arrival of the Enlightenment in America in the eighteenth. Theologians everywhere were grappling with the challenges to Christianity posed by science, which was lifting the veil on nature's workings and, ultimately, raising questions about God himself. The questions were serious enough that the Christian faithful believed they had to reassert the primacy of God, demonstrate the accuracy of the Bible, and explain the relevance of the Trinity. Many, like Samuel Clarke and John Witherspoon, fought fire with fire—they used science itself to make their case for religion. Reason was their watchword as they combated the skepticism of Arians, Socians, deists, philosophers, and others.[9]

Jacob Green, as a result, was hardly alone as he studied his Bible and pondered the meaning of faith. He approached the review of religion in an enlightened manner—his exploration was reasoned, rational, systematic, measured. The views of men, he warned in one early entry in his daybook, tended to run to extremes. He would avoid that pitfall and, instead, coolly examine the various controversies of the different ages. Jacob's perambulations began with the customs of the ancients, including the Druids, and the hostility that early Christians faced. His review then carried him on to Jewish history, the "absurdities" of Roman Catholicism, and the views of everyone from Peter Lombard to the Socians. In his rough jottings—many sentences were half thoughts and lacked punctuation—Jacob did not advance his own arguments. Instead, his purpose was to poke and to prod at

*Fig. 3* Green often wrote in a form of shorthand developed by Englishman James Weston. This example is from a 1776 notebook of Green's that is stored in his papers at Princeton University.

conventional wisdom as he worked his way up to the arguments of modern times. He was fascinated by the seemingly irreconcilable—those who relied on reason to determine God's existence versus those who turned to revelation. As he studied Christian history, Jacob kept returning to his core questions, stressing the importance of learning which parts of the Bible represented truth and which were inspired by God. He devoted "chapters" in his daybook to analyzing God's powers—the Trinity, the Holy Spirit, and God the Son, among many others. In attempting to answer such questions, Jacob examined the origins of the world, the authority of the scriptures, and the nature of sin and evil.[10]

As he laboriously analyzed this coda, Jacob devoted one day a week (usually Wednesdays) to a second daybook, covering nearly one hundred pages, that broke down the mechanics of good writing and sermonizing. Here again he drew on his Harvard education and his experiences in the Great

# Stenography Compleated,

### Or the Art of

# SHORT-HAND

### Brought to Perfection;

*Being the most Easy, Exact, Speedy, and Legible Method extant:*

### WHEREBY

*Can be Joined in Every Sentence, at least* Two, three, *four, five, six, seven, or more Words together in One, without taking off y Pen, in y twinkling of an Eye. And that by the* SIGNS *of the* ENGLISH *Moods, Tenses, Persons, Particles, &c.*

### Never before Invented.

*By this New Method any, who can but tolerably write their Names in Round-hand, May with ease (By this Book alone without any Teacher) take down from y Speakers Mouth, any Sermon Speech, Trial, Play, &c Word by word, though they know nothing of Latin, And may likewise Read one another's Writing distinctly, be it ever so long after it is written. To perform these by any other Short-hand Method extant, is utterly* Impossible, *As is evident from y Books themselves.*

### AUTHORIZ'D BY HIS MAJESTY,

*And Attested by many Gentlemen, at the Beginning hereof.*

Compos'd by JAMES WESTON, the only Author and Professor of this New Method.

### LONDON.

*Printed for the* AUTHOR *and Sold by him, at the Hand and Pen, over-against Water Lane, in Fleet Street.* MDCCXLIII.

J. Cole sculp.

*Fig. 4*   In London, James Weston published a manual in 1743 explaining how his shorthand system worked.

Awakening, focusing on Cicero and on how a "discourse . . . [can] move a heart." Jacob wrote these daybook entries as if he was delivering a lecture to a classroom of college undergraduates: he would lay out his thesis and proceed to construct a carefully reasoned argument in support of that thesis. An important task for Jacob was determining in his mind what constituted bad writing. Such writing, he decided, "is weak and languid; i.e. what faintly conveys the authors sentiments." Bad writers, he continued, "say nothing to inform the understanding, convince the Judgment, or please the Imagination . . . there is something awanting; which lies in this, that the discourse is not filled to make [an] Impression." In other words, bad writers are boring—they are "pedantic" or bombastic.[11]

Good writing, by contrast, is "simple, natural, nervous, diffuse, sublime," according to Jacob. Out of that list of attributes, "simple" and "natural" were the most important ones to him. He admiringly cited the writing in the Old Testament: "The thoughts are natural, & the choice of words is natural." He also praised Demosthenes and Cicero, who managed to be eloquent and persuasive without giving the "appearance of art & study, or of affectation." Effective writers, Jacob strongly felt, take care to "accommodate to the capacities of the hearers. This is a most important Rule of Eloquence." The implications for the minister trying to win over souls to Jesus Christ were obvious. Sermons "ought to be plain & simple," Jacob advised; regular English was much more effective than relying on "dead languages." When delivering these sermons, the "Speaker ought generally, if not always to appear calm, composed, & without any emotion at all."[12]

This was not surprising advice coming from someone who considered himself a poor public speaker. Yet in another sense it *was* surprising, considering how much Jacob admired Whitefield and Tennent. The powerful, emotional preaching of the leading awakeners had moved him profoundly, and he was recruited to Hanover to serve as an *evangelical* minister. Instead, Green's views reflected his careful study of the ancients; the treatises of his contemporaries, especially Jonathan Edwards; and the rhetoric of the Enlightenment. Simple was best; calm reason was more persuasive than fervid outbursts. Jacob's Harvard coursework taught him that a good sermon should be built around four parts—*invention*, the process by which the speaker determines the subject matter; *arrangement*, by which the speaker places his argument in proper order; *style*, the determination of the proper language to use; and *delivery*, by which the speaker decides what voice and body language to employ.[13]

Jacob's writing and preaching style was far closer to Edwards than to the classic rhetoricians or to the Great Awakeners. Green rejected the two extremes in sermonizing—he found his "rationalist" peers too elitist, too learned, too argumentative, but he was not comfortable with the evangelical style of Whitefield and others that stressed emotion and the ability to deliver a sermon extemporaneously. Instead, Green found a kindred spirit in the famed minister from Northampton, Massachusetts. Edwards sought a middle ground in preaching that merged sound thinking *and* emotion. Edwards wanted to win over the "head" by going through the "heart." To achieve this task he relied on vivid natural imagery that appealed to the emotions. Edwards at times was almost mystical in his use of language, stressing the beauty of nature and the wondrous ways of God.[14]

Jacob's search for the middle ground is evident in his daybooks. He evinced little patience for college-educated ministers, who he said were more interested in showing off their education than in imparting sound evangelical principles to his listeners. He stressed that the careful minister should avoid excessive emotionalism, but he went on to say that emotionalism has its place in good writing and sermonizing. "We must be careful to set on the proper considerations before the Mind in the natural order; i.e., we must put first the plainest, & then the more complex, views of things"—all with an eye toward awakening the emotions in hearers. To pull off this feat, Jacob stressed, "a speaker must feel the emotions in himself." He likened the process to a "contagion"; when the speaker feels warm emotion, he can pass it along to his audience. But if the speaker feels a "coldness," he will cut a "very sorry figure" and fail to move his listeners.[15]

The most important aspect of Green's education during this period was his study of Jonathan Edwards. It was Edwards who quieted his mind on Calvinism and enabled him to solve the key riddle about predestination— why should anyone act morally? As Green put it in his autobiography, Edwards did the most to "bring me off from all the notions that bordered on Arminianism," the idea that man could achieve salvation on his own, that he had the free will to change his own fate. This doctrine, derived from the teachings of Jacob Arminius in the sixteenth century, threatened all that Calvinism stood for. The attack was serious enough that Green was tormented by questions about man's culpability in sin and his ability to reform his ways. The role of free will only baffled him further during these early years. In 1744, Green hesitantly decided "that I think a man may be a free agent without having any power to believe, for a man may act freely and chuse to do one thing without being able to do the contrary to it, so a sinner may act freely in chusing to go on in sin without being able to chuse holiness."[16]

Looking for better answers, Green read Edwards's writings intently, especially his renowned *Freedom of the Will* and his *Inquiry Concerning Qualifications for the Sacraments*. Edwards had several concerns in these tracts. With the Enlightenment and "rational" religion advancing methodically in the mid-eighteenth century, he wanted to counter the attacks on Calvinism, especially by answering those critics who said that John Calvin's rigid theological system built on the doctrine of predestination undermined a person's moral responsibility. Edwards carefully set out to reconcile free will (the notion that individuals are free to do as they please) with Calvinism (the idea that an omniscient God controls all). Edwards reconciled the seemingly irreconcilable by distinguishing between natural necessity and moral necessity. An all-powerful but loving God governs through the latter—in his greatness he grants individuals the power to choose within the limits that God has decreed. As one recent biographer of Edwards explained, God "created intelligent beings who were free to choose what they wanted in the most significant ways possible in a God-governed universe. Their choices were fully their own, and they were morally responsible for their choices."[17]

Green was impressed with this line of argument, and he came to believe that Calvinism's critics were the inconsistent ones. Green noted in his autobiography that most skeptics were "partly Calvinists, and partly Arminians." An intellectual muddle, in other words: the skeptics "dare not look the Calvinistic principles through, follow them to their source, and receive them with all their consequences. . . . They believe the perfections of God, and that he foreknew all things," yet they were unwilling to accept that God controlled all.[18]

Green fleshed out his Edwardsean insights in a series of sermons and tracts that he published in the 1760s, beginning with a published sermon in 1764 on baptism and culminating in 1770 with a short pamphlet that summarized his views. Like Edwards, Green rested his theories on one sturdy foundation: God is all-powerful, loving, and good. In staking his claim for God's greatness, Green again acknowledged the conundrums that it created: if God is so powerful and good, why does he permit evil? If he is so loving, how can he be so cruel as to save some sinners but not others? And if God truly controls all, then are not humans powerless to achieve salvation? And are they not blameless for current or past sins?[19]

Unlike the confused explanation he gave in 1744, he answered these perplexing questions in the 1750s and later by constructing an Edwardsean
defense, distinguishing between what he termed natural inability and spiritual inability. The difference between the two concepts was great, Jacob
asserted. "Natural Inability, is the Want of Power or Faculty to do what Persons have a Will to do, what they choose and desire to do," he explained. "A
Man that has lost his Hands cannot do the Work that others do, tho' he
might wish and desire to. . . . The Man without Hands . . . [is] under a natural Inability." By contrast, spiritual inability involved a conscious choice by
the individual to do good—or ill. For the sinner, "the Motives to do good
and avoid evil, have no considerable Weight with him. His wicked Disposition overcomes the Motives to good. . . . The Sinner is not blind and deaf
like him that is without sight and hearing; the Sinner has Eyes to see, and
ears to hear, and an understanding by which he may consider, but he has no
Heart to read, hear or consider."[20]

Green well knew that skeptics would accept this as only a partial explanation, that they would counter with the observation "*That Persons have not
Power to alter their bad Will and Inclination; and that they cannot help being
of such a bad Heart and Temper*" (Green's emphasis). To answer such objections, Green drew on Edwards's concept of the will. "If any Person has a
Will to love God or Holiness," Green explained, "there is then Nothing in
the Way, he does the Thing; he loves God and Holiness." In other words,
spiritual inability represented the "want of Will and Inclination." In defining the will, Green and Edwards were tackling head-on the advances of liberalism and the Enlightenment. These "modern" values, espoused most
powerfully by John Locke and René Descartes, placed a premium on individual rights by asserting that people have the freedom—the free will—to
act as they choose. Individuals, in other words, were responsible for their
own actions.

Edwards and Green agreed that free will involved a person's ability to
choose. But where they differed from Enlightenment apostles was in assign-
ing the agent ultimately responsible for bestowing such an important right.
For liberals, free will resided within individuals; for Edwards and Green, it
resided with God. Both men reached this conclusion after traveling down the
same path. It all began with an understanding of the supreme deity: he was
sovereign, the creator of the universe and all within it. In his loving greatness,
God decided to grant individuals the right to act. Edwards explained the
presence of sin through his concepts of natural necessity (ingrained, naturalistic

reactions to things such as physical pain) and moral necessity (habits of the heart where God gives one the choice of what to do), while Green called it natural inability and spiritual inability. For both men, God was the one who bestows choice, or free will, on individuals. Sinners, Jacob maintained, "are acquainted with their Duty. They know what is Right and what is Wrong; they know the dreadful Consequences of Sin, and the happy Effects of Holiness. Heaven and Hell are set before them." Jacob added, though, that it was impossible for the unregenerate to achieve his or her own salvation; only God can bestow that: "'Tis impossible to choose a new Heart. . . . 'Tis contrary to the Nature of Things."[21]

Having satisfied himself that free will can be reconciled with Calvin's predestinarian teachings, and that individuals *do* have a choice to act morally or to sin, Green next worked out his views on the church's role in this Calvinistic world. Who should belong to the church—only the elect (i.e., those who are saved)? Or should everyone, including the unsaved, be allowed to join and participate in the sacraments? The writings of Englishman Isaac Watts, the Calvinistic theologian and hymn writer, guided Green on this question of church purity. Green analyzed Watts's *Rational Foundation of a Christian Church*, which was nearly four hundred pages and published in 1747, and praised it as "the most rational and scriptural, of any thing I have seen upon these subjects." From Watts, Green worked out the role of reason in religion and the rationale for instituting a purer church with stringent admission standards. "Wherein soever Revelation gives us plain and certain Rules for conduct, Reason itself obliges us to submit and follow them," Watts explained. "Where the rules of Duty are more obscure, we are to use our Reason to find them out, as far as we can, by comparing one Part of Revelation with another, and making just and reasonable Inferences."[22]

From there, Watts showed the importance of reason to church formation. "*The Light of Reason* teacheth, that there must be a mutual Consent, Compact, or Agreement, amongst such Persons as profess the same Religion, to walk according to the Directions and Dictates of it." Perpetuating the church by admitting properly qualified members, he continued, was essential. On this issue, Watts cited both reason and the New Testament: common sense dictated that members with like views band together, and that these members "will think it proper to cast such Persons out of their Fellowship, that they may not infect the rest, nor dishonour their Religion." But the New Testament also taught that the Christian church must take "take Care that they be kept pure, and free from Scandal, by separating themselves from evil Members, and by casting out those that depart from the Truth, or are guilty of gross Immoralities."[23]

Green agreed with Watts that only the elect can be full church members, and he decided by the early 1760s that he must fight for a purer church and, eventually, a purer society. He would, in other words, push to create a church where only the truly repentant could be full members, and he would work to cleanse society of some of its most pernicious shortcomings, including the holding of fellow human beings in bondage. Where to begin, though, in this audacious crusade to change the world? Green chose a logical place—his home church on Hanover Neck. He would institute a far stricter policy toward church membership and the partaking of the sacraments in Hanover. Green formally announced this shift in a sermon on baptism that he delivered to his congregation on November 4, 1764, but he began his effort several years earlier. Green then expounded on his views in two long tracts that he published in 1768 and 1770.[24]

The baptism issue had been bedeviling Puritan New England since the days of the Great Migration in the 1630s. Who, exactly, was eligible for baptism? An adult who could show he was of the elect? An infant who was the offspring of full church members? Or could the children of the unregenerate be baptized, too? These seemingly mundane questions masked a far more serious one: how pure should the church be? In the heady early days of New England's founding, Puritan radicals came down on the side of purity by baptizing only those children of parents who were communicant members. However, following the adoption of the "halfway covenant" in 1662 by a synod of clergy, the Puritan movement became more "liberal" on these questions. The halfway covenant permitted the offspring of partial members to be baptized, and the practice gradually took hold throughout New England under the prodding of Solomon Stoddard and other reformers. Soon, many Puritans were asking whether the same liberalizing tendencies should be applied to the other sacrament, communion. Stoddard, of course, answered yes. Those individuals who lived scandal-free and sought to become Christians should be permitted to partake in the Lord's Supper, he argued. Stoddard saw the administering of the sacraments as a recruiting tool to bring more people to Christ.[25]

Because of Dickinson's influence, Green had followed the Stoddardean position during his first decade as a Presbyterian pastor. In the November 4 sermon, Green informed the congregation that he had changed his mind; he also explained at length the centrality of baptism to his vision of a purer church. The act, he told the congregants, "signifies the washing away [of] our native and contracted guilt and defilement," and as such qualified baptism as a seal. Receiving baptism meant that its recipient was one of God's "visible people"—he or she was of the elect, in other words, one of God's chosen saints. Because of baptism's great importance, not everyone automatically qualified for it.[26]

In explaining why, Green returned to the Calvinistic conundrum about behavior and free will. God is all-powerful, yet we all have a choice; thus moral behavior falls into two categories—"natural and instituted duties." The former, he said, involved basic acts of human decency, such as living honestly and ethically: "Every rational creature is bound to perform them, and sins less while he endeavours to perform them." The latter was different. Instituted duties involved Christian duties mandated by God, and Green cited three examples—the gospel ministry, baptism, and the Lord's Supper. Not all individuals are cut out for the ministry, he said; they are called to it. "Nor may any draw near to God in the reception of the sacraments, (which are instituted duties) unless they are such persons as he declares qualified for them." Adults have to qualify for baptism, Green stressed, and those "who openly continue in the sins of drunkenness, profane swearing, uncleanness, and the like scandalous vices" were disqualified.[27]

But, according to Green, the standards were high for baptizing infants as well—their parents had to be in good standing with the church and be able to qualify for communion. Here, Green was raising the bar ever higher: it was not enough for an individual to have been baptized in childhood and to attend services as an adult; parents who wanted their children baptized must "renew the covenant . . . [and meet] the same qualifications, as if they were to be baptized themselves." They must be full members, in other words. Green was thus rejecting the key Arminian premise that baptizing anyone was a way to draw more people to the church. What was the point, then, of baptizing babies? Green answered that the act signaled something important: it bestowed "God's seal or mark" on children and demonstrated to them that God will be watching over them. It also signaled that these children would be under the care of the church and "watched over in a kind friendly manner."[28]

Green outlined the specific requirements that adult applicants must meet to qualify for baptism. The first was "a competent degree of christian knowledge; . . . God must be worshipped with understanding." The second was that "they must be free from scandalous sins and offensive behaviour."

Moreover, applicants have to "be actually engaged in the positive and practical parts of religions. . . . They must manifest a relish for religion, and the company and conversation of godly people; a reverence for the holy name of God."[29]

In making his case for such rigorous standards, first succinctly in the 1764 sermon and then at length in his later tracts, Green fell back on his core Puritan beliefs and the arguments of Jonathan Edwards and Isaac Watts. The Puritans' covenant of grace defined his understanding of what constituted a "proper profession" by seekers. The covenant represented "a command and a promise" between man and God, Green told his congregants. On man's part, he is to "acknowledge his sin, the evil he has done, the miserable condition he has brot himself into." For those who repent, God will then grant "eternal happiness" and "the enjoyment of God himself." By embracing the covenant of grace, Green stressed, a seeker shows that "we prefer God and Christ to everything else; that we love his will, and take his word for our rule; that we hate sin, and watch against it. Now, persons that can say this, have true religion."[30]

In this way, covenantal theory underlay Green's view of the sacraments and a pure church. It was impossible for God to "enter into covenant with unregenerate men," he said. Both sides, he reiterated, made promises to each other. Breaking that promise rendered a seeker unfit—"dangerous" even—to partake in the sacraments. God "has appointed his faithful servants to profess their regard to him, & exhibit the evidence of their compliance with his holy Covenant . . . and to seal it in certain Sacraments: And that God on his part has appointed certain sacraments . . . to be signs themselves of the good that shall flow of them that comply with his covenant." He warned that he could not permit someone to partake of one sacrament (baptism) but not the other (communion): "Such a person cannot act right in one Sacrament, while he is under so great Errors as to the other." Thus Green concluded that the same demanding standards for baptism should be applied to communion—only the regenerate can come to the Lord's Table.[31]

In making these arguments, Green rejected the halfway covenant and everything he once liked about Stoddard's inclusiveness. Admitting the unregenerate, he explained, "gradually weakens & destroys chh. discipline." It gives sway to the uncommitted and undermines the purity of the devout. Because of the dangers of admitting the unsaved, it was important for the church to maintain some separation from the world. "The door of the church is not to be opened to take in all the world," he told his Hanover congregation. "The church and the world are distinct things according to scripture." If the church let in sinners, it would "flatter" them and "let them build up self-righteousness." It would also "tend to destroy the peculiar love, union, and communion that ought to be among chh. members." And it would put the unregenerate in positions of power—they would have a say in the running of the congregation and the choosing of ministers and church officers. Most of all, letting the unregenerate in would lower the barrier between the church and the world, allowing the sins of the outside to infiltrate the church and pollute it. In advocating for a purer church, Green also wanted to head off the threat posed by the regenerate who stray from God's ways. Stoddardeans and other rationalists cast a forgiving eye on these backsliders, but Green felt they must be dealt with sternly through excommunication, a harsh punishment that most congregations tried to avoid. "What's so terrible in excommunication?" he wondered. He defended it as the best way "to shew them, & others, that they belong to Satan, & that these sins [if] continued will shut them out of heaven & leave them to go to hell with all the unregenerate."[32]

Green began to make concrete changes in Hanover as early as 1757. The most important one was to tighten the standards for baptism and for admittance to communion. From 1747 to 1756, during his Stoddardean phase, Jacob performed an average of eighteen baptisms a year, with a high of twenty-two in 1755 and a low of fourteen in 1748. In the 1760s, he did about seven baptisms a year—less than half of what he had done a decade earlier. To determine whether someone was worthy of admission to the sacraments, Green summoned the applicant to a meeting, where he questioned the person on his or her spiritual state. It was a task, of course, that Green took seriously. He likened the minister's role to that of a "doorkeeper" who is "under solemn obligations to take care, that those they admit be duly qualified according to the rules of God's word." Yet Jacob leavened his tough stance with a touch of humility. "Gospel ministers," he conceded, could "not pretend to discern the heart [of seekers], or determine who are internally gracious." Instead, based on these interviews, Jacob admitted to the sacraments those persons "who make an understanding profession of faith, repentance, and new obedience, and whose behaviour and practice gives reason to think their profession is sincere."[33]

The tightening of standards created no fissures within the congregation. Quite the opposite. In his autobiography, Green observed that it was his Stoddardean "sentiments" of the 1740s allowing looser admission practices that were unpopular with most members. Implementing tougher standards did not result in any overt protests in Hanover or lead to Green's ouster, noteworthy outcomes when contrasted with Edwards's experience in Northampton. When he succeeded his grandfather as congregational pastor, Edwards continued Solomon Stoddard's liberal (and popular) policies on admission to the church and the sacraments. But, like Green, Edwards was never comfortable with the looser standards, and after intense study he, too, concluded that such permissiveness was false and unbiblical. His decision to abandon the halfway covenant and end Stoddard's standards caused an uproar in the church. The protests were so virulent that they contributed to Edwards's dismissal as pastor in 1750.[34]

Nothing like that occurred in Hanover. Instead, Green pressed on with the task of building a stronger Presbyterian faith. Presbyterianism was a growing force in Morris County in the prerevolutionary years, and the denomination's strength radiated outward from Hanover. Up to the mid-1750s Hanover Township—a large territory that encompassed Whippany to the south and Dover to the north—had the only Presbyterian church in the area. As the old 1718 meetinghouse deteriorated and the Presbyterian population grew, the presbytery finally agreed in 1755 to build two more meetinghouses, one at Hanover Neck (Green's home church) and one at Parsippany. Jacob also served as Parsippany's minister until 1760, when the congregation got its own pastor. By 1775, the Presbyterians had nine congregations in Morris County, the vast majority in Hanover and Morris Townships. By comparison, six other faiths (Baptist, Quaker, Congregationalist, Dutch Reformed, Lutheran, and German Reformed) had only one church in the county each. Thomas Bradbury Chandler's Church of England had none.[35]

Green's contributions to Presbyterianism's growth in Morris County were both intellectual (he worked out the Calvinistic doctrines that underlay the creation of a purer, stronger church in Hanover) and mundane (he began keeping records and introducing Presbyterian structures to the congregation). During these years, Green matured as a leader. Gone was the nervousness and indecisiveness from his first years on the job. He emerged from his theological studies convinced that he had to act, and his congregation was solidly behind him. It suffered from none of the New Light–Old Light splits that bedeviled other Presbyterian churches.

Ironically, this future champion of laymen's rights shared the view of his New England compatriots that the minister was the undisputed leader of the congregation. In a Puritan world, the pastor was a highly respected person who was seen as a member of the local aristocracy. Green brought this mind-set with him to New Jersey, and he ruled the congregation for many years strongly, almost haughtily. When he tightened admission standards in the 1760s, he did so without getting the approval of the elders or the presbytery. Green interviewed candidates on his own and decided by himself whether someone should be admitted to the church or the sacraments. When Green concluded that the person was worthy of admission, he passed along his rec-ommendation to the church.[36]

Hanover, of course, was a *Presbyterian* church, and this meant that it placed limits on Green's authority. When he arrived in 1745, Hanover already had deacons in place—but no elders. Green may have seen himself as the congregation's undisputed leader, but he also well understood in these early years the strengths of the Presbyterian system. To lead effectively, the pastor needed allies among the laity. Without such support, Green could meet the same fate as his two predecessors. Jacob thus moved quickly to get elders in place. In June 1747, a few months after he was formally installed as Hanover's pastor, five men were selected as elders. All were from leading families and possessed the stature and wealth to help Green lead; two (John Ball and Joseph Tuttle) were longtime deacons and thus the only officers when Jacob came to Hanover.[37]

The Ball family was among the earliest arrivals to Hanover: Caleb migrated from Newark about 1710, bought land on Hanover Neck, and became a part owner of the forge known locally as the "Old Iron Works." The Tuttles came later than the Balls but achieved greater prominence. Joseph Tuttle pur-chased land in Hanover in 1725 and added to it in 1734, when he bought 1,250 acres at Hanover Neck. As a wealthy landowner, Joseph became a county freeholder at Morris's founding, and he worked with Green for years as deacon and elder. They were close enough that Green wrote the inscrip-tion on his gravestone when Tuttle died in 1789 at the ripe old age of ninety-one, with Green praising Tuttle's leadership and "virtuous honor." Joseph Kitchel came from a large landowning family in Hanover Neck, where the new meetinghouse was built, and the Kitchells held a variety of posts in the county. Joseph farmed part of a 1,075-acre tract that he and his brother John inherited from their father.[38]

Besides relying on the help of the congregation's elders and deacons, Green had two boards at his disposal—a parish board that assisted with the financial details of running a church, and a Presbyterian session of elders that handled discipline and "other matters of record," according to its minutes. The parish board met periodically in the prewar years, but the session did not convene regularly until 1771, some six years after Jacob formally tightened admission standards to the church and the sacraments. For more than twenty years, in other words, Green pretty much acted alone in matters of church doctrine, although he likely consulted with the elders and had their support when he wanted to make changes.[39]

The main concern of the parish board was replacing the decrepit meetinghouse. In 1754, the board selected a five-person committee, including elder Ephraim Price, Jr., to oversee the construction of an edifice just to the east of the 1718 meetinghouse on land donated by Henry Burnet. The committee was in charge of raising money, supervising construction, and handling a host of other mundane details, such as deciding what to do with salvageable parts from the 1718 meetinghouse (it voted to give Parsippany the pulpit, the seats from the gallery, and the windows and glass). Because money was so tight, building the replacement was no easy task. Construction dragged on for years, and the parish board struggled to complete the project.[40]

In April 1758 it appointed a new four-person board to again try to raise enough money to finish the meetinghouse. Seven years later, the parish board gave the go-ahead to plaster the building. Two years later the church was still unfinished. Green was not pleased with the slow progress or with how the meetinghouse itself was shaping up. The money shortage meant that the congregation was relying on temporary seating and not pews; it also meant that the seating arrangements were haphazard. People sat wherever they wanted. In 1769, Green asked the board to reconfigure the church interior so that pews would replace the "common seats" in the west gallery and in an unfinished section. Jacob had several goals in mind when he made this proposal. Two were seemingly routine. The congregation would assign pews so that people would know where to sit, and it would charge rent, thus raising badly needed revenue for the church. But he also wanted to improve discipline and encourage piety within families: families would sit together in cordoned-off pews (thus promoting unity) and parents could better keep an eye on their children (thus promoting order). In taking this position Green was once again showing his traditional, even aristocratic mien. In New England and elsewhere, the renting of pews reinforced the traditional order of colonial society: the wealthy and the powerful sat in front, in the choicest seats; the less well-off sat in the back or the gallery. Church seating, as a result, reinforced society's gradations, and it helped to maintain order. The elite led; followers followed. Jacob shared this view, and he saw pews as an important aid in building the kind of congregation he wanted. Green felt so strongly about the need for pews that he volunteered to pay for them himself—a startling offer since Green felt he was badly underpaid. The board accepted his offer, although it promised to reimburse him later.[41]

To aid his efforts to raise standards among members, Green donned the cloak of a teacher. It was a task he performed daily. Green preferred meeting with congregants in private meetings, where he posed questions to them "and [would] hear them answer . . . as they thought proper." On other occasions Green encouraged members to submit questions to him, which he treated as an opportunity to deliver a lecture: "At these meetings I thought it proper to speak upon some things, and in a manner, that would not have been proper for the pulpit." He also encouraged discussion among attendees. Green worked hard to establish a rapport with his membership. He made a point of visiting every single family early in his pastorship, devoting two days a week to this task: "When I came to the house, and the family was collected together, I first prayed with them; and then I began with the youngest, and so proceeded on till I came to the heads of the family—asking questions and discoursing, according to their several capacities."[42]

Prayer was an important part of these private meetings as well, and Green set aside at least one day a month for such sessions, "when my elders and I have, by turns, prayed and sung, &c. These days I have found useful in keeping up some sense of religion." Green demanded a lot from his membership—and from himself. He understood that he led by example; as he put it, "I have been very sensible that my own personal religion was of great importance to myself, and to others." He thus fasted at least once a month: "On these fasting days, I used to write my wants, or the things that I would, for each day, bear particularly on my mind before God." He would then mediate on these wants and write out a series of resolutions.[43]

One evangelical tool Green had little use for was the revival. This was somewhat surprising, given his support of the Great Awakening, his belief in evangelism, and his assertion in his 1770 tract that one way to end all the arguing over admission standards was to spark a revival of religion and create more qualified applicants for the church. Yet in the prewar years, Green led only three revivals: in 1756, 1764, and 1774, and most can be traced to personal causes. In 1756, Jacob's first wife, Anna Strong, died, and to assuage his grief, Jacob threw himself into his work. "I was for a twelve-month after that event remarkably stirred up, quickened and engaged," he explained. "I prayed and preached with an increased sense of divine things." The impetus for the 1774 revival came from another unfortunate development: Green suffered an "apoplectic fit" (in the words of his son Ashbel) so serious that his family and congregation feared he would die. The crisis produced soul-searching within both Jacob and church members. Although seemingly close to death, Jacob retained "perfect possession of his intellectual facul-ties," Ashbel said. He asked his eldest daughter to read from the gospel of John, which "produced in him a kind of holy rapture." Meanwhile, when doctors warned that Jacob might not make it through the night, neighbor-ing ministers and the Hanover congregation gathered to pray for his life. Their intercession, according to Ashbel, produced miraculous results: "The man who expected to be in eternity before morning—an expectation in which physicians as well as friends concurred—was in the morning, free from almost every threatening symptom of his disease." A relieved Jacob turned the episode into a lesson on God's goodness, and he pressed on with the revival. "In this sickness, I had remarkable views of divine things, and received uncommon tokens of favour from my people, who were then full of religion," Jacob recalled.[44]

But overall, this most serious of men was uncomfortable with the histri-onics of the revival, and pressing outside obligations kept him from feeling the spirit. Instead, the sermon remained Green's primary teaching tool and his preferred medium for bringing people to Christ. The sermon was the high point of the service, and it provided a forum for Green to inculcate religious and educational values to his parishioners. As his daybooks and sermon notes reveal, he put a tremendous amount of thought into the ser-mon. In a typical week, according to his diary, he delivered at least two of them—one on Sundays in Hanover, and one during the week at other Pres-byterian churches in Morris County or at members' houses. Often he gave a series of sermons on one theme that could last six weeks or more. Green wrote his weekly sermons on scraps of paper—some in Weston's shorthand, others in partial sentences. These sermons were more than outlines, though. Throughout his forty-five-year career in the ministry, Jacob never possessed the confidence to speak extemporaneously as a George Whitefield would. Yet the meticulous preparation also reflected Jacob's values. His approach was a hybrid between the latitudinarian and urbane sermons favored by many of his Harvard classmates such as Jonathan Mayhew, and the emo-tional and pietistic sermons of most Yale-trained pastors. His style, in other words, was closer to a Jonathan Edwards—studious, carefully prepared, well argued, but seeking to arouse an emotional response from the audience. Jacob carefully stated his thesis or argument based on the day's biblical text (in fact, in his daybook, he stressed that the minister should select the text first and the discourse second), and he proceeded to defend it in clear, at times compelling prose, backing up his main points with everyday metaphors that his listeners could easily grasp.[45]

Green was remarkably consistent in his message. He wanted to change people's behavior and get them to reform their ways. For him, that was the key to bringing them into the invisible church. He had little use for millennial themes. Nor, unlike many evangelical preachers and itinerants (especially Methodists on the frontier), did he discuss his own trials: his struggles to achieve a rebirth and avoid backsliding remained private. Instead, out of the hundreds of sermons that he delivered in the prewar years, one theme predominated: the importance of moral responsibility and the need for sinners to recognize the imminent dangers. In 1768, in Morristown, Green took to the pulpit at the Presbyterian church there. He drew his inspiration from the gospel of John and John's warnings about arrogance—"You search the Scriptures, for in them you think you have eternal life," with his main point coming from chapter 5, verse 40: "But you are not willing to come to Me that you may have life." From that key line, Green delivered his sermon lesson, expounding on the threats from unregeneracy. "Unregenerate sinners," he told his listeners, "are loath to believe that they are so bad, so wicked & blamable as they really are. They are willing to believe & at length do believe that they are not so very bad." Jacob's purpose in these sermons was to get people to understand the nature of sinning and the offensiveness of sinners' behavior. "Light & happiness are to be obtained by coming to him or complying with the terms of salvation," he told his listeners. In a line that reflected his views of an unregenerate's spiritual inability, he added, "But sinners will not come, they are unwilling to comply." They are, in other words, blind to the saving grace of Jesus Christ.[46]

Green believed he was delivering an effective sermon if he acted as "an advocate for Virtue & Religion; to attain that improvement of Understanding, that purity of heart, dignity & even severity of Character." And he could do that only if he spoke from the heart and with a deep knowledge of his subject. "The authority of the speaker does not arise from superior station; or power annexed to the office," he noted in his daybook. "But it is of a more sacred kind, founded in superior wisdom & Virtue. An uncommon Eloquence gives a superiority over the Minds of Men: but wisdom seen & acknowledged gives a greater & stronger superiority than Eloquence can give."[47]

Week after week, he tried to get Presbyterians and other attendees to understand what was at stake. Hell awaited the unregenerate and "the fallen race of Adam." Green constructed one such sermon around a passage from Mark 9:47–48: "And if your eye causes you to sin, pluck it out. It is better for you to enter the kingdom of God with one eye, rather than having two eyes, to be cast into hell fire." From that text, Green delivered his stark warning. "Hell is a place with a real material Fire," he explained. "Sinners will receive the greatest punishment they are capable of both in body & Soul." The punishment was so severe that they faced something akin to torture—their bodies would "be kept alive in the midst of a burning fire."[48]

Heaven or hell? It was up to God. "You are in God's hands," Green declared in a 1769 sermon. He alone will determine when you die and whether you will receive a spiritual pardon. "Consider what poor brittle clay you are in the hand of an angry God. You are but as clay in the hand of him the potter who can make you the vessel of his wrath whenever he pleases. Your life . . . is in his hand." God's wrath, Green continued, "is very terrible; when he riseth up none can stand before him."[49]

Some of this language, especially references to an angry God, echoed Edwards's teachings. Yet Green's intent was more than to scare people. He also described the joys of heaven that awaited the elect. But upstanding Christian behavior was essential if someone was to demonstrate that she was among the saved. Many a sermon began by describing the dangers awaiting the sinner before segueing to the eternal rewards available to the repentant; the wrathful God was also a loving God. The 1769 sermon warning of God's terrible vengeance concluded by urging people to open their hearts to him— "God is willing to be reconciled to you," Green stated plainly. The Lord, he continued, "has endowed man with a rational & spiritual substances. . . . He has given us passion of love & hatred, hope & fear, joy & sorrow. . . . And all these things God has appointed to work to getting for our Good." The happy conclusion: "God has told us if we are obedient all is glorious & perfection."[50]

Green's weekly sermons thus softened Calvinism's hard edges and appealed to the enlightened rationalist among his audience. Yes, God decided all, and, yes, hell awaited the unsaved, but there was much the good Christian could do to avoid such an awful fate. As Green explained in one sermon, "Mankind has Reason & Understanding & Understanding & Light . . . the Fall has not destroyed man's Reason & Understanding . . . mankind are capable by these to know & discover the Faith respecting God & his Perfections as is clear from Roman 1:20–21"—a passage that emphasized "since the creation of the world His invisible attributes are clearly seen."[51]

Subtle, Jacob Green's views were not. The indecision of the late 1740s and early 1750s was gone, replaced by the 1760s by a clear, forceful expression of his religious beliefs.

## The Loyalist Down the Road: Thomas Bradbury Chandler, Anglican Convert

Unlike in the case of Jacob Green, there was little doubt that Thomas would attend college, and there was no need for him to wait on tables once he got there. He enrolled at Yale and, based on the Chandler pedigree, was ranked seventh in the incoming class of twenty-seven students. Like Jacob, Thomas was a natural student, becoming known at college for his piety and learning. Although Yale and Harvard had their peculiarities (Harvard was far more "liberal" and latitudinarian than was its Connecticut rival), Thomas's course of study differed little from Jacob's. Thomas studied the ancient languages, logic, natural philosophy, metaphysics, ethics, and all the other things a young gentleman needed to become a minister. He graduated from Yale in 1745, a year after Green left Cambridge.

He was nineteen.

Chandler thus knew at a far younger age than did Green that he wanted to be a minister, and he suffered from none of the insecurities that beset his Presbyterian counterpart. Chandler was raised a Congregationalist and hailed from a family with deep roots in the Puritan church. But Congregationalism was not a good fit for this fifth-generation Chandler. He studied theology under someone more congenial to his tastes and proclivities—Samuel Johnson, an Anglican and the future president of King's College in New York City. Johnson and Chandler developed deep bonds of affection, with the former serving as Thomas's mentor. (Thomas later wrote a reverential memoir of Johnson's life.) Johnson, for his part, recognized how gifted Chandler was, praising him as "a truly valuable person, of good parts and competent learning . . . and of good morals and virtuous behavior."

From Johnson, Thomas learned the ways of the king's church. The Church of England was a state-established institution that had, following the reforms of King Henry VIII, become an arm of the government. The monarch was the church's supreme earthly leader who appointed the bishops who ran the church. In Puritan New England, the state wanted each congregation to encourage people to turn to Jesus Christ. In England and its foreign domains, the state wanted its church to produce two things—good Christians *and* good citizens. It saw the two goals as complementary. Devout Christians attending church regularly would make for orderly, loyal subjects of the king. For the state, the church was to reinforce the government's power, and the state was to reinforce the church's power. Samuel Johnson was a good High Church Anglican who was wholeheartedly devoted to the Henrician legacy. He backed the state church and all that it stood for; in an age when Protestantism was expanding and roiled with factionalism, he was dismissive of dissenters, especially of the Puritan variety. Thomas recalled that his mentor had "an early dislike" of Congregationalism because it gave too much power to the people. Johnson found lay exhorters "ignorant" because they uttered "the most horrid expressions concerning God and religion." He especially disliked Presbyterian Jonathan Dickinson, an early mentor of Jacob Green, because he was "a true zealot against the Church."

Under Johnson's guidance, Chandler converted to Anglicanism and was quickly identified as a rising star in the king's American church. Within two years of leaving Yale, he watched the offers for his services pour in. In 1747, two churches asked him to serve as a catechist; instead, he accepted the advances of St. Peter's Church in Westchester, New York. He did not remain there long. St. John's Church in Elizabeth Town, New Jersey, was so impressed with Chandler that it persuaded him to join it in December of that year, despite the fact that he remained too young to be ordained as a minister. Thus, as the winter days shortened and the afternoon shadows lengthened, Thomas Bradbury Chandler packed his bags and headed to East Jersey—dissenter country, bastion of Presbyterianism and Whig radicalism, and the home of that detested "zealot" Jonathan Dickinson and his protégé Jacob Green.[52]

# 3

*Father*

The center of Jacob Green's domestic universe was a handsome one-and-a-half-story parsonage on Hanover Neck (fig. 5). It was an unpretentious house befitting the domicile of a Presbyterian pastor ministering to a country church—a residence that was approximately half the size of the mission house that Jonathan Edwards resided at in Stockbridge, Massachusetts—but the parsonage, with its symmetrical windows and centered doorway, did offer up a touch of rustic Georgian elegance. Inside was a mix of the practical and the pious, the simple and the elegant. Green's growing family attended to their household chores while the patriarch retreated to his book-lined study to write his sermons and peruse his diverse library of theology, philosophy, history, and literature. Jacob may have preached simplicity in his sermons, but his domestic space demonstrated he had a taste for the refined. His family dined on queensware and pewter plates—luxuries few could afford in early America—and for amusement members could play a forte piano.[1]

Outside the parsonage was a complex landscape that reflected the myriad interests of a financially struggling country parson. The house sat on ten acres surrounded by cornfields and cleared swampland; within shouting distance were a barn and a tenant's farmhouse. Across the street was Jacob's Latin academy, where for a time he taught school to approximately eight boys from throughout Morris County. A little farther on, about a quarter of

*Fig. 5*  The Greens lived in a simple but handsome parsonage that the Hanover congregation built, and finally finished, in 1758. It sat on ten acres and was surrounded by cornfields and cleared swampland. Drawing by Stephen Manson.

a mile from the parsonage, was the new meetinghouse, which finally replaced the dilapidated structure that greeted Jacob in 1745. And farther still was the gristmill that Green partially owned on land he used to farm.[2]

In important ways, the completion of the parsonage in spring 1758 represented another step toward stability for the thirty-six-year-old parson, with the house helping to anchor Jacob in this Presbyterian world as he pondered the larger questions concerning God and society that so consumed him in the two decades before the American Revolution. Before the congregation agreed to build the parsonage in 1754 (construction began in 1757), Jacob and his family lived in a small house in lower Whippany that he had built largely at his own expense after his arrival in Hanover Township in 1745.[3]

Between 1745 and 1756, Green experienced the highs of seeing four children born and the lows of his wife's death—his beloved Anna. Although such setbacks were not unusual for the times (one of his deacons endured the deaths of five wives), they tested Green's faith and darkened his mood as he struggled to establish himself in a new colony. Jacob had arrived in Hanover in 1745 as a bachelor and remained one for two years, an eternity in the harried life of a country parson with a demanding flock to tend and a large territory to oversee. In 1747, things changed for the better when he married Anna Strong. How the young couple met is unclear—Jacob was loath to discuss such intimate details in his autobiography, and two sons from a later marriage who wrote about their upbringing never knew her. Anna hailed from the fishing and farming community of Brookhaven, New York, on the western end of Long Island, within hailing distance of New York City. The paths of Jacob and Anna likely crossed during one of Jacob's trips to synodical meetings in Newark or New York.[4]

Despite his silence about their courtship, Jacob loved her. The marriage produced four children in eight years—three daughters and a son. The first child, who was born in the fall of 1748, only a year after the wedding, was named in honor of her mother. When Anna died of "a consumption" in November 1756, according to Jacob, her death left her husband badly shaken. Describing Anna as a "tender amiable Wife," her gravestone reflected the grief that her passing produced: "A Blessing to her Relatives in Life / Her Death their Loss beyond expression grate." For Jacob, a strict Calvinist who viewed the powers of God as absolute and magisterial, Anna's early death at age thirty-one was portentous. It sent him into mourning and caused him to become even more reflective about the questions that had occupied him for years—the tenuousness and brevity of life, the power and mystery of God. To work through his grief, Jacob began preaching more intently, which led to his first "revival" in Hanover—in addition to more emotional preaching, he divided the congregation into four sections for catechizing and "conversed with the youth every week." This quickened activity led to a revival of religion and a "special outpouring of the Holy Spirit" among congregants, according to his son Ashbel. Jacob thus strove to turn his personal tragedy into something positive. He would use his revival as an opportunity to strengthen the congregation and spark a resurgence of piety among Hanover's populace. The loss of his wife also strengthened Green's Calvinistic faith. "I prayed and preached with an increased sense of divine things," Jacob wrote years later. "I would thank God; for I would give him the glory of exciting and quickening me." It was a marked contrast to his feelings in 1745, when he struggled to understand the paradoxes posed by Calvinism.[5]

In October 1757, as carpenters readied the parsonage for their minister and his children, Green remarried. The marriage was both a bow to the practical needs of family and a signal that Green was moving on in the wake of his wife's death. Jacob had several young children to raise and a household to run. He needed a helpmate. The woman who filled this void and took Anna's place at the hearth was Elizabeth Pierson, and there is little doubt about how the two met. She was the daughter of a Presbyterian pastor named John Pierson, who ministered to a congregation in nearby Mendham, after having served earlier in Woodbridge, New Jersey, and was well-known and respected in church circles. He was born in 1689, was a Yale graduate, and was a Puritan descendant who gained a reputation as a Presbyterian moderate. As a close friend of Jonathan Dickinson's, Pierson possibly got to know Jacob in Elizabeth Town. Pierson was also a founder of the College of New Jersey, and they may well have connected through that association. Regardless, John came to live with his daughter and new son-in-law after he retired from the pulpit, and he spent his remaining years in the Hanover parsonage.[6]

The second marriage, like the first one, produced a bushel of children—seven in twelve years, beginning in 1758 with the birth of Elizabeth and ending in 1769 with the arrival of John Wickliffe (only six survived; the biblically named Benoni was born in 1760 and did not live to see his first birthday). The match between Jacob and his bride was excellent. Besides a strong physical attraction, the couple shared a commitment to the Presbyterian Church and a love of books. "Both my parents were eminently pious," noted Ashbel, the talented third child of Jacob and Elizabeth who was born in 1762. "My mother [was] always praying with the family, when my father was from home." Together Jacob and Elizabeth introduced their children to Calvinistic religion and to the disciplined ways of Presbyterianism. Ashbel, a brilliant scholar who became a Presbyterian minister, was struck by just how stern his upbringing was: "In no other family have I ever known the Lord's day to be observed with equal strictness and solemnity." On Sundays, after Jacob had returned from church services, the parents gathered the children for "instruction and devotion," according to Ashbel. Writing in his old age, some seventy years later, Ashbel could still vividly recall seeing his father "sitting in his arm chair, and without book, and commonly with his eyes shut, asking in regular order every question in the Westminster Shorter Catechism, helping or correcting those [children] who could not repeat it perfectly."[7]

Jacob, of course, had strong views about the parental role in religion. The church, he passionately believed, could not do it alone; it was up to fathers and mothers to instill discipline in their children so that they could take their rightful places in the church upon reaching adulthood. "Warn your children," Green advised his Presbyterian congregants in one sermon. "Reason with them; shew them what they are doing. Give them advice; pray with and for them." The overarching point, he stressed, was to "bring the case often before God. He has the hearts of all in his hand. He can sanctify and make your children obedient." But children bore a responsibility, too; Green warned them that their actions had consequences and that poor choices could not be dismissed later as the follies of youth. Several misbehaviors especially concerned Green. Foremost was the child who disobeyed his or her parents; Jacob labeled such disobedience "a great sin, most contrary to the express command of God." By contrast, obeying thy parents "is a divine precept." The second serious transgression was "frequenting bad company," a sin that often led to further misbehaviors—fornication, excessive drinking, "sensual lusts," profaneness. For those youths who did engage in such acts, Jacob lectured that they had but one recourse: "Yield yourselves up into the hand of God. . . . Look to the mercy of God in Christ."[8]

Jacob relentlessly preached these values to his youthful congregants at church and to his children at home. He expected Ashbel and his other children to memorize key church doctrines—and he expected them to understand what they were reciting. Green liked to pose questions to his parishioners, and he used the same technique at home. According to Ashbel, after repeating the Westminster catechism the children had to answer questions "on five chapters previously prescribed." Jacob would then quiz them about the text he had preached on "and what we could recollect of the sermons we had heard." Ashbel's younger brother Calvin had similar recollections: "When I was young my father made it a point to chatechise us on Sabbath nights at 5 o'clock in summer and 6 o'clock in winter. He spent about one hour and a half instructing us." Jacob also encouraged his children to read beyond the Bible, including poetry, and these Sunday sessions were a time for them to describe their readings. "The whole," Ashbel said, "was concluded sometimes with a short address from my father, and always by an impressive prayer. No secular business, nor conversation on secular subjects, was allowed in the family, except that which related to milking the cows, and relieving the necessities of other brute animals."[9]

For Jacob and Elizabeth's offspring, growing up in such a demanding religious household obviously posed its challenges. Other children at other times did not handle such demands so well. In the late eighteenth century, James Finley came of age in a Presbyterian household much like the Greens. His stern father was pastor of the Presbyterian congregation at Cane Ridge, Kentucky, and he too made his children repeat the Westminster catechism. The father followed up with questions, just as Jacob Green did, but he did not always get the answers he wanted. In his autobiography James Finley recounted one tense exchange with his ministerial father:

> "James, do you pray?" I replied, "No, father, I do not."
> "Why do you not pray, my son?"
> "Because I do not see any use in it. If I am one of the elect, I will be saved in God's good time; and if I am one of the non-elect, praying will do me no good, as Christ did not die for them."

Young James Finley took pleasure in challenging his father. Questioning the tenets of his father's Presbyterian faith was a way to rebel against his Calvinist upbringing. Nor did young James confine his rebellion to the home—he also argued with his father's congregants about the shortcomings of Calvinism. He argued so much with church members, including the congregation's elders, that "I became very obnoxious to the high-tone Calvinists, and they looked upon me as very dangerous to their young people."[10]

The Green children caused their father no such embarrassment. Instead, they spoke lovingly of their parents and of their upbringing. For Ashbel, his years "under the paternal roof" were happy ones. And his brother Calvin, who was three years younger, spoke fondly of both parents but especially of his mother. "When I was 3 or 4 years old my Mother would take me by the hand and lead me to meeting and back again. There was a little foot path on one side of the road that I always walked in when I went to meeting," Calvin wrote in his short autobiography. "Oh, the best of Mothers to take care of me when young."[11]

These two sons did have mildly rebellious streaks. Excessive drinking was one of the biggest sins that Jacob railed against, but that did not stop Calvin from imbibing at the encouragement of acquaintances. "I heard some people say all must get drunk once," he recalled. So he did, on wine, and he got violently sick for his trouble. Calvin said he never got drunk again; "I think once is a plenty." In his autobiography, Ashbel confessed that he caused his parents some grief through his "acts of disobedience, and [through] the youthful and irregularities in which I indulged." He was surely exaggerating; Ashbel was well behaved throughout his childhood. "My early religious education preserved me, during the time I lived with my pious parents, from open and profligate vice," he said at another point, and it enabled him to keep his "native corruptions" under control.[12]

Ashbel did stand up to his father on one important issue. Jacob had peremptorily decided that of his four living sons, the oldest and the youngest should be "scholars" and the middle two should be "farmers or mechanics." As the second-oldest son, Ashbel was thus supposed to work with his hands. From an early age, however, Ashbel loved books and the classroom. Ironically, Jacob was partly responsible for Ashbel's rebellion. The Sunday sessions, where Jacob encouraged his children to read broadly, including poetry, planted a seed in Ashbel. His love of books further sprouted because of Jacob's insistence that his children, even those who were not destined to be "a professed scholar," master reading and grammar. Ashbel loved reading so much that for a time, in his own words, he "thirsted for the fame of a poet," and in his poetic compositions he drew the praise of his mother. Jacob did succeed in discouraging Ashbel from becoming a poet—he told his son "to aim at a good prose style, and to let poetry alone"—but not from attending college. Ashbel had an important ally in this quest: his mother. She "favoured" his desire to attend college, and Jacob eventually went along with it.[13]

Ashbel's experience was interesting on two levels. It mimicked Jacob's upbringing as a child: Jacob, too, was supposed to learn a trade, but he instead rebelled and ended up attending college. And the incident shows just how traditional Jacob Green's views of parenting were. He remained very much the controlling New England patriarch, with strong views of what his sons should do (he expressed no such concern for his daughters). During his lifetime he set up all his sons on nearby farms but kept ownership of the land until his death; his daughters received only money when he died in 1790, although he did bequeath one-third of his real estate to his wife—another sign of his conventionality. Green's approach to his sons resembled the behavior of fathers in Andover, Massachusetts, and other New England villages during the prerevolutionary years. By keeping title to their lands, these fathers maintained a degree of control over their sons, who sought independence by acquiring farms of their own and starting families.

Inheritance practices, as a result, were designed to extend patriarchy. A family's wealth rested on land, and the father in turn controlled the land and thus his sons by keeping title to these holdings.[14]

In Jacob's case, he carefully accumulated land after his arrival in Hanover in 1745. He first bought 120 acres in lower Whippany, then supplemented this purchase through the years until he had enough land for the four sons born during his second marriage. Calvin, the second-youngest son in Green's second marriage, lived on eighty acres; Ashbel, the second-oldest son, received fifty acres and the rights to Jacob's ownership in a grist- and a sawmill, as well as the two-acre lot that the mill sat on and the eighteen acres that surrounded it. The oldest son, Pierson, got the plantation that straddled Essex and Morris Counties, while the youngest, John Wickliffe, was bequeathed the fifty acres that constituted the "rest of the Willow meadow place."[15]

Jacob is not so easy to classify as a "traditionalist," however. Unlike many fathers of English descent who practiced primogeniture, Jacob did not favor the oldest son. In fact, Pierson in some ways was treated the most harshly. He received a smaller portion than did Calvin, and Jacob accorded him even less freedom than he did for Calvin: Jacob placed Pierson's seventy-five acres in a trust administered by three church members for the support of Pierson's family. Calvin apparently got the largest farm because, unlike the scholarly (and mildly rebellious) Ashbel, he was the most committed to farming. Thus Jacob was fairly unconventional on this front; he did not practice primogeniture like most English patriarchs, yet he did not treat his sons equally like most German-speaking colonists did. But he *did* favor his sons over his daughters; only the young men received land. Green's daughters got money, and the amounts varied. Elizabeth, the eldest daughter in his second marriage, received $240 while Dorothy got $210 in Spanish dollars and Keturah $210 in regular money. The children of Abigail, the daughter from his first marriage who was dead, divided up $160.[16]

Despite his cultivated mind and his rock-solid commitment to the church, Jacob retained a fondness for the agricultural pursuits of his New England childhood. "Indeed, he had such an opinion of the importance of knowing how to manage a farm, that he engaged a pious and distinguished farmer of his congregation, to take charge of my elder brother and myself," Ashbel recalled. This congregation member taught the two boys all aspects of farming. "In consequence of this," Ashbel said wryly, "I became acquainted with every species of farming business; from which, as it has turned out, I have derived very little other advantage than being able . . . to cultivate a large garden with skill and success."[17]

Calvin apparently had no academic inclinations, and he dutifully followed the path that his father set out for him. In his teens he learned farming, first from a tenant farmer named Jeb Roberts and then from William Ball. In 1781, when Calvin was sixteen, Jacob informed his son that it was time to master a trade, and he sent Calvin to learn shoemaking and tanning from a friend and neighbor named John Smithson. Jacob also informed him that "I must know what it was to get a living," Calvin wrote in his autobiography. "He said I must pay him for my board which was a dollar a week and he would pay me for my work. I thought it a little hard at first but I soon found it was for the best." Calvin's reward for his loyalty and hard work was to receive the largest tract of land from Jacob, the main plantation, and a ten-year supply of hay after his father's passing.[18]

As Ashbel's experience indicated, Jacob did want all of his children— including his daughters—and grandchildren to receive some schooling, and he usually took care of their education himself. Across the street from the parsonage he built a schoolhouse that he used to teach his children and fee-paying pupils. Some of the students even boarded with the Greens and later with Calvin, who reported housing four of the Latin academy students. The academy combined the functions of a modern elementary school—Jacob taught grammar, arithmetic, writing, and reading—as well as college preparatory for the more advanced, where they learned Latin and other skills needed for higher learning. Ashbel's early education included mastering grammar: when he was only seven years old Jacob had him reading "Cheever's Accidence" and Latin; Calvin reported being able to read from the Bible by age six. And, true to character, Jacob ran his school with a stern hand. Ashbel explained that his father took on pupils "on the condition, that he should direct their studies" and that students would need to recite their lessons. "He would discharge them, if they were idle, or failed to make progress, according to their capacities."[19]

A number of Jacob's students, including Ashbel and the youngest son John Wickliffe, went on to enroll at the College of New Jersey at Princeton. Two others who attended Princeton were Samuel Beach, who was born in 1761, and Mahlon Dickerson, who was born in 1770. Samuel and Ashbel were friends. They enrolled together at Princeton in spring 1782 as juniors, roomed together, and helped revive the college's American Whig Society. Beach became a tutor at his alma mater, and he later studied law under Richard

Stockton. Dickerson was from a wealthy background. His family, which migrated to Hanover from Long Island, achieved affluence through land-holding, iron mining, and manufacturing. Young Mahlon first studied Latin under Caleb Russell in Morristown, then attended several other schools before ending up at Green's academy in 1786. Under Jacob's firm guidance, Mahlon studied math, geography, and languages. A year later he entered Princeton and thrived, going on to become a successful businessman and politician (he served as New Jersey governor, U.S. senator, and secretary of the Navy).[20]

Jacob's daughters apparently were as literate as their brothers, if Jacob's will is any indication. In dividing his prized library of approximately one hundred books, Pierson, Calvin, Elizabeth, and Keturah were each allowed to select any ten volumes from their father's holdings. His widow, Elizabeth, was accorded the same right as well. This bequest was an important sign that Jacob believed in education for women.[21]

Yet among the many causes that Green took up during the revolutionary era—emancipation, currency reform, education, laymen's rights—female equality was not one of them. In the end, religion defined (and circum-scribed) Jacob's views on family and education. In his household, he had but one overriding concern: to raise good Christians who would lead exemplary lives. All—husbands and wives, sons and daughters—needed to be able to read the Bible so they could study it on their own and grasp its many lessons. Parents also must discipline their children and mold them to be devout Christians. One task was to prepare their children for the afterlife; helping their children avoid sin was a second essential task. Thus, Jacob's views of child rearing were quite conventional by the standards of New England and of evangelism throughout early America, and they stood in stark contrast to Enlightenment values emerging in the mid-eighteenth century. John Locke saw the human mind as a tabula rasa at birth, a canvas that parents would color in as their children advanced in age from infancy. He and other enlightened writers rejected original sin and the views of many Protestant theologians that children were inherently depraved. In modern terms, Locke and his followers placed nurture over nature, while evangelicals believed that nature (i.e., God's will) was paramount. Jacob Green was no Lockean when it came to family; he was a Presbyterian Calvinist who believed that the Lord controlled all. Even his own children needed to show they were of the elect—they could not become members of the Hanover congregation until they had demonstrated this elemental fact.[22]

Such views were the product of Jacob's New England upbringing and his years of studying the Bible and other religious texts. He grew up in a covenantal, Puritan world that stressed the role of patriarchal families and of neighbors in maintaining religiosity and the proper functioning of society. The first line of defense against sin began with the family. "Families are the Nurseries of all Societies," Cotton Mather exclaimed. "Well-ordered Families naturally produce a Good Order." In such a society parents were to receive plenty of help from the dense kinship networks that permeated the New England countryside. Puritans believed in "a holy watchfulness" whereby the entire village would contribute to society's spiritual health. The church, supported by an intricate web of kinship and neighborhood networks, punished fornication, drunkenness, and other sins as an affront to God. Good Puritans came down hard on miscreants because bad behavior by individuals violated the covenant and could lead to God punishing the entire community. Presbyterian divines agreed that the marital relationship was divinely sanctioned and that the family was to serve as an extension of the church. Thus Jacob's admonitions on sin and the importance of parental discipline were as natural to him as breathing. He was raised in a New England community that preached the importance of the moral order, and he joined a church that shared the same values. Green, as a result, brought his own children up the same way—right down to trying to dictate which children could go to college and which should learn a trade.[23]

Yet the tug of family was quite strong, and it exerted a reciprocal pull on religion. When Jacob died in 1790, he left no money to the church or other charitable causes. His entire estate went to his family. His evangelical values—which preached the equality of all before God—were tempered somewhat by traditional family values. He set his sons up on nearby farms and kept them as close to him as possible. Green, in essence, was replicating his experience in Stoneham: Calvin and Pierson had land nearby; Ashbel's land bordered Jacob's main farm; Jacob's brother Benjamin followed Jacob to New Jersey and settled in Hanover, too. Naming patterns further show just how important family was to the Greens—Pierson was named after his mother's father; the oldest daughter in both marriages was named after her mother; another daughter was named after Jacob's mother; the children, in turn, named their children after siblings and relatives.

In important ways, family helped define the Presbyterian congregation in Hanover. Families sat together at Sunday services (indeed, Jacob encouraged this by insisting that the new meetinghouse contain pews), joined the church together, and prayed together at home. Their role was so important that parish boards did all they could to support families, encouraging parents to discipline baptized children and recommending "serious people" to spend the last Thursday of every month in prayer. Mothers played an especially important role in promulgating piety; women constituted a majority in the congregation (they represented 57 percent of the church membership between 1747 and 1790) and were a driving force in the religious education of the young in the home. For all of Jacob's efforts to bring his children to Jesus, it was Elizabeth whom Calvin cited when he recalled his religious upbringing. She spent more time with Calvin and his siblings on a daily basis, and it was his mother who led him to the meetinghouse on Sundays and other days. Even when he was an adult, Calvin's mother had an outsized role in his religious life. In 1789, a twenty-four-year-old Calvin had not yet formally joined his father's church. That year, "my mare died. Quite a loss to me. I began to pray in secret. I thought it time to begin [evaluating the state of my soul]," Calvin recalled. As he prayed, "I began to think of the things of another world," reading the Bible and grasping "that Christ is willing to save as great a sinner as I." But Calvin was unsure what he should do next, so he turned to his mother, not to Jacob. And Elizabeth advised him that "the Lord had begun a good work" and that he and his wife were "under conviction." Only then did Calvin approach his father about joining the congregation. Jacob treated his son no differently than he did any other seeker. He asked Calvin many questions, and stressed the need to pray. Satisfied with Calvin's answers, Jacob told him that he and his wife "ought to join the church," and they did so in October. Thus, quite literally, it was often the mothers who led their families into church membership. Women were usually the first to join the congregation; their husbands and children followed later.[24]

Although Hanover's meetinghouse stood at the geographic center of the community, the pulse of the church was really in the surrounding countryside, where, on their family farms, parents and children gathered to read the Bible and to pray. Not all family members were full church members, of course, but nearly all family members attended church. Kinship networks, as a result, served as a feeder that delivered seekers to the meetinghouse door. Many young people, including the Green children, found marriage partners through the church community: between 1746, when records were first kept, and 1781, 54 percent of children of members married into a family belonging to the congregation. Thus in 1767, Anne Green married a Tuttle;

in 1769, Abigail married a Broadwell; and in 1776, Elizabeth married a Brad-ford. Jacob's brother Benjamin, meanwhile, married a Dalglish in 1750. Over the years, Kitchels married Beaches, and Tuttles married Balls. With each marital union, the ties among families and between families and the church grew ever tighter.[25]

Families also served as feeders to congregational posts: Tuttles repeatedly served as deacons and elders. Prices could be found on various committees, as could Dalglishes and Beaches. From generation to generation, on down through the Revolution, the same families were active in the religious, social, and economic life of the community. In 1740, when Hanover Township became a part of the newly formed Morris County, its first two freeholders were a Tuttle and a Ball.

Kinship, however, functioned somewhat differently in Hanover than it did in other Presbyterian strongholds because of the American church's eth-nic divide. On one side of this divide were settlers of Scotch and Scotch Irish heritage; on the other were those of New England descent. The former had a much stronger ethnic identity than did the latter. Scottish Presbyteri-anism was forged in the northern lands of what became the British Isles amid a heated rivalry with the Church of England, a rivalry that resulted in fierce political and military clashes. Centuries of conflict with England bred a strong sense of Scottishness among adherents of the Presbyterian faith in Scotland and Ireland, where more than one hundred thousand Scottish Presbyterians migrated to Ireland in the late seventeenth century.[26]

Some 225,000 Scotch Irish came to the New World between 1718 and 1775, far more than the second-largest white immigrant group, the Germans. These Scots and Scotch Irish scattered to frontiers as far north as the Maine woods and as far south as the Carolina backcountry. A large number came to central New Jersey as well. Regardless of where they settled, these settlers formed tight communities centered on Presbyterianism, a Scotch Irish her-itage, and hostility to all things Anglican and Catholic. The settlement of Williamsburg Township in South Carolina was typical. Ulster emigrants founded it in 1734 along the Black River about a hundred miles from Charleston. To instill a sense of community in this frontier outpost, the set-tlers moved quickly to organize a Presbyterian congregation. In late 1736, within two years of the settlement's founding, "the people began to form into a religious society, built a church and sent to Ireland for a minister," set-tler Robert Witherspoon recalled. Their loyalty to the homeland was strong. The first person to be buried at the church graveyard was Witherspoon's grandfather, a man Witherspoon described as a devout Presbyterian: "He was well acquainted with the scriptures—had a voluability of expression in prayer and was a zealous adherent to the reformed protestant principles of the church of Scotland." A "great aversion to episcopacy"—the Church of England—infused the elder Witherspoon's beliefs, as it did for other community members. Thus, in places like Williamsburg, ethnicity and Presbyterianism became entwined: ethnicity reinforced religious identity at the same time that religion was reinforcing ethnic identity. The two worked in tandem, with church services becoming, in the words of one historian, "a symbolic rite of affirmation to one's ethnic association." Robert Witherspoon put it another way. Williamsburg's Presbyterians "were servers of God," he noted. "They were well acquainted with the scriptures and were much in prayer. . . . In a word they studied outward piety and inward purity." By worshiping together at their Presbyterian church, Scotch Irish settlers constructed sturdy communities that rested on the foundation of family, kinship, ethnicity, land, and religion.[27]

Family, land, and Presbyterianism were equally important in Hanover, but Scottishness did not define this community. A New England heritage did. The Greens and Hanover's settlers, as a result, carried a different set of cultural baggage to East Jersey than did the Scotch Irish who arrived in central Jersey. They were less clannish, more open to outsiders, and (ironically, considering the events of 1776) less hostile to England. They could be disdainful of their Scotch Irish brethren and their brand of Presbyterianism. Green, in fact, went so far as to deny that he was "a Presbyterian, according to the church of Scotland." His remark was telling. Hanover's earliest settlers came from Long Island, Connecticut, and other Puritan strongholds. In temperament and spirit they were closer to the Congregationalism of New England than to the Presbyterianism of Scotland. Presbyterians of a New England bent rejected Scottish subscription, which required strict adherence to the doctrinal creed and articles of the Scottish kirk. For the Scottish branch of the church, subscription was a way to preserve purity and to maintain unity in the church's furious contest with English episcopacy. Ministerial candidates who did not subscribe to Scottish doctrines were kept out of the Presbyterian Church. Green and his New England compatriots had little patience with the Scottish view. In the New York Synod, subscription served as another kind of test—those who backed it wanted the Scotch Irish branch to control the American Presbyterian Church, and those who opposed it favored the New England one. Jonathan Dickinson, Green's old mentor, led the fight in the synod against the Scotch Irish contingent.[28]

But the differences between the Scottish and English Presbyterians should not be overstated, either: family was important to both groups. It was especially important to Jacob Green. For him, the task of bringing people to God began with the parents, who were to lead by example and teach their children to avoid the sins of the world. The reform of society, in short, began at home.

*The Loyalist Down the Road:*
*Thomas Bradbury Chandler and Elizabeth Town*

Home was now Elizabeth Town.

In some ways, this picturesque village was an awful lot like Woodstock. Both towns were founded by Puritans in the seventeenth century, although migrants from Long Island started Elizabeth Town while settlers from Massachusetts founded Woodstock. Both were agricultural villages with small family farms. Both were prosperous. Elizabeth Town, though, was no inland village, miles from a port city. Chandler described it as being "situated on a very Public Road in the most populous and thriving part of the Province." Located on Newark Bay, it took advantage of its proximity to a growing New York to become the largest community in East Jersey, a distinction it enjoyed until the Revolution.

With the exception of his decadelong exile during the Revolution, Chandler never moved again. It was Elizabeth Town where he found his soul mate and raised a family. In 1750, three years after his arrival, Thomas married Jane Emott, a village resident. They were a perfect match in temperament and breeding. Jane's father, Captain John Emott, was successful and respected, and her mother, Mary, was the daughter of Elias Boudinot, Sr. The newlyweds lived in the glebe near the village center on the town creek. The stone house itself was quite old when Thomas moved in—it was built in 1696—but he was able to enlarge it in 1765 as his family (and his library) grew.

Thomas and Jane had five children: four daughters and a son. The eldest was William, who was born in 1756, and the youngest was Mary, who arrived in 1774. While the Chandler clan back in Woodstock remained safely ensconced in its Congregationalist world, Thomas created an Anglican one in Elizabeth Town. His wife fully shared his religious and political views, as did his children. William attended King's College, an Anglican bastion, in New York City and graduated from there in 1774. During the Revolution he fought for the king as a captain in the loyalist battalion known as the New Jersey Volunteers.

With his domestic affairs in order, Thomas was able to devote his full energies to the spiritual tasks at hand. At the top of his list was waging battle with the dissenters in Elizabeth Town and its environs. Stately St. John's was an island of Anglicanism in a hostile sea of dissenters—Presbyterians primarily, but also Baptists, Congregationalists, Lutherans, and others. "As to Roman Catholics, we have none in this Province," Chandler wrote in one report. "The Chief Enemies of the Church are the English Dissenters of different denominations who are thrice as numerous as its Professors and more active against us than our friends are for us. Of their open opposition indeed for some years past we have no great reason to complain; but the secret arts whereby they are endeavouring to undermine the principles of the Church amidst the fairest professions of Friendship."

Unlike Jacob Green, Chandler detested revivalism and the emotional preaching that defined it. George Whitefield had visited Elizabeth Town and St. John's during his legendary 1740 tour, and in winter 1764 he wanted to return to the village. Chandler had other ideas. One of his missions, he believed, was to douse the flames of revivalism, and Whitefield's desire to preach again at St. John's presented Chandler with a golden opportunity to take a stand against enthusiasm and radical religion.

It was a lonely crusade. Even his own parishioners wanted to hear the famous revivalist speak and were upset when Chandler barred the door to Whitefield. In a July 1764 letter, Chandler defended his actions—and revealed his distrust of popular religion, his fear of dissenters, and his belief that the Church of England had to send bishops to America if it were to thrive in the New World.

"My Tranquility which never before was interrupted was somewhat disturbed in the Winter past by reason of my refusing my pulpit to Mr. Whitfield, who signified his desire of preaching in my Church. This unluckily was at a time when no Clergyman had yet refused him since his last coming into the country, and after his having had the free use of the Churches in Philadelphia, which last consideration was what led my people to expect and desire that I should receive him into mine," Chandler began. But he felt he had no choice—Whitefield's views were simply too dangerous to the state church.

Moreover, Chandler believed that Whitefield was beyond redemption—he saw "no evidence of his reformation" regarding "his undutiful and schismatical behaviour." The membership at St. John's found Chandler's reasoning unpersuasive; as Chandler conceded, "a great part of my people remained unsatisfied and appeared to be much offended at my incompliance."

For Chandler, the incident reinforced an upsetting conclusion. In the colonies, the dissenters reigned supreme over the English church: "It is a great hardship upon the Church in these Colonies that its friends must act only on the defensive, the times being such as to render it imprudent and unsafe to venture into the Territories of its Enemies." This inferior status rankled him—"we are stigmatized as factions"—and the danger for him was that the colonists would see Anglicanism as just another church. "If we are altogether silent on these heads our own people grow indifferent and in time may think it immaterial whether they are in communion with the Church."

Chandler saw at least two solutions to the dissenter problem, one modest and one more ambitious. He would take up his pen and seek to demolish the dissenters through the force of his logic and the power of his arguments. More ambitiously, he wanted to fortify the church by bringing one or more bishops to America. This was a long-held dream for American members of the Church of England, and St. John's wardens had also complained that the colonial church was badly outgunned by its rivals:

> The situation of our circumstances is still such that unless we have a Minister constantly to officiate and reside amongst us, we can have a melancholy prospect before us—Our congregation will decrease and we have too great reason to fear that in time it will hardly deserve that name. For as long as the Dissenters in this town have five Ministers settled, constantly to officiate in publick, to visit them in private, ready to serve on any particular occasion . . . and we can have none with us but once in three weeks, or a month . . . as long as this is the case with a prospect of being better provided for, the difference is so great in their favour that most of our People might be persuaded to think it their duty in that condition to join with the Dissenters.

The lack of American bishops bothered Chandler for another, more emotional reason: the dissenters were allowed to erect church edifices to their liking but the king's church was not: "The Dissenters in this country, of Every Denomination, have the full Enjoyment of all they can desire towards rendering their respective Forms of Ecclesiastical Government and Discipline compleat—the Moravians in our neighborhood are allowed a Bishop—and the Papists in Canada have the same Indulgence. . . . And yet the only Crime we are conscious of, with Regard to the Public, is, that we belong to the national Church."

The more Chandler thought about it, the more he became convinced that securing bishops was the solution to the church's problems in America.[29]

# 4

## *Farmer-Miller-Physician-Teacher*

The blessings were growing, and so were the burdens. In 1768, Jacob and Elizabeth had nine children (four from Jacob's first marriage) and a tenth would be born a year later. The Greens' financial problems were growing along with the family. Jacob's salary as minister of Hanover's Presbyterian church, he complained bitterly to the congregation in December 1768, failed to keep pace with the increased demands placed on him as the family provider. When Green accepted the congregation's call to stay in Hanover in 1746, the members paid him fifty pounds a year, raising that salary to sixty pounds and finally, by the late 1760s, to seventy pounds. But that amount was still inadequate, Green said. Worse, he could not count on receiving the full amount because members were often lax about paying their dues.[1]

Green's deteriorating finances placed him in an impossible position. Jacob strongly believed that ministers should not become involved with the marketplace, or "secular" affairs as he called it. The gospel should always be a pastor's main concern. Yet Jacob's family needed to be clothed, housed, and fed, and he said he lacked the money to adequately do that. Because of his religious scruples, he resisted taking on outside work in the first ten years of his pastorate to make ends meet, as so many country parsons did. Instead, Green concentrated on his pastoral duties: visiting families, holding church services across Hanover Township, writing sermons, counseling the needy, baptizing infants. The dilemma, though, never went away. As his debts mounted after 1746—Jacob calculated they reached 200 pounds within a few years of his arrival in Hanover—his anger grew. By the end of 1768 he could not contain himself any longer, and he poured out his frustrations in a long, angry letter to the congregation.[2]

Disputes between ministers and congregations over inadequate or unpaid salaries were common in early America, but this conflict was particularly explosive because of its timing and its religious dimensions. Green had announced to the congregation a few years earlier that he was instituting higher standards for church membership and participation in the sacraments. At the same time, he was busy writing lengthy tracts explaining the need for a purer church. Yet at home, as his financial pressures were growing and he was trying to reform the church, his own congregation was letting him down—it was, he lamented, failing to meet its most basic obligations. "There is a covenant between minister & his people," Green pointedly reminded the congregation in his 1768 address. "They are as much bound to do duty to him, as he is to do his duty to them." Jacob charged that the congregation over his first two decades in the pastorship repeatedly failed to uphold its end of the bargain. "Considering the covenant . . . between Minister & people," he continued, "I cannot but look upon my people as covenant breakers." Hanover's failure not only angered Green, it led him to cast an even more critical eye on society as he began to implement his reforms. At home, he was seeing firsthand the failings of the colonists, and these failings directly influenced his writings and his reform program.[3]

The dispute over Green's maintenance reflected a complex, and shifting, economic and religious relationship in the prerevolutionary years. Hanover had a reputation as a poor place, and congregation members routinely blamed hard times when they did not pay their church dues. Yet the township was growing in the 1740s and 1750s, boasted a diversified economy in the 1760s, and enjoyed a status in the 1770s as the second-wealthiest township in Morris County. It had far more stores and taverns than many of its neighbors and, over the course of Green's forty-five-year pastorship, was generally prosperous. Indeed, by 1779, Hanover had the county's second-highest number of improved acres; the most cattle; the most forges; the most mills; and the most slaves. Such rankings were especially impressive because the other townships in Morris County were also doing well. In 1725, the county was largely unsettled frontier. As late as 1745 it had a population density of less than one person per mile; by 1772 population density stood at twenty-five people per square mile. And the economy grew accordingly, with agricultural and industrial output rising. As tax lists and wills show, Hanover's wealthier citizens were able to purchase some of the finer things in life—they sat at mahogany tables, ate from silver bowls, and rode in four-wheeled carriages. The township's less-well-off inhabitants, meanwhile, had enough purchasing power to support nine stores and six taverns—the second-largest number of commercial offerings in the county.[4]

Hanover owed its rising economic power in the prewar years to the twin pillars of agriculture and industry. One sign of the former's importance was the ubiquitous presence of mills. Hanover had nine sawmills and seven gristmills in 1779, the most in Morris. Its main crops were corn, wheat, rye, and barley, and farmers raised potatoes and peas as well. Peach and apple orchards and distilling were prominent. The township also benefited from its proximity to New York City, Newark, and other major towns. Markets were close by, enabling farmers to sell their produce in Elizabeth Town and elsewhere. Hanover benefited from this proximity in another way: many a New Yorker decided to retreat to the quiet of New Jersey to farm. One notable example was Philip Van Cortlandt. After graduating from King's College in 1758, he lived on Long Island and worked in New York City as a merchant. In 1772 he and his wife moved their nine children to the village of Whippany in southern Hanover Township. There they lived at Dashwood, an elegant home on a hill that served as the center of a thriving farm. In Hanover, larger farms ran five hundred acres and up. One prosperous farm sold in 1769 totaled five hundred acres, with one-third of the land in meadow. It also had fifty acres of boggy meadow that produced hemp and corn, and an apple orchard of four hundred trees. Herd sizes averaged ten cows, twenty sheep, and five horses.[5]

The second economic pillar was industry. Forges were present in Hanover from the beginning and helped to spur settlement; John Budd and John Ford arrived in the area in 1710, selecting a site along the Whippany River for the forge the partners soon opened. The operation, which became known as the "Old Iron Works," manufactured iron from ore and sold it in Newark and Elizabeth Town. In the 1740s, as Green settled into his ministry, the number of forges jumped, thanks to Hanover's rich natural resources. The township was blessed with water, iron ore, and charcoal. Hanover also had the most tanyards in Morris County—eight, or twice as many as neighboring Morris Township had.[6]

As happy as this overall economic picture was, a closer look showed that things were not so rosy in the 1760s, when Green was making his ill-timed plea for money. The colony's economy, including in Morris County, was struggling: currency was scarce, markets were flagging, and debts were rising. When Hanover's church members cited straitened circumstances in 1768, they were not exaggerating. Times were hard. For all of its growing strengths, Hanover even in the best of times could not match the wealth of a Perth Amboy or an Elizabeth Town. It was a not a city. It was an agricultural hinterland in the western interior of a small colony. Its economy was solidly middling, neither wealthy nor poor. Farm sizes averaged 150 acres—smaller than in the Chesapeake but larger than in New England and in nearby Morristown, where farms averaged seventy-one acres in the 1770s.[7]

The complexity of this situation placed Green in a quandary. Overall, Hanover's economy was growing, and he passionately believed that its Presbyterian inhabitants possessed the resources to better support its pastor. He also believed that the church should come first and that the members had a covenant to uphold. Yet Green issued his plea for money during an economic downturn, and only a few years after the congregation had built his family a parsonage and undertaken the construction of a new meetinghouse at great financial sacrifice. He must have looked like an ingrate to many members.

In one regard, Green was simply venting in his 1768 address to the congregation. For years he had known what he had to do. If he wanted more money, he would have to go out there and earn it. Thus, well before 1768, Green had begun taking on outside jobs, with various needs dictating the timing. The first activity he undertook was farming. When he arrived in Hanover in late 1745, the congregation did not provide him with a house. He fended for himself until his marriage to Anna Strong in 1747, when he borrowed money and used part of her dowry to purchase 120 acres in lower Whippany for fifty pounds—a respectably sized farm that was well within the norm for Hanover Township. Green then built a small house largely at his own expense, raised a crop of corn on two to three acres, cleared some swampy land, and later grew wheat and vegetables, including turnips. He insisted, defensively, in his 1768 letter to the congregation that he did not spend much time in the fields, and he was quite right. Green's labors as pastor took nearly all of his time during these early years; besides, he did not much like the work himself, and never did. Growing up in New England, Jacob worked hard to escape the drudgery of farm life so that he could concentrate on his studies.[8]

Operating a farm was no economic panacea. It required a sizable capital investment, even for part-time farmers. Besides the expense of buying land

and constructing a house and support buildings, Jacob needed to hire labor to plant the crops and bring them to harvest. His first marriage produced only one son, and another son was not born until 1761. To meet his labor needs Green first turned to slavery, a somewhat surprising decision given his later career as an abolitionist. His decision to buy a slave, though, was not really so surprising: it was not at all uncommon for ministers to own slaves in the colonial period, and Jacob had been introduced to the practice as a child, when family members in Massachusetts and Connecticut owned a few slaves. He was reintroduced to the practice upon his arrival in New Jersey—slavery was growing in East Jersey, including in Hanover. New Jersey's slaveholdings were tiny compared with the Chesapeake and South Carolina, and most farmers never established large plantations. William Kelly of Morris County possessed one of the area's largest holdings—he had more than twenty slaves working as field hands on a two-thousand-acre farm. Most farmers in Hanover and Morris owned one to two slaves and used them to help in the fields; others put them to work in the forges and mills. Jacob was quite typical in his decision to buy one slave and use him to help out on the farm. Lacking the time to work in the fields himself and with no sons to handle the myriad chores of farming, Jacob had his slave fill the role of an indentured servant.[9]

Then he suffered a double blow. Anna died in 1756, and a few months later his "Negro" did so as well. The emotional toll on Green was great but so was the financial hit. A cash-strapped Jacob lost his investment in the field hand; with "my worldly circumstances low," he did not have the resources to buy a replacement. Green was forced to hire temporary help to mow his grass, cut his wheat, and haul his hay, among many other things. But relying on paid labor was expensive—he complained to the congregation that the cost was an extravagant forty pounds a year.[10]

Over time, other solutions presented themselves. Green was able to rent part of his land to tenants, a strategy that brought in income and allowed him to avoid the expense of hiring farmhands. Most of all, as his sons came of age, he put them to work farming—much to Ashbel's dismay, who "became acquainted with every species of farming business" despite his disdain for the plow. Calvin, meanwhile, worked as a farmer throughout his teen years before learning several trades, including tanning and shoemaking. Despite graduating from the College of New Jersey in the late 1780s, John Wickliffe also farmed.[11]

Small as it was, the Greens' farm was a busy, diverse place, consisting of grain fields, meadows, and orchards. They raised two of the most common crops found in Morris County, corn and buckwheat. They also grew, among other things, rye and flax. Ashbel reported that the farm had "a considerable number" of cows and other "brute" animals. At the time of Jacob's death in 1790, he owned three heads of cattle, three pigs, and four horses—smaller than the average county herd size of ten cows but larger for horses. In many places in the middle colonies, horses were considered something of a luxury; they were expensive to feed and maintain. Three horses alone required eighty bushels of grain, meaning six acres had to be devoted to their care. The Greens likely used their horses for plowing and to haul the wagon they owned.[12]

Orchards were an important part of the local economy, and the Greens used theirs to raise apples, which they turned into cider. The women—Jacob's wife and five daughters from his two marriages—played an important role in these agricultural activities. The household contained four spinning wheels, one weaver's loom, and one quilting wheel. The women spun wool, baked bread, milked cows, churned butter. The farm was sufficiently large to keep the family well clothed and fed with meat, vegetables, and bread, but it was not lucrative enough to relieve Green's financial stress. He was no plantation owner growing a cash crop, spending his days surveying his fields and overseeing a workforce of indentured servants or slaves. The day-to-day grind of running a family farm never interested him; God came first, always, and his decision to labor in the Lord's garden instead of his earthly one cost him financially.[13]

Besides renting out part of his land to a tenant, Green used his tracts to branch into other moneymaking activities. In 1758, when the congregation finally built a house for the Green family, Jacob sold part of his former farm to raise cash. On that tract the new owner constructed a gristmill, with Green becoming partial owner. (He also owned a sawmill and a distillery.) Green apparently lent out what cash he did have—at his death, Green was owed eight-five pounds in bonds and notes; he also possessed one state certificate worth eighty-four pounds.[14]

Green saw his sale of land and his investment in the gristmill as a worthy compromise that allowed him to meet his familial and religious duties. "Once built, [the mill] would help my worldly circumstances, without involving my mind in worldly cares," he explained in 1768, before adding defensively, "I did it as the most holy way to subsist among a poor negligent people." Green's defensiveness—and his dig at congregation members—said volumes about his relations with his church in the 1760s. The members were upset that their pastor had gone into the milling business. "People did not like my scheme," he reported. "It was commonly said, that it did not belong to Ministers to engage in such things." Green reacted with indignation: "When I found that people would neither support me, nor let me support myself, it not only cooled my affection toward them, but produced some degree of Alienation." He was so upset, he said it affected his sermonizing: "It was hard to preach to my people with that affection, that ought to be between minister & people."[15]

The dispute over the mill was not easily resolved. Although the membership remained disappointed with Green, Jacob retained his part ownership in the gristmill and he took on even more activities, including operating a kiln for bricks and working as an estate lawyer. Another noteworthy activity was cerebral: in November 1758, Green became interim president of the College of New Jersey at Princeton when Jonathan Edwards unexpectedly died after only two months in office. For Green, who had served as a trustee since 1748, his appointment as president served as a welcome distraction during a tense time over his milling activities. His temporary removal to Princeton—he served as president until May 8, 1759—allowed a cooling-off period for both sides. According to Green, his withdrawal to Princeton "took me out of my present distresses at home, & seemed to turn peoples affections something more toward me." Members apparently viewed their pastor with more respect and recognized that Green's talents presented him with other opportunities on larger stages. To Green's relief, they began to pay their dues more punctually: "I returned home to them with more cordial affections than I had had for them for some years. I preached to them with more heart & courage than before."[16]

This beneficial state of affairs did not last long, however. Old grievances quickly resurfaced once Jacob was settled back in at Hanover Neck. The mill remained controversial: "People's regard toward me disappeared; they neglected payments, & I had but little success in the ministry." Green decided to give the congregation a choice: raise his salary, or allow him to practice medicine as a physician. After the "great noise & clamour" over his partial ownership of the mill, Green apparently had learned a lesson. He would consult with congregation members before taking on additional "secular" activities. The change in tactics aided his cause. The congregation remained unwilling to raise his salary, but it was agreeable to him working as a doctor.[17]

Taking on yet another new job elicited mixed emotions in Green. It was an additional unwelcome demand on his time, and an additional distraction to handle. In his autobiography, Green had nothing but harsh things to say about this period of his life. "When I entered upon worldly schemes, I found them in general a plague, a vexation, and a snare," he wrote. "If I somewhat increased my worldly estate, I also increased sorrow, and incurred blame, in all things, except the practice of physick." Working secular jobs violated his deepest religious principles and forced him to join a commercial revolution that right-thinking ministers everywhere feared as a grave threat to Christianity. Indeed, the Great Awakening of the 1740s partly arose out of the belief that a growing economy was harming religion. From the earliest days of his pastorship, Green decried those Christians who on Sunday chose the business of money over the work of the Lord. His message, delivered with relentless consistency over forty years, was that people must put God first and affairs of the world second. So, how could he now turn around and pursue wealth for his family? His 1768 address to the congregation was, in part, a long, defensive attempt to explain why.[18]

Practicing medicine was a bit different, though. In early America, physicians were in short supply, and Hanover badly needed Green's services. Taking on the care of sick patients allowed Jacob to regain some of his popularity. But it also made sense on another level. In this religiously charged, Calvinistic world, illness carried a spiritual component. A person's physical health was seen as being linked to his or her spiritual health. When one sinned, bad things often followed. Lewis Bayley, author of the seventeenth-century tract *The Practice of Piety*, summed up this belief well: "Sicknesse comes not by hap or chance . . . but from mans wickednesse." Ordinary Christians took this message to heart. As one historian concluded about Puritan New England, "People looked on [ministers] as healers who could relieve sickness in their souls and distemper in the body social." Numerous preachers, as a result, worked as physicians. Get right with God, they stressed, and one could get right in the body. Ashbel Green indicated that his father thought along the same lines. "His charges for medical services were always moderate," Ashbel wrote. "And he often united, at the bed-side, and in the family of the sick, the duties of the physician, and the minister of the gospel."[19]

The Enlightenment saw much progress on the medical front, including the development of the first rudimentary microscopes, the use of inoculations, and the tentative first steps toward the professionalization of medicine. At places like Yale, professors were delivering lectures on anatomy and pathology to students, who could earn a bachelor's degree in "physic" and go on to study under a doctor. Yet the practice of physic remained primitive on the eve of the American Revolution. Most doctors, including Green, received no formal training in medicine. Jacob learned the craft from observing other doctors in the area and from studying textbooks on his own. He approached this task with his usual diligence and thoroughness. His 1790 will indicates that he relied on two texts—Richard Brookes's *General Practice of Physic* and Lorenz Heister's *General System of Surgery: In Three Parts*. Both books shed light on Green's approach to medicine and his ability in the years before the American Revolution to blend religious belief and Enlightenment principles. Brookes was an acolyte of the Enlightenment who used his textbook to lecture on the importance of careful observation of disease and the rigid study of medicine. He had no kind words for folk medicine, warning physicians to avoid following "quack" remedies. Short chapters dealt with everything from "Catarrbal Fevers" to the measles and toothaches. Much of his advice must have resonated with Green, for Brookes the physician did not lose sight of Brooks the humble follower of God. "The more we enquire into the Nature of Man," he wrote in the textbook's preface, "the more Reason we have to admire the Wisdom and Power of the Creator; and the greater Occasion to confess our own Ignorance."[20]

Heister's work—a primer on surgery—further indicates how ambitious Green's practice was. Heister, who was born in 1683 in Frankfort-on-the-Main and taught medicine, botany, and surgery at leading German universities, was considered the founder of scientific surgery in his native land. His *General System of Surgery* went through at least seven editions between 1718 and 1779, and it offered instruction on how to treat "Wounds, Fractures, Luxations, Tumors, and Ulcers of all Kinds." Like Brookes, Heister stressed the need for physicians to study and observe.[21]

In embracing these medical texts and their Enlightenment underpinnings of reason and careful study, Green apparently ignored the works of physician-ministers. For instance, John Wesley, founder of Methodism, had written one of the most popular medical texts used in the colonies, a 1747 treatise called *Primitive Physic; or, An Easy and Natural Method of Curing Most Diseases*. Unlike the scientific rigor of the work of Brookes and Heister, *Primitive Physic* relied on time-honored remedies, such as halting a nosebleed by placing white paper under the tongue and mending a broken shin by placing a dry oak leaf around it.[22]

Green was not immune to the lure of certain traditions; according to Ashbel, his father did bleed patients, a centuries-old treatment that sought to restore the "humors" to balance by withdrawing blood from patients in copious amounts. But Green also embraced newer techniques, especially the use of inoculations. All in all, he had a wide-ranging practice befitting the needs of a country parish. Because of the demands on his time and the extensiveness of his practice, Green needed help. He first enlisted the services of Ashbel, who described how his father "called on me to prepare medicines, sent me to let blood, to inoculate for the small-pox, and to extract teeth." Ashbel spent so much time helping his father out "that I obtained the common appellation of doctor before I had ever seen a college." When Ashbel moved on to ministering and other activities, his youngest brother, John Wickliffe, apparently took his place—it was Wickliffe who inherited his father's treasured medical texts upon Jacob's death in 1790.[23]

Through arduous labor, Green was able to cut his debts in half, from 200 pounds in the 1750s to 100 pounds in 1768. According to a 1779 tax list, he paid a tax of 163 pounds—one of the highest totals in Hanover. And when he died in 1790, his estate was valued at 503 pounds, more than double the average estate of 195 pounds in the 1786–90 period in Hanover Township. Moreover, he acquired many of the trappings associated with wealth: a large library of expensive books, a forte piano, two silver bowls, two sets of silver spoons, and fine china. This improvement in his finances came at a cost, however. Under constant strain and overworked, Jacob was often sick and nearly died in 1774. His extracurricular activities, with the exception of the doctoring, remained unpopular. And as his fortunes improved, Green as early as the 1760s found himself accused of being wealthy, a charge he indignantly denied. He told the Presbyterian membership in his 1768 address that he remained poor, that his salary was inadequate and "badly" paid, and that the expenses of his family outstripped his resources. Indeed, "all unbiased persons would rather be astonished that I have been able to subsist," he huffed. Jacob even denigrated the parsonage that the congregation built for him in 1757—he dismissed it as "just an House to live in," adding that he had to spend about seventy pounds of his own money "to make it comfortable."[24]

He felt abandoned in another regard. Green believed that the congregation's lay leaders had failed to back him up in the dispute over money: "I cannot but blame, the leading men in this place, who have heretofore been my Friends, that they so much alone, or encourage people, in their injurious way of thinking that I am not in much want." Things were so bad during this period that Green considered asking the presbytery to dismiss him from the Hanover pastorship. He refrained from taking this fatal step, however. One reason, he explained, was that seeking action from the presbytery would offend his Calvinistic sensibilities: "It has always been a principle with me, not to be very active in disposing of myself, but to leave myself to the disposal of providence." He came to Hanover in the first place at the direction of providence, "& here I suppose it my duty to stay, till God in his providence Shall open a door for my removal, or call me elsewhere."[25]

Reliance on providence had its limits, though. Green felt he had a duty to speak up and let the congregation know just how upset he was about the lack of financial support. In presenting his arguments, he conceded that he was not perfect, that he was aware of "a sense of my own short-comings & deficiencies in the work of the ministry," and that he had an obligation to fulfill his pastoral duties to the best of his abilities. But he insisted "that slackness & negligence in duty, was first in them, & not in me," and that his "covenant-breaking" congregation had to try harder to meet its obligations.[26]

Neither side looked particularly good in this fight over salary. Green's 1768 address to the congregation was bitter, angry, defensive, and over-wrought. The congregation could be petty in its treatment of Green, lax in paying his salary, and inconsistent in its approach to him (it ignored his requests for full payment of his salary, then questioned his commitment to the church when he was forced to take on outside work to make ends meet). Yet the breach was not permanent, and the two sides got through this ugly period by compromising. The parish board in April 1769 formed a commit-tee to procure firewood for the Green family, thus addressing one of Jacob's specific complaints. It also agreed at that meeting to apply pew rents to Green's salary. In 1771 and 1772, the board began taking more forceful action against those congregation members who were in arrears on their dues.[27]

Green, for his part, played the good soldier after unleashing his anger in the 1768 letter. He did not quit or seek his dismissal from the Hanover pas-torship. True to form, he worked harder on all fronts. Still, the dispute left deep scars. It caused him to think even deeper about religion, the economy, and society. It colored his views of politics and the colonies as the crisis with Britain worsened in the early 1770s, by convincing him even further that a moral reformation was needed. It made him realize, in a very personal way, just how much change was necessary. The crisis, he was coming to understand, was about more than politics. In American society, there was a moral sickness. People were too absorbed with their selfish lives and needs; as the experience in Hanover showed, they were putting their own wants ahead of the church's.

This painful realization led Green to write one of his greatest creations, the best-selling *A Vision of Hell*, which lampooned society and all the ungodly behavior he was witnessing in Hanover and elsewhere. The tract, which was first published in 1770 under the pseudonym Theodorus van Shemain, begins simply, with a narrator recounting how "in the month of May, in the year 1767, in a morning after I had been some time out of bed, I was musing upon the low state of religion, and the great progress of vice; I considered how the devils would rejoice and triumph in the decay of piety." From this innocent reverie the speaker falls into a trance, where he experiences a "visionary view, or clear representation of HELL." The next nineteen pages detail his visit to the underworld. Inhabiting this dark place are nine devils, ranging from Beelzebub to Lucifer, who meet to discuss how to advance their design of "promoting sin, and bringing sinners to hell."[28]

As the narrative unfolds and the devils plot how to ruin God's kingdom, Green brings out the knives. The first to feel his jabs are those members of the laity—and they are a large group—who do not adequately support their minister. The devil named Apollion proposes a simple way to harm the ministry: "If we can bring people fully to believe, that ministers ought not to have a salary . . . sufficient for their comfortable subsistence, we shall do much to overthrow the ministry; for Clergymen, poor wretches, cannot subsist on nothing." The devil named Mammon agrees that withholding salary is a great way to harm the clergy's effectiveness—"it will keep ministers from many places, where otherwise they would be labouring to pull down our kingdom." He adds, "I [would] love to see their hearts sink under a view of the ingratitude of their people."[29]

The devil Belial suggests another "easy" way to undercut the minister— get people "to raise evil reports, falsehoods, and lies, concerning a minister, especially if he is faithful, and spread these reports among the people. We have friends in every place, male and female, who delight in this work." Moloch concurs, adding that parents are another key ally in this effort. He proposes "that we should tempt and stir up parents to talk against ministers, before their children. By this the young ones will be prejudiced, and embold-ened to condemn, and speak slightly of them." As a result, the ministry will become "useless to the rising generation."[30]

The devils lampooned a wide range of misbehaviors inside and outside of church. One misbehavior: those congregants who fall asleep a mere five minutes into the sermon. A second: those congregants who let their neighbors get away with sleeping in church because they are "afraid of offending" them. Other congregants may be awake, but their minds are wandering during the service because they are "fully engaged in viewing the dress and habits of others: New cloaths and new fashions will employ their thoughts." Vanity was thus a third, and major, problem. The devils agree they can undercut religion by inducing churchgoers "to employ their thoughts, and spend much time in dressing, and adorning themselves." Such persons seek to draw attention to themselves, thus undermining the real purpose of church services—to concentrate on the holy word through reading, hearing the sermon, and prayer.

Sabbath-breaking was yet another serious problem. The devils plot how "to influence persons to vain and simple discourse in going to, and from the house of God, and between exercises of public worship. Some may be tempted to talk upon, and contrive frolicks; some tell stories; some talk of their farms, oxen, houses and the like." They will be so focused on these frivolous diversions, Apollion explains, that they will neglect the sermon and the "truths delivered" in them.[31]

Fellow ministers did not escape Green's barbs. The nine devils agree that their biggest enemy is the minister who is able to preach clearly and powerfully. Effective ministers bring people into church; ineffective ones don't. The devils concur that they must "induce bad men to enter into the ministry. . . . The gospel in the hand of a slothful man does us but little hurt." The devils also laud the incessant bickering within the Protestant world; arguments over theology and heated rivalries among sectarians greatly help their cause by turning people away from God.[32]

The tract ends on a somber but hopeful note. The devils are gleeful about their prospects in a post–Great Awakening world where piety is declining: "Oh! What multitudes of souls will now come to hell to increase our torment." Another adds, "We will torment you forever." At that point, the narrator wakes up and his trance ceases. He understands it was merely a dream—but a dream that contained important truths. He decides to publish his experience so that others may learn of the dangers they face. But in speaking out, he risks the wrath of Lucifer and his satanic allies. Green then drives home his point: "I fear them not, while I trust in God. . . . Jesus Christ is stronger than Satan, and they that trust in him shall overcome the evil one."[33]

Green's purpose in *A Vision of Hell* was to shame people and, through satire, to get them to see how selfish their behavior was. And by getting people to see and understand the dangers of self-love, he was hoping to get people to return to church and to turn to God. It was a message he was to deliver again, and again.

* ◆ *

## *The Loyalist Down the Road: Thomas Bradbury Chandler and the Bishop's Cause—an Introduction*

The bishop's cause was the center of Chandler's universe, the sun around which his other views revolved. In this one issue merged all his hopes and dreams for church and state, God and seeker, king and subject. Unlike Jacob Green, who was using his reform cause to try to propel society forward on a variety of fronts, Chandler was using his in an attempt to restore society to something that had long passed. Chandler looked longingly to the days before the Glorious Revolution and the English Civil War, when the union of church and state was strongest. For that very reason, few religious issues were as politically charged as Chandler's attempt to bring a bishop to America.

Episcopacy was so controversial in Western Christianity for reasons of theology and politics. Protestant reformers felt the office was unbiblical because it departed from Jesus Christ's presbyterian model; equally important, they felt it was tyrannical and corrupting because of the great powers held by bishops and the fiscal resources needed to support them. The animosity toward the episcopal structure began with the bishop of Rome: the Catholic pope, according to these reformers, not only presided over Christendom through an office with no biblical foundation; he also he lived in princely splendor in the Vatican and accumulated all the earthly treasures of a king.

In England, Protestant reformers had additional complaints: the reformation of Henry VIII, who broke away from Rome in the 1530s, did not undo enough of these popish corruptions. They were little happier with Elizabeth I, when she assumed the throne from "Bloody Mary," her Catholic half sister, in 1558. The Elizabethan settlement saw the restoration of Protestantism and the Common Prayer Book. But numerous Catholic practices continued in England, including signing with the cross, kneeling at the communion table, observing saints' days, using wafers—and continuing an elaborate church hierarchy resting on episcopacy.

The unhappiness was so great that a new reform movement arose during Elizabeth's reign called Puritanism, whose mission was to rid the English church of its popish remnants. But the differences between dissenters and episcopalians went deeper than matters of ceremony; Puritans also challenged Henrician conceptions of church and state and the very essence of hierarchical society. When Henry seceded from Rome so he could marry Anne Boleyn, he created a state church overseen by the monarchy. Henry's doctrine of royal supremacy declared that the king was the supreme ruler of the national church, and that the king had direct, God-given control over the cure of his subjects' souls. Henry's motivations were both religious and political; an intermittingly pious man when he was not killing his critics, he truly did believe that a monarch was God's chosen one who had the responsibility for the welfare of his children. But his political motivations were equally powerful—Henry wanted the church to reinforce the powers of monarchy. The state church would foster control through both persuasion and brute force. All were required to attend Sunday services, where priests would deliver royal-approved discourses on political and spiritual matters. Church courts, meanwhile, tried to enforce conformity: they punished people for "heresy," for failing to attend church services, for not paying tithes, for sexual immorality. Henry executed numerous people, including a bishop, who refused to take the oath of supremacy acknowledging his powers and the new church.

Under Henry and later monarchs during the Tudor and Stuart reigns, the nation's twenty-six bishops were important cogs in the government's machinery of control. They served in the House of Lords, providing a reliably safe bloc of votes for the king. They enjoyed powers of censorship, vetting the publication of books; they licensed teachers. Many also worked as civil servants and administrators. Holding such great power, and enjoying the perks of patronage, many bishops became quite rich and lived in "palaces" that further offended Puritan sensibilities.

During the reign of Charles I in the 1620s and 1630s, the episcopal office became even more controversial, for the driving force in the Church of England during this period was William Laud. As archbishop of Canterbury, Laud strengthened the church courts, using them to persecute Puritans and other dissenters. Moreover, he and Charles declared a virtual war on Calvinism—they forbade the teaching of predestination at Cambridge and Oxford and extolled the glories of Arminianism. As these heavy-handed attempts to impose conformity produced growing discord during the 1630s, Charles became even more convinced that episcopacy was essential to his survival, and he refused all dissenter attempts to oust the bishops, declaring that those who wanted to end the office "aim at nothing but the overthrow of royal authority."

The combined insults of Arminianism, episcopacy, and persecution, perpetuated by Laud and his bishops, helped spark the English Civil War, which began in 1639 and led to the executions of Charles (1649) and Laud (1645). The victorious parliamentarians and their Puritan allies abolished the office of episcopacy, and many bishops were imprisoned or sent into exile. Upon the restoration of the monarchy in 1660, Charles II brought the bishops back, only to see the office again weakened in the Glorious Revolution of 1688. The bishops, it must be stressed, survived all these twists and turns, as did the notion—albeit a watered-down one—that a proper realm functioned best when church and state worked together.[34]

# PART II

*Revolutionary Thinkers and the Trials of War*

# 5

## *Polemicist*

Jacob Green, radical? In 1770, the answer may have not been so clear to his contemporaries. The mounting crisis with Great Britain was radicalizing a growing segment of the American population, but Green was keeping quiet, at least publicly, about all things political. He wrote no tracts denouncing the Stamp Act or lambasting Parliament's attempts to tax the colonies. At home, he was a stern patriarch who ruled his household in time-honored ways; at church, he guided the congregation with the firmness of an English lord. To an enlightened apostle of Jefferson's ilk, his reform causes must have seemed parochial, even quaint: Jacob Green in 1770 could be found in his pulpit, urging his parishioners to give up drunkenness, swearing, and gambling. He railed against "grasping" and selfishness, and he talked incessantly about the need to purify the church—a cause he pursued with the same relentless focus that Thomas Bradbury Chandler pursued an American bishop for the Church of England. Taxation without representation? The rights of man? Green said nothing about these momentous issues.

Green's pen, though, was quite busy in the late 1760s and in 1770, and the series of tracts he wrote were instrumental in his journey to the revolutionary firebrand of 1776 that he became. For it was in these tracts that Green put the finishing touches on the beliefs that would sustain him during the war and serve as a catapult to a wider range of reforms in the late 1770s and early 1780s. Like Chandler's quest for a bishop, the immediate issue was seemingly narrow: how to construct a pure church. Green admitted as much, apologizing in one tract for not discussing supposedly more momentous issues. But creating a pure church meant everything to him, and it sprang from his deeper desire to keep Calvinism relevant during the Enlightenment and to confront the perplexing paradoxes that bedeviled the movement. His efforts to tighten standards for church membership set off a spirited debate in New England and led him to assume the role of a polemicist to defend his views.[1]

In Protestant intellectual circles in the 1760s, theologians were still fretting over the Enlightenment and Arminianism and what they portended for Calvinism. The angst was perhaps greatest in New England, where Congregationalists divided into three warring camps: liberals, who were Christian humanists and devotees of Enlightenment reason; Old Calvinists, who were guardians of the faith; and New Divinity men, who took a middle ground that defended Calvinism from the onslaught of science while seeking to make its harsher aspects more palatable to skeptics. In important ways, Green's heart was with the New Divinity movement. As an admirer of Jonathan Edwards, he shared much with the movement's leading practitioners, especially Samuel Hopkins and Joseph Bellamy. All three men believed in high standards for the church, distinguished between the saved and unsaved, and largely (but far from completely) followed Edwards's teachings on the will, with all its ramifications for Calvinism and the proper ordering of society. Green, though, was the most forceful of the three in boiling the dispute among the three camps down to one central proposition—whether the church should admit "graceless persons."[2]

Green first laid out his ideas for a purer church in 1764, when he delivered his "Christian Baptism, a Sermon," and in 1767 when he published "Sinners Faultiness, and Spiritual Inability, Considered in a Sermon."[3] The two sermons introduced hearers to key elements of his philosophy—the need for high standards in admitting members to the sacraments, including baptism—but it was not until 1768 that Green comprehensively explained his vision in a published tract. *An Inquiry into the Constitution and Discipline of the Jewish Church*, which was published by Hugh Gaine, a New York printer, covered seventy-four pages and constituted a frontal assault on the Stoddardeans and their beliefs. The advocates of open church membership, Green wrote, were misguided and wrong to assert that allowing the unregenerate to partake in the sacraments could prod them into reforming their ways and lead to their being saved. Admitting the unregenerate "has a Tendency to flatter them with vain Hopes, ease their guilty, Consciences, and build them up in Self-Righteousness," he declared. In other words, it gave them false hope that they were of the elect and that by partaking in the sacraments they were gaining God's favor.[4]

Green built his case around the nature of the covenant. "When God speaks of the Covenant [of grace], he sums up in this: *He will be their God, and they shall be his People: He is to them a Father, and they are his Sons and Daughters.*" To be accepted into the covenant, Green continued, a person "takes God for his God, loves him supremely, and heartily submits to him, in, and thro' Jesus Christ." In return, God "will justify them, adopt them into the Number of his Children, and become their Father, and their God: . . . he will give them the Influence of his Spirit; afford many Privileges in this World, and give them Heaven at last." Such blessings were bestowed only on the saved. "All unregenerate Sinners ought to know," Green exclaimed, "they are Enemies to God and Holiness, that they hate the Way of Salvation by Christ, and that consequently God abhors them." Green rejected Arminian arguments "that many unregenerate Persons have some good Principles, mean well, and have some sincere Regard for and liking to God in his proper Character." That may well be true, Green noted, but it also was irrelevant because God alone determined who was saved. One could not "work" one's way to salvation. And for Green, the unsaved would never be able to completely change their ways—they could *partially* amend their bad habits, but that would not get them very far.[5]

Such were the dangers of admitting the unregenerate to the sacraments. It would not lead to them being saved; it would mislead them into thinking they could be saved. Such a charade, Green concluded, would hurt the church itself—the participation of the unregenerate "open[s] the Church to the World of ungodly Men, so greatly as to profane gospel Ordinances: And take in so many carnal Ones, as to interrupt, if not to destroy, Brotherly Love and Christian Communion."[6]

Green's raising of the ramparts against the unpure attracted much criticism in New England, where, in the words of the Reverend George Beckwith of Lyme, Connecticut, it led to "debates and perplexities among some of our people." The clamor was loud enough that Beckwith decided he had to speak out. Beckwith was a Yale man, the longtime pastor of the north parish in Lyme, and a social conservative who wanted to maintain traditional New England society and the established church in Connecticut. His biggest fear was that Green's crusade would undercut the established church by driving people away from Congregationalism to the Church of England, where standards were more lax. And by weakening the church, Beckwith warned in a 1769 tract, Green could "bring the country into the ancient state of heathenism"—an alarming development whereby the unsaved remained outside the visible church.[7]

Beckwith did agree with Green "that no person under scandal" should be allowed to participate in the sacraments. However, Beckwith said the problem was determining who was worthy of admission. Should individuals be judged by how they behave when out in the world (their external behavior)? Or should they be judged by what was in their hearts (their internal behavior)? Had they undergone a conversion and committed to Jesus Christ? For Beckwith, people who were misbehaving publicly should not be allowed to partake in the sacraments. *Visible* behavior was the key, he stressed. Lying, cheating, drinking, whoring—all were grounds for exclusion. Determining the state of someone's heart was something else, however, something far more difficult to ascertain: "A person is rendered scandalous . . . by overt acts in speech or behaviour; and not by any invisible state of the mind, which we can never know," he explained. The church, he continued, "has no right . . . to make any judgment at all on the invisible state of others minds or hearts." Only God knew the inner thoughts and beliefs of a seeker.[8]

Beckwith's tract restated an old argument in the Calvinist world. He was a Stoddardean who sided with the 1662 synod in Boston that permitted the "halfway covenant." For these Congregationalists, children of partial members had the right to be baptized. Visible professions of faith were all that were necessary to join the church and participate in the sacraments, according to Beckwith, and he drew on biblical history to buttress his case and to counter Green's use of the Bible in *An Inquiry into the Constitution*. The apostles formed the first churches with no firm idea of who was saved or not; Beckwith noted, "They admitted [the first members] upon a visible, doctrinal profession of the Christian faith, and promise of obedience to the laws of Christ; leaving the matter of their invisible state to God, the alone judge of hearts." The standards were not terribly high, anyway, Beckwith maintained. The Asian churches "had more hypocrites than truly godly in them," while "the Lord himself termed [the church in Laodicea] *wretched and miserable, and blind and naked*, destitute of true godliness" (Beckwith's emphasis). Beckwith's conclusion: "Now if the apostles themselves, with their great, yea supernatural light, could not act with any certainty of this rule, but were so often mistaken; how much less can ministers and churches now?" For Beckwith, the church should apply only one standard—that a seeker profess a faith in Christ and promise obedience to him. The church, he said, was under no obligation to ferret out "secret hypocrites" but instead should be encouraging people to repent and to reform. The church should be inclusive.[9]

Beckwith's criticisms did not especially perturb Green; he had dealt with these issues at length in *An Inquiry into the Constitution*. Indeed, Green believed that Beckwith's pamphlet "contains so little, that is properly against me, I did not think there was any need of a reply." But, of course, Green did respond because he believed that Beckwith had distorted many of his arguments, and the Connecticut minister's misrepresentations may well "lead some less thinking people astray, or at least to keep them in ignorance and error." Green patiently emphasized a point that he had made many times in many forums, including his 1768 tract: "The dispute is not whether we can infallibly know the hearts of others, or be certain who have true grace. . . . I hold not this." Nor, in Green's mind, was the dispute over whether "unregenerate men have a right in the sight of the church, whenever they exhibit credibly evidence of a supreme regard to God." They did. Instead, Green maintained that the issue was over whether the clearly unregenerate, who behaved sinfully and knew they were unregenerate, could partake in the sacraments. He passionately believed they could not. Nor could the church "receive persons considered as unregenerate, while they exhibit not credible evidence that they are real saints."[10]

Green also said that Beckwith distorted his argument over baptizing children, when the latter claimed that Green would deny baptism to those infants who were the offspring of parents denied the right to come to the Lord's Table. "Mr. B. has several times misquoted my words, and misrepresented my sentiments," he complained. Green denied ever saying that parents had to come to the Lord's Table before they had the right to baptize their children. Instead, what he said in his sermon was that the "last qualification for baptism [was] that persons come into full communion *with a design* to partake of the sacrament of the Lord's-supper" (Green's emphasis). They did not, he stressed, actually have to take communion.[11]

Green's biggest problem with Beckwith was the Connecticut minister's fuzzy use of covenantal typology. "In my view," Green wrote in his response to Beckwith, "the whole controversy, in a great measure turns upon the nature of the covenant, of which the sacraments are seals." Green saw the covenant of grace and the sacraments as one; you could not participate in one without the other. Beckwith's failure to understand this elemental truth was the great flaw of his whole system, he said: God did not enter into covenant with the unregenerate, and therefore the unregenerate could not participate in the sacraments. For Beckwith and his fellow Stoddardeans to be persuasive, Green lectured, they needed to show "the nature of that covenant, the terms of it, the design of it and in what manner unregenerate men, as such, can engage in it." Green, however, felt that was impossible. The best they could do was argue for the existence of an external covenant—a sort of secondary covenant for members of the visible church. But Green denied such a thing existed. As he put it in *An Inquiry into the Constitution*, Beckwith and others "talk something of an external Covenant, that God can enter into with the Unregenerate; but they will not explain themselves, or tell where such a Covenant is mentioned in Scripture, or how God does, or can make or seal Promises to the Unregenerate." God, Green insisted repeatedly, did *not* enter into covenant with the unregenerate. He entered into covenant only with the saved, and this pact was the *only* way for someone to become eligible for church membership and communion. The covenant, in other words, constituted a promise made by God and the saint: the saint would behave, and God would allow him or her to come to the Lord's Table. *An Inquiry into the Constitution* elaborately drew on Old Testament history to show how this was so. Green organized chapters around such topics as "Of Israel's Covenanting in Moses's Time" and "What was the Nature of the Covenanting that God required of that People?"[12]

Green's short response to Beckwith did little to quiet the critics. Hugh Knox, an Irish-born Presbyterian minister with whom Jacob had corresponded for years, publicly entered the fray in 1770 when he published *A Letter to the Rev. Mr. Jacob Green, of New Jersey, Pointing Out Some Difficulties in the Calvinistick Scheme of Divinity* . . . Like Beckwith, Knox was troubled by the harshness of Green's Calvinism and its seeming rejection of the unsaved. And like Beckwith, Knox wondered how Green could raise standards without knowing what was in someone's heart. But Knox's concerns were much broader than Beckwith's and his criticisms were more serious. Knox was troubled by the paradox of Calvinism itself: if God was all powerful, why did he save some people and not all? How do you account for sin if the Great Maker was as loving and controlling as Calvinists believed? In confronting Green's drive for purity, Knox revisited the issue of free will that Jonathan Edwards had so ably explored in the 1750s.

Knox did find some of Green's arguments persuasive, although the compliment he paid to his friend from Hanover was backhanded. "You speak as one fully and deliberately convinced of being in the right; and indeed the oftner I read your sermons on baptism, the more force I think I see in your arguments," Knox offered up in praise, before adding, "And yet I really think, on the supposition that your doctrine is right, the practice of it should be introduced with great prudence and caution, and not before it is well understood by a people." The problem, Knox said, was that "no human means will ever be able wholly to exclude hypocrites" from the church. His point was similar to Beckwith's: higher standards would paradoxically *weaken* the church because "the disgrace of having one's children unbaptized, in a christian country, might not induce multitudes to wriggle themselves into the church, by solemn lies and hypocritical professions, rather than to be under it."[13]

The bulk of Knox's tract, an outgrowth of his correspondence with Green over several years, dealt with free will. Green's work built on the writings of Edwards, and Knox properly lumped the two theologians together. Edwards's and Green's task was to reconcile free will with Calvinism. Edwards's insight was to distinguish between natural necessity and moral necessity. An all-powerful but loving God governed through the latter—in his greatness he granted individuals the power to choose within the limits that God had decreed.[14]

Green postulated a similar theory, although he called it different things at different times. In his daybook of 1754–55, Green first ruminated on the *sins of necessity* versus the *sins of commission* (the behaviors one was powerless to change, versus those behaviors one was responsible for). In his crucial 1764 sermon on baptism, he described *natural duties* (the need to live honestly and ethically) and *instituted duties* (those tasks that God directed one to do). In a sermon that he published in 1767 called "Sinners Faultiness, and Spiritual Inability, Considered in a Sermon," Green settled on his key terms— *natural inability* versus *spiritual inability*—which built on his earlier theories. Under natural inability, an individual was powerless to change a behavior: "A deaf Person may choose and desire to hear the Word preached but cannot." By contrast, spiritual inability involved a conscious decision by the individual to commit sin—she is "a careless Sinner who has Sight [but] neglects to read it [the Bible] for Want of Heart." Sinners, Green continued, take "a great Delight in and Bias to that which is wicked. . . . The Motives to do good and avoid evil, have no considerable Weight with him."[15]

Knox praised Green's sermon explaining this theory as "excellent," and "the distinction between *natural* and *moral* inability, I have ever thought an important and useful one."[16] But he was merely being kind, for Knox went on to challenge the whole concept as ultimately unworkable. Knox criticized both Green and Edwards for developing "a scheme, wherein all things are so *fixed, ordered* and *disposed* by a divine predetermination and decree, that, by a *necessity of consequence*, they must come to pass." Moreover, he continued, "this scheme you seem to think *necessary* in order to maintain the *supremacy* and *sovereignty* of GOD, and the absolute dependence of the creature." When God determines the actions of humankind, even evil ones, Knox noted, that destroys "moral agency"—the incentive for an individual to perform good works. Knox believed that Green's careful definition of natural ability did not eradicate this shortcoming: "It is as *impossible* for the *non-elect* or *reprobate* to be saved, or to *do* or *obtain* any thing *spiritually good*, as it is for me to remove a mountain." For those consigned to condemnation, "they [are] under a natural impossibility of salvation." More cruelly under this doctrine, Christ was not sent to save them—"to *them* no saviour was sent; for *them* no saviour died . . . and to *them* no salvation is really and sincerely offered."[17]

Knox also questioned Green's concept of spiritual inability. Green had preached that "the want of power [which is spiritual inability] is the want of will. . . . Man lost his spiritual ability, or good will, or inclination to do good, by the depravity of human nature at the fall." The implication here was that there was nothing a sinner could do to overcome Adam's transgressions unless God bestowed on the individual a good heart and the will to change. Such a dark view of the Fall—which was gospel among strict Calvinists of the time—bothered Knox tremendously: "I am of opinion that it is a sinner's *own* guiltiness, and self-contracted vileness and pollution, which *most* distresses him at that time. . . . *Original sin*, or what I would rather choose to term it, *original corruption* (for I know of no original sin, properly so called, but the first transgression of *Adam*) is only of *secondary* consideration, as the source from which actual transgressions flow." Knox thus placed misbehavior on the individual—he or she was responsible for his or her actions.[18]

The obverse of this belief was that the individual had the power to change his or her behavior. Knox did not carefully distinguish between motivations, as Green did with his natural inability versus spiritual inability and the implication that some behaviors were unchangeable. People *could* change, Knox declared, and they could do so simply by turning to Jesus. Knox thus placed far greater stock in Christ's atoning goodness than did Green and other strict Calvinists: "I am inclined to believe, that CHRIST has *repaired*, yea *much more* than repaired, the ruins of the fall. . . . I am induced to believe . . . that no human infant will ever suffer eternal torments, on account of any *original sin* or *corruption* whatever." Most of all, Knox believed that "no human creature shall ever finally perish, but by his *personal* and criminal abuse." Christ's crucifixion offered everyone the chance "to be *as happy* as *Adam* could have been by keeping the covenant of life."[19]

The upshot of these bold assertions was that Knox bestowed "a liberty of choice" on humans, similar to John Wesley's doctrine, that was far broader and more generous than what Green and Edwards allowed in their doctrines on free will. In Knox's view, God created humans, made them rational, and left it up to them whether to walk down the right path or not. As he explained in a letter to Green, Knox said that "the simple prescience of GOD, can have no manner of influence on this event. The thing happened, indeed, just as GOD foresaw that it would; but it happened wholly by the fault of the creature."[20]

Despite this expansive definition of free will and his pointed questioning of Calvinistic beliefs, Knox drew back from the implications of his arguments. Unable to escape the conventions of his age, he still believed that God was all-powerful and, more surprisingly given his previous arguments, that God still preordained who was saved and who was not. Knox suspected "that the number of the *saved* and *damned* are from eternity *known*, and . . . *fixed* and *determined* in the divine idea, and that none ever will accept the offers, or submit to the terms, of the gospel salvation, but such as GOD from eternity *foresaw* and *foreknew* would do so."[21]

Not surprisingly, Green found Knox's views on free will and Calvinism a muddle. Green asked him in a letter, "Does GOD's foreknowledge depend on his decree; 'or his decree upon his prescience'?" Knox's candid response was "I do not know." He pointed out that the scriptures were not conclusive "on this nice metaphysical speculation." Green also asked Knox whether God purposely placed creatures in "a state of trial, so as to leave them in the greatest equilibrium; could he foresee how these creatures would acquit themselves?" Knox's answer was "Yes, certainly; otherwise his prescience, and consequently his knowledge, could not be infinite." Knox also admitted that Edwards's famous *Freedom of the Will* baffled and confused him: "I find it an immense toil to follow him in his reasonings, and profess that there may be many fallacies in them, which I am not able to detect."[22]

Knox's confusion was understandable, because Edwards simultaneously argued that individuals had the power to choose and that God controlled all. This seeming paradox rested on a careful definition of the will. The will was not an independent agent, according to Edwards. A person did not control his or her will; God did. And because God controlled the will, he controlled the power of choice. How to explain a person's bad decisions and the endless choices one faces in the course of the day? Edwards's answer was clever: as the creator and ruler of the universe, an all-powerful, infinitely wise God bestowed on his creation multiple courses of action, and they were free to choose within those ranges of actions which path to follow. Green agreed with Edwards on these points, observing, "If any Person has a Will to love God or Holiness, there is then Nothing in the Way, he does the Thing; he loves God and Holiness." Unlike Knox, both Green and Edwards believed that individuals could enjoy no meaningful freedom because God was so powerful. They only had the *illusion* of freedom. Green described the will as "the Fountain of Power in the Soul, and to suppose a Power in the Soul over this Power, is an Absurdity." And this meant that sinners could not change their fate through free will. "Some seem to propose, that Sinners should will and choose a [good] Thing . . . which is impossible and a Contradiction," Green said in his sermon "Sinners Faultiness, and Spiritual Inability, Considered in a Sermon." In other words, it was impossible for the unregenerate to achieve his or her own salvation; only God could bestow that.[23]

Knox compiled his correspondence and published it as a tract in London in January 1770. Two years later, he sent Green a copy of the publication from Saba and apologized for its tardiness ("It Came out from England about 3 months Ago, & should have been Sent unto you Sooner, were it not that passages to your Coast are a little unfavorable in the depth of the winter"). Green chose not to publish a response to Knox. Instead, he wrote another long tract that was dated June 29, 1770—almost five months to the day after Knox published his *Letter to the Rev. Mr. Jacob Green*—that revisited his views on the broader controversy.[24]

"An Humble Attempt Truly to State the Controversy" was Green's final attempt to explain his position and to mollify his critics. In many ways, it was a plea for civility and common sense: "I heartily desire, that persons on both sides of this controversy may endeavour to bring matters to an amicable [close]. Why cannot this be done, if we are friendly on both sides? And why should we be otherwise!" Any compromising would have to be done by his opponents, however, because Green did not budge from his position on the need for purity in the church. Nor did he directly acknowledge the arguments of Beckwith and Knox. He did, however, implicitly acknowledge the force of Knox's views by further developing his own suppositions on the unregenerate and better explaining the causes of sin. "The two great sources of human actions, are self-love, & supreme love to God," Green wrote. "All that is done in the world may be Supposed to flow from these." The latter, of course, constituted "true virtue, or holiness": the saintly venerated God and placed love of him before anything else. The not-so-saintly placed his own needs first, and for Green "there is no worse principle in human Nature" than such selfishness: "All the bad actions, & horrid wickedness in the world springs from self love & no other source."[25]

Thus self-love was one key to understanding the sinful behavior of the unregenerate, according to Green. It was the wellspring of their actions. It led them to grasp for money, to seek finer clothes, to assuage their pain in drink, to swear without restraint. Most seriously, Green said, self-love corrupted their hearts. The unregenerate cared more about themselves than about God; "All the unregenerate look to something more than to God, [they] *Serve the creature more than the creator.*" The polluting nature of self-love also harmed the unregenerate's ability to change. When they prayed, when they tried to change their ways, they did it for themselves and not for God. Prayer, instead, "should be a sort of solemn mediation upon the subject in the presence of God. And this is proper for all the unregenerate." This meant, for Green, that the unregenerate "should acknowledge how hard his heart is, & how destitute of any proper desires of spiritual God." Humbleness was essential; surrendering to Christ was pivotal.[26]

Green's self-love doctrine, which so neatly captured the follies of human behavior, did not resolve the basic conundrum facing Calvinism, however. Was there *anything* the unregenerate could do to "earn" salvation? Emphatically not, Green answered. He reiterated that a divine being preordained who was saved and that it was God's decision, and God's alone, who could become a saint; an individual was powerless to overturn this divine edict. Moreover, "An Humble Attempt" repeated Green's belief that the will was synonymous with the soul, and that God (and not the individual) controlled it. In doing so, the tract had terribly harsh things to say about the unregenerate: they were destined to go to hell because the Lord was so mad at them. "God stands in the Sinners way. Sinners are now . . . to be hurt by God," and the sinner should tremble at this prospect, Green warned: "God is dreadfully angry with them . . . their guilt is daily increasing; they are heaping up fuell for hell if they should yet die out of Christ."[27]

Such assertions seemed to amply vindicate critics' complaints that people had no incentive to behave virtuously under Calvinism. Green, though, had an answer: if one truly loved God and was under the light of the Gospel, a person *could* be regenerated. Green could make this seemingly inconsistent argument because of a second conundrum bedeviling Calvinism: no human truly knew whether he or she was of the elect, and no human knew whether *another* human was of the elect—not the pastor, not the congregation, not the seeker's family. Only God knew. Because of this inherent uncertainty among mortals, a sinner could change his ways and visibly demonstrate to the world that he was of the elect—that he had repented, amended his behavior, and returned to righteous living; when he did all that, he could justifiably proclaim that his reformation was at God's behest and that he was a member of the invisible church. Green offered up an important caveat, however: these changes had to be done for God's glory and not for the glory of the individual. One had to turn to Jesus, to accept that he was the Savior. Then one had to truly change his or her ways. She had to open her heart to the saving truths by surrendering to the Lord; this surrender would then open the floodgates to further change. "A Soul enlightened with Gospil truths, is a fit organ for grace of God to operate in & by. A Soul must act according to its light & knowledge," Green explained. Even more hopefully, God in his infinite goodness decided to save some of the most wicked. "His method," Green said, was "to put his grace where there is light."[28]

Such a possibility of redemption was a powerful incentive for people to reform their behavior, Green believed. *All* Christians could hope that they were among the elect. Green boiled this exciting prospect down to a simple, terse equation—repent and believe: "God proposes to man eternal happiness upon his repentance & Faith." The Lord can make this promise to the "fallen man" because of the covenant of grace, and it meant that sinners could hope that they would be converted. "Why?" Green asked. Because of God's forgiveness: "Why truly God has taken them in hand, & is using the means with them that he does with those that he brings home to himself, & not because they are more friendly to God & divine things."[29]

This was Green's answer to the arguments of Beckwith and Knox that Green's purity crusade was undermining the church by driving people away: the covenant of grace was a powerful spur to good behavior because, in Green's words, it consisted of a command and a promise. Humans were to obey God and do their duty by living righteously. God would then deliver to them his promise of eternal happiness. In this sense, the covenant of grace was quite simple. "When any one of the human race does thus repent & believe he is in Covenant with God," the Lord, in turn, "will grant some visible sign, or token" that an individual is in covenant. These visible signs made it apparent to the church who was of the elect—and who was not. The reverse was true as well: irreligious behavior indicated one was not of the elect and thus was not eligible for full church membership and participation in the sacraments. Hence, in Green's estimation, constructing a pure church was entirely feasible. A pastor and his congregation *can* deduce who was worthy of admission. Yet it involved more than negative evidence; "there must be something Positive," he explained in the appendix of *An Inquiry into the Constitution*. "Profession of Religion, and Practice or Behaviour agreeable, is the Rule to judge by," he wrote. "Agreeable Practice and Behaviour, implies the Exhibition of a Taste and Relish for Divine Things; the Ways of God, and godly People."[30]

Green thus categorically rejected his foes' arguments that it was impossible to raise standards and was self-defeating to do so. Green, in fact, believed that the Stoddardeans had it backward: barring the visible sinner from communion was the most effective way to spur a change in behavior. He recounted the time a minister (presumably Green) refused to baptize a man's child and would not allow the man to take communion, despite the seeker's insistence that he was qualified. His rejection "was a shocking thing to the man; he turned it much in his mind" until he realized that he was indeed unfit to partake. So he vowed to reform his behavior, became "eminently pious, & became an officer in the church."[31]

Green's views on church membership informed his opinion of society and politics. British North America was filled with fallen men and women, great sinners who were driven by self-love and not love of God. He did not have to look far for evidence of such behavior. Green was bitterly disappointed with his own congregation, which he felt was acting selfishly when it refused to raise his salary and often failed to pay the full amount. In 1768, he called it a "slackness & negligence in duty" on their part.[32]

Green also worried about the many temptations that people faced, thanks to an expanding American economy that was turning the colonists into consumers. Partaking of a "consumer revolution," people now had more money to spend and more choices on which to spend it. Materialism was growing and religiosity was dropping. The Great Awakening, he sadly concluded, was long over and so were its beneficial effects. Thus Green's drive for more rigorous church standards faced its sternest test not from foes like the Reverend George Beckwith but from a materialistic society that was seemingly turning its back on God. Green certainly understood the enormity of his challenge. "I am very Sensible that our Sentiments are not calculated to take place in a low State of Religion. They are not likely to prevail in a time of degenerancy," he concluded in "An Humble Attempt." "I have no expectation that our plan, or Notion of chh communion will generally take place while religion is in its present low State." Thus, if Green was to implement a pure church, he would also have to fight to purify society. Green was confident he could improve society's morals, and in the late 1760s he began working out how. He decided on a multipronged effort. First, he instituted tighter admission standards at home, in Hanover, and devoted his weekly sermon to the need for individuals to improve their behavior. Then he sought to build support in Protestant intellectual circles by publishing several tracts and sermons expounding on his arguments with the hope that other pastors at other churches would follow his example. Then he composed *A Vision of Hell* in a successful attempt to reach a mass audience among the laity (fig. 6). *A Vision of Hell* was his most important effort because he reached so many people with the tract's release. Published in 1770, it went through more than twelve printings and became a best seller. Paul Revere did the engravings for the second edition.[33]

Despite the dark title, Revere's ghoulish illustrations, and Green's bitter personal experiences that underlay so many of the themes, the tract was written with great wit and dwelled little on hell itself. Green served up no lurid descriptions of the underworld and the awful fate that awaited the damned, unlike many of his fellow ministers who terrified audiences with their tales of burning fires and dreadful pits of glowing flames. Instead, through satire he poked fun at contemporary religion and its low standards. Indeed, one scholar likened *A Vision of Hell* to C. S. Lewis's *Screwtape Letters*, and the comparison is apt. Green wrote with a relatively light touch to make two points—life posed all kinds of temptations for the weak or unaware, and religion in the colonies was wanting.[34]

Green's purpose in *A Vision of Hell* was to shame people and to get them to see how selfish their behavior was. And by getting people to see and understand the dangers of self-love, he was hoping to get them to return to church and to turn to God. The tone and the imagery of *A Vision of Hell* were aimed at a mass audience. The tract relied on straightforward prose and

# A VISION OF HELL,

And a DISCOVDRY of some of the *Consultations* and *Devices* there, in the Year 1767.

## BY THEODORUS VAN SHEMAIN.

And the Lord said unto Satan, Whence comest thou ? Then Satan answered the Lord, and said, From going to and fro in the earth, and from walking up and down in it.       Job 1. 7.

Your adverfary the devil, as a roaring lion, walketh about feeking whom he may devour.       1 Pet. 5. 8.

Satan himself is transformed into an angel of light. 2 Cor. xi. 14.

Lest Satan should get an advantage of us : for we are not ignorant of his devices.       2 Cor. ii. 11.

## BOSTON:

Printed and Sold at John Boyle's Printing-Office, next Door to the *Three Doves* in Marlborough-Street. 1767.

*Fig. 6*   Paul Revere of Boston did the two primitive drawings for Green's best-selling tract *A Vision of Hell*. Employing medieval imagery, Revere showed four grinning devils jubilantly waiting at the mouth of hell (represented by a fire-breathing monster) for their next victims.

biting sarcasm to make its points. It was written in the form of a story, describing a journey that was meant to entertain and educate. Gone were the dry theological arguments that Green used in his debate with Beckwith and Knox.

The illustrations were important as well. Easily recognizable to Protestants of all stripes, the cartoonish figures appearing in the drawings reinforced the tract's themes. The first edition contained a woodcut of the heavenly city Zion and its enemies. Labeled "tyrant sin," it featured the pope, several devils, Turkish Muslims, and young women in revealing dresses—all enemies to right-thinking Protestants. As mentioned above, Revere's two illustrations appeared in the second edition. The one on the title page was based on an earlier illustration of Revere's that appeared in 1768 called "A Warm Place—Hell." That 1768 illustration, in turn, was modeled on an earlier English one. All of these illustrations drew on medieval imagery, as well as longtime themes in literature, that depicted hell as a fiendish place of fire and burning lakes, populated by devils with pitchforks and other frightening creatures. Revere's drawing for Green's tract, as a result, was easily recognizable to the colonists; it showed four grinning devils jubilantly waiting at the mouth of hell (represented by a fire-breathing monster with huge mouth agape) for their next victims. Not that anyone would miss such an explicit message, but Green reinforced the point by reprinting four biblical passages just beneath the illustration. The passage from 1 Peter was representative: "Your adversary the devil, is a roaring lion, walketh about seeking whom he may devour."[35]

The second illustration appeared on the tract's final page. Green's narrator has concluded his journey with calls for the seeker to turn to God and avoid the awful fate of spending eternity in hell: "Oh, that poor sinners on earth would shun the devil's snares, and trust in God! . . . If they would resist the devil he would be made to fly from them. Jesus Christ is stronger than Satan." Below these hopeful words was a drawing of a man standing below dark clouds, next to a skeleton holding a pitchfork pointing downward.[36]

Green's strategy during these prewar years says much about the man, the minister, and the reformer. He was no George Whitefield (or even a James Davenport) who went on speaking tours in an effort to spark a second Great Awakening. He was too shy and too poor of a public speaker to undertake such a thing. Moreover, he said little about the new birth and devised no strategies to lead people to one, despite the fact he had heard Whitefield preach in person and was offered a job with him. In his own congregation, he held few revivals and never preached on the new birth and what it entailed. His focus, instead, was on individuals' behavior, and his primary weapon was his pen. In the pulpit, he delivered well-crafted sermons on the need for personal reform that he either wrote out in longhand or outlined in Weston's. Outside the pulpit, he published frequently between 1767 and 1770, composing carefully written tracts arguing for pure churches composed of well-behaved members. He wrote *A Vision of Hell* with the same goals in mind for a broader audience, and it sold spectacularly.[37]

So, was Jacob Green a radical in 1770? Well, yes and no. His attempts to purify the church and clean up society in the years leading up to 1770 were the first steps in what would become an audacious program to change society. In the prerevolutionary years, Green rejected the halfway covenant and other compromises of religious reformers. Yet his frame of reference during this period remained "traditional." He had not yet overcome his New England mind-set. His tenets remained the longtime Puritan values of salvation, self-examination, and godly living. Seventeenth-century covenantal theology remained critical to him. Mutual obligations defined society and an individual's place within in it—one owed allegiance to God, to one another, and to one's community. Green talked incessantly about the obligations that congregation members owed each other. Sometimes it was financial support of the church, as the 1768 dispute over his salary showed. Often it involved heartfelt faith. And always, according to Green, good Christians had an obligation to help their fellow man, including rebuking neighbors for sinful behavior. "Our usefulness in the world very much depends upon our being Suitably free from failings, oddities & disagreeable conduct," he explained one Sunday.[38]

In holding fast to such traditional beliefs, Green was rejecting many of the intellectual currents swirling around him during the Enlightenment of the mid-eighteenth century. He especially rejected the profit motive, the enlightened notion espoused by Adam Smith and other economic thinkers that the pursuit of money by individuals collectively benefited society. For Green, such a theory was preposterous. Pursuing wealth was un-Christian and violated the covenant. Those individuals who strove merely to make money were vain and selfish, he preached in his sermons and writings; they were interested only in self-love and not in the Lord. *A Vision of Hell* ridiculed profit-seeking economic behavior as crass, with the devils sagely agreeing on how easy it was to seduce those individuals who panted after wealth. Such people wanted to get rich and to acquire the finer things in life, including elegant carriages and fancy clothes. As the devil Nifroch put it, "New cloaths and new fashions will employ their thoughts: Others shall think of themselves and their own dress and finery, and how others view and admire them."[39]

Green was especially appalled at the idea of someone wanting money for money's sake. Merchants, planters, and others who engaged in such behavior were putting money ("grasping") ahead of the church. As *A Vision of Hell* noted, these people were only part-time Christians: on the Sabbath, "he meets with persons with whom he can do many errands, and transacts much business. . . . He attends church two or three hours and thinks he is a good christian, without knowing what christianity is."[40]

Like his Puritan forebearers of the seventeenth century, Green saw commerce as a threat to the church *and* the state. Virtuous, disciplined men were to put the needs of God and the community first. They were to rise above petty private interests and act virtuously for the good of the whole. He did not develop his religious views in a vacuum, however. Green wrote his 1768 congregational address and his religious tracts, including *A Vision of Hell*, at a time when the colonists and Great Britain were arguing over the right of Parliament to tax Americans. Although Green was no politician, he was watching political developments closely and reading New York's Whig newspapers faithfully. He grasped the implications of what was happening and understood that the radical challengers to British rule constituted a "secular" movement that was defending colonial rights *and* preaching the need for individuals to reform their behavior to advance the needs of a republican state. It was a movement that wanted to reorder society to prevent the arbitrary abuse of power. It was a movement that stressed that virtuous, disciplined men had to work together if the community were to thrive.

It was, in short, a movement that represented a tremendous opportunity for Pastor Green and his vision of reform.

*The Loyalist Down the Road: Thomas Bradbury Chandler
and the Bishop's Cause—a Fight Renewed*

The episcopal controversy had a long history behind it by the time Thomas Bradbury Chandler took up the cause in the 1750s. He was no innocent in the coming fight. Chandler had learned his history, and learned it well, from

Samuel Johnson. Johnson, the brilliant Yale-trained theologian who had defected to the Anglicans in the "Yale Apostasy of 1722," was convinced that the church's survival in America rested on the sending of bishops to the colonies. Johnson had a Laudian hatred of "rigid Independents" (primarily Puritans) and a Henrician belief in the union of church and state. Chandler fully absorbed these principles from his mentor. Indeed, he accepted them so thoroughly that Chandler pursued a bishopric with even greater vigor than did Johnson. Besides writing extensively on the subject, he organized annual gatherings of Anglican ministers beginning in 1758, where they honed their strategy of pressing for episcopacy, drew up petitions to send to London, and approved incendiary tracts to lob at their dissenter enemies.

Chandler's cause remained an uphill fight, however. Given the long history of animosity toward the episcopal office, the Crown well understood that sending a bishop to America would set off a firestorm in New England and the Mid-Atlantic colonies. For years, Johnson and others had been pleading their case to no avail. The first sustained campaign for a bishop began in 1701, when the Society for the Propagation of the Gospel was founded. This missionary group was seeking to make the Church of England a force in the colonies, and it wanted a bishop to aid that cause. Its campaign drew the support of Queen Anne, and a bill was prepared for Parliament. But when Anne died in 1714, so did the society's efforts to obtain a bishop. In 1741, the bishop of Oxford, Thomas Secker, revived the campaign by pressing anew for a colonial episcopate. He got no further than the SPG did, because of the raging political headwinds against bishops.

Chandler, though, was undaunted by this history of failure. He decided the backers of American episcopacy needed to try again, and he used the conventions of 1765 and 1766 to rally anew the northern clergy to his cause. His timing was not good. The Stamp Act crisis had both sides on edge—the Americans were fearful they were about to lose their liberties; the Crown and Parliament were angered that their attempts to raise revenue had created such a violent backlash. American radicals were immediately suspicious when they heard that Chandler and his allies were reviving their episcopal plans.

In turn, Chandler's reaction to the latest American opposition was exasperation. The office, he patiently pointed out in his *Appeal to the Public in Behalf of the Church of England in America*, was administrative, providing two important tasks: ordaining ministers and disciplining them once in office. Without bishops, the church was rudderless. For proof, one did not have to look far, Chandler said. The American church was in "wretched

Condition . . . for want of Bishops." An American bishop would be the leader of the church's colonial branch, the stern hand who would provide structure, wisdom, and guidance to the clergy and the flock. "When it is said, that the Church of England in America, without Bishops, must be without Government," he explained, "this is to be understood in a qualified Sense. For where there is absolutely no Government at all, there can be nothing but Disorder and Confusion, without any Appearance of Regularity."

Then there were the practical considerations, Chandler continued. "The Clergy can evidently do but little without a Bishop . . . proper Care cannot be taken of them by a Bishop who has the immediate Inspection of a large Diocess in England, and resides at the Distance of Three Thousand Miles." With a bishop absent, "the Clergy are independent of each other, and have not Ecclesiastical Superiors to unite or control them." Although most ministers were hardworking and dedicated, Chandler noted that the American church possessed no way to deal with the incompetent or the corrupt: "If a Clergyman shall disgrace his Profession in an open and scandalous Manner, a Bishop residing in the Country can suspend him immediately."

Last was the difficulty of ordaining American candidates for the ministry—without a bishop nearby, they had to cross the Atlantic Ocean to reach London at great expense and danger. Ship's passage, in Chandler's reckoning, averaged 100 pounds sterling per person. "To Men of Fortune this is an inconsiderable Sum; but Men of Fortune must not be expected to devote themselves to the Service of the Church in America." Taken together, the cost and the danger of an Atlantic voyage contributed greatly to the shortage of Anglican clergy in America: "In the Province of New-Jersey there are Twenty-one Churches and Congregations; Eleven of these are intirely destitute of a Minister, and there are but Five Clergymen to do the Duties of the other Ten." But, even when candidates did hazard the ocean crossing, "another glaring Disadvantage, to which the Church in America is manifestly subject, arises from the impossibility that a Bishop residing in England, should be sufficiently acquainted with the Character of those who go Home from this Country for Holy Orders."

Sensible reasons, all. If Chandler had stopped there when presenting his case, he might have won over a sizable number of people of good sense and will. But he did not stop there, for Thomas Bradbury Chandler had an incurable case of logorrhea; he simply could not resist adding why bishops were so important to society. American Whigs took notice.[41]

# 6

## *Revolutionary*

As Governor William Franklin entered the council chamber in mid-January 1775, he calmly surveyed the waiting members of the New Jersey legislature before beginning his carefully prepared speech. In his tone and words, Franklin exuded reasonableness, and he was almost apologetic as he launched into yet another defense of the king. "It is not for me to decide on the particular Merits of the Dispute between Great Britain and her Colonies," he began. "Nor do I mean to censure those [who] conceive themselves aggrieved for aiming at a Redress of their Grievances. It is a Duty they owe themselves, their Country, and their Posterity."[1]

The governor then got down to his real purpose: lecturing the legislators on the seriousness of the widening colonial rebellion and their responsibility to resist the radicals who were fomenting it: "You are their legal Representatives, and you cannot without a manifest Breach of your Trust, Suffer any Body of Men, in this or any of the other Provinces, to usurp and exercise any of the Powers vested in you by the Constitution." For all his outward assurance and calm, Franklin understood that his and the Crown's positions were tenuous and deteriorating. He told the gathered members that the colonies were at a crossroads, with one path "evidently leading to Peace, Happiness, and a Restoration of the Public Tranquility, the other inevitably conducting you to Anarchy, Misery, and all the Horrors of a Civil War."[2]

Franklin's stark assessment encapsulated the fears of many Americans, including Thomas Bradbury Chandler, in 1775 and 1776: if the colonies did not compromise with the Crown, they faced war and ruin. "What must the consequence of a rebellious war with the Mother Country, any person of common sense, if he will take the liberty to exercise it, may easily foresee," Chandler declared in 1775. "Even a final victory would effectually ruin us; as it would necessarily introduce civil wars among ourselves, and leave us open and exposed to the avarice and ambition of every maritime power in Europe or America."[3]

Jacob Green would have none of that. Ever the intellectual and the student of society's ills, he came to a conclusion opposite from Franklin's and Chandler's—that independence from Great Britain would mean salvation, affording the colonies the opportunity to grow and blossom materially and spiritually. Dismayed that so many in the middle colonies (especially in New Jersey) disagreed with him, and impatient that so many hesitated to take the final step and declare independence, Green published an influential tract in April 1776 that sought to refute all the arguments for reconciling with king and Parliament. *Observations on the Reconciliation of Great-Britain and the Colonies* was another classic Green production: calm, reasoned, analytical, and, ultimately, influential in New Jersey because of all that (fig. 7).[4]

The phlegmatic tone, however, could not mask the direction that Green's thinking was taking during these tumultuous years. Jacob was becoming, in the words of his son Ashbel, an "ardent" revolutionary who loved liberty. By crystallizing his beliefs on religion, politics, and reform, the American Revolution further radicalized him, and he wholeheartedly embraced the independence movement because he saw it as a heaven-sent opportunity to throw off the British yoke and institute badly needed changes on a broad front to improve society. The independence movement, in short, meshed perfectly with the causes he had been pursuing since the early 1760s.[5]

In his zeal for independence, Green vaulted ahead of many of his fellow citizens in New Jersey. A political backwater with a regionally based economy, the colony had few direct dealings with the British Empire. New Jersey's economy remained small and agrarian in 1775. It had no newspapers as the war neared. It lacked a formal revolutionary organization until 1774. On top of these challenges, New Jersey's Whig movement had to contend with one of the most experienced royal governors in British North America, William Franklin, who came to office in 1763. Benjamin Franklin's son was an avid supporter of the Crown and a talented politician who did all he could

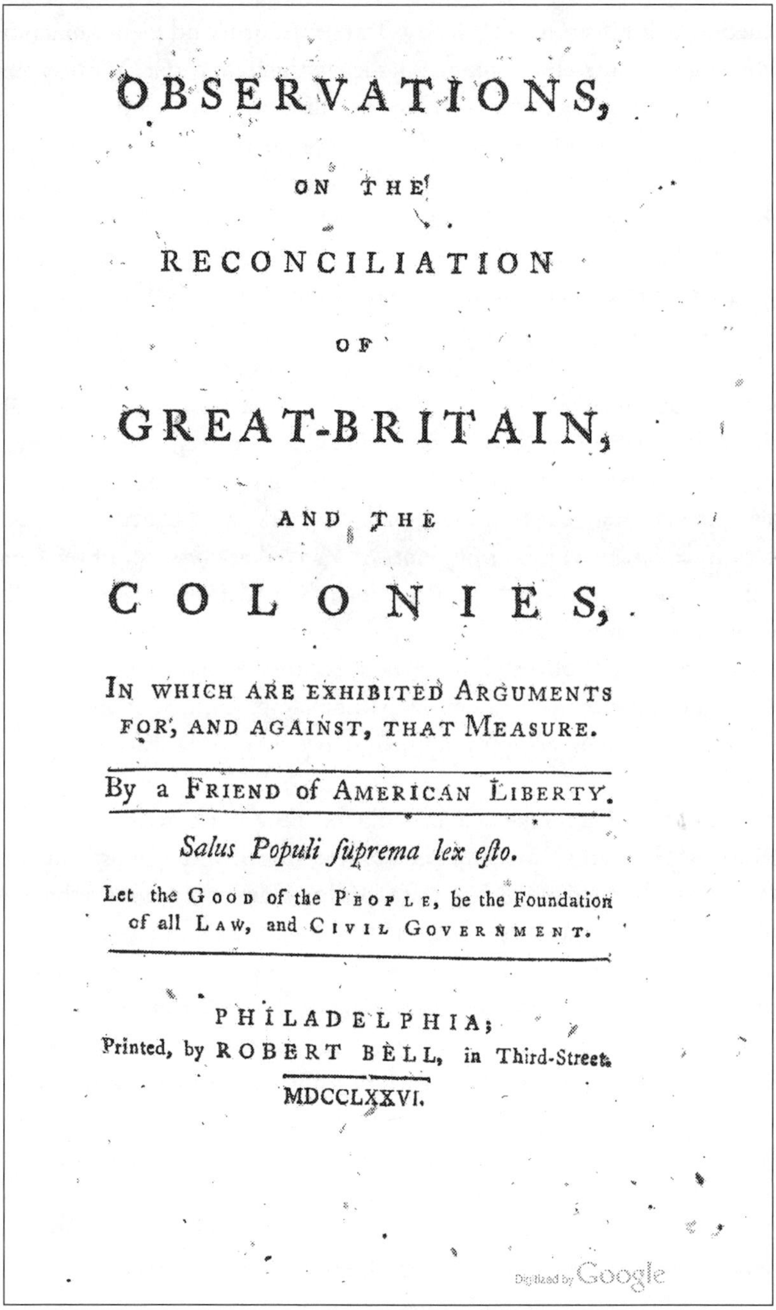

# OBSERVATIONS,

## ON THE

## RECONCILIATION

### OF

# GREAT-BRITAIN,

### AND THE

# COLONIES,

In which are exhibited Arguments
for, and against, that Measure.

By a Friend of American Liberty.

*Salus Populi suprema lex esto.*

Let the Good of the People, be the Foundation
of all Law, and Civil Government.

PHILADELPHIA;
Printed, by ROBERT BELL, in Third-Street.
MDCCLXXVI.

*Fig. 7* Green's lauded tract advocating independence sold widely, partly because it was printed in both New York City and Philadelphia. This version was offered by Philadelphia printer Robert Bell for only one shilling.

to encourage loyalism in New Jersey. The governor found plenty of support among the colony's elite, among Anglicans (including one Thomas Bradbury Chandler), and among West Jersey's substantial Quaker population. In 1776, the percentage of New Jersey's loyalist population was more than twice as high as the colonial average: about 36 percent, versus 16 percent elsewhere.[6]

But New Jersey's small radical faction had a number of things going for it, including the support of the Presbyterian Church. Presbyterianism was the largest, most influential Protestant church in the colony, and its membership by 1774 had come to dominate East Jersey's revolutionary movement at all levels, from the county committees in such places as Morris County to the delegation sent to represent New Jersey in the Continental Congress. Elizabeth Town's main Presbyterian congregation was especially important. Its members included William Livingston, the Whig writer and future governor under the 1776 state constitution; Abraham Clark, who signed the Declaration of Independence; Elias Boudinot, who served as president of the Continental Congress; and several generals, including Matthias Ogden and Elias Dayton. The support within Presbyterian ranks extended beyond the pews to the highest councils of the church: the New York Synod, which was led by John Witherspoon, was firmly in the patriot camp, and it sent out a pastoral letter in 1775 to members warning them to get ready for a war that was close at hand.[7]

Besides providing intellectual backing for the Whig movement, Presbyterianism supplied geographical bases of support, one of the most important being Green's home county. Morris (as well as Hanover) was a Presbyterian-Whig stronghold that counted few loyalists among its inhabitants. Unlike Monmouth and some other places in New Jersey, Morris was socially and religiously cohesive. From the earliest days of the Stamp Act crisis, the county backed the radicals in their fight against the Crown. When Parliament enacted the "Intolerable Acts" in 1774, Morris was the third county in New Jersey to condemn it. Morris also took the lead in New Jersey in raising money and supplies for Boston. Presbyterian-dominated Hanover Township was equally ardent for independence. Its seven-member committee of observation, four of whom were connected with Green's church, enjoyed wide support in the township. It enforced the rules of the Continental Association, banned the circulation of James Rivington's "incendiary" loyalist newspaper in the township, and denounced "a wicked Ministry" that was seeking "to disunite and divide us."[8]

As in other places, the fuse for rebellion was lit in New Jersey during the Stamp Act controversy of 1765. In March of that year, Parliament imposed duties on colonists' documents and papers. Americans protested, deriding the duties as a tax. In June, Massachusetts called for an intercolonial meeting, but New Jersey initially declined to participate. A group of lawyers met in Perth Amboy, however, and agreed to boycott the stamps and not conduct any legal business. In September, James Parker of Woodbridge published the *Constitutional Courant* and helped stir up opposition to the Stamp Act in his colony. Gradually opposition in New Jersey to various British measures grew, and Assembly members agreed to send representatives to the Stamp Act Congress, which was scheduled to meet in New York City.[9]

The New Jersey legislature, meeting in November 1765, endorsed the actions of the Stamp Act Congress and backed a resolution denying Parliament's right to tax the colonists without their consent; the resolutions concluded that Parliament's attempt to impose the Stamp Act on America was "unprecedented, and not to be thought of without the greatest anxiety."[10] Parliament's retreat on the Stamp Act in March 1766 was temporary: in 1767, it passed the Townsend Acts, a new collection of duties on glass, paper, paint, and tea. These revenues set off another round of protests in New Jersey, with public meetings of citizens and the legislature denouncing Parliament anew, and the Assembly drawing up another petition. In Morris County, opposition to the Townsend duties and to other British acts (including the quartering act) was strong.[11]

When the Townsend Acts were repealed in 1770, revolutionary agitation quieted in New Jersey. Instead, local issues dominated colonial affairs, including arguments over a loan office and a politically explosive controversy over how to handle the theft of 8,000 pounds from the East Jersey treasury. In 1769 and 1770, riots broke out in Essex and Monmouth Counties owing to tensions over debts and proprietorial policies. The lull in the imperial debate ended in 1774, when Parliament enacted the Intolerable Acts to punish Boston for its destruction of tea from the East Indies. New Jersey promptly joined its sister colonies in protesting. Every county in New Jersey held meetings to denounce the British government's actions, including the Administration of Justice Act of May 20, 1774, which sought to suppress township government. It was Essex County, home to Thomas Bradbury Chandler, that took the lead in New Jersey, passing a series of resolutions protesting the Intolerable Acts. More important, Essex issued a circular letter that called on other counties to send delegates for a general meeting to be held on July 21, 1775, in New Brunswick. To elect delegates and form committees of correspondence, counties across New Jersey held meetings in June and July. A few weeks later, on July 21, New Jersey's first Provincial Congress convened. It pledged to help Boston, agreed to abide by a colonial-wide nonimportation agreement—and reaffirmed the colony's loyalty to the king.[12]

So it went on down to January 1776. Many petitions were approved, boycotts implemented, and resolutions passed. A majority of New Jerseyans supported the defense of colonial liberties, but most hesitated to take the final step and back independence. Ensconced in the Presbyterian-Whig stronghold of Hanover, and utterly convinced that reconciliation with Great Britain was impossible, Green grew impatient with (to borrow the memorable words of a letter writer from Somerset County) "the ignorant, the weak, and the timid" within the colony. Green concluded he had to enter the political fray. It was a step he did not take lightly, for this decision violated one of his most cherished beliefs—that men of the cloth should not become involved in politics. But he felt his participation was unavoidable—the colonies had to declare independence and undertake the reforms that he felt were needed. Thus, sometime in the opening months of 1776, he began laboring over a tract that he would publish in April as *Observations on the Reconciliation of Great-Britain, and the Colonies.* To keep up appearances, he published the tract anonymously, signing it as "a Friend of American Liberty." (His authorship was a poorly kept secret, however.)[13]

His *Observations* was an answer to the arguments of Chandler and others that independence could not be won and was something to be feared. Indeed, the belief was widespread that secession would result in disaster. Chandler wrote two powerful tracts in 1774 warning "ignorant and deluded Americans" of the folly of breaking away from Great Britain. In *The Friendly Address to All* Reasonable *Americans*, he maintained that a Continental Congress led by "the madmen of *New-England*" was rushing Americans into a war they could not win. The colonists, Chandler warned, lacked the armies and fortifications to withstand Britain's military might—America's borders "are open and accessible on every quarter, and have not a single fortress to cover them, nor one regiment of regular troops to defend them." With no military to speak of, the colonies would face disaster: "The country that is now 'fair as *Eden*,' will become a field of blood, overspread with desolation and slaughter. I tremble, and my blood retires to my heart at the prospect of such amazing anguish and misery." His description of America as "fair as *Eden*" was telling. Chandler saw no evidence of tyranny on the British side. "The Frame of the English government, for the admirable wisdom of its structure, has always been the wonder of the world," he declared. "And under its protection and mild influence, the subjects of Great-Britain are the happiest people on earth." America was thriving under the Crown's benign rule, and he strongly believed that Britain—and not Continental Congress—would be the best protector of civil liberties (although Chandler did concede that the Stamp Act was unwise).[14]

Green devoted the first half of his tract to the arguments of Chandler and others for reconciling with the Crown. The remainder of *Observations* presented in a question-and-answer format Green's case for independence. For Green, the crux of the matter was simple: "Shall we be reconciled to Great Britain, so as to be under her government, or shall we be independent?" That question led to a more crucial one: "Have we a right to be independent?" The answer to the latter, he vigorously argued, was yes. In direct contradiction of Chandler and other British apologists, Green maintained that Britain had forfeited its right to govern the colonies by breaking the compact between the ruler and the ruled.[15]

It was a very Lockean (and radical) argument for rebellion, with Green noting that "in a state of nature . . . every man had a right to enjoy himself. . . . And in that state of nature, each man had a right to defend and vindicate himself, if assaulted or injured by others." Green, like other Whig radicals, posited that "the whole design of civil government or magistracy, is the good of the people." When the government fails to protect its citizens, the people have a right to rebel. "What obliges us to submit to British government? It is not for want of will and disposition, in her that she does not proceed against us to the utmost," he wrote. "She has endeavoured to crush us, and expected that what she has done would have accomplished it. Britain expected by her armed force, the Fishery Bill, and others of the same cruel kind, by starving and blood shed, to have reduced us to an entire submission."[16]

Green was especially angered by the Crown's dual strategy of mixing force with persuasion to try to bring the rebellious colonists to heel. "How strange is it that Britain should declare us rebels, seize our effects, and try every way to hurt us, at the same time that she proposes an accommodation, and appoints Commissioners to treat with us!"[17]

The opening section of *Observations*, however, was largely devoid of anger. Green wanted to win over the reader with his calm tone. He placed the blame for the imperial crisis squarely with the British Crown: "She has acted directly contrary to all her obligations to protect and defend us, most unjustly pronounced us rebels, and treated us as such." With these preliminaries out of the way, *Observations* moved to the second, and more lengthy, section that sought to refute the loyalist arguments for reconciling with the Crown, the main one being that a war for independence was unwinnable. As Thomas Paine did in *Common Sense*, Green pointed out the difficulties that Britain faced in trying to "victual" an army and navy across the great expanse of the Atlantic Ocean. But even if the Crown found a way to supply its troops, "an army of 25,000, and 10,000 sailors, would by no means subdue us," Green declared. "We can raise five to one against this number."[18]

Green also dismissed the argument that independence would leave the former colonies vulnerable to attack from other European powers, such as the French and Spanish: "If we were once Independent, it would be the interest of all the European nations to keep us so." *Observations* disagreed with the belief that it would be dishonorable for the Continental Congress to declare independence while petitioning for a reconciliation. "Our petition and offer of reconciliation, should be viewed only upon condition, that Britain would redress our grievances, repeal several acts of parliament, and place us in as good a condition as were in 1763"—and that time had long passed, Green concluded. Britain had had a chance earlier to achieve peace but failed to do so: "Since that time, much of our precious blood has been spilt; one of our best generals slain, several large towns burnt, and others cannonaded."[19]

For Green, there was no turning back. It was too late to reconcile with Great Britain. And that fact did not scare him—quite the contrary. Unlike Chandler, he found the prospect of independence exhilarating. Besides "avoid[ing] tyranny, and oppression," he noted, the colonies would have the freedom to form a representative government that, Green believed, would be more efficient and effective than British rule. "If we are independent, our taxes will be inconsiderable, compared with what they will and must be, if we are under regal government." No longer would the government have to support "hangers-on" or "placemen and pensioners."[20]

Green shared Paine's disgust with hereditary government. When a ruler ascends to the throne by birth, "we must take the chief magistrate as he is; sometimes an infant, sometimes with scarce common sense . . . sometimes ambitious, fierce, and cruel, using all the power of the nation to promote tyranny." The British government, in Green's view, was thus holding back colonial development with its high taxes, suffocating mercantile regulations, and corrupt, inefficient government. The Navigation Acts, which required all exports to British North America to pass through English ports, had long vexed the colonists and stymied the development of colonial industries. By throwing off the dead weight of British regulations, Green predicted, American energies would be unleashed: "This land of liberty will be glorious on many accounts: Population will abundantly increase, agriculture will be promoted, trade will flourish, religion unrestrained by human laws, will have free course to run and prevail, and America [will] be an asylum for all noble spirits and sons of liberty from all parts of the world."[21]

Green's stolid, workmanlike prose in *Observations* carried none of the pyrotechnics of Paine's *Common Sense* (or Chandler's tracts for that matter). Paine's work, which was published in January 1776 and by one estimate sold five hundred thousand copies in the first year, was blunt, direct, sarcastic. Where Green politely avoided ridiculing the king, Paine lambasted the Crown as "exceedingly ridiculous," "a mere absurdity!" With gusto, Paine trashed the entire institution: "In England a k——hath little more to do than to make war and give away places; which in plain terms, is to impoverish the nation and set it together by the ears. A pretty business indeed for a man to be allowed eight hundred thousand sterling a year for, and worshipped into the bargain!" Green, by contrast, blandly asserted, "Hereditary government tends to keep a continual opposition between the court and the country: So that a courtier and a patriot are opposite characters, which is the greatest absurdity in nature, if the design of civil government is properly viewed."[22]

Yet it was the tract's calm tone that made *Observations* so influential in New Jersey and the middle colonies. As the foremost historian of New Jersey politics in the 1760s and 1770s concluded, "The popularity of Green's *Observations* was probably due to the manner of presentation and the fact that it appealed to all elements of the population. Forthright and plausible, the piece stands in stark contrast to the usual reckless and irrational productions of radical publicists." Green's approach certainly reflected his temperament. By nature he was a disciplined, serious man who kept his emotions in check and largely avoided the outbursts of a Thomas Bradbury Chandler and of evangelicals.[23]

But the moderation of *Observations* was also quite calculated. In all of his writings, Jacob Green the Calvinist routinely used the language of the Enlightenment that he imbibed at Harvard—he believed that reasoned and careful appeals to the rational mind were the best ways to influence people.

As far back as 1754, Green was concluding that the most effective arguments were those that were simple, direct, reasonable. Nearly all of his writings, with the exception of *A Vision of Hell*, carefully laid out his arguments point by point in an introduction; Green then proceeded to prove his thesis by expounding on individual points in the order he laid out in the introduction. It was a classical, Socratic approach, as this Harvard graduate posed questions and proceeded to answer them. Over the years Green perfected such a didactic approach in his writings and sermons. Sometime over the winter of 1776, he began composing his political tract that would be published as *Observations*. Green took great care, going through at least two early drafts before sending a final version to printer John Holt of New York in February or March. About ten pages of two drafts are extant, and both surviving drafts deal with the section on independence. Green did not extensively rewrite any passages as he reworked the tract. Instead, he labored to find the right tone, trimming phrases here and there and substituting words that he felt were more appropriate to the arguments he was making. Both drafts were more critical of the Crown in places than was the published version. Other changes were routine editing, as Green tightened his arguments and smoothed out the phrasing.[24]

His goal was to make *Observations* even more reasonable and persuasive to those colonists unsure about independence. For instance, the passage about the king's hangers-on deleted the phrase "so many reduced by luxury and other ways." In another place, he changed "and those that were entrusted with the management of the affair, would *unavoidably* be suspected of bribery" to "would *probably* be suspected of bribery." Green was forthcoming about his strategy, noting at the tract's outset, "Whenever the settlement of our affairs is attempted, it should be with great deliberation and calmness. Self-interest, party spirit, heats and animosities should have no part in a matter of so great importance."[25]

But, of course, Green wanted to convince the colonists that reconciliation was impossible and impracticable by 1776, and the wording changes in his drafts reflected his desire to achieve universal appeal for his tract. One change was especially telling. In several places Green edited out the word "liberty" for a more Lockean tone. One such place was Argument I for independence, where Green cited the biblical injunction that a divided house cannot stand. In the first draft he wrote, "The incroachments upon our *natural Liberties* by regal officers are so well known to every man, that has any acquaintance with public affairs, that I need not enlarg." But the published version referred to "incroachments upon our *natural rights* by regal officers." And in Argument VI, where Green maintained that "if we are independent, we shall be less liable to internal tumults," he noted that "our people have more such high notions of liberty, have been used to meet, form and publish resolves and *assert their liberty*, and have succeeded so well in our present attempt, that it will be difficult to prevent such attempts for time to come if they are put under B.G." The final version put it this way: "Our people have such *a sense of liberty*, have been so used to meet, form, and publish resolves, and *assert their rights and privileges*, and have so well succeeded in our present contest with Britain, that it will be very difficult to prevent something similar for time to come, if they are put under British government, especially if they think it is without necessity, and contrary to their natural rights."[26]

Besides being well written, *Observations* achieved prominence in New Jersey for several other reasons: Green was the first, and only, New Jersey resident to publish a tract between 1763 and 1776 supporting independence. The colony's writers were relatively quiet in the prewar years. At a tavern in Cumberland County, Whigs posted a handwritten newsletter called the Plain Dealer every Tuesday from December 25, 1775, to February 12, 1776. And in December 1775, "Lycurgus" published an essay in a New York newspaper advocating independence. Thus *Observations* filled a void in New Jersey. Moreover, neither of those earlier efforts had the reach of Green's statewide tract, which was published first in New York by Holt's *New-York Journal* in early April (ensuring wide distribution in East Jersey) and a week or so later in Philadelphia by several newspapers (ensuring wide distribution in West Jersey). Also aiding its spread was the tract's cheap price. Philadelphia printer Robert Bell sold *Observations* for only one shilling, "with large allowance to those who buy per dozen." By contrast, Bell charged three shillings for *Plain Truth*, a tract that took on Paine's *Common Sense*. In New York City, *Observations* was even cheaper—good patriots could buy it for only six pence. (Holt charged less than Bell because his version had no appendix.) All of these factors meant that the tract sold briskly enough that Bell brought out a second edition.[27]

Articulate and well reasoned, *Observations* greatly aided the Whig cause at a pivotal moment in the revolutionary drama. It helped reassure colonists nervous about the prospects of the independence movement. To broaden its appeal, it carefully mixed Whiggish themes with a few Calvinist ones, although the former was emphasized—the Crown was out to enslave America; a conspiracy was afoot to deprive the colonists of their liberties. But the tract also sprinkled religious allusions throughout, maintaining that the Revolution was not merely a glorious cause but also a divinely inspired one. When Green asked in *Observations* whether the colonists have the right to be independent, he answered, "We all believe an over-ruling providence, we have appealed and applied to God in our present struggle; we believe that the sovereign of the universe, the judge of all the earth, disposes of nations and kingdoms, and that sooner or later he will visit for iniquity."[28]

Whereas loyalists such as Chandler feared that a militarily weak collection of American states would fall prey to power-hungry European nations, Green was serene because of his religious faith. Besides making the cold-eyed (and ultimately correct) calculation that France and Spain would want to strike a blow against the British Empire by helping the rebellious colonies, Green was confident that God would protect Americans. "Our cause is good," he explained, "and we have the Great Disposer of all things to confide in, and apply to." He was so confident of God's backing because the colonists would be throwing off the supposedly corrupt British government and replacing it with one that was "most equitable, rational, natural." Moreover, this would be "a government most favourable to religion as well as liberty, and the natural rights of mankind. In this way we have abundant reason to think that God will smile upon and bless us . . . and prevent the evils that earth or hell may devise against us."[29]

Green viewed liberty as a gift from God to humankind. As he put it in a letter he wrote later in the war, liberty "is such a blessing, such an amiable object, that there is a natural thirst and desire for it in all the human race. This cannot be eradicated, but is as fixed and inseparable from nature as self-love is." However, human nature has a dark side, Green continued: "None of the human race care to be deprived of Liberty, and yet almost all mankind have, and always have had, a strong and strange disposition to deprive others of it." He attributed this sorry state of affairs to fallen man. Since Adam's time, "tyrannical persons" have launched attacks to enslave others; Green then recited a catalog of wars described in the Bible from Chedorlaomer in Genesis 14 to the battles in Judges. "Why have the followers of the meek and lowly Jesus been persecuted, and such rivers of Christian blood been shed?" he asked. "It was because they claimed liberty of conscience; liberty to think and choose religion for themselves."[30]

Thus Green's understanding of liberty differed significantly from John Locke's. Locke argued forcefully in his *Second Treatise of Government* that whenever the ruler and legislature overstepped their bounds, "they *forfeit the power*, the people had put into their hands . . . and it devolves to the people, who have a right to resume their original liberty." Later thinkers in the eighteenth century fleshed out this insight, arguing that the will must be sovereign so that individuals can freely choose their government.[31]

But for Calvinists, this was a particularly dangerous argument because it undercut God's power. If people were free to do what they wanted, where did that leave God and the Calvinist belief that he controlled all? Jonathan Edwards grappled with this issue for years before coming up with his elaborate definition of free will that sought to preserve God's sovereignty while accounting for people's apparent ability to act freely. He began by narrowly defining the will as a term for a person's power of choosing. The will itself does not choose, Edwards stressed; the person does. In making such a distinction, Edwards was taking aim at Arminian definitions of liberty. "Their notion . . . is that there is a sovereignty in the will, and that the will determines itself," he said. Edwards countered that the will itself is not an agent. The person is the agent, and it is the person who acts, not the will. How much freedom does God give a person, and how controlling is God? Edwards answered that God allows people to choose on their own through the agency of moral necessity, meaning that individuals are morally responsible for the choices they make. Thus for Edwards, God bestowed the power of liberty on individuals to act—but he did so at a price. With freedom came responsibility, according to Edwards: in a God-created universe, *liberty is the chance to act morally*; it is the chance to know and obey God.[32]

This obligation to know God infused the Calvinist view of liberty and free will. True liberty meant that people were to obey God. They were to act morally, not selfishly. Such a belief carried over into the political arena. Governments were to act morally, too, and Calvinists judged them by the same standards that they applied to individuals. Great Britain, of course, came up short in this moral reckoning. Green viewed England and its government as corrupt and depraved. From 1765 on, as the revolutionary crisis built, Green and other Calvinists increasingly saw the Crown and Parliament as selfish and venal. His lament in *Observations* about England's "hangers-on" was echoed elsewhere in the Calvinist world. A bloated government was not only wasteful of taxpayers' money; it was a sign of the rulers' vice and profligacy. To support such profligacy, the British government was becoming increasingly predatory and tyrannical. The Crown had to raise taxes and fees to support its hangers-on and to pay for excessive spending, and it did so against the wishes of the people.[33]

Green and his fellow Calvinists thus viewed the imperial crisis on an individual and a national level—both needed to reform. Independence would free the colonies from a corrupt overlord, and it would give Americans a chance to reform their own ways. Green's two wartime letters on liberty made this connection explicit. So did a fast-day sermon he delivered in April 1778 and published in 1779. In this Calvinistic sermon, Green maintained that the American Revolution, including the British tyranny that led to it, were all part of God's grand design. A "great and glorious God . . . has seen from the first how our American troubles came on, and how they have proceeded. He permits the British court to oppress us, and has excited our resentment; excites us to stand for our liberties civil and religious." According to Green, God allowed something so inexplicable in an attempt to rouse the people to fight for their liberties *and* to change their sinful ways.[34]

In his second letter on liberty, Green warned that Americans would lose their hard-won freedoms if they were not vigilant. And how was liberty lost? "The answer," he wrote, "is that vice is the general, radical cause of this loss." For Green, vice posed a grave threat to liberty on at least two levels. The first danger was that "it provokes God to . . . punish a sinning people, by permitting usurpers and tyrants to seize on their natural rights." As evidence, Green cited the accounts of Israel in the Book of Judges and "the histories of vicious nations." The second threat came on the individual level: "Vice has a *natural* tendency to the loss of Freedom. Idleness and prodigality will reduce men, and make them dependent upon those that are rich, which will endanger freedom." In other words, it allows the unscrupulous to dominate the meek and to assert their will on society and government; elections are no longer open and fair, and republicanism becomes corrupted.[35]

Despite the assertion in *Observations* that Americans were morally superior to the English, Green for years had seen a society racked by sin. In early 1776, he still believed that faith was slipping, vice was rising, and society was sinning. British corruption abroad merely added to his fears about corruption at home. Yet, despite all these shortcomings, his mood was hopeful, even confident as war approached. For Green, the Revolution would not simply be a political contest waged to determine who would rule the American people. It would be a moral revolution as well. It would be a chance to end the corruption—both political and spiritual—of the times.

It was an argument that had plenty of support in other quarters. John Witherspoon was a Presbyterian minister who headed the College of New

Jersey in Princeton and became active in the patriot movement. He served on and off in the Continental Congress from 1776 until 1782 and was the only clergyman to sign the Declaration of Independence. On May 17, 1776, Witherspoon delivered a forceful sermon titled "The Dominion of Providence over the Passions of Men." Like Green, he too was supremely confident that America would be more than a match for England's military might. "There are fixed bounds to every human thing," he explained. "When the branches of a tree grow very large and weighty, they fall off from the trunk. The sharpest sword will not pierce when it cannot reach. And there is a certain distance from the seat of a government, where an attempt to rule will either produce tyranny and helpless subjection, or provoke resistance and effect a separation."[36]

Like Green's letters on liberty and his fast-day sermon, Witherspoon's "Dominion of Providence" linked the military conflict with personal reformation. Witherspoon called the crisis "a season of public judgment." "Can you have a clearer view of the sinfulness of your nature, than when the rod of the oppressor is lifted up, and when you see men putting on the habit of the warrior, and collecting on every hand the weapons of hostility and instruments of death?" Those who will be falling in the first battles "have not many more warnings to receive," he warned. Like Green, Witherspoon believed that God was on the colonists' side. But whereas Green couched this belief in vague generalities, Witherspoon did not. He saw direct evidence of God's intervention in the contest with Britain: "What surprising success has attended our encounters in almost every instance? Has not the boasted discipline of regular and veteran soldiers been turned into confusion and dismay, before the new and maiden courage of freemen, in defence of their property and right? . . . Some important victories in the south have been gained with so little loss, that enemies will probably think it has been dissembled." For Witherspoon, God "is the Lord of hosts, great in might, and strong in battle."[37]

And Witherspoon went much further than Green in directly linking a change in individual behavior to success on the battlefield. "The best friend to American liberty," he explained, is the one "who is most sincere and active in promoting true and undefiled religion, and who sets himself with the greatest firmness to bear down [on] profanity and immorality of every kind." Witherspoon told his audience that all Americans should serve as guardians of morality but that certain "classes of men" were especially important in the fight against sin: "Magistrates, ministers, parents, heads of families, and those whom age has rendered venerable. . . . I must particularly recommend this matter to those who have the command of soldiers inlisted for the defence of their country. The cause is sacred, and the champions for it ought to be holy." In case anyone misunderstood his message, Witherspoon concluded his sermon by explicitly linking religious behavior and the fate of the rebelling colonies: "I beseech you to make a wise improvement of the present threatening aspect of public affairs, and to remember that your duty to God, to your country, to your families, and to yourselves is the same. . . . It is the man of piety and inward principle, that we may expect to find the uncorrupted patriot, the useful citizen, and the invincible soldier. God grant that in America true religion and civil liberty may be inseparable."[38]

Witherspoon's sermon was a tour de force in its balancing of John Locke with John Calvin. One of Witherspoon's biographers cites "The Dominion of Providence" "as a near-perfect exemplar of the melding of Christian and liberal political theory." Throughout the sermon, Witherspoon moved back and forth, almost effortlessly, between religious and Whiggish arguments. Green drew on both, too, in *Observations* and in his fast-day sermon, but not to the extent that Witherspoon did. In the former tract Green did not so explicitly link Whiggism and religion. Instead, he justified a war for independence in Lockean terms: government existed to promote the welfare of the people; tyranny was unacceptable. When government violated the compact between the ruler and the ruled, the people have a right to rebel.[39]

*Observations* was an example of Green's ability to tailor his arguments for his audience. (*A Vision of Hell* was another.) Although religion undergirded everything he wrote and believed, he was not afraid to embrace the language of the secular and to downplay the religious when it suited his purposes. By contrast, many Whig preachers baldly combined the political and the religious, sometimes in inflammatory ways. One example involved Moses Mather, a Congregationalist minister from Connecticut who was three years older than Green. He delivered an especially incendiary sermon in 1775 that he liked so much he later had it published in Hartford. Built around Old Testament texts (unlike Green, who worked almost exclusively with the New Testament), the sermon began with a thunderclap: "At a time when we are called upon to surrender our liberties, our religion, and country; or defend them at the point of the sword, against those, that were our friends, our brethren." Mather cared little about offending the sensitivities of the moderate or the conservative. His purpose was not to persuade the undecided but to bludgeon the arguments against independence. The British were oppressors; Americans were slaves. British cruelty, he thundered, ran so deeply that Americans had no choice but to physically fight for their liberties, and Mather almost gleefully pointed out that the ensuing fight would be bloody. "The fairest fruits are always most obnoxious to the birds of prey: English liberties . . . were obtained, sword in hand . . . and what rivers of blood have been shed, to maintain and defend them," he wrote. Americans, he continued, will face the same trials: "Let us gird on the harness, having our bosoms mailed, with firm defiance of every danger; and with fixed determined purpose, to part with our liberty only with our lives."[40]

Green's restrained language in *Observations* was especially striking when compared with the writings of Mather and even Paine. Thomas Paine the deist freely used religious language in his political tracts while Jacob Green the devout Calvinist did not. Besides quoting extensively from the Old Testament, Paine's *Common Sense* deployed sentences with cadences redolent of the Bible. For instance, in arguing that the colonies would be better off if they maintained distance from Europe, Paine wrote, "Every thing that is right or natural pleads for separation. The blood of the slain, the weeping voice of nature cries, *'Tis time to part.* Even the distance at which the Almighty hath placed England and America, is a strong and natural proof, that the authority of the one, over the other, was never the design of Heaven." Paine did not stop there; he went on to say, "The reformation was preceded by the discovery of America, as if the Almighty graciously meant to open a sanctuary to the persecuted in future years."[41]

The designs of the Almighty were never far from Green's thoughts either, but in composing his *Observations* this minister donned the robes of an Enlightenment apostle. He peppered the tract with such words and phrases as natural rights, the people, rational, state of nature—all of which could easily have come from the pen of Thomas Jefferson or John Locke. Biblical cadences were absent from his tract; the vernacular of Enlightenment philosophy was not. Note his impassioned defense for the righteousness of independence: "We have not run presumptuously into danger, nor are we proposing an independency that is unjust or unreasonable. What we propose is the most equitable, rational, natural mode of civil government." Green was quite comfortable using these phrases, and *Observations*, as a result, was possibly even more Lockean than *Common Sense* was. This "Friend to American Liberty" (as Green called himself) knew his audience and how to reach it.[42]

Hence, he published *Observations* in April 1776 to wide acclaim in New Jersey and the middle colonies. The tract cemented his reputation as an ardent patriot and thrust him further into revolutionary politics. As *Observations* was making its way into taverns and firesides throughout the spring of 1776, pressure was steadily building in New Jersey and elsewhere for the colonies to declare independence. In early May, Rhode Island cut its ties to the Crown, and Virginia began preparing to write a state constitution. On May 10, the Continental Congress, in an attempt to move along the laggards, passed a resolution recommending that the colonies adopt governments "best conducive to the happiness and safety of their constituents." It approved a far stronger statement several days later, on May 15, when John Adams penned a preamble to a resolution declaring that royal authority had to be "totally suppressed and all the powers of government exerted under the authority of the people of the colonies." Later, on June 7, Richard Henry Lee of Virginia proposed "that these United Colonies are, and of right ought to be, free and independent States, that they are absolved from all allegiance to the British Crown."[43]

Decision day was fast approaching, and New Jersey would have to figure out where it stood—with the revolutionaries, or with the king. The provincial election scheduled for the last week of May became a referendum on independence. The election of pro-secession candidates would mean that the next session of the Provincial Congress would declare for independence and write a state constitution; support for royalist candidates would mean that the colony would remain loyal to the Crown. Thus the publication of Green's *Observations*—especially the April release in Philadelphia—was perfectly timed. It appeared just as the independence drama was reaching its climax in New Jersey. How many people it swayed for independence is impossible to know, but subsequent events provided strong evidence of the tract's importance to the revolutionary debate.

When Morris County elected its five-member delegation in late May, a whopping twenty-nine candidates ended up on the ballot, including one who did not want to be—Jacob Green. He left behind no account of this election. But someone likely put his name forward over his objections; according to Ashbel, his father "was so far from seeking to obtain a seat in that congress, that he did all he could to avoid it, short of absolutely refusing to serve." Regardless of how Green's name ended up on the ballot, the outcome was never in doubt in this Whig stronghold. Voting commenced at

Morristown on May 27 and was held over a six-day period in the county's five townships (table 1). The Provincial Congress loosened suffrage requirements: earlier rules stipulating that only freeholders with at least one hundred acres could vote was changed to "every person of full age, who had resided one whole year in any county immediately proceeding the election and was worth at least 50 pounds in real or personal estate." With loyalist opposition virtually non-existent in Morris, a radical slate easily emerged. The top-five vote getters in order of finish were Jacob Drake, Silas Condict, Ellis Cook, William Woodhull, and Jacob Green (table 2). Green finished well behind Woodhull, a Presbyterian minister from Roxbury, who had 343 votes to Green's 291. Drake, the top vote-getter, received 491. Green owed his election to two factors. He had a strong base of support in Hanover, where turnout in this election was highest: out of 525 votes cast, 186 votes (or 35 percent of the total) came from Hanover. Mendham, by contrast, accounted for a mere 5 percent of the total and Pequannock 15 percent. And with so many Hanoverians voting, the township was able to elect two members to the delegation—Green and Ellis Cook, a wealthy blacksmith who was active in revolutionary politics. It was the only township in Morris with more than one representative.[44]

Table 1  May 1776 vote for Provincial Congress

| Township | Votes cast (n = 525) | Percentage of total |
| --- | --- | --- |
| Hanover | 186 | 35% |
| Morris | 120 | 23% |
| Roxbury | 118 | 22% |
| Pequannock | 73 | 15% |
| Mendham | 28 | 5% |

Source: Poll list, May 1776, for delegates from Morris County to New Jersey's First Constitutional Convention.

Table 2  Winning candidates in Morris County

| Candidate | Township | Votes |
| --- | --- | --- |
| Jacob Drake | Roxbury | 491 |
| Silas Condict | Morris | 487 |
| Ellis Cook | Hanover | 485 |
| William Woodhull | Mendham | 343 |
| Jacob Green | Hanover | 291 |

Source: Poll list, May 1776, for delegates from Morris County to New Jersey's First Constitutional Convention.

Undoubtedly, however, Green's victory was attributable to the popularity of his political arguments. Indeed, historian Larry R. Gerlach concludes that Green in May 1776 was as important and influential in New Jersey as that other Presbyterian firebrand, John Witherspoon: "Especially significant [on the congressional scene] was the appearance for the first time of John Witherspoon and Jacob Green. These two Presbyterian clergymen, perhaps the most outspoken and influential advocates of independence in the colony, personified the new temperament of the Congress."[45]

Green most likely felt a swirl of emotions upon his election. Some embarrassment, because he believed a man of cloth should stay out of politics. Some trepidation, because his political duties would take him away from the far more important task of saving souls and reforming society. But surely he also felt a surge of satisfaction, maybe even pleasure. After all, his *Observations* had won wide praise and given him a chance to directly fight for something he passionately believed in. With his election to the Provincial Congress secured, Green would be heading off in June to Burlington for a legislative session that would determine whether New Jersey took up arms against the king and became an independent state.

*The Loyalist Down the Road: Thomas Bradbury Chandler and the Bishop's Cause—a Friend of Episcopacy and Hierarchy*

Chandler the writer resembled a locomotive building up steam on a hilly incline. His tracts began slowly and learnedly as he chugged his way through the opening pages of his treatise. But as he approached the crest of the hill— the point where the sheer justice and importance of his cause became overwhelmingly obvious to him, and where the sheer stupidity of his opponents became equally obvious—he hurtled over the top and with increasingly unstoppable velocity poured out his true thoughts and feelings.

Such was the case in Chandler's *Appeal to the Public*. He knew both the controversial history of episcopacy and the reasons for American opposition to the office. Still, he could not help himself when he was trying to convince everyone of the absolutely obvious need for bishoprics and the total rightness of his cause.

After laying out his reasons for an American bishop in the calmest, most thoughtful tones he could muster, Chandler went on to confirm the worst fears of American Whigs by candidly revealing what he thought of republicanism and monarchy—he disdained the former and loved the latter. The Church of England, he explained, was a bulwark for the Crown. "Episcopacy and Monarchy are, in their Frame and Constitution, best suited to each other," he wrote near the end of *An Appeal to the Public*. "Episcopacy can never thrive in a Republican Government, nor Republican Principles in an Episcopal Church." King and church, he continued:

> are mutually adapted to each other so they are mutually introductive of each other. He that prefers Monarchy in the State, is more likely to approve of Episcopacy in the Church, than a rigid Republican. . . . It is not then to be wondered, if our Civil Rulers have always considered Episcopacy as the surest Friend of Monarchy; and it may reasonably be expected from those in Authority, that they will support and assist the Church in America, if from no other Motives, yet from a Regard to the State, with which it has so friendly and close an Alliance.

These arguments horrified leading Calvinists and Whig radicals. They, too, knew their history—they remembered what William Laud had tried to achieve in the 1630s during his attempts to strengthen the state church and the episcopal office. Chandler's candid defense of an episcopal church and a monarchical government brought knowing nods from American radicals. And the timing of Chandler's crusade brought further knowing nods—he wanted to strengthen the Church of England (at the expense of dissenting sects) and thus the Crown and the British government (at the expense of American liberties), all during the 1760s, when a new king and a reinvigorated Parliament in the aftermath of the Seven Years' War were seeking to bring order to the British Empire by increasing governmental revenues and powers. William Livingston, for one, noted the great financial burdens involved with episcopacy—bishops needed their palaces, coaches and horses, cathedrals, and supporting bureaucracy manned by high-salaried assistants. The dissenters well understood something else. Bringing a bishop to America, they warned, would create a popish-like hierarchy that had no place in the colonies and a Protestant church—it elevated ceremony over the purity of the Bible and undermined the liberties of individual congregations.

Chandler's crusade for an American bishop was thus also a clash of two worldviews. In a Chandlerian world, Jacob Green's emerging democratic ethos of religious liberty and laymen's rights, in a society dominated by the hardworking farmer and artisan, were nowhere to be found. Instead, Chandler would replicate a hierarchical society in the colonies where the wellborn would lead and loyal subjects would follow, worshiping in a church based not on the Word but on sacramental ceremony. Such a prospect horrified Green and other Whig radicals. In his autobiography, Green simply dismissed the whole episcopal edifice in one terse sentence when he declared, "Nor am I an Episcopalian, according to the church of England." In his 1776 *Observations on the Reconciliation of Great-Britain*, he more pointedly denounced hierarchy and the British system of government as tyrannical and oppressive. The Whigs feared that bringing one or more bishops to the colonies would add to government corruption, lead to higher taxes, and increase London's reach into the lives and affairs of Americans. As Green explained in his tract, "By independency we shall avoid tyranny, and oppression. If we submit to British government, we shall be continually cramped with Governors, and other officers appointed by the crown. All those in authority over us, will be such as suit the ambitious designs of Great Britain, however contrary to our interest." And in a 1781 tract on church government, he rejected Chandler's assertion that bishops constituted a superior order to pastors, elders, and the laity. Power, Green declared firmly, must reside with the congregation, not with a bishop.

The wide gulf between the two sides so angered Chandler that his successive tracts attacked the American radicals in increasingly vitriolic terms. In *The Friendly Address to All* Reasonable *Americans on the Subject of Our Political Confusions*, written during the tumult over the tea act, he implored Americans everywhere to wake up from their "slumber" and open their eyes to the danger surrounding them: "madmen of New-England" were fomenting an illegal rebellion that would cost everyone their liberties.

The stakes were especially high for American members of the Church of England, according to Chandler. Those who backed the "fanatics" from New England were putting "power into the hands of those who will use it against you. . . . Their inveterate enmity to the Church of England, has polluted the annals of British history. Their intolerance in England, towards the members of the Church, when the sovereign power was usurped by them, is recorded in characters of blood; and the same spirit was dreadfully triumphant in New-England." The descendants of New England's founders "are the very persons that will govern you, if the projected revolution should take place. As they have now broke loose from the authority of Parliament, which for some time past restrained them from mischief, they begin to appear in their natural colours. They have already resumed the old work of persecuting the Church of England, by every method in their power."

New England intolerance meant that Anglicans faced a choice, Chandler continued. Church members could back the New Englanders "and renounce your principles relating both to religion and government, or you can expect no quarter under the administrations of such intemperate zealots." For Chandler, of course, this was really no choice at all. Good Anglicans should side with their king and their church: "This Church has always been famed and respected for its loyalty, and its regard to order and government. Its annals have been never stained with the history of plots and conspiracies, treason and rebellions."

The best way for America to protect its liberties and preserve its prosperity, he advised, was for it to retain its ties to the Crown: "Of all the subjects of Great-Britain, those who reside in the American Colonies have been . . . by far the happiest: surrounded with the blessings of peace, health, and never-failing plenty—enjoying the benefits of an equitable and free constitution—secured by the protection and patronage of the greatest maritime power in the world." Chandler conceded that the Stamp Act "was so contrary to all our ideas of American rights . . . that there was no difficulty in repealing it." But this one misstep did not alter a fundamental fact: the real threat to liberty came not from Parliament but from the growing independence movement and its extralegal creation, the Continental Congress.[46]

# 7

## *Politician*

Green's arrival in Burlington, New Jersey, in mid-June 1776 was a signal moment for him in his fierce advocacy for independence. Characteristically, he had nothing to say about it. An ocean away, Thomas Bradbury Chandler wasn't talking much either—he had fled to London in 1775 and was a helpless spectator as the long-running revolutionary drama was reaching its climax in the summer heat of 1776. Green, it can safely be said, was all business as he took his seat in the Fourth Provincial Congress during the second week of June. He saw his task as twofold: he wanted to ensure that New Jersey broke away from the rule of King George III, and he wanted a republican government to take the Crown's place. He apparently cared about little else; when those two critical missions were accomplished, Green abruptly departed from Burlington and never again served in political office. He left to others the task of running the state government and arming the militia that would defend it.

As uncomfortable as Pastor Green was in the role of politician, he was not intimidated by his congressional surroundings. In his younger days, he had rubbed shoulders with such leading religious figures as George Whitefield and Jonathan Edwards. As a trustee and interim president of the College of New Jersey, Green had gotten to know some of the colony's leading public figures, including the governor. This Harvard graduate also was no stranger to the intellectual centers of New England and New Jersey.

Burlington was a handsome town, elegant even, its prosperity fueled by the considerable wealth of Quaker and Anglican divines. The brick houses of merchants and lawyers dominated the narrow city streets. As West Jersey's chief town and capital, it was home to the province's largest markets. Its port gathered up beef, pork, and other foodstuffs for shipment to Philadelphia and the West Indies. Its markets and fairs sold the produce of neighboring farmers. Since 1702, the legislature had split its time between Burlington and Perth Amboy. Yet, aesthetics aside, Green may well have wondered why he and the other congressional delegates were meeting there. Burlington was no Whig stronghold. West Jersey's Quakers were neutral and the province's Anglicans were mostly loyalist. It was East Jersey, not West, that supplied the sinews of radicalism and independence. As late as November 1775, Burlington's residents could be found petitioning the Third Provincial Congress against independence. Burlington, however, had two things going for it in June 1776: it was close to Philadelphia, where the Continental Congress was in session. And it was not Perth Amboy, the Anglican stronghold in East Jersey.[1]

On the afternoon of June 11, after an opening prayer delivered by the Reverend John Witherspoon, the Provincial Congress got under way when enough delegates were present to constitute a quorum. Sixty-five members had been elected in May—more than the forty-seven sent to the Third Provincial Congress but fewer than the eighty-seven at the Second Congress. The delegates in Burlington presented a relatively new face to the revolutionary movement. Only nine of them had served in the colonial Assembly, and only twenty-three had attended the Third Provincial Congress. Most, including Jacob Green, were newcomers to the political scene, although experienced hands oversaw the legislative sessions: Samuel Tucker was reelected as president and William Paterson as secretary. John Hart became vice president.[2]

After examining the certificates of election and selecting officers, the delegates agreed to keep the doors shut and the proceedings secret to ensure candor. On the following day, June 12, Green cast his first recorded vote—he helped defeat an attempt by more conservative members to require a quorum of two-thirds to conduct routine business. Instead, a simple majority would be enough to hold votes. This resolution was more than routine housekeeping. From the beginning, the Provincial Congress struggled with poor attendance. It could not begin as scheduled on June 10 because of the lack of a quorum, and it had to delay the morning session the following day for the same reason. For all major votes, including on the momentous questions of independence and whether to approve the state constitution, only about half of the delegates were on hand. The attendance problem only worsened over time.[3]

One of the delegates' first tasks was to determine what to do about the royal governor, William Franklin. Weakened as his position was, Franklin remained in office and was doing everything he could to thwart the independence movement. One ploy was to call for the Assembly to meet on June 20, a last-ditch attempt by the governor to undercut the Provincial Congress and, in the words of one observer, "to distract and divide our counsels, and thereby to throw us into much confusion." On June 14, the delegates approved a motion that Franklin's summons be ignored; Green joined with the majority, and the resolution passed easily. In rapid succession, the delegates then backed a string of resolutions that held Franklin in contempt for violating the May 15 resolve of the Continental Congress; convicted him as "an enemy to the liberties of this country"; called for his arrest; and ended his salary. Green again voted with the Whigs on all of these resolutions except for the one cutting off the governor's pay. On the latter motion, only three delegates sided with Franklin, but Green's name was in neither the "yea" nor the "nay" column.[4]

The ousting of Governor Franklin was a virtual declaration of independence, for it effectively ended royal government in New Jersey, and the Provincial Congress proceeded with plans to form a state government. The delegates at this juncture had few doubts about the wisdom of independence, although they received a number of petitions between June 11 and June 24 urging them to keep the current form of government. New Jerseyans remained divided on the question, but the independence movement was clearly gaining ground. All but one of the pleas for the status quo came from loyalist-infested Monmouth County; the other was from the north ward at Perth Amboy, an Anglican stronghold. By contrast, the petitions urging independence and the formation of a new government came from a broad swath of New Jersey's population. Two of the earliest and more important petitions arrived from "sundry" inhabitants in Perth Amboy, "praying that the government under the king of Great-Britain may be suppressed, and [that] this congress would point out and establish some more suitable form of government." A third petition more pointedly requested "that a new government be established; and that a speedy and absolute independence upon Great-Britain be proclaimed."[5]

On Saturday, June 22, the delegates elected five members (including John Witherspoon) to represent New Jersey in the Continental Congress, and they directed them "to join with the delegates of the other colonies in Continental Congress in the most vigorous measures for supporting the just rights and liberties of *America*." More important, the Provincial Congress instructed the five-man delegation to back independence from Britain. Two days later, on June 24, the Provincial Congress took another significant step toward secession from the British Empire when it selected a committee of ten "to prepare the draught of a constitution." The measure was uncontroversial enough that the journal kept by the Provincial Congress didn't bother recording the vote; it merely ordered that the ten appointed members ready a draft.[6]

At the committee head was a familiar name—Jacob Green, who was given the honor over a host of other patriot luminaries, including John Cooper and John Covenhoven. Green, of course, was no lawyer. He had written virtually nothing on constitutional theory. And he was a Presbyterian minister with zero political experience before June 11. But he was the author of *Observations on the Reconciliation of Great-Britain and the Colonies*, a widely praised tract that cemented his reputation as a staunch supporter of independence. Most likely, the delegates wanted a noncontroversial figure to oversee such an important committee, yet someone who possessed gravitas as a revolutionary. After deciding to send John Witherspoon to the Continental Congress, they turned to another radical minister—Jacob Green—to oversee the committee charged with producing a constitution.

He did not come to the task fully unprepared. In the main body of *Observations* and in myriad other writings, Green sketched out his positions on civil government, and these reflected his extensive reading into the leading religious and Whig literature of the day. In addition to his studies of the Bible and Christianity, he was a careful reader of John Holt's *New-York Journal*, the leading radical Whig newspaper in New York City. According to Ashbel, Jacob eagerly awaited the publication's arrival each week. It was "brought by stage from New York to a tavern, about half a mile distant from my father's, where I was commonly on the watch for their arrival," Ashbel recalled in his autobiography. "As soon as this took place, I seized the one which belonged to my father, and carried it to him with all speed . . . and he either perused it in silence, or by his order it was read to him by one of his children."[7]

Like so many other colonial writers, Green borrowed liberally from Lockean thought. "In a state of nature, as in the first ages of the world, or before mankind were formed into societies for civil government, every man had a right to enjoy himself," he wrote in *Observations*. For Green, such a complete freedom was contingent on man not "injur[ing] . . . any of his fellow creatures." Given humankind's weaknesses since the Fall, civil government became necessary for the protection of all, and it was government's job—and specifically the job of the civil magistrate—"to defend and protect the people, in the peaceable enjoyment of their properties and privileges." On this, Green the radical Presbyterian minister and Chandler the conservative Anglican minister would agree: government was a necessary institution with an important role to play because of the moral failings of man.[8]

But unlike Chandler, Green was no lover of hereditary government. As a student of history and the Bible, he believed that too many such governments had become "tyrannical and arbitrary." Worse yet, many had come into power without the acquiescence of the people. Nevertheless, in good Chandlerian fashion, Green conceded that once men left a state of nature, they had no choice but to form civil societies and turn power over to a magistrate, who would rule for them. But Green did not see this abdication of power on the people's part as a blank check to the government. "The proper business of the civil magistrate was, is, and ever will be, to defend and protect the people, in the peaceable enjoyment of their properties and privileges," he maintained.[9]

The perfect government, he continued, was one "most adapted to answer the ends of government, according to the word of God." In other words, "a government most favourable to religion as well as to liberty, and the natural rights of mankind." Successful governments, Green concluded, protected the freedoms of its subjects while also encouraging them to worship God and live upright lives as devout Christians. Here, Chandler and Green would again agree, but the latter did not go as far as the former in designating a role for government as moral enforcer. Chandler passionately believed that church and state should actively work together to promote the spiritual, and that a state-supported church like the one in England was preferred over squabbling dissenter churches spreading confusion and anarchy. Chandler saw other purposes as well for government—he wanted to maintain hierarchy and the authority of the Crown. For him, the threat to liberty was not from a grasping Parliament and Crown but from the "mobs" in America who aspired to lead. His writings positively dripped with contempt for "the people." In his *American Querist*, he asked whether "ignorant men, bred to the lowest occupations, who have no knowledge of the general principles upon which civil society should be always established—are any of them qualified for the direction of political affairs?" There was no doubt what Chandler's answer was. Nor was there any doubt about what he thought of the Continental Congress. He blasted it as "an iniquitous and tyrannical government," a "government of unprincipled *mobs*."[10]

Chandler also feared that Americans' religious liberties would be lost if independence was won. He warned that Anglicans, Quakers, Baptists, and German and Dutch Reformed had the most to worry about, because the "republican zealots and bigots of New-England" would be in charge of the independent nation and they would move quickly to discriminate against dissenters. Green did not deign to answer such an argument. Instead, he pressed in *Observations* for a "religion unrestrained by human laws," explaining in a footnote that "'tis not enough to say every religious sect should be tolerated, for no one should be established." On this issue, Green demonstrated far more confidence in the individual than he had earlier, maintaining that "every man not only have the right, but [should] be encouraged to think and judge for himself in matters of religion." He also felt strongly that no one "should be allowed to molest, disturb, or encroach upon another" in matters of faith. Green had confidence in individuals' ability to make the right choice; Chandler did not.[11]

Green's confidence in the Continental Congress was high as well; he went out of his way to praise Congress for having "done worthily. They have nobly exposed their lives and estates in the cause of liberty." Green had no doubt that Americans were ready for true self-government: becoming independent and forming republican governments will result in *fewer* "tumults and rebellions" than under monarchy, he maintained. He could make that confident declaration because "our people have now such a sense of liberty; have been so used to meet, form, and publish resolves, and assert their rights and privileges" that their impressive vigilance will prevent British-like tyranny from recurring. Indeed, Green expected liberty (among other things) to flourish after independence was gained.[12]

Of those governments that qualified as the most successful, Green had no doubt—it was those that followed the will of the people and did not possess a strong central power. Although church and state should be kept separate, he believed that God would "smile upon and bless" a republican-style government that ruled honorably and equitably. Chandler may have seen the British government as the perfect protector of civil liberties, but Green strenuously believed that Great Britain was failing at this most basic of tasks.

"If we are under British government, we can make no laws to our advantage, unless Britain views them so," he asserted. "Not a new county can be formed, or choose representatives without leave from home. If we are independent we may yearly choose such rulers as suit us best." Green saw annual elections ("or once in three years") as the most effective way to ensure that rulers are "put on a level with their fellow subjects" and can be held accountable for "mal-administration."[13]

Green's views on "the people," however, were more nuanced than his pronouncements first suggest. In one place in *Observations*, the author sounded positively Chandlerian: Green warned at the beginning of the tract that there was no place for "self-interest, party spirit, heats and animosities." Green, in other words, shared the elites' nervousness about full-blown democracy and the risks of what "mobs" might do if they assumed too much power; virtuous citizens, instead, should act for the public good and not for the selfish interests of the individual. Chandler put it far more harshly in his writings (he derided radical leaders as "hairbrained fanaticks"), but Green, too, feared factions and selfish behavior. The disinterested make the best leaders, according to the conventional thinking that Green and Chandler shared.[14]

Two groups were *not* members of the "disinterested" taxonomy, in Green's view—the wealthy and the poor. Green distrusted the motives of the former and was leery of allowing the latter to participate in elections. "For those that [are] very opulent, and those that are dependently poor, will in general rather destroy than preserve the freedom of elections, and the freedom of our country," he wrote in a 1780 newspaper essay. Classical republican theory had long held that the poor would be too beholden to its betters to participate in the life of the polity; their lords would tell them how to vote. But classical Whig theory had also long held that only the better sort possessed the qualities to act virtuously on behalf of the community. Green rejected that reasoning. He placed his faith not in the wellborn but in the middling farmers and tradesmen. These common folk, and not the elite, were the best protectors of freedom, he maintained.[15]

The outlines of Green's Whiggism were thus fairly clear as he assumed the chairmanship of the committee appointed to write New Jersey's first state constitution: authority should rest with the people, under a republican system that would contain checks to prevent tyranny while still protecting civil liberties, including that of religious expression. Serving with him on the committee were four delegates from West Jersey and five from East Jersey, including one from Morris County (Silas Condict). The committee thus tilted eastward toward the more rabidly revolutionary section of New Jersey, and Morris was the only county to have two representatives on the panel. Several members were quite prominent in New Jersey politics. John Cooper of Gloucester County was treasurer during the colonial period and served briefly in the Continental Congress before being elected to the legislative council in 1776. John Cleves Symmes was a well-respected lawyer and legislator who went on to become a state Supreme Court justice. More interestingly, the committee was overwhelmingly Presbyterian: seven of the ten members were members of that church—a fitting testimonial to Presbyterianism's influence in New Jersey's revolutionary movement.[16]

As the committee readied to meet, it had few models to draw on from its sister colonies. By late June, when Green was convening his committee, only New Hampshire and South Carolina had written new constitutions (the former approved its charter in January 1776, the latter in March), although Virginia was hard at work on its revolutionary framework of government and would approve its constitution on June 29. Green's committee, though, was well versed in Whig constitutional theory. It had John Adams's treatise on government to draw on, as well as New Jersey's earlier, and progressive, charter that governed the legislature for nearly a century.

To say that Green's committee moved fast would be an understatement— it produced a constitution within forty-eight hours. The panel worked in secret, left no minutes, and did not divulge who wrote the document. Historians have been speculating ever since on how the committee could have produced a constitution so quickly. Most of all, they have wondered who authored it.

Charles R. Erdman, Jr., who wrote a dissertation on the 1776 constitution, came up with two theories: a committee member brought a draft that he had written before the Provincial Congress met; or the committee "appointed a sub-committee of Jacob Green and Jonathan D. Sergeant who, working feverishly, produced a constitution in forty-eight hours." Erdman dismisses the latter theory as implausible, both because of the difficulty of producing a constitution from scratch in under three days and because Green was a minister with no legal training and no inclination toward constitutional writing. Other historians, though, *did* suspect that Green was the author. His first biographer, Joseph F. Tuttle, was convinced that Green carried a draft to Burlington, and based his conclusion on an analysis of Green's *Observations* and its companion tract called "The Plan of an American Compact with Great Britain." Tuttle, incorrectly, believed that Green wrote "American Compact" and used it to draft a constitution; he also asserted that the brevity and tone of the constitution sounded just "like him." A few later historians echoed Tuttle's findings, but most others did not find his theory convincing.[17]

Erdman and a recent historian of the New Jersey constitution, Julian P. Boyd, are convinced that Sergeant, a young but talented lawyer, was the author. Born in Newark, New Jersey, in 1746, Sergeant enrolled in the College of New Jersey's grammar school in 1755 and graduated from the college in 1762 after getting his bachelor's and master's degrees. He then studied law under Richard Stockton, who in 1776 was a fellow delegate in the Provincial Congress. Sergeant served as clerk in the first Provincial Congress and won the praise of John Adams and other revolutionaries, including John Witherspoon. In February 1776 Sergeant was elected to Continental Congress, and Erdman and Boyd see his time there as crucial. He was in Philadelphia during the pivotal month of May, when the Continental Congress debated and passed the May 15 resolution. He was likely exposed to the work of the Virginians—Thomas Jefferson was preparing drafts for his state's first constitution, and George Mason's Declaration of Rights was printed in a Philadelphia newspaper that month. Sergeant requested, and received, a copy of John Adams's influential *Thoughts on Government*.[18]

In June, Sergeant returned to Burlington to serve in the Provincial Congress, and Erdman and Boyd strongly suspect that he carried a draft of the constitution with him. Sergeant's arrival, in their view, was all part of a grand bargain among Princeton friends: John Witherspoon and Richard Stockton would serve in the Continental Congress, and Sergeant would attend the Provincial Congress and sit on the constitution-writing committee. In a cryptic passage in a letter to John Adams, Sergeant came close to admitting authorship: he told Adams that he was "really forced to bear a principal part" of the work at the Provincial Congress because the delegates were "plain men" who were "hardly competent in the penning of a common vote." (That quotation can be read as a dig at Jacob Green.) Such a theory remains conjecture and is no more proven than Tuttle's belief that Green wrote the constitution. But Boyd and Erdman are correct that Green apparently gave no real thought to constitution making; his focus was on persuading Americans to sever their ties with Great Britain. It is also highly significant that his son Ashbel, who was in possession of Jacob's papers and did so much to let posterity know of his father's achievements, did not claim authorship for Jacob. If Jacob had written the constitution, Ashbel likely would have said so after his father's death.[19]

Although the authorship remains unproven, the other facts are not in dispute. The committee of ten produced a constitutional draft within two days. The Provincial Congress referred the draft to a committee of the whole; under the leadership of John Covenhoven, this committee discussed its provisions for two and a half days. The Provincial Congress then spent less than a day debating the constitutional draft. On July 2, the delegates approved the constitution, and a thousand copies were printed for distribution throughout the newly independent state; leading newspapers reprinted it in full, including Green's favorite paper, the *New-York Journal*, on July 18. On July 15, the delegates decided on rules for electing the inaugural legislature, and on August 21, the Provincial Congress met for the final time. The new state legislature replaced it on August 27, electing William Livingston as the state's first governor.[20]

Although Green's committee left behind no record of its deliberations, Jacob likely found much to admire in its handiwork. Tuttle was right on one count: the constitution, in true Green fashion, was succinct and simply written. It also adhered to the broad principles he outlined in *Observations*. The constitution's preamble was Lockean: "Whereas all the constitutional authority, ever possessed by the kings of *Great-Britain* over these colonies, or their other dominions, was by compact, derived from the people." Some of its language echoed Green's *Observations*: "And whereas in the present deplorable situation of these colonies, exposed to the fury of a cruel and relentless enemy."[21]

The constitution mixed the conservative and the radical in ways that Green probably approved of. Some Whigs in 1776 wanted the emerging state constitutions to reject the British model with its checks and balances and adopt a one-chamber legislature. As one newspaper essayist explained in mid-June, several governmental branches "cause perpetual contention and waste of time"; worse, they can lead to oppression by allowing "ill disposed aspiring men" to gain control of the levers of power. New Jersey's drafters rejected such arguments. They created a two-chamber legislature consisting of a General Assembly and a legislative council that fulfilled the functions of a Senate.[22]

The bicameral structure was clearly intended to provide balance and a modicum of checks on democracy. Both chambers elected the governor. Both had the authority to initiate a bill. Both had to approve a bill for the measure to become law, a stipulation that effectively gave each chamber a veto over the other. Several conservative elements from the colonial period survived in the new state constitution, including the idea that the council was to serve as a check on the lower (and presumably impulsive) house. The drafters accomplished this by ensuring that wealthier and supposedly wiser men would occupy the higher chamber. Whereas a candidate for the Assembly had to be worth only five hundred pounds or more, someone seeking a seat in the legislative council needed to be "worth at least *one thousand pounds*, proclamation money, of real and person estate"; this higher standard meant that farmers and tradesmen of middling means would have a hard time qualifying for office. Moreover, as a further rein on rampant democracy, the drafters continued the practice of allowing only independent men with a stake in society to vote; they decided that a voter had to be worth at least fifty pounds "proclamation money, clear estate in the same." Finally, as in colonial times, the council was to work more closely with the governor by serving as "a privy council to advise the governor in all cases, where he may find it necessary to consult them." In case anyone misunderstood its intentions, the constitution explicitly decreed that the council shall "in all respects be a free and independent branch of the legislature."[23]

In all these ways the constitution was conventional and even conservative—it rejected radical calls for a unicameral legislature and instead created a bicameral body that gave each chamber a check over the other. Chandler, who praised the British constitution as the best on earth, would have been pleased with the balance of the New Jersey document. And the balance was surely a positive for Green as well: he worried about the tyranny of the ruling class *and* of the people. As his later fight with the American Presbyterian Church showed, he opposed placing too much power in one governing body. He saw decentralized authority as the best guarantor of democracy. The conservative clauses in New Jersey's constitution, however, were counterbalanced by several important "liberal" elements. The constitution placed more power with the people's chamber, the Assembly. It barred the council from preparing or even altering any money bills; instead, the Assembly controlled the purse strings. The constitution also emasculated the governor's office, taking away his veto, his appointive powers, and his ability to prorogue the legislature. Last but not least, elections for both chambers and for governor were to be annual. This requirement must have pleased Green and upset Chandler: the people, and not the Crown, were to be sovereign.[24]

Green was also likely happy with the provisions on religious freedom since they so closely resembled his thoughts in *Observations*. Article XVII of the constitution decreed "that no person shall ever within this colony be deprived of the inestimable privilege of worshipping Almighty God in a manner agreeable to the dictates of his own conscience." The article made it illegal to compel someone "to attend any place of worship, contrary to his own faith and judgment." Also banned were the formal establishment of religion and the taxes required for its maintenance. This was standard stuff, including the *limits* placed on religious freedom, for these safeguards applied to Protestants only. Article XIX made clear "that no *protestant inhabitant* [emphasis in original] of this colony shall be denied the enjoyment of any civil right merely on account of his religious principles." Further, office holding was limited to "all persons, professing a belief in the faith of any protestant sect." Catholics and Jews thus need not apply. On balance, New Jersey's charter was a classic Whig document—suspicious of executive power, anxious to elevate the people's role, within reason. The constitutions of the other twelve states could all say the same.[25]

Yet several aspects of the document must have rankled Green. The impediments to office holding were hardly democratic in an era of laymen's rights—a cause dear to Green's heart. He was suspicious of the wealthy, yet the upper chamber was virtually reserved for these men. Worse, the constitution was silent on slavery. In *Observations*, Green had harsh things to say about slaveholding, deriding the practice as "a dreadful absurdity!" He also denounced the hypocrisy of slaveholders: "What a shocking consideration, that people who are so strenuously contending for liberty, should at the same time encourage and promote slavery!" The constitution, however, left the institution intact, meaning the practice of holding human beings in bondage would continue in New Jersey until after Green's death.[26]

Another likely problem for Green was that the charter, which was passed two days before the Continental Congress adopted the Declaration of Independence, hedged its bets. The final clause declared "that if a reconciliation between *Great-Britain* and these colonies should take place, and the latter be again taken under the protection and government of the crown . . . this charter shall be null and void." The constitution further waffled by referring to New Jersey repeatedly as a "colony" instead of a "state." Such hesitation, designed to mollify those moderates who retained hope of a last-minute reconciliation with Great Britain, must not have pleased the author of a tract rejecting any such thing. It certainly bothered the radical Whig delegates. The final clause was controversial enough that the Congress revisited the issue on July 3, a mere one day after the constitution's passage, when it voted on a resolution asking the delegates whether the constitution should be printed immediately or deferred "in order to reconsider, in a full house, the propriety of the last clause." Seventeen delegates supported printing the constitution immediately; only eight supported deferring it. Green's committee of ten was divided on the question. Three panel members voted to defer—including Sergeant, the purported author of the constitution—and three voted to print the constitution immediately. Four members—including Green—did not vote at all.[27]

Recorded votes show that Green's committee was divided sectionally (East versus West Jersey) and ideologically (radical versus moderate/conservative). Two key votes—the July 2 one approving the constitution, and the July 3 one on the concluding clause—demonstrate not only that reality but also that the compromises of the document itself left both radicals and conservatives unhappy for different reasons. The wording of the July 2 and July 3 resolutions further showed the complexity of the situation as New Jersey took the momentous step of declaring its independence and setting up a state government. The pivotal July 2 vote was not a straightforward one asking delegates whether they approved of the charter. It asked instead "whether the draught of the constitution, formed on the report of the committee of the whole, be now confirmed, or be deferred for further consideration?" Those who backed the constitution but wanted some changes made could conceivably vote for the latter. Five committee members, including Green and Sergeant, voted "for now." Two members voted to defer, and three did not vote at all. The two who voted to defer—Samuel Dick and Elijah Hughes—were both from West Jersey; of the five supporting immediate ratification, three were from East Jersey.[28]

Yet the events of the next day show that these votes were not so black and white. Radicals were unhappy with the charter's concluding clause, and they wanted it debated further. So the situation became reversed: two out of the three committee members voting for delay were from East Jersey; two out of three members voting for "printing now" were from West Jersey. Sergeant and Symmes who voted on July 2 to confirm the constitution voted on July 3 to defer; Dick did not change his vote—he again wanted the constitution deferred. Conservative-leaning delegates, especially those from West Jersey, still hoped things could be worked out with Britain. Radical Whigs, especially those from East Jersey, wanted the break from Great Britain to be final.[29]

The constitution was so hastily reported out of committee that panel members may not have had time to register their objections. Instead, Green's panel apparently left it up to the committee of the whole and the full Congress to work out the differences. As the split votes reveal, the resulting com-promises meant that some committee members were unhappy with the final product.

Green's position on all this is unclear. Apparently he viewed the July 2 vote as final—he was voting for ratification of the constitution, and he saw his job as finished when the delegates approved adoption. That was Ashbel's take on events: his father departed "as soon as the main business—the for-mation of a constitution for the State—was completed[; he] refused to return, although pressed to do so." But, of course, the constitution wasn't final. The July 3 vote could have delayed implementation and opened the constitution up to revision, albeit on the final clause only. So it was puzzling that Green did not stay another day to vote. Possibly he was unaware that the issue of the concluding clause would be revisited. Or maybe he saw the whole thing as academic; he could have reasoned that independence was a done deal and that the clause would remain inoperative. At the time, rumors were rampant that the British were about to invade New Jersey (indeed, many delegates had already hurried home because of such fears), and Green may well have understood that invasion would kill the conservatives' final hopes for reconciliation.[30]

It is unclear when exactly Green headed home, but his failure to vote on July 3 indicates that he had left Burlington. It's inconceivable that he would not have voted on something so important if he had remained in atten-dance. Ashbel, writing years later, reported that Jacob departed after the constitution was approved, but his chronology was vague: "As soon, how-ever, as it [the constitution] was ratified by the Congress, he [Jacob] left that body and returned, after about a month's absence, to the duties of his pasto-ral charge." Given that Green arrived in Burlington on or about June 10, "a month's" attendance at Congress would carry him to about July 10—which was unlikely since he did not vote on any more bills.[31]

Regardless, Green's time in Congress was brief but historic. During a whirlwind four weeks, the delegates ousted a royal governor, backed inde-pendence from Britain, approved a state constitution, and furthered prepa-rations for war. Green arrived in Burlington with a reputation as a radical Presbyterian Whig, and he did not let his constituents down. The five-person Morris delegation represented one of the most unified and pro-independence counties in the state, and the members were in full agreement between June 11 when the congressional session got under way and July 3 when Green left Burlington. All of them backed the motions to arrest Franklin and cut off his salary, although Green did not vote on the latter. All supported the critical prefatory vote of June 21 "that a government be formed for regulating the internal police of this colony." Surprisingly, though, only Ellis Cook and Green (the two from Hanover Township) participated in the most momentous vote of all—the July 2 resolution approving the constitution. Morris delegates Silas Condict, Jacob Drake, and William Woodhull did not vote. Condict's absence was especially intriguing, for he was on Green's constitutional committee. And, interestingly, not one delegate from Morris voted on July 3 when the Congress decided not to reconsider the last clause of the constitution. Possibly they all had joined the exodus of delegates from Burlington: within a few days of the July 2 vote, attendance had fallen to one-third of the original number.[32]

With so much accomplished in so short a time, the delegates and their fellow New Jerseyans turned their attention to the next pressing task: preparing for war. On July 2, the very day they voted on the proposed state constitution, British General William Howe landed twenty-five thousand English and Hessian troops off the New Jersey coast, on Staten Island. After evacuating Boston in mid-March, British warships had begun appearing in the area on June 25. Staten Island would be the staging area for an invasion of either Long Island or East Jersey, and that chilling fact set off a wave of panic throughout the state, especially along the exposed coast near Staten Island. Some residents began evacuating their homes, with one observer reporting to the Provincial Congress that "the frontier inhabitants" were "moveing the[ir] Household goods & effects" in wagons and carts. William Livingston, who was named brigadier general of the New Jersey militia and was organizing the state's defense, recorded in vivid detail the chaos that was unfolding in early July when the Provincial Congress was debating the constitution. The residents were "greatly dispirited" and in "such Confusion," Livingston wrote in July 3 from Elizabeth Town, and they feared they were at the enemy's mercy because so many members of the militia were off in neighboring New York.[33]

The remaining delegates in Burlington responded by stepping up military preparations. They requested, and received, two tons of powder from the Continental Congress, which they then ordered be distributed to the most exposed counties in East Jersey and a few in West Jersey, including Burlington. The delegates also took steps to deal with the growing loyalist problem. With a large British army so close to New Jersey, according to the Congress's journal, "a number of disaffected persons have assembled in the county of

*Monmouth*, preparing, by force of arms, to oppose the cause of *American* freedom, and to join the *British* troops, for the destruction of this country." The Provincial Congress thus ordered militia from Burlington and Monmouth counties to "proceed, without delay, in order to quell the aforesaid insurrection."[34]

Green arrived home in early July to a county making final preparations for the coming invasion. The arduous task of forming a militia, arming it, and training it had begun a year earlier, after the opening battles of the Revolution at Lexington and Concord on April 19. Those two battles, along with the action at Bunker Hill, were turning points in Hanover and surrounding townships, according to Ashbel: they succeeded "in awaking a high military spirit, not only among the men, but the boys also, of our land in general." During the last six months of 1775, the county raised five companies of minutemen led by William Winds and William Dehart, and it supplied these troops with five hundred pounds of powder and a ton of lead. When the Provincial Congress ordered each township in the state to form one or more companies of eighty men, Winds took the lead in Morris, forming a regiment and commencing drills, with other residents organizing a troop of light horse.[35]

Forty miles away, in New York City, General Washington and his army were dug in after leaving Boston in mid-April 1776. He had guessed correctly that the British would move on New York after abandoning Boston, and he began strengthening defenses and marshaling his forces. At his disposal was a "flying camp" of five thousand militia from Delaware, Maryland, New Jersey, and Pennsylvania that was led by General Hugh Mercer and was deployed along the Jersey coast facing New York. Morris militia under Colonel Jacob Ford headed to the flying camp in June. Other troops from Morris were sent to reinforce Long Island, in case Howe decided to launch his invasion there.[36]

All the preparations, though, were grossly inadequate, and Livingston's letters in this tense time were a litany of the militia's shortcomings: the units were short of men, officers, arms, and training, and (as Chandler had repeatedly warned) they were up against a powerful enemy with the world's largest navy and the ability to strike wherever it pleased. The flying camp, which was deployed from Perth Amboy on up to Bergen County, was stretched dangerously thin and was too small for its assigned task of defending the coast. On July 4, Livingston begged Washington to send him "a few experienced Officers" to help him prepare the militia for the fight ahead: "Our

Men are raw & inexperienced—our Officers mostly absent—want of Discipline is inevitable." Washington was sympathetic and fully understood the dangers that New Jersey faced and how "justly excited" the residents were. "I have concluded to discharge the Militia from this Place [New York]," he told Livingston, "except those from Morris County whose internal Situation is such as to leave them nothing to fear from the Enemy." Washington sent the militia to Bergen, with orders to harass the enemy if they attempted to land troops there. But he rejected Livingston's plea for experienced officers because he had none to spare: "I would gladly comply . . . but I have few of that Character." Washington also tried to reassure Livingston by noting that the Continentals had received no indication that Howe was going to move soon.[37]

Both sides used July and early August to continue strengthening their forces. Washington briefly considered attacking Staten Island, but bowed to the advice of his officers and instead concentrated on readying the region's defenses. In an attempt to bar the British navy from operating north of New York City and surrounding the American forces, troops built two forts along the Hudson. One was on the New Jersey side, directly across from Fort Washington on Manhattan, with the intention of placing the British frigates in a withering cross fire. American troops worked feverishly on the high bluffs of the New Jersey Palisades to finish the post before Howe unleashed his army of thirty-two thousand on rebel forces. When done it was a four-sided affair surrounded by some three hundred huts that were extensive enough to house three thousand soldiers. In mid-October the citadel was renamed Fort Lee in honor of General Charles Lee.[38]

Unfortunately for New Jersey's quavering residents, the forts were as impotent as General Mercer's flying camp. They lacked the firepower and accuracy to stop Howe's armada, which numbered some three hundred ships (the British fleet was so vast that one awed American soldier thought that "all London was afloat"). New York's situation was even more dire than New Jersey's. Washington had sent Lee to the city in mid-January with orders to prepare a defense. He took one look at all the waterways surrounding Manhattan and realized the situation was nearly hopeless. With virtually no American navy to worry about, Howe could land wherever he pleased. Indeed, Lee warned Washington in a letter that the city "is so encircled with deep navigable water that whoever commands the sea must command the town." The Americans' one slim hope, Lee concluded, was to a build a series of fortifications on the western end of Long Island, on Manhattan, and in

New Jersey. Despite the long odds of successfully defending New York, Washington felt he had no choice but to try to keep the city in American hands because of its political significance. Thus, in early July, an American army of about twenty thousand troops could be found huddled in southern Manhattan, awaiting a British attack. Besides being badly outnumbered, the army was, in Washington's laconic words, "extremely deficient in arms . . . and in great distress for want of them."[39]

The inadequacy of American defenses became apparent on the afternoon of July 12. On that day, Howe dispatched two warships—the forty-four-gun battleship *Phoenix* and the twenty-eight-gun frigate *Rose*—to test the rebels' defenses. The two ships, accompanied by a schooner and two supply tenders, sailed up the Hudson, lobbing cannon balls at Manhattan as they went. Lee's fortifications sprung into action; one of the first batteries to open fire was at Red Hook, followed by batteries at Governors Island. One witness calculated that the rebels got off 196 shots—with none hitting its mark. The batteries on the New Jersey side fared no better. In fact, when the guns at Paulus Hook opened up, the British ships fired back and drove the artillerymen from their stations. The fleet of five ships continued up the river, unharmed. When the fleet reached Fort Washington, the Americans discovered, according to one participant, that their guns were too high on the bluffs to be effectual.[40]

New Jersey was exposed. The only thing left was for Jacob Green and his fellow New Jerseyans to await the onslaught to come.

---

## The Loyalist Down the Road: Thomas Bradbury Chandler Flees to London

As Green waited impatiently for the colonists to declare independence, Chandler was fretting that the independence movement was becoming stronger. Green saw the Revolution as a chance to achieve a moral reformation; Chandler feared the opposite would happen, that anarchy would ensue if the colonies achieved independence. For a lover of the state church and the Crown, the radicals' scariest accomplishment was their ability to construct a parallel system of government that operated through local committees and congresses.

This ability to bypass the legally constituted state in the early 1770s left Chandler in a rage, and he again took up his pen to thunder against the threat to royal authority. *In What Think Ye of the Congress Now?* written in 1775, he warned the American people that the true tyrants resided not in London but in Philadelphia. In this caustic, forty-eight-page tract, he laid out his case against patriot organizations, at times in mocking tones: the "Gentlemen of the Congress" were not true representatives of the people, but were usurpers overstepping their bounds and "increase[ing] the evil, which they were sent to remove."

More darkly, Chandler foresaw calamity if the colonies were foolish enough to take up arms against the greatest military power on earth: "That we should have expectation or hope of being able to conquer or withstand the force of Great-Britain, is to me astonishing. I doubt not but the Americans are naturally as brave as any other people; and it is allowed, that they are not wanting in numbers. But they are without fortresses, without discipline, without military stores, without money. These are deficiencies which it must be the work of an age to remove; and while they continue, it will be impossible to keep an army in the field."

Chandler charged that members of the Continental Congress were fanatics who were ignoring the will of their constituents: "They have altogether neglected the work they were sent upon; that the powers delegated to them by their constituents, for the good of the colonies, were prostituted to the purposes of private ambition; and that all their proceedings as far as we can judge, were instigated and directed by New-England republicans, to the utmost confusion of the Colonies, the disgrace of their constituents, and their own infamy." The tyrannical nature of Congress, Chandler believed, meant that good Americans should reject it and everything it recommended: "We manifestly owe them no obedience at all; we owe them no respect as a body: Much less are we bound to plunge ourselves headlong into that abyss of misery and destruction which they have opened; an abyss, which indeed must soon swallow us up." Chandler's opinion of the committees of correspondence was no better, nor that of the Sons of Liberty. The extralegal patriot organizations all deserved the same fate, he concluded. Failure to restrain Congress and the committees, Chandler warned, would result in the loss of liberties for all Americans. To prevent that, "we must rescue our necks from the *yoke* of the Congress, and our legs and arms from the *fetters* of Committees. This is the bondage we have most reason to dread, as it is equally oppressive and disgraceful."

Chandler's attempts to secure an American bishop, his unswerving loyalty to the king, and his harsh attacks on the independence movement made him a pariah in his hometown and across British North America. His outspoken defense of the king would have brought him trouble in most places, but it was his misfortune to be based in Elizabeth Town, New Jersey. The village was no Anglican stronghold; it was home to some of the most powerful Presbyterian politicians in New Jersey's revolutionary movement. The political environment of 1774–76 presented these Whig leaders with several thorny problems; the biggest was persuading the rest of the colony to take the fateful step and declare independence from Great Britain. But closer to home they had to deal with an embarrassing problem—the presence of Thomas Bradbury Chandler.

The patriots' early efforts to silence Chandler began in 1774, when the Elizabethtown Association authorized the burning of Chandler's *Friendly Address to All Reasonable Americans*, declaring that the tract was a threat to American liberties. With the outbreak of fighting at Lexington and Concord in April 1775, the pressure on Chandler intensified. Friends were now warning him that the Sons of Liberty and others were no longer content with burning Chandler's writings; his life itself was in danger. If the tone of his diary is any indication, Chandler reacted calmly to these threats to his personage. Yet he grasped that he was in real trouble, that these were not idle threats. When the pressure became intolerable, he fled on May 15, 1775, to New York City, taking only "some Articles of necessary Apparel." He left behind his wife, Jane, and their five children. Chandler was hoping that his exile would be short and that he would be able to return home promptly.

His hopes were dashed. In New York, "I found every Thing in the utmost Confusion, and the Friends of Government under the severest Persecution; I therefore lodged at Mr. Kempe's, the Attorney General, as a Place unsuspected, and less liable to Insults, than where I commonly used to lodge in the City." Word of Chandler's arrival spread to "that turbulent Faction, which had assumed the Government of the City, [and they] were making Enquiries after me, and determined to pay me a Visit." Chandler laid low for a day and tried to figure out what to do. His heart told him to return to Elizabeth Town and his family; his head told him otherwise, as did his friends. They "recommended" that he sail to England, and Chandler agreed he would have to go into exile. And thus, on the evening of May 16, "I contracted with Capt. Joseph Winder for a Passage to Bristol in the Ship *Exeter*, and staid that Night at Mr. Kempe's."

Chandler, however, had to figure out how to stay safe until he could board the *Exeter*, which would not be sailing for several days. A Captain James Montagu came to Chandler's rescue and allowed him to board the *King-Fisher*, a ship that Chandler described "as the only Place of Safety near New-York." There, Chandler remained until Saturday, May 20, when the *Exeter* docked at "the Hook." Chandler was now back among friends: "Dr. [Myles] Cooper [president of King's College] and I shifted our Lodgings to the *Exeter* to be ready for our voyage; there we were kindly received by our Friends Mr. [Samuel] Cook, and Capt. [Michael] Kearny, who were to be our Fellow-Passengers."

Still, the waiting went on. Eighteenth-century ships were at the mercy of the winds, and the *Exeter* was unable to depart for several days. Finally, on Thursday, May 25, 1775, the conditions turned favorable. In stark contrast to his political tracts, Chandler described his departure calmly and unemotionally: "Having waited till this Time for a proper Wind, we put to sea in the Morning, turning out with a Head Wind, in Company with more than 20 Vessels, most of which were bound to European Ports. We saw the *Asia*, of 64 Guns, from Boston, go in to the Hook, and come to an Anchor. At Evening the Land appeared to be distant about 6 Leagues."

The view of shore receded, and so did Chandler's dreams for an American bishop leading a Church of England to dominance in a land that remained loyal to the king.[41]

## Host

At 11 p.m. on November 19, 1776, nearly five thousand British troops under the command of General Cornwallis began boarding the flatboats that would carry them across the Hudson River to New Jersey. It was a miserable night for a river crossing—a cold, heavy rain pelted the soldiers in their woolen redcoats, and thick fog shrouded the towering Palisades that loomed ahead. But little went wrong for the British on this moonless night and in the immediate days ahead. When the sodden soldiers debarked at a dock in Closter, New Jersey, about six miles north of Fort Lee on November 20, and climbed a precipitous path up the Palisades, the rout was on and New Jersey's problems were just beginning. The economy was in tatters, the new state government was barely functioning, and New Jersey was virtually defenseless against the British onslaught.[1]

The Green family felt especially exposed during this dangerous time. The parsonage was in the far eastern reaches of Morris County, seven miles from Morristown and less than a mile from the Essex County line, which meant that the family was "in very hazardous circumstances," according to Ashbel Green. "For on the retreat of General Washington, and the pursuit of the British army . . . we were within twelve miles of the enemy's line of march." The family also felt exposed because of Jacob's prominence as a Presbyterian firebrand. He had advocated independence, publicly criticized the Crown, and led the committee that wrote New Jersey's first state constitution. "On these accounts," Ashbel observed, "he was peculiarly obnoxious to the tories."[2]

With the rebel army in headlong retreat in late November and the British methodically advancing, rumors were rampant. One was "that a party of the enemy's cavalry was to be detached, to seize a number of the leading whigs in Morris county, and my father, of course among the rest," Ashbel recalled. Jacob's friends urged him to flee and "retire to an obscure part of his parish for safety." He resisted, until one rumor proved to be particularly credible. Jacob and his wife scurried off, leaving the house in Ashbel's charge: "My father's instructions to me were, to treat the enemy, if they came, with the greatest civility." He also told his son to feign ignorance, and to inform the British that he knew not where his parents had gone: "Happily, however, the British did not come, either on that night, or at any other time." George Washington's assessment of Morris County proved accurate—this Presbyterian-Whig stronghold nestled in the Watchung Mountains was relatively safe from the British. Jacob and his wife—the "fugitives," as Ashbel wryly described them—returned home and "were all mortified that they had fled when they might have remained in safety."[3]

The embarrassment Jacob experienced as a fugitive was a harbinger of things to come. Living in a small state that quickly succumbed to British arms, Green never really got to enjoy the glories of the revolution that he had helped bring about. With the British punishing New Jersey for its treasonous behavior, Jacob witnessed firsthand all the shortcomings of the revolutionary movement: Continentals on the run from the enemy; a militia afraid to fight; moral shortcomings everywhere. Thus quite quickly—by 1778—Green's excitement and confidence following the British evacuation of Boston in March 1776 had given way to disillusionment. Not that Green had been naive about the risks the revolutionaries faced in the war's opening days; he was an astute observer of colonial society and human nature. More so than many other Whigs, he well understood the challenges the independence movement would face and the shortcomings that bedeviled American society. Despite all that, Green's disappointment with his fellow Americans was palpable, and it led him to reassess his beliefs and his hopes for the Revolution. With the war reshaping his thinking, thoughts expressed in his earlier writings emerged more forcefully in his revolutionary essays and sermons, and he became even more convinced that Americans *had* to change their ways. For Jacob the teacher and exhorter, the war provided valuable lessons about the economy and society that he soon would be applying outside the pulpit.

In 1775, Green and other leading revolutionaries envisaged the war as a test, and they were confident that the colonists would pass it because of their supposed moral superiority over the corrupt and decadent British. Green's confidence only grew after the British evacuated Boston in March 1776 and sailed for Nova Scotia. He gloated to a neighboring loyalist that "the whole power of Britain could not conquer the single province of Massachusetts Bay," and he predicted that the Crown would never be able to crush the rebellion. Green was not alone in his giddiness. As historian Charles Royster so famously described, a "Rage Militaire" swept the colonies in 1775 and grew in early 1776 after the British withdrawal from New England. Americans celebrated the victory with gusto and were confident that American arms would make short work of the British.[4]

Green and others were soon regretting such words. Many militia units refused to turn out when Cornwallis crossed the Hudson River on November 19 and entered New Jersey; some that did show up quickly fled to the safety of their homes. One Continental Army officer was positively livid with New Jersey's residents and its government during this chaotic period. "This State is totally deranged, without Government, or officers civil or military in it that will act with any Spirit," Brigadier General Alexander McDougall fumed in a December 1776 letter to Washington. "The Militia are without leaders and many of them not in the Power of the enemy are dispirited." Washington was not much kinder. "The Militia from the Counties of Morris & Sussex turn out slowly and reluctantly," he noted in a letter to New Jersey Governor William Livingston. "Designing Men have been purposely sent among them to influence some and intimidate others, and except Gentlemen of Spirit and Character will appear among them and rouse them, little can be expected."[5]

The feeling was mutual. One reason New Jerseyans panicked at the British approach was that they were so unimpressed with the ragged Continentals who were supposed to defend them. Before marching to Jersey, the rebel army had suffered setback after setback in neighboring New York. The first rout came on Long Island in late August, followed by the retreat from nearby Manhattan in mid-September. More setbacks (at Throg's Neck, Harlem Heights, and White Plains) ensued, leaving the troops dispirited and mutinous. When the British captured two key forts, Washington and Lee,

New Jersey's position became militarily impossible. The British had a large army and navy in place to crush the state's rebel movement.

The mission of Washington army's from late November to mid-December hardly inspired public confidence, either: the Continentals were not trying to drive the invaders out of New Jersey; they were merely trying to live to fight another day. The tired troops shuffled southward toward Philadelphia, barely staying ahead of the slow-moving colossus that was the British army. Led by Cornwallis and reinforced by General William Howe's troops, the invading army grew to nearly ten thousand. It was a large, well-supplied force that, thankfully for Washington, was slowed by its very size; by one estimate, the force required seventeen tons of food a day. Some one thousand horses pulled its extensive baggage train.[6]

Thomas Paine was with Washington's army during the retreat through New Jersey and watched the fiasco unfold. He complained bitterly that the British commander, William Howe, was more interested in "a ravage than a conquest." Yet he reserved his harshest criticism for New Jersey's residents. The Continental troops, he insisted, retreated "with a manly and martial spirit. All their wishes were one; which was that the country would turn out, and help them to drive the enemy back." It did not happen. In *The American Crisis*, a series of pamphlets he began writing in December 1776, Paine poured out his frustrations with New Jersey and other states in the Mid-Atlantic. "Why is it that the enemy hath left the New England provinces, and made these middle ones the seat of war?" he pointedly asked. "The answer is easy. New England is not infested with tories, and we are." The tract's legendary opening words were even more mortifying for New Jersey's civilians: "These are the times that try men's souls. The summer-soldier and the sun-shine patriot will, in this crisis, shrink from the service of their country."[7]

Paine, though, was doing more than tearing down the hapless militia in the early days of the New Jersey invasion. He composed *The American Crisis* at the urging of his fellow officers, who wanted him to boost morale. Civilians—those summer soldiers and sunshine patriots—were easy targets for someone as truculent as Paine, but the tract was also a sign that the army faced severe morale problems of its own. If the Continental Army disintegrated and the British succeeded in pacifying New Jersey, the Revolution could be dealt a fatal blow. The stakes were high, and Paine (and Jacob Green) knew it. The revolutionaries, they well understood, would have to pay a steep price if they wanted to secure their freedom. Thus, in *The Ameri-*

*can Crisis*, Paine tried to buck up discouraged revolutionaries, Continental soldier and civilian alike. "Tyranny, like hell, is not easily conquered: yet we have this consolation with us, that the harder the conflict, the more glorious the triumph," he wrote. Paine simply could not believe that tyranny would win. He closed *The American Crisis* by urging squabbling Americans to unite, and pointing out that posterity will be judging the revolutionaries: "Let it be told to the future world, that in the depth of winter, when nothing but hope and virtue could survive, that the city and the country, alarmed at one common danger, came forth to meet and to repulse it."[8]

The uplifting passages could not mask the reality of what was unfolding in New Jersey. The British came to New Jersey. Many patriots ran. Things were going so well for the British that Howe issued a proclamation on November 30, 1776, promising "a free and general Pardon" to "all Persons speedily returning to their just Allegiance." Needless to say, he and the king's supporters were pleased with the response. The *New-York Gazette* reported on December 16, "The People of New-Jersey fly to the [British] Army in great Numbers, rejoicing that they have once more obtained British protection." The *Gazette* writer was confident that these residents were rejecting "the Iron Rod of Tyranny, with which the Republican Faction so long had oppressed them." Most New Jerseyans, however, were hedging their bets because of the British success on the battlefield. Some eagerly switched sides and took up arms for the king; Cortlandt Skinner successfully raised six battalions of loyalist forces known as New Jersey Volunteers. Other residents, especially in Bergen and Monmouth Counties, ended their neutrality, trading with the British or refusing to sell goods to patriot forces. Such subtleties mattered little to revolutionary leaders; Paine called loyalists cowards, and Washington despaired at the number of New Jerseyans accepting pardons: "The conduct of the Jerseys has been most Infamous. Instead of turning out to defend their Country . . . they are making their submission as fast as they can."[9]

Despite Washington's displeasure with the slow-moving militia from Morris, at least it turned out and fought, unlike soldiers in other places. More important, the county quickly became a safe haven for the reeling patriots. It was no Monmouth, a county to the south torn by dissension and civil war. Morris's residents were united in their support of the Revolution. Its radical population combined with geography to make the county a virtual fortress: Morris lay behind the Watchung Mountains, and militia were posted to guard its key passes. These "mountains" were really little more than hills—a series of three long ridges resting on volcanic rock—yet they were imposing enough to constitute a barrier against British encroachments and were high enough to allow sentinels to track enemy movements all the way to New York City. Indeed, in the astute words of Ashbel Green, the hills "were kind of a natural barrier for the camp and military stores at Morristown. A hundred men might have defended some of the passes over these hills against a thousand."[10]

Refugees from throughout the state—including Governor Livingston's family, which relocated to Parsippany in spring 1777, not far from Green's church on Hanover Neck—flocked to the county's safe confines during the British invasion and its aftermath, and General Lee with an army of 2,700 troops took up residence in Morristown on December 8. A thousand county militia under the command of Jacob Ford and others joined him. Thus fortified, the revolutionaries began to rally. Lee sent Ford and the Morris militia to raid Woodbridge, where they seized four hundred cattle, two hundred sheep, and numerous horses. The militia harassed British foragers and hindered enemy communications. Washington and the main army, meanwhile, crossed into Pennsylvania on December 8 to regroup. On December 25, they recrossed the Delaware, captured Trenton in a daring early-morning attack, and nine days later won again at Princeton.[11]

The stunning victories meant that the enemy's supply depot at New Brunswick now lay open, and it was an inviting target for Washington. The capture of Brunswick, with its bountiful supply of arms and cash, would be so significant that Washington believed it could win the war for the Americans. But six grueling weeks of marching had seen Washington's army retreat and then counterattack, and the Americans were too exhausted to pull off another surprise against the British. Instead, Washington understood that his troops needed to rest. Seeking a safe place to recover, he did what hundreds of refugees had already done—he looked west, to Morristown and Morris County.

Washington's appearance at Morristown in early January 1777 culminated a wild ride for Jacob Green and his family: despair in early December, elation in late December. Yet the new year meant work, and lots of it, for Washington's army of five thousand needed to be housed, clothed, and fed. The men lacked proper winter gear, including such basic items as coats and shoes. They also lacked tents, meaning that county residents within fifteen miles of Morristown had to open their doors to the soldiers and their officers. Thus, in 1777, Jacob Green moved from the rhetoric of revolution—writing pamphlets and a constitution—to the nitty-gritty of supporting the soldiers who were charged with winning the war. One of the first things the Green family did was to take in fourteen officers and soldiers, and Pastor Green encouraged his congregants to do the same.[12]

With army provisions so inadequate, a second critical task was feeding the troops, and kitchen hearths across Morris began churning out soup, vegetables, and meat for the men. The third task was organizing relief efforts. The military's needs were especially acute when the troops first stumbled into town. Besides having to take care of those newcomers to Morristown—and a staggering two thousand men were ill when they first marched into the village—the army left behind numerous wounded in Princeton hospitals in the aftermath of the fierce one-day battle. Churches throughout Morris took the lead in the relief work, as they transformed themselves into social service agencies. In Hanover, Green and his fellow Presbyterians collected clothing, shoes, blankets, and linen for those men still convalescing after the Battle of Princeton.[13]

Green's stature in the community as a revolutionary and a man of God meant that he represented civilians in dealings with General Washington, including the serious issue of what to do about the smallpox that menaced the army and threatened to spread to Morris residents. By February, the threat was so serious that Washington's staff decided that all the troops needed to be inoculated—a controversial procedure at the time, and one that many people feared. The army's task was delicate. It had to undertake a massive inoculation without causing a wave of panic among the civilians who were housing and feeding his men. But, of course, it proved impossible to keep the news from Morris County's residents. Word spread that soldiers were infected with the disease and that the general, acting on the advice of his medical staff, wanted to undertake a massive inoculation. For the safety of civilians, Washington ruled that the families quartering the men should be inoculated as well.[14]

Washington's plan caused an uproar, and Green, "accompanied by some of the most respectable men of his congregation," rode by sleigh to Morristown to question the general about the inoculations and to relay peoples' fears. When the Hanover Presbyterians met with the tall, lanky general, Green did most of the talking. He first donned the cloak of the good soldier, telling Washington "that he well knew that in military operations it was not unusual to make a *certain* sacrifice of a number of lives, to ensure the success of a battle, or for the general good of the community." Green the Calvinist stressed that he and his fellow congregation members "were prepared to submit . . . to their destiny." But then Green got to his real point, arguing that such a sacrifice was unnecessary and that Washington should separate the troops from the populace "so as not to subject the whole to the contemplated calamity."[15]

Washington was not swayed, according to Ashbel's account of the meeting: "Their apprehensions, he was confident, were altogether groundless; that the inhabitants would find . . . that the proposed measure was no calamity at all." Most powerfully, Washington pointed out to Green that if he followed the pastor's advice and quarantined the men, the families who had shared close quarters with the troops would have no guarantee that they had not been exposed to the virus. Without the inoculation, they could die and the smallpox could spread to the rest of the civilian population. Green grasped the power of this reasoning, Ashbel said, and "my father and his friends came back perfectly reconciled to the measure." According to one early historian of Hanover, "Mr. Green unfolded a thorough plan for the inoculation of all belonging to his congregation and urged—even commanded—them to comply with it." The Hanover church, as did other congregations, became a smallpox clinic where the inoculations were done. Army surgeons and area physicians performed the inoculations, with ministers tending to the sick. Green's warnings about dying for the cause proved prophetic—smallpox killed sixty-eight people alone in Morristown in 1777. Outside the village, records are incomplete, but at least two ministers (one in Bottle Hill and one in Mendham) also died.[16]

Green took the lead on another front: he had his parish put up and nurse ailing, newly released American prisoners of war. In December 1777, months after Washington's army had moved on from Morris County, the British freed a number of POWs being held in New York City. Some were imprisoned aboard ship in the East River in conditions so wretched that thousands died before the war ended; others were kept at a sugarhouse and at churches. Most of those freed that month were weakened from malnutrition and disease; indeed, "a number of them were so debilitated by famine and disease, that they fell down and died in the streets of New York, before they could even reach the vessels appointed to transport them," Ashbel said. Twelve of "these pitiable objects" were taken to the Greens' parsonage; when the wagon pulled up, they had to be helped into the house. The family swung into action, "cleansing and clothing them, preparing for them suitable food, and in every way ministering to their necessities." After the immediate crisis passed, the Greens sent ten of the former prisoners to other families within the parish. Two remained at the parsonage.[17]

All this activity meant that Jacob Green was seeing the war up close, in all its majesty and ugliness. New Jersey's militia overcame its feeble start to become one of the best performing in the new nation and helped keep the British on the defensive. The overall military situation improved by 1778, and the main theater moved south to South Carolina and Virginia in 1779. For Green, however, the improving situation did not ameliorate the problems he was witnessing within the revolutionary movement. One disturbing aspect was the violence of the Whig movement.[18] Rebels harassed the king's supporters and threatened them with bodily harm, and worse. When the British were overrunning the state in late 1776 and the loyalists had the upper hand, the king's supporters pillaged rebel strongholds and joined in armed attacks against rebel units. The revolutionaries fought back, giving as good as they got. A second phase of this civil war began in early January 1777 when the tide had turned and British and Hessian forces had retreated to Paulus Hook and New Brunswick. The revolutionaries began exacting revenge on these "Criminals," and the anger extended to the highest reaches of government: Governor Livingston vowed to "make rough work with [those British supporters who] have been active against us." Loyalists who did not take oaths of allegiance to the revolutionary government could have their property confiscated, and Whigs resorted to violence to compel compliance.[19]

A loyalist who lived within a mile of the Greens' parsonage came to fear for his life, and this presented Jacob with a moral dilemma. Good Whigs had little to do with loyalists, and this loyalist was particularly repugnant. Ashbel described him as "an English emigrant, a man of considerable property, and not a little hauteur, who had drunk as deeply into toryism as my father had into whigism." In his *Observations on the Reconciliation of Great-Britain*, Green had said that "I do not pretend to reason with professed tories," but that was not literally true. In the days leading up to independence, Jacob had argued repeatedly with the neighbor, deploying every argument in his Whig arsenal, including his main points from *Observations*, to try to bring him around to the patriot cause. In these debates, Green sounded positively Jeffersonian. Like the famous revolutionary to the south, he denied, in Ashbel's recollection, that the Crown "had nursed [the colonies] up from infancy, defending us against the French and Indians." But Green's arguments had little effect on the neighbor. And as the rebels' military situation deteriorated in the waning days of 1776, the tory "became so publicly audacious, that some young men and ardent whigs, in a neighbouring town, were reported to have declared that they would tar and feather him." The report, according to Ashbel, "frightened him half out of his life."[20]

The loyalist turned to an interesting place for protection from rebel mobs—Jacob Green and his Hanover congregation. It was a complete capitulation, Ashbel reported. "He acknowledged that he had done wrong in speaking against the American cause, said he was sorry for his imprudence and violence, and was willing to promise most explicitly and solemnly that if he might be forgiven, and be permitted to live in peace and safety, he would be silent on the American controversy." Jacob now had a choice. He could turn his back on a British supporter and let his fellow Whigs deal with him. Or this Christian and man of God could help someone in need. It was not the easiest of decisions. Faced with the same choice, a minister in a neighboring town whom the loyalist had also appealed to for help ignored him.[21]

Green chose differently—he took pity on the neighbor. Not that Green was a saint. His initial reaction to the loyalist's story of impending violence was skepticism: he "had not heard a word about the tarring and feathering of his alarmed visitant," Ashbel said. The neighbor, who was painfully aware of the fate of loyalists elsewhere, insisted on making a public confession, and the two men worked out a plan to execute it. Jacob wrote down the confession for the loyalist and instructed him to appear in church. That Sunday, with the man standing in the pew before the congregants, Jacob read the confession from the pulpit. The man spent the remaining war years at his Hanover farm, "without any disturbance." But relations between Jacob and the neighbor remained frosty. According to Ashbel, when the danger of tarring and feathering had passed, the loyalist "seemed to suspect it, and treated my father with greater distance after, than before that occurrence."[22]

More menacing to the Greens and other residents in East Jersey was the plundering of the civilian population by soldiers of all stripes and the nonstop foraging wars fought by raiding parties from both armies. The Hessians were especially notorious—and feared. Civilians saw them as thieves and as mercenaries whose sole interest was in enriching themselves. New Jerseyans thought little better of British regulars; William Livingston summed up many people's views when he told the legislature in late January 1777 that the British invasion was marked by "Devastation & Murder . . . with Barbarities unknown to civilized Nations."[23]

Yet Americans' behavior was also odious. New Jersey's militia officers, Livingston charged, were leading their men "into every Kind of Mischief; one Species of which is that of plundering the Inhabitants under Pretence of their being Tories." The Greens could attest to the accuracy of that assertion. A company of light horsemen surrounded the Greens' parsonage at midnight one evening in 1777 and placed armed guards at the doors and windows so no one could escape. Emerging from their darkened bedrooms, the Greens were unsure whether the men were British or American; they also did not know what the intruders wanted. Jacob's wife, Elizabeth, feared the worst—that the soldiers were British and had come to arrest her husband, and she urged him to hide. He refused, got dressed, and "opened the doors of his house to the invaders, and asked them to declare their purpose," Ashbel recalled. "It was then discovered that they were not British dragoons, but a lawless band of American cavalry." The Americans, who obviously did not know who Jacob was, announced that they were searching for Tory property, and Jacob let them in, "beg[ging] them to take care of their candles, and not set fire to his dwelling." The soldiers "were soon satisfied that they had come to the wrong house" and withdrew.[24]

On another occasion, American troops stole poultry from Hanover farmers, including the Greens. Elizabeth was distraught that the soldiers had made off with "a fat turkey that had been reserved for Christmas dinner." Green, who was such a stern critic of vice and the shortcomings of American society, was surprisingly patient with the men's bad behavior and even tried to justify it. They were hungry, he told his family, and he cited a passage from Proverbs to explain why they should be forgiving in this instance: "Men do not despise a thief, if he steal to satisfy his soul when he is hungry."[25]

Housing soldiers carried another kind of risk. The two former POWs living with the family were battling serious fevers, and Ashbel got sick and nearly died. His parents placed him in a trundle bed in their bedroom, wrapped both of his wrists with a blister plaster, and nursed him back to health. One of the ex-POWs, meanwhile, could be violent and posed a physical threat to the family. Ashbel described the man as "an athletic Irishman" who in a high delirium bolted from the house one Sunday when everyone but Ashbel was at church. The man "threatened vengeance to any one that should attempt to control him," Ashbel recalled, "and his fever gave him a strength that was formidable." It took three to four "stout" men from the congregation to subdue him. According to Ashbel, the two former prisoners recovered only slowly—it took about three months before they were well enough to go home.[26]

The family faced a spiritual threat as well: its members were exposed to the vulgarity of soldiers. In time-honored fashion, the troops swore—loudly and profusely. Washington and other revolutionary leaders recognized that the epithets risked offending the populace, and the general tried to crack down on the practice, telling the troops in a general order that "his feelings are continually wounded by the Oaths and Imprecations of the soldiers whenever he is in hearing of them." State and Continental articles of war, meanwhile, prohibited profanity, and "An American" lambasted the practice in an essay in the *New-Jersey Journal* that was addressed "to the TRIBE of SWEARERS." All of this was for naught, of course. Facing death in combat and days of numbing deprivation, the soldiers cursed the world around them. The men who lived with the Greens could swear with the best of them. Their rough language and uncouth manners, according to Ashbel, scandalized this devout Presbyterian family. Six children were living at home at the time, including Keturah, who was nine years old in 1777, and Calvin, who was twelve. Before the war, these young children grew up in a tightly controlled household that revolved around the Bible, church, and a strict code of Christian ethics. Jacob and Elizabeth railed constantly against swearing, citing it as one of the gravest offenses to God.[27]

The soldiers' presence upset much of this, and Jacob's reaction was to try to wall his family off—literally—from the vulgarity. When the Greens housed the army officers for about two months in the summer of 1777, Jacob divided the house in half, with the two parties sharing only the kitchen. But, of course, this was not much of a solution in a parsonage that Jacob had complained in the prewar years was too small. Now it was housing some eighteen people, and it must have been horribly cramped. Wall or no wall, the family was in regular conduct with the men, and the officers' coarseness left a lasting impression on young Ashbel. The men were Virginians, he recounted, "and they were the most shockingly profane in their common conversation of any men I have ever known. Their language, at times, was absolutely horrifying to any ear not accustomed to blasphemy." Ashbel was further shocked that they had no interest in reading any of the books from Jacob's fine library. Instead, they amused themselves by firing their rifles in shooting contests and by playing cards. "Such was their devotion to cards," Ashbel recalled, "that when one of their number died . . . it was with difficulty they could be restrained from playing while the corpse was yet in the house." Ashbel did not describe how his father handled such blasphemy, but card playing and swearing violated everything he believed in. And given later events, Jacob clearly was observing and taking notes.[28]

The former prisoners who stayed with the Greens in late 1777 and early 1778 offended the family in other ways. The Irishman told the family that he was going to return to the Continental Army when he was well enough so he could treat the prisoners just as poorly as they had treated him. Jacob had long preached the importance of Christian forgiveness, and Ashbel pointedly described the soldier's attitude as "very bad," although he had to concede that the man's thirst for revenge "was the natural result of the cruelty he had experienced on a mind not deeply imbued with the principles of humanity or religion." In other dealings with Continental officers as a lowly private in the Morris County militia, Ashbel found them not only "profane" but also quite willing to "avow infidel sentiments." None, he said, "ever formally reasoned against Christianity, either with me or in my hearing, yet their known opinions and loose practices, had a degree of influence in leading me to question the truth and authority of divine revelation."[29]

Ashbel's military service exposed him to even more kinds of vice, and worse. It also posed a terribly difficult question for his father. Would Jacob be willing to see his most talented son die for the cause? On one level, it was a relatively easy question to answer. Patriots expected patriots to fight, and Presbyterians in New Jersey were among the most patriotic in the new nation. Hanover Township's Presbyterian families sent their fathers and sons off to war in large numbers. Kinship and the congregation became feeders for the military: 36 percent of the Hanoverians who were in the militia or army were from families affiliated with Green's Presbyterian congregation. The ranks, as a result, were filled with the leading Presbyterian families—the Kitchels, Beaches, Munsons, among others. The pull of family, home, and church was so strong, though, that Hanoverians overwhelmingly preferred service in the militia over that in the Continental Army. About 85 percent of township residents were in the militia. Only 6 percent donned the army's blue uniforms (another 8 percent did stints in both the militia and the army). Those numbers compared favorably with the other Presbyterian-dominated townships in Morris County, where a total of 1,552 men served: 69 percent in the militia, and 9 percent in the army (9 percent served in both). Overall, Hanover Township supplied 17 percent of the troops from Morris County during the Revolution.[30]

Yet, on another level, the issue of military service was not so simple for Jacob; he had to weigh what was best for himself and his family. Jacob apparently never considered serving as a military chaplain. One reason might have been age: he turned fifty-four in 1776 and his health was not strong enough to withstand the rigors of being in the field. A more likely reason was that Jacob concluded he could be of greater service to the revolutionary cause as a pastor and as a reform-seeking writer. But if his fascination with the military contest whirling around him was any indication, it was not the easiest of decisions. According to Ashbel, his father "could not always content himself to remain out of sight of the conflicts which took place between the British troops and the militia of this neighborhood." Jacob, in short, liked to watch the action in the field, often on horseback "at a short distance, on an elevated spot."[31]

Ashbel's service presented a different kind of quandary for Jacob—but, apparently, only for this one son. Ashbel's older brother Pierson, who was born in 1761, enlisted in the Continental Army as a private early in the war and served until the end of hostilities in 1783, first in "Spencer's Regiment" (also known as the Fifth Battalion of the Jersey Line) and then in Capt. Jonathan Holmes's company in the Second Regiment. Ashbel was different. As he approached adulthood, it was becoming clearer how gifted he was as a scholar. Jacob dropped his plans to turn Ashbel into a farmer and instead began thinking about his son's future in the classroom and the pulpit. The British invasion of New Jersey threatened such dreams. Where would a teenage Ashbel be best suited—staying in the classroom as a student and a teacher, or trying his hand in the military with a musket? Militia service allowed him to do both, and that middle ground was what the Greens decided to pursue. Ashbel began his martial training when he was fifteen, and he was permitted to formally join the militia when he turned sixteen. Presbyterian connections eased the way: Ashbel served as a private in a unit commanded by a church member, Enoch Beach, who was a captain in the county's eastern battalion.[32]

Militia duty was dangerous work at a dangerous time. Ashbel became involved in 1777 when the much-maligned militia was taking the fight to the British and making the redcoats' lives miserable: whenever they ventured out from their garrisons, they faced harassment from New Jersey's part-time soldiers. Militia picked off the enemy from behind trees, ambushed British foragers, and destroyed bridges and supplies. The harassment was so bad that a loyalist reported, "Not a stick of wood, a spear of grass, or a kernel of corn could the [British] troops in New Jersey procure without fighting for it."[33]

Ashbel's early service began innocently enough. The Morris militia was ordered to march west to the Delaware River to protect the residents of Minisink from a possible Indian attack. Ashbel served as an orderly sergeant for this task, where he observed the militia's shortcomings up close. His unit reached Minisink after a rapid march, and posted no guard to keep an eye out for Indian allies of the British. Fortunately, no enemy appeared, so Ashbel's company amused itself by hunting deer-and failed to kill any. "I believe the greatest danger experienced by any one of the whole expedition, was in crossing and re-crossing the Delaware in an Indian canoe, which none of us knew how to manage skillfully," he observed with bemusement.[34]

Ashbel had plenty of harsh things to say about the officers he encountered, but he was impressed by Brigadier General William Winds, another Presbyterian, who commanded the militia. (Ashbel called him Wines.) Winds was an imposing figure, according to Ashbel: a "gigantic frame and strength" who possessed great courage. "But the most remarkable thing about him was his voice," Ashbel recalled. "It exceeded in power and efficiency . . . every other human voice that I ever heard." Winds put his voice to good use during a skirmish in the winter of 1777 near New Brunswick, when the general and his troops ran into a large British foraging party and were greatly outnumbered. "Before the British came within musket shot, he thundered at the top of his voice—'Open to the right and left, and let the field pieces come in.' The British were without field pieces as well as himself, but expecting a deadly fire from the American artillery, they faced to the right about and hastily retreated."[35]

Ashbel saw his first serious action shortly after the Morris militia returned from the Minisink. British troops from New York City were again foraging in New Jersey, detaching shallops and a frigate up the Hackensack River to gather hay in the countryside. The Morris militia, Ashbel recalled, gathered at the Acquackanonk Bridge on the Passaic River about ten miles north of Newark. Winds expected the foragers to advance on his position, but when they failed to, he decided to attack a fort the British had established near the Hackensack to aid in the foraging. As the militia approached the fort, the British unleashed a cannonade, the first time that Ashbel had come under fire. It was an unforgettable moment for him: the "cannon ball came over us, a little above our heads, with that screaming and whizzing kind of noise . . .

as it passes through and seems to torture the air." Ashbel was full of bravado at this point, likening the sound to the famous description of gunfire as "the most pleasant music I have ever heard."[36]

Winds placed about one-third of his troops, including Ashbel, in a ravine and directed them to hide; when the British troops passed, they were to "rush out and attack their rear with our utmost vigor." There the men sat for more than an hour until one of them became impatient. The soldier walked into an open field and challenged the British to come out of their fort. They declined the offer: "The enemy probably had not a larger force than was barely sufficient to man the fort, and we could not provoke them to leave." So the militia marched away, encamping at a spot about a mile from the fortification.[37]

For Ashbel, the high of being under fire was dissipating. He was experiencing the miserable lot of the common soldier: lots of marching, little action, and even less food. He went eighteen hours without eating anything but an apple and a piece of bread. When the troops were readying to breakfast the following morning, "intelligence was received that the enemy was marching in force, to cut off our retreat." It proved to be a false alarm, but the men had to abandon their meal and make a forced march. Now Ashbel was even more tired and hungry: "The excitement which had kept up my spirits was over. I was exhausted with hunger, want of rest . . . and was seized with a kind of apathy, or stupor, which rendered me indifferent to every thing—careless even, whether I lived or died."[38]

Already Ashbel was beginning to confront the moral dilemmas he faced as a soldier. His Presbyterian upbringing had taught him that killing was wrong, and that good Christians were to love thine enemy. His doubts only grew when he finally fired his gun at another human being. That momentous event occurred after several days of rest, when the militia learned that the British foraging party was finally ready to board its shallops and return to its base at Staten Island. A militia captain by the name of Outwater asked for volunteers to march to the Hackensack and try to cut off the boats as they made their way down the river to rendezvous with the frigate that would carry them to New York. About thirty men, including Ashbel, agreed to go.[39]

The militia unit was too late, though. As it approached the river, a family informed the men "that a number of boats had already proceeded down the stream, and that others were then in the act of passing." The militia hurried on and were mortified "to see one boat after another reach the protecting frigate." To move closer to the British entailed crossing a deep inlet that could be forded only by walking over a log. When about ten of the men refused to advance farther, the others left them behind. After Ashbel and the twenty men had crossed, "we saw a lagging boat, the last of the thieving squadron, beating down the stream against a head wind. We hurried forward, and took a position which proved to be within reach of the frigate's cannon." The men crouched down in a sedge and waited. When the boat was within range, they opened fire, with enough force to silence the guns aboard the boat. The boat then drifted to safety at the opposite shore. The frigate, meanwhile, fired its cannons, forcing Ashbel and the others to hide behind a large haystack. When the militia retreated behind the haystack, the British aboard the boat emerged from their hiding places and taunted the Americans, "revil[ing] us as a set of rascally rebels."[40]

The captain asked for volunteers to take "a good shot at those blackguards in the boat." Only Ashbel and one other man raised their hands—and Ashbel considered the man a miscreant who was trying to redeem himself after stealing "ornaments" from the women in the family who had helped the militia earlier: "I scorned to go in his company, but my pride would not permit me to retract my offer. I asked for the best gun in the company, as I did not think my own was good at a long shot." Ashbel selected an old hunter's gun that had a long barrel and headed toward the river, with the thief trailing behind. Ashbel's plan was "to creep into the sedge, sit on the ground, take good aim with my piece rested on my bended knee, and the moment after I had fired, to fall backward, and lie as close as to the ground as possible" in case the foragers returned fire. It went according to plan, with one problem: the soldiers aboard the boat were again hiding. Ashbel was forced to fire at the hay on the deck, "behind which I thought it most likely they were skulking." He doubted he hit anyone, and did not remember if the British returned fire. After lying still for some time, Ashbel crept out of the sedge and rejoined the others crouching behind the haystack.[41]

Later, however, Ashbel was mortified that he might have killed someone. Writing a letter to his son years later, Ashbel said that his anguish remained. "In my serious moments," he told his son, "I have frequently taken of my volunteering an attempt to take the life of an individual, on board" the shallop. "Never for a moment, have I doubted the lawfulness of defensive war," he continued. "And if ever there was a purely defensive war, that of our revolution, in my deliberate judgment, possessed this character." But reflecting on his acts, and studying "all the best writers on the subject," led Ashbel to conclude "that any act or operation not calculated to shorten the conflict, is unjustifiable." Ashbel believed that the incident fell into the latter category: Captain Outwater was wrong to order the attack on the boat because it "was completely out of our power, and the destroying of an individual could have produced no sensible influence in shortening the war of our revolution." No military commander would have agreed with him on this point; the militia's harassing of the British helped drive the latter from New Jersey. Nor would have many Protestants. As the research of historian Keith L. Griffin shows, the Reforming tradition permitted Christians to "wage war upon [a] just and necessary occasion." In *Observations*, Jacob stressed that rebellion was "just" when the ruling magistrate violated the will of the people. Still, in Ashbel's mind, Christians were permitted to fight only defensive wars; he was uncomfortable with offensive operations, and time did little to change his mind. The mature Ashbel harshly criticized the young Ashbel: "The part I acted, was rash, foolish and criminal—calling for regret and repentance." His participation led to him to seek "divine forgiveness" for trying to kill another person, and Ashbel believed that God had forgiven for this and "other transgressions."[42]

For Jacob, the distinction between offensive and defensive war may not have mattered by mid-1778. What loomed larger was the reality that Ashbel could be killed. It's also likely that the perniciousness of military life and its threat to Ashbel's religious foundation factored into Jacob's thinking. Three years into the war, Jacob apparently had seen enough. The result, according to Ashbel, was "that my father, with a view of keeping me from mingling too much in military affairs, devised a plan" to get his son out of military service. The Greens took advantage of a state law that "excused every teacher of a school of fifteen scholars from all military duty." So, after only one year of military service, the seventeen-year-old Ashbel began teaching first English and then classics at a school big enough to exempt him from further duty. The evasion embarrassed Ashbel in his later years. He tried to justify the family's actions by praising "our revolutionary patriots [for] provid[ing] for the instruction of the rising generation." But the flimsiness of this justification was obvious even to Ashbel, who claimed that he took advantage of the law only to avoid training exercises: "I still kept my soldierly equipments in constant preparation for actual hostility, and whenever an alarm occurred, I immediately dismissed my school and repaired to the place of rendezvous."[43]

Ashbel's service thus represented the outer limit of Jacob's revolutionary commitment. He was not willing to see his most promising son die for a cause that he had long championed. His partial retreat was also a sign of his growing disgust with the revolutionary movement: the looting, the harassing of loyalists, the weakening of religion. He had seen it all firsthand. On April 22, 1778, Jacob told the world just how disgusted he was, using a fast-day sermon to decry the selfishness engulfing the patriots.[44]

God, Green told his listeners, was angry with Americans because of their many sins, citing the "infidelity, profane cursing and swearing, [and] neglect of religion." For Green, these sins were "breaches of the first table of the law." They were, he explained, sins against the Lord. He conceded that many people don't see much harm in swearing, but for Jacob, that made swearing all the less excusable: "To affront God to his face by profaning his sacred name is shocking. . . . To dare the power and justice of God, and call for damnation on themselves and others, is folly and wickedness beyond what I am able to express." Equally upsetting to Green was that this sin was spreading at a time when it should have been lessening. "What an amazing increase of this sin in our land in a few years! What an increase of it in our army since it was first constituted!"[45]

The Revolution, in Jacob's view, was harming religion in another important way: people were ignoring the Sabbath. Worse, "the house of God, and the worship of God are despised." Likely recalling Ashbel's experiences with Continental officers, Green pointed out that "the man that conscientiously scruples to comply with fashionable vices is shunned, is treated with a sneer if not hooted at." Perhaps most dangerously of all, selfishness was increasing, a sin he carefully defined as "that which is opposite to public spiritedness and general benevolence. . . . A selfish person will promote his own private interest at the expence of the public. He will injure and oppress others to advance himself." This definition was a variation of Green's depiction of human behavior as self-love, which he described in his 1770 tract "An Humble Attempt to State the Controversy." With the war's arrival, Americans should have been working together for the common good. "But instead of a public spirit . . . in us all, there has been in many . . . the most insatiable avarice, and a greedy grasping at every thing within their reach." It was a sentiment that Washington, Paine, and other patriots would heartily agree with—they, too, bitterly decried the war profiteering and other failures of the civilian population.[46]

Green found the hypocrisy of his fellow revolutionaries especially galling: "Those among us who act upon the principle of getting what they can from others, by taking advantage of their wants and weakness, are practicing the same thing which we are now opposing in Great-Britain." They were, in other words, using the war to pursue their own interests, to "extort" from the public that which they wanted: "These extortioners and oppressors among ourselves, would if circumstances concurred and favoured, act as cruelly as the British ministry has done." God, he warned, was watching this behavior and weighing it against "the conduct of our British oppressors." And he did not like what he saw: "God with indignation beholds our selfish, avaricious, oppressive practice: And we may well suppose that for this, among other evils, he corrects us by continuing the war upon us." It was a shocking statement in many ways—Green was in essence saying that the Lord wanted the war to drag on to teach its participants a lesson; there would be no victory against the British until the Americans changed their ways: "Let the inhabitants of the land fear and take warning; repent and reform that we may not continue under the divine displeasure, and fall under still heavier judgments."[47]

Green delivered a dark, damning sermon—one of the most severe in his forty-five-year career as a minister. It captured perfectly his foul mood after nearly three tumultuous years of war. The revolutionaries were failing, and the moral reformation was sputtering. Yet Green did not believe the cause was lost. He still was hopeful the Americans were going to win. Most of all, he still believed in the goodness of the Lord and felt that God was on the side of the Americans. "God is yet waiting to be gracious," Green told his listeners as he wound up the sermon. "He deals with us as with a people whom he designs to save and not destroy." Despite all their shortcomings, Americans retained a measure of goodwill with God: "He remarkably appears for us, and prevents our ruin; yea, gives us advantages against our enemies." God, in the end, was testing the Americans—they have to persevere, to overcome the challenges they were facing on the battlefield and off it. Or as Green put it, "Things are yet in our favour. Though the war is protracted, and we are so long held under the rod, yet all things shall be for the best in the end. Nothing less than what we suffered would have done for us."[48]

The cause remained glorious, and Jacob Green had unfinished business as a reformer.

### The Loyalist Down the Road:
### Thomas Bradbury Chandler in Exile

It took about ten days for the *Exeter* to reach the Grand Banks, where the weather and the seas turned "rough," in Chandler's words. The Atlantic was so stormy that the passengers and crew were unable to fish. It was turning piercingly cold, anyway, and being on deck, exposed to the driving winds and pitching sea, must have been uncomfortable. Chandler described seeing "a large Island of Ice, by which time we experienced the Weather to be almost intolerably cold." By June 24, a month after setting sail from Sandy Hook, the passengers were anxiously scanning the horizons in hopes of spotting Ireland's coast, "but [we] were disappointed, owing chiefly, as we afterwards judged, to the bad Steerage of the Ship." Another six days passed until land was indeed near, when the wayward *Exeter* approached Lundy, an island about twelve miles off the southern English coast, at 4:00 in the morning. At 10:00 a.m. that day, a pilot boarded the ship and guided it up the English Channel within, by Chandler's reckoning, a mile of the Devonshire coast. Although it was now summer, the weather remained unforgiving—Chandler lamented in his diary that it was "blustering and stormy."

On July 2, the *Exeter* anchored at Kingroad, and Chandler and Myles Cooper—an ally in the bishop's cause—scurried off, breakfasting at the White-Hart Inn in Bristol and attending services at St. Stephen's, a fourteenth-century church on the River Frome. Chandler's early weeks in England were spent playing tourist. One of his first stops was the British Museum, where he admired the Magna Carta. He also dined at St. James Palace, a castle-like structure with gothic towers built by Henry VIII in the 1530s that by Chandler's time had become the principal London residence of the monarchy. Chandler sat at a table with the king's chaplains, where "it was there asserted, and universally admitted, that no less than 2,000 Stage-Coaches set out from London every Monday, and that the Number of Horses belonging to the City is 70,000; and that there is a Clock in the Palace, which requires winding up but once a Year."

During these early months in exile, Chandler experienced London's seamier side—his pocket was picked three times. The first time, the thief made off with a handkerchief, even though "it was closely buttoned"; the same thing happened again only five days later, despite Chandler's vigilance. The Lord's house proved to be no sanctuary, either. In March 1776, a pickpocket divested him of his watch as he stood among the crowd at the church door. Chandler was so upset at this loss that he shelled out three shillings to run an advertisement offering a reward of two guineas for its return. Not that he was under any illusions about its return. He suspected "a Gang of Villains" was responsible for the theft, for "another Gentleman at the same Time and Place lost his Watch, while he was standing with the Plate to collect the charitable Contributions of the People."

Chandler's emotions during this difficult time ran the gamut. He missed his family terribly and was bitter at the rebels (as he always called them) for forcing him to flee Elizabeth Town. He especially missed his beloved Polly, the youngest daughter who was a mere seven months old in 1775 when he hurriedly departed from Elizabeth Town. In a poignant letter Chandler wrote in early 1779, he lamented that "she was but a Green Gosling when I left her; and my Absence has been so long that, on the first Sight, I should probably not know her." For this doleful state of affairs, he gave "thanks to those dear creatures, the American Rebels, and *our* americanized Generals! But this is too tender a subject."

Yet Chandler remained busy and partook of all that London had to offer. The intellectual atmosphere was especially invigorating. One of his first stops during his exile was Oxford. He wandered the city's streets, visited the study of philosopher Roger Bacon (who died in ca. 1292), and explored all the colleges, making stops at the Observatory and "the grand Library" of Christ's Church. Chandler got to mingle with Oxford's dons, attending one sumptuous party that took place on a "grand Barge, and [we] were attended by another, containing Servants, Provisions, Liquors, &c. for the Company." He haunted many a library and art gallery, perusing the books and examining the collections of the statues from antiquity. When he left London in 1785, he needed twenty-two boxes to transport all his books home. Chandler, who earned a nice pension from the Crown as a reward for his loyalty, indulged his taste for the refined as well. He bought, among many other things, a mahogany case containing forty-eight knives and forks with silver handles, and later added "a compleat set of Tea china, blue and gilt."

Lonely as he was for his family, Chandler was never alone. He made the daily rounds, visiting fellow American exiles, government officials, Anglican leaders, and others. A Friday in August 1775 was typical: "Dined with the Archbishop of Lambeth, in Company with Charles Townsend Esqr., one of the Lords of the Treasury, &c. Was treated with the most cordial Kindness, was shewn by his Grace all his Gardens, and by his Lady all the rooms belonging to the Palace." As the passage indicates, the visits were both social and business. Chandler gave British officials his take on American affairs and tried to glean as much information as he could about British war policy, which he then passed on to loyalists in America. As always, Chandler was not shy about sharing his opinions. In consultation with several others, Chandler developed his own peace plan and managed to obtain an audience with Lord Germaine on December 14, 1775, after the latter was appointed to the superintendency of the American department. Chandler congratulated Germaine on his new job and said he hoped the latter would be able to restore "Peace and Tranquility to that unhappy country." With a touch of self-importance, Chandler noted in his diary that he was appointed "spokesman" by the American gentlemen in London.

Despite having been forced to leave America, Chandler retained his confidence that British arms would prevail over the rebels. In 1777, he implored Samuel Seabury, who was based in British-occupied New York City, to keep his confidence that the king's forces would triumph: "For God's Sake, keep up your Spirits a little longer . . . every Thing will end well at last. The next campaign will crush the Rebellion, in all Probability. Another large Army is now going over from hence."

Chandler also had a great deal of confidence in John Burgoyne, believing the general's Canadian-based army possessed enough men and arms to prevail in its invasion of New York State. Burgoyne's surrender at Saratoga in October 1777 thus came as a great shock. Chandler got word of the disaster sometime in November or December, and "we were all struck into Confusion by an Arrival from Quebec, with an Account . . . of Gen. Burgoyne's having been obliged to surrender his Army to the Rebel Forces. Although we were apprehensive of the great Difficulties and Hardships our galiant General had to overcome we were not prepared for the News of such a compleat overthrow."

The setback made him apprehensive, but his optimism was mostly unshaken. Even the Americans' alliance with hated France in early 1778 did not greatly worry him. "As to a war with France, it is generally expected, and we are not badly prepared for it," Chandler wrote in a June 1778 letter to Seabury. He also categorically rejected any talk "of nominal or *real* Independency" for the rebels. Most right-thinking people in Britain believed that the army could still dispatch the upstart Americans, and Chandler agreed. But beneath the brave talk, Chandler was not so serene. He concluded his letter to Seabury by confessing, "For my Part, I have done with forming Opinions upon any public Affairs, having been so often baffled and defeated in my fairest Expectations."[49]

# PART III

*Reformers on the Home Front*

# *9*

---

## *Crusader*

Disappointed yet determined, Green saw 1779 and 1780 as a time of possibility. Like the rest of the American public, he was war-weary. The fighting was never ending, and the British showed no signs that they were ready to quit. (In London, Thomas Bradbury Chandler was exhorting the administration to squash any talk of peace with the rebels and "to fight it out" to the end.) The Continental Army was steadily becoming more professional, but it still lacked the ability to deliver a knockout blow to the enemy. Worse, its hardships continued, even worsened. The national government's finances were in a state of near collapse by late 1779, and the Continental Congress lacked the resources to pay the troops and to keep them clothed and fed. With virtually no money for supplies, procurement officers could only issue promissory certificates to farmers and shopkeepers, who often refused to sell to the army. When George Washington and nearly eight thousand troops entered winter quarters in Morris County in early December 1779, the men went hungry and froze in the cold—during, as cruel fate would have it, one of the harshest, snowiest winters on record. The troops, as a result, endured their most miserable winter yet, shivering at a mountain redoubt outside of Morristown that exceeded Valley Forge in suffering.

A few miles away in Hanover, the Green family was stoically dealing with these latest calamities. Ashbel was still studying. Pierson was still in the Continental Army. Calvin was still learning farming. Their father, though, was strangely energized despite the sputtering Revolution and its dispirited patriots. His blistering fast-day sermon, delivered on April 22, 1778, and published in 1779, was cathartic for him. After cataloging the patriots' many failings in his sermon, and after watching the financial chaos—empty treasury, depreciating currency, rampant inflation—continue into the new year, Green embarked on a grand program of reform that he saw as essential to saving the Revolution and society. One cause was fairly obvious. Green railed against the moral stain known as slavery. He had for years opposed human bondage and took a swipe at it in his 1776 tract, *Observations on the Reconciliation of Great-Britain and the Colonies*, and in his fast-day sermon.

Green's second cause was somewhat more surprising. He wrote a series of newspaper essays urging reform of the fast-sinking continental currency and offering his thoughts on the public debt. Although *Observations* touched on economics, Green had never devoted an essay to such an arcane worldly subject. That he did so in late 1779 and the early 1780s says a great deal about how politicized he was becoming four years into the Revolution, for in the prewar years his primary concern was reforming people's religious behavior—grasping for wealth was wrong; the Lord should come first.[1]

By 1779, Green's concerns were far wider. The survival of an infant United States was at stake, and its disastrous finances could bring the whole tottering house down. Hence, Green offered a detailed, sophisticated plan to halt the depreciation of the currency. Such a reform would strengthen the national government and give it the means to adequately finance the military effort. But reforming the currency also had a moral and religious dimension for him. The rapid depreciation of paper money was harming the most vulnerable members of society—the widows and orphans. Worse, in Green's view, it was enriching speculators and crass moneymen and encouraging people to grasp for wealth. Thus, restoring America's finances required a moral and religious reformation—people would have to start saving, which would require them to act less selfishly. Lastly, Green was concerned about the political implications of a depreciating currency. The worsening economic conditions for farmers and tradesmen threatened American liberties. He proposed a comprehensive solution to these complex, interrelated developments. The currency must be reformed, and farmers and tradesmen—the backbone of American society and the sinew of its democratic system—had to stop falling into debt and becoming dependent on the wealthy.

In formulating these views, Green once again drew on long years of study and observation. As a child living in the Massachusetts Bay Colony, he had witnessed firsthand the havoc that a depreciated currency could wreak. When his father died, Green was left an orphan and his mother a widow. Young Jacob inherited some land, but its value had depreciated by the time he was ready to go to Harvard. In Ashbel's recollection, the depreciation was searing. "[My father's] experience in early life had taught him a lesson on this subject which he well remembered. His paternal inheritance had been materially diminished, by the depreciation of the money denominated 'Old Tenor,' in the then province of Massachusetts Bay." According to Ashbel, Jacob was also upset that some of his friends were duped into "selling their farms and houses, on the offer of what appeared to be an enormous price." These childhood wounds were apparent in his newspaper essays: when Green discussed the victims of depreciation, widows and orphans topped his list. He felt real anger at the plight of these "helpless persons." Equally upsetting to him was that moneymen were taking advantage of them. In Letter I he called them, among other things, "engrossers, forestallers, extortioners, and avaricious traders."[2]

Throughout the eighteenth century, all the colonies had struggled with a money shortage, largely because of British mercantilist policy. London banned the coining of colonial money. In the 1660s, Massachusetts was the first colony to suggest starting a private bank that would issue paper money; in 1681 the bank opened, only to quickly fail. Barred from coining money, most colonies resorted to land banks: a borrower would secure a loan by using land as collateral. The land bank, in turn, would issue the loan through bills of credit that functioned as paper money. The system actually worked well in New Jersey. The first land bank opened in 1723, and it loaned 40,000 pounds over a twelve-year period. Things went so well that the colony opened a second loan office in 1733 and a third in 1735. But British merchants hated the land banks, because they did not want to accept colonial paper bills as legal tender, and the Crown repeatedly barred New Jersey from opening any more loan offices. Then, in 1764, Parliament passed the Currency Act. Decrying "the great quantities of paper bills" in the colonies, the act banned the use of bills of credit as legal tender. With no specie supporting the bills of credit, the colonies' paper money quickly depreciated. Debtors, including many small farmers, wanted to pay their debts with the bills; merchants opposed that.[3]

Things got no better once the colonies declared independence. Lacking both reliable revenues and the power to tax, the Continental Congress had taken to printing paper money to pay its bills. The amount at first was relatively small: $2 million in June 1775, but the emissions quickly soared as the war got under way in earnest in 1776. By the end of that year, $25 million was in circulation. The value of the currency, which was not backed by taxes or specie, began its alarming drop in value. By 1779, when Green was ready to take up currency reform, the situation had escalated into a full-blown crisis. Congress had doubled spending in 1777, had tripled it in 1778, and was spending even greater sums in 1779—a staggering $10 million a month. (Net new emissions totaled almost $200 million in the 1775–79 period.) The combination of depreciating dollars and rising war spending sent prices soaring—more than fivefold in many places. A chastened Continental Congress sought to defend its behavior in the opening month of 1779: it pointed out in a circular letter that "necessity" forced it to emit paper money, because the ongoing war required prodigious sums of money to wage. Still, Congress conceded that "the paper currency multiplied beyond what was competent for the purposes of a circulating medium." It tried to reassure the states that it was taking steps to correct the problems, and it again urged the states to contribute taxes to the national confederation.[4]

Green made his case for currency reform in five influential essays in the *New-Jersey Journal* that, according to Ashbel Green, "were republished in almost all the newspapers at that time in our country." They attracted enough attention that a satirist in the *Independent Ledger* of Massachusetts mentioned Green's work while poking fun at all the schemes to reform the continental currency. Green's first letter appeared on November 16, 1779, and he composed it in response to a circular letter that the Continental Congress had sent to the thirteen states two months earlier, on September 13. The congressional letter blamed the depreciation on two interrelated causes—one natural, one artificial. The former was simple, the letter declared. Congress had printed too much paper money. The latter was "a more serious subject," as the circular letter delectably phrased it, but it came down to the reality that the people had lost faith that paper money would keep its value. The lack of faith, in turn, caused the bills to depreciate even further. Congress estimated that $160 million in bills was circulating by 1779, but that the government had collected only $3 million in taxes. It decided to cap emissions at $200 million, leaving the government just $40 million more to emit in paper money. In a burst of good intentions, Congress vowed to release this remaining $40 million only when "absolutely necessary for public exigencies." It again pleaded with the states to meet its obligations, and it resolved that any emissions above the $40 million would be funded through taxes.[5]

Green was unimpressed with this plan, although he was his usual tactful self, praising the overall letter as "excellent." But he allowed that the letter "contains some things not fully understood, and some things respecting which the public would be glad to query." He first disputed Congress's somewhat convoluted distinction between natural and artificial causes of the depreciation. The delegates had tried to explain the concept by writing, "Supposing . . . that 30,000,000 was necessary for a circulating medium, and that 160,000,000 had issued, the natural depreciation is but little more than as five to one; but the actual depreciation exceeds that proportion, and that excess is artificial." Green cut through the legislative-ese and said that the excessive emission of bills was the sole problem, although he agreed that the subsequent depreciation did cause people to lose confidence in the bills. Green then honed in on the underlying problem—bills not backed by specie were destined to fail. "Hard money is the soul and spirit of paper," he observed, "for as the spirit keeps the body moving, and as the body without the spirit is dead so is paper without hard money."[6]

In his second letter, which was published in the same issue of the *New-Jersey Journal* as the first essay, Green explored the seemingly innocuous question of whether it was possible for the continental dollars to regain their original value. Congress and other economic thinkers were focused on how to halt the depreciation of paper money and return the bills to their original value—laudable goals all. But Green warned that returning the continental currency to its original value would carry serious drawbacks. Speculators at the top could be unfairly enriched, while the small debtors (middling farmers and tradesmen) at the bottom could be badly hurt. Speculators had "amassed vast sums of continental money" for practically nothing, in hopes that the United States would someday redeem the money at full, or close to full, value. And, for Green, the hoarding of money for speculative purposes raised a fundamental question: was it fair to heavily tax the country for up to twenty years so that these speculators can "receive four, eight, fifteen, or twenty times as much as they gave for their money?"[7]

Conversely, he wondered, what would happen to the ordinary citizen if the money were to be fully redeemed? Letter II walked the reader through the complexities of this problem and described the devastating effects of inflation. Green drew on an example that everyone in an agrarian society could easily grasp: a farmer buys a farmstead that was worth 1,000 pounds seven years before depreciation set in, but because of the falling value of money he is forced to purchase it for 8,000 pounds. This farmer pays 6,000 pounds upfront to the seller and gives bond for the remaining 2,000 pounds. His taxes, meanwhile, have soared because of inflation—the value of his livestock and other movables rose to nearly 5,000 pounds from a prewar value of only 300 pounds. The farmer struggles to pay his higher taxes, to support his family, and to pay off his bond. When he falls behind on his payments, "he is arrested for the two thousand pounds, which he owes; his farm is seized and sold." But his problems are just beginning if the value of the currency is returned to its original value: the farm he bought for 8,000 pounds would fetch only the original price of 1,000 pounds, and the same thing would happen with the sale of his estate—it would produce only the pre-inflation value of 300 pounds. The farmer is left bankrupt; "his farm itself is gone; his moveable estate is gone; and he still owes seven hundred pounds good money," Green explained. "In some such ways must multitudes unavoidably be ruined if the money is made good."[8]

This concern neatly framed Green's solution to the currency problem, which he spelled out in his third letter. Green wanted a controlled depreciation that would protect the interests of the small debtor while reviving the finances of the national government. He urged the Congress to emit $10 million in new money (a later letter amended that figure to $15 million) and use half of that amount to gradually retire the old bills at a rate of twenty to one. Congress should impose taxes to cover the remaining debts and ensure the soundness of the new emission, but Green wanted any taxes to be levied fairly and equitably. And that meant, Green reasoned, finding a balance between taxing and funding—that is, obtaining a loan in hard money from a European country. His overall concern was, again, to protect the interests of the common citizens who had sacrificed so much during the war. Excessive taxation would be ruinous and unfair to them, he warned: "How unjust, how cruel would it be after the war is over to tax our soldiers, those orphans, and other persons mentioned, who have done so much already?"[9]

In these five essays and three subsequent ones on taxes, several important themes emerged. One was Green's linking of private behavior and public virtue. Frugality by individuals would allow the larger community (the nation) to pay off its wartime debts. Indeed, Green saw farmers and tradesmen as key: "Those are the most useful members of society." They filled the battalions that formed the core of the army; they grew the crops that fed the troops and the civilian population; they manned the forges that made the muskets and the cannons that the troops fired at the enemy. And these farmers and tradesmen were the ones who would pay the bulk of the taxes that would retire the public debt and allow the United States to put its finances on a sound footing.[10]

From this premise came a second, even Jeffersonian theme: the independent yeomen and tradesmen would allow democracy in the new nation to flourish. Green's essays, as well as his two letters on liberty, dripped with contempt for the rich and were wary of allowing the poor to vote: "For those that [are] very opulent, and those that are dependently poor, will in general rather destroy than preserve the freedom of elections, and the freedom of our country." This was a classic Whig notion, with an American twist: only those with sufficient property can make informed, independent decisions at the ballot box. Classical republican theory had long held that the poor would be too beholden to their betters to participate in the life of the polity; their lords would tell them how to vote. But classical Whig theory had also long held that only the better sort possessed the qualities to act virtuously on behalf of the community. Green scathingly rejected that reasoning. In 1780, nearly two decades before the Jeffersonian party had emerged, he was placing his faith not in the wellborn but in the middling farmer and tradesman. These common folk, and not the elite, were the best protectors of freedom.[11]

Green expressed this theme most baldly in his two letters on liberty, which appeared at the same time as his last two essays on the public debt. "The very rich and the very poor, will both conspire to destroy freedom of elections; the rich by aspiring, and the poor by being dependent upon them," he wrote in his second letter on liberty, which was published on May 10, 1780. "When persons are so poor as to become dependent, their freedom of voting at elections is gone." Remaining independent required diligence and hard work on the part of the yeomen. Green's essays stressed that farmers must live within their means and avoid debts. Should a large number of them fall into bankruptcy, "it would be an unspeakable damage to our country. I would therefore intreat my fellow countrymen to preserve their station, live frugal, and not involve themselves in private debts, nor bring themselves into a dependence upon others." In his second letter on liberty, Green stated that he would welcome "something like an equality of estate and property"—a notion that would be considered communistic today—because it would best preserve civil liberty. But Green was no dewy-eyed idealist. He quickly added that such equality of property "cannot be expected." Instead, he preached repeatedly in many forums—newspaper essays, pamphlets, the pulpit—on the need for "common people" to maintain their independence by living frugally and virtuously. People needed to work hard and live disciplined lives. It was, he believed, the key to the health of the souls of both the nation and the individual. To reinforce this theme, Green signed his essays "Eumenes." In *Plutarch's Lives*, luxury and ease corrupt the Macedonians and lead to the downfall of their armies and their renowned general, Eumenes, who commanded Greek and Macedonian troops fighting on behalf of Alexander the Great's son.[12]

Green's essays sparked a spirited debate in the *New-Jersey Journal*. One letter writer grasped the social implications of Green's plan to reform the currency through a controlled depreciation. "It breathes forth strongly the breath of liberty and justice to the oppressed," "A Friend to Liberty" exclaimed in the December 14, 1779, issue. He found it "reasonable" to "give to everyone the true value of his money. . . . By this method the truly helpless widow and orphans, and other innocent sufferers, will be redressed—our public expences lessened and brought within our power."[13]

But most letter writers took issue with Eumenes. "Reason" wondered "what would foreigners and posterity say when told, that Congress, to prosecute the war, issued bills of credit to be of *equal value with gold and silver*, but in a short time thereafter, decreed that *one silver*, or new *paper dollar should be the full value of twenty dollars*, for which they gave their obligation?" Reason's criticism was mild compared with that of "Standfast," who took on both Eumenes and "True Patriot," an essayist for the *New-Jersey Gazette*. "I should suppose [the essays] were wrote at the instigation of the British emissaries, had I no evidence of their proceeding from reverend heads, whose mouths are daily employed in petitioning the Almighty in fervent prayer for the establishment and welfare of these United States. Their plans of taxation are unprecedented, and evidently calculated to ruin us." Standfast believed that the two "reverend heads" were out of their element. "They may, for ought I know, be well enough acquainted with church government," he said, but he was sure "they have very little knowledge of the government of the states, and the principles of national policy." Standfast wondered whether Eumenes had bothered to read the Articles of Confederation and Congress's letter to the states. He found Green's plan misguided and dangerous, because it was "imposed upon the public under the specious pretence of doing justice to individuals. I confess there is [some] injustice in having twenty dollars made good in the hands of the person who received them only for one dollar," he continued. "Yet, if we extend our ideas as far as that period, we shall find, that he will pay nearly as much of his money out of his hands in order to redeem it in the present mode of taxation, as in any other way." Standfast in this letter and one of March 29, 1780, defended the Congress and "its superior wisdom," and he beseeched the public to stand fast and support "due authority." He had no doubt that Congress's plan "will, in the end, prove fully effectual in raising the value of our currency."[14]

"A Farmer," writing in the *New-Jersey Gazette*, shared Standfast's skepticism of the various reform proposals floating about and instead placed his faith in the Congress: "Hence then, my brave fellow-citizens and farmers, let us rely on the virtue of our rulers; let us cheerfully comply with the requisitions of Congress; let us no longer heighten our calamity by furnishing the means by which we suffer."[15]

Green had anticipated these criticisms and knew that his questioning of Congress would generate controversy. He tried to head it off in Letter I by arguing for the right of a citizen to question his rulers. "We venerate the Congress," he began, "but they know, and we all know, that their conduct is to be looked into. . . . Every friend to his country has a right, with modesty and humility, to query and propose any thing for the public good; especially respecting our currency." As for the personal attacks on his "reverend head," he let them pass without comment—except for one. A letter by "Unshaken" got under Green's skin and prompted him to append a postscript to Letter V that opened with a series of insults: Green dismissed Unshaken's essay as "so weak a performance [that it] cannot make any considerable impression on persons of sense." He went on to say that "most of his arguments (if any thing he has advanced may be called argument) are such feminine ones, as Deane Swift says, directly tend against the cause they were designed to defend." Yet Green *did* respond to Unshaken's arguments, because this critic had raised a serious question that was on the minds of nearly everyone: what was to stop the next round of emissions from depreciating? One correspondent in the *Gazette* put it well. After the Congress calls in "all the money, and give[s] in return one dollar for twenty . . . what is to be done then? Is the same scene of iniquity to be again repeated—are thousands again to be ruined by a second inundation of paper money?" Green forcefully said no. The key to his plan, he reiterated, was to keep the new round of emissions to $15 million and to obtain a small loan of hard currency: "I think I may defy Unshaken, or any body else, to produce an instance where paper money has depreciated, if there was a proper quantity of hard money circulating among it, and where the authority of the whole State was engaged to support the credit of the paper money." In other words, paper money would keep its value if it was issued in a limited amount and was backed by specie and taxes.[16]

Green's commonsense approach was clearly stated and well thought out, and it found support in other forums. The feeling was growing throughout the nation that the government would have to raise taxes to head off depreciation and to better support the ill-clad and poorly supplied army. Certainly the desire for proper revenues had plenty of backing within the Congress. Its circular letters constantly begged the states to meet their financial obligations. But the idea of raising taxes was also gaining support outside the legislative chamber. Thomas Paine came up with one of the most creative cases for raising taxes. In *The Crisis Extraordinary*, published on October 6, 1780, in Philadelphia, he pointed out through elaborate calculations that Americans' tax burden was far lower than that of their English brethren: the British tax rate was "above eleven times heavier than the taxes we now pay." The Crown, Paine claimed, went to war so it could impose the same burdensome taxes on Americans. Thus, in Paine's view, the stakes were quite high in year 5 of the Revolution. If Britain defeated their former subjects on the battlefield, the Americans could expect to see their taxes soar. That being the case, wouldn't it be "best to raise two millions to defend the country and govern it ourselves, and only three quarters of a million afterwards, or pay six millions to have it conquered, and let the enemy govern it?" he asked.[17]

In New Jersey, a True Patriot was also beating the drum for tough measures. Like Eumenes, he wanted the old paper money retired at a rate of twenty to one, with new emissions backed by a combination of hard money obtained through loans and taxes. (He also called for price regulations, which Eumenes dismissed as impracticable.) Yet the idea of raising taxes was particularly unpopular in New Jersey because of the state's significant economic weaknesses. Unlike Virginia and other states, it had no western lands to sell. And unlike New York and Pennsylvania, it had no thriving ports from which to collect import duties. The government could tax but two groups—its farmers and artisans—and these two groups vociferously complained that they were already shouldering too much of the financial burden.[18]

As the debate grew louder and the financial crisis worsened, the Congress in mid-March 1780 decided it could not dither any longer. It voted to retire the old bills in stages and to issue new ones at a "proportion of one to twenty"—similar to what Eumenes recommended. To head off depreciation of the new bills, the Congress tried several expedients. It decreed that the bills would "be redeemable in specie, within six years after the present," and would bear an annual interest rate of 5 percent. It voted to retrieve the old bills through taxation at the rate of $15 million a month through April 1781. Simultaneously, it would hold the new emission to $10 million, exactly what Eumenes recommended in Letter III (although he went with $15 million in Letter IV). But lacking coercive powers of taxation, the Congress was again forced to rely on the voluntary cooperation of the states if this latest plan was to work. The Continental Congress would not destroy the old bills until the states paid their taxes, and it would emit no new bills until the taxes were paid. The timing of the emission would thus depend on the states— the congressional act decreed "that the said new bills shall be struck under the direction of the Board of Treasury, in due proportion for each State, according to their said monthly [tax] quotas." In all, the Congress planned to send 60 percent of the new money to the states, and it asked them to use the bills to meet the supply requests of the Continental Army.[19]

As Ashbel Green recognized, the plan was strikingly similar to what his father had recommended. The old money would be pulled out of circulation in stages. New money would replace it, also in stages. The bills would be backed by taxes, and their emission would be limited to $10 million. More-over, these emissions would replace the old at a ratio of one to twenty—one new bill for twenty old ones. The plan drew praise from many quarters, including from a surprising source—Unshaken, although he could not resist taking one final dig at Eumenes. "By this plan," Unshaken wrote in a short letter to the *New-Jersey Journal*, "public faith is preserved, the extremes pro-posed by the tribes of scribblers, avoided, and not withstanding Eumenes's prophecy to the contrary."[20]

Green did not comment directly on Congress's latest plan. Instead, in three essays he wrote after the passage of the Currency Act, he looked ahead to the day when the war would be over and the United States would need to pay down the public debt. Understanding that Congress's call for additional taxes would be unpopular, especially in his home state, Green used these essays to argue for a solid financial base to pay off the public debt. But in publishing the essays, Green was also returning to his favorite theme: if a disciplined government was to retire its debts, it would need a disciplined citizenry living within its means and willing to pay higher taxes. These three essays, in other words, once again brought together the political and the religious.[21]

One fear of Green's was that prewar spending habits would quickly return when the Revolution ended. "Should the war cease, we must not expect to flow in ease and luxury immediately," he warned. "We must not expect the principal advantages of this contest to come in one day." In Letter I on the public debts and taxes, which was published in the *New-Jersey Journal* on April 5, 1780, Green stressed that the wartime sacrifices were not yet over: "Taxes must be as high as industrious frugal farmers and tradesmen can well pay, without reducing them so as to prevent their managing business to advantage." Yet the founding generation must be willing to sacrifice, he maintained—it had an obligation to itself and to posterity to sacrifice so it could afford the tax burden and lower the public debts: "We must be very frugal, live as much as possible within ourselves, live low . . . not to superfluities, but to pay our public debts, which we have necessarily contracted by the war." In his second letter, Green conceded that paying down the debt would not be easy. In fact, he warned that the popular measures—selling western lands, confiscating loyalist estates—would go only so far. A broad and comprehensive tax program would be needed, he said, and farmers and tradesmen would have to make significant changes in their lifestyle if they were going to be able to handle this burden. Frugality, in other words, was badly needed. "We must . . . be laborious, be frugal, above all be virtuous," Eumenes recommended. "If we abstain from excesses and extravagancies; if we shun vice in general and live in love and equity among ourselves; if we fear God and serve our generation according to his will, we need not fear any difficulties."[22]

In these three essays in 1780 and 1782, Green anticipated the charged debate that was about to explode in New Jersey in the mid-1780s over taxes and currency reform: should the state heavily tax its citizens and rely only on hard money? Or, with the postwar economy struggling, should it lower taxes and issue more paper bills? Abraham Clark, a Presbyterian layman from Elizabeth Town who was a longtime member of the state legislature and the Continental Congress, was a kindred spirit of the parson from Hanover. Like Green, Clark championed the cause of the debtor class and attacked moneymen and speculators. When the war ended in 1783, he pushed legislation to help the farmers and tradesmen in debt and fought hard for the issuing of more paper money. Opposing him was, among others, Governor William Livingston. Livingston saw debtors and paper money as the biggest threats to the state's economic well-being; in typically sarcastic language for this longtime polemicist, he argued that the state should retire its paper bills and replace them with hard money. For Livingston, debtors were lazy ne'er-do-wells who were simply trying to get out of paying their taxes to the state and their debts to their creditors. Clark countered with a pamphlet that echoed much of what Green had argued several years earlier—the bulwarks of a successful republican society were the farmers and mechanics, and currency and tax policies must be designed to protect their interests.[23]

Green stayed on the sidelines for this debate, which largely ended in May 1786 when the legislature approved a bill that revived the old land-bank schemes from the colonial period. By 1786, Green had moved on to other issues and causes. He likely was satisfied with his essays—he had said his piece and said it well. Indeed, Green's arguments were far more nuanced than those coming from the pens of Livingston and Clark. Green's essays on taxes sought a middle ground that would protect the interests of debtors and creditors: he argued strenuously that *everyone* should pay their fair share of taxes, but he warned against imposing excessive burdens on farmers and other debtors. Yet he would have agreed with Livingston that the reluctance to pay taxes could be the sign of a moral failing. But unlike Livingston, Green understood that ordinary citizens made real sacrifices during the war and that most were not merely shirking their postwar responsibilities.

The religious dimensions were much more important to Green than they were to Clark and Livingston—for Green, of course, it always came back to religion, even for worldly subjects such as taxes and currency. Viewing societal challenges holistically, he saw the problems with currency as yet another opportunity to share his message about the need for a reformation in behavior. In his final published essay on taxes, which appeared on June 19, 1782, Green compared the patriots' ordeals during the war to that of the Israelites in the wilderness. Like the Israelites, Americans had to rise to the occasion and meet their obligations. "In a little while after our proper exertion we shall rest in our good land like Israel in Egypt after their tedious journey in the wilderness," he explained. "God has favoured us and smiled upon us through the war, and shall we now provoke and tempt him, by our reluctance and unwillingness to pay our taxes which are the means to accomplish the end we desire."[24]

As important as finance was to Green's program to reform society, a second crusade loomed even larger for him—eradicating the horror of slavery. It was an issue that had been bothering him for years. Slaveholding was not only common in New England, it was common among Congregational ministers. Many a pastor, including Jonathan Edwards, had one or more slaves working as servants in their household. So did John Pierson, Jacob's father-in-law and a retired Presbyterian minister, who was living at the parsonage with the Green family. In a 1771 estate inventory, Pierson was listed as owning one slave, a child. And Jacob Green himself briefly owned a slave in the early 1750s. It was not a happy experience. A cash-strapped Green had gone into debt to buy the slave, only for the slave to die in 1756 when "I lost my negro, in a manner that was affecting." He apparently never owned a slave again. Ashbel, who was born in 1762, six years after the slave's death, never mentioned that his father was a slave owner, either because he did not know or because it was too embarrassing to admit. Instead, he wrote that "it is among [my] earliest recollections . . . that [Jacob] had a perfect abhorrence of African slavery, derived from parental influence."[25]

Clearly, Green had become uncomfortable with the practice by the late 1760s and early 1770s; the independence movement then helped turn him into an abolitionist. Green had no doubts that the British were seeking to enslave the colonists. Further, like other Calvinists such as Samuel Hopkins and Levi Hart, he had no doubts that a freedom-loving people had no business enslaving other human beings. In *Observations on the Reconciliation of Great-Britain, and the Colonies*, Green took time out from criticizing king and Parliament to condemn the hypocrisy of slaveholding among Whigs. America, he noted, professed to be "an asylum for all noble spirits and sons of liberty from all parts of the world." Yet the colonies—north and south alike—allowed slavery, and they continued the practice even after declaring independence from the Crown. "What a dreadful absurdity!" Green lamented. "What a shocking consideration, that people who are so strenuously contending for liberty, should at the same time encourage and promote slavery!"[26]

Green resumed his attack two years later, when he delivered his hard-hitting fast-day sermon in spring of 1778 that lambasted the revolutionaries' sinful behavior. Slaveholding, he told his congregation, was "one of the great and crying evils among us." As in *Observations*, Green noted the hypocrisy of revolutionaries who were fighting for political equality to deny freedom to Africans and their descendants. The sin of slavery, he argued, was as great as the sin of Britain denying America its liberties—in fact, in some ways it was greater. Britain was merely *attempting* to deprive Americans of their liberties; "we in America have a long time been in actual violation of it." In decrying slavery and its attendant cruelties, Green argued for the humanity of blacks. "Is not the hard yoke of slavery felt by negroes as well as by white people? Are they not fond of liberty as well as others of the human race?" he pointedly asked. Freedom, he continued, was "the natural unalienable right of all."[27]

But, Green said, slaveholding was more than hypocritical; it subjected the young United States to ridicule: "What foreign nation can believe that we who so loudly complain of Britain's attempts to oppress and enslave us, are, at the same time, voluntarily holding multitudes of fellow creatures in abject slavery." Worse, it subjected Americans to the ridicule of someone far more important—God. Holding a fellow human being in bondage was so cruel and inhumane, Green said, that it constituted "the most crying sin in our land" and risked bringing down the wrath of the Almighty. Slaveholding itself also imperiled the war effort—Americans could lose if they did not get their house in order.[28]

Green rejected slaveholders' contentions that the Bible condoned their owning of Africans. The Bible, he maintained, clearly condemned the holding of slaves: "Apostle Paul ranks men stealers (which is the sin we are guilty of by negro slavery) with murderers of fathers and murderers of mothers, whore-mongers . . . liars." On a more basic level, slavery violated the Christian commandment to love thy neighbor. Holding another human in bondage, Green reasoned, was a hateful act that ran counter to everything Jesus preached on love and humility. In making this argument, he was rejecting the views of his mentor, Jonathan Edwards. Edwards believed that the Bible *did* condone slavery, because the New Testament did not expressly condemn human bondage and would have if God had believed slavery to be a sin. But Green's antislavery arguments brought him into line with other Calvinists, especially those who belonged to the New Divinity movement, such as Samuel Hopkins and Edwards's son, Jonathan Edwards, Jr.[29]

For all his "radicalism" on this subject, Green the realist never lost sight of the great hurdles that abolitionism faced because of the popularity of slavery and the distractions of war. He thus pursued a dual track, proposing a short-term and a long-term solution to ending slavery. The long-term solution was for the legislatures in each state to pass laws gradually emancipating the slaves. In a postscript to his fast-day sermon that he published, Green laid out the details of his emancipation plan: "All that shall hereafter be born, and all that are now under five years old, should be free, the males at twenty-one years old, and the females at eighteen." Those slaves between the ages of five and ten years of age would be freed when the males turned twenty-three and the females twenty. In this manner he went on to list emancipation dates for every age group, ending with those between fifty and sixty to be freed in one year and those older than sixty "to serve during life, in order to be taken care of and provided for by their owners."[30]

Green was convinced that his proposal was the most practical and realistic for the country. By gradually freeing the slaves, the economic interests of slave owners would be protected while a great moral wrong would be righted. Yet his plan's prospects were so uncertain that his short-term solution was to encourage slaveholders to free their slaves on their own. They did not need to wait for the legislature to act, he pointed out, and he appealed to their sense of humanity and to the dictates of reason: "If those masters had a true spirit of freedom; if they abhorred the very nature of slavery, they would soon free themselves from such a blot in the character of freemen."[31]

As much as Green abhorred slavery, he concluded that its eradication could not take priority over winning the Revolution. Thus he drew back from his dire warnings that the revolutionaries could lose the war because of slavery. "I doubt not but we may succeed against our British oppressors even if we should not free ourselves from the guilt of enslaving others," he stated. The reason was that the "cause of Britain is most unjust, and our contest with them is most righteous." But Green noted that the Americans would have a much stronger case if they ended slavery. "Our neglecting to reform in this matter may protract the war to a distressing length," because God would punish America by allowing the war to continue.[32]

Thus Green's reasonableness and his commitment to the Revolution were leading him in contradictory directions. Slavery was wrong, he declared, and should be abolished right away; otherwise, Americans could lose the war because of divine punishment. Yet abolishing slavery immediately would be hard to accomplish, so Americans should wait, and they could still win the war anyway because Britain was a bigger sinner. And in a final inconsistency, he was dismissive of those who argued that emancipation had to wait until the war ended. To the contrary, he believed it was the perfect time to end slavery—emancipation would please God and encourage him to "free us from our calamities." By waiting until the war ended, "we might as well say that we cannot, in this difficult time, raise men for our army, because we are so straightened for help, and need our men at home."[33]

Despite all these twists and turns, Green left no doubt about where he stood on the great moral issue of slavery. He opposed human bondage and condemned those patriots who defended the practice. In New Jersey, his diatribes against slavery in the 1770s placed him in the vanguard of revolutionary-era abolitionism and helped to stir up agitation on the question. Ironically, the American Revolution hindered, rather than aided, the state's nascent abolition movement—because of the immensity of the war effort and the need for unity to fight a powerful enemy. Although some slaveholders fired up over the Declaration of Independence did free their slaves, New Jersey and other state governments made manumissions harder out of fear that the former bondsmen would flock to British lines. Moreover, the war neutered one of the biggest, longtime critics of slavery, the Quakers, who had opposed all aspects of the peculiar institution from slave importations (they urged the New Jersey legislature in 1773 to make them illegal) to disowning those Friends who held slaves (the Philadelphia Yearly Meeting took this step in 1776).

The war, however, marginalized the Quakers politically, and the slavery debate remained relatively quiet in New Jersey until Green began his campaign in 1778 and 1779. Its impact was uneven. One influential lawmaker who apparently read Green's essays was an old colleague from the Provincial Congress, John Cooper, a Quaker from Gloucester County, who served with Green on the committee that drafted the state constitution. In September 1780, Cooper published an essay in the *New-Jersey Gazette* that echoed one of Green's key arguments: failure to cleanse the stain of slavery from the new nation would invite divine retribution. "Can we imagine our prayers to Almighty God will meet with his approbation, or in the least degree tend to procure us relief from the hand of oppression, whilst the groans of our slaves are continually ascending mingled with them?" Cooper asked. "I fear, indeed, that not only our prayers, but our publick fastings, are an abomination in his sight." Like Green, Cooper warned that the hypocrisy over slavery would prolong the war—"how can we hope to prevail against our enemies, whilst we ourselves are tyrants, holding thousands of our fellow-creatures in slavery under us?" (Cooper, though, called for immediate emancipation, unlike Green, who urged a gradual emancipation.) Outside events further gave a sense of momentum: in 1780, Pennsylvania became the first state to pass an act gradually emancipating the slaves within its borders.[34]

But the headwinds lashing the abolition movement were fierce, even overwhelming. Although fighting in New Jersey had lessened by the late 1770s, the British threat to the state was too dire for the legislature to even contemplate ending slavery. Governor Livingston learned that the hard way. In mid-1778, convinced that slavery was "utterly inconsistent, both with the principles of Christianity & Humanity," he submitted a message to the Assembly urging it to pass an emancipation law. The Assembly not only declined to consider passing such a bill, it persuaded the governor to withdraw his message because it felt, in Livingston's words, that the state was in "too critical a Situation to enter on the consideration of it at that time." Cooper fared no better on December 1780, when he sought to introduce a bill in the Legislative Council to abolish slavery throughout the state. The council denied him permission to even introduce the act. About the same time, the Assembly refused to consider two memorials from Morris County and one from Hunterdon "praying that a Law may be passed for the Abolition of Slavery."[35]

The Legislature *was* willing to pass bills ensuring that slaves could not aid the British. One such bill gave justices of the peace the authority to order the removal of slaves from areas near enemy territory; several localities also passed statutes authorizing the militia to disarm both free blacks and slaves. The legislature, fearing that freedmen would be unwilling to work and would become burdens to the community, had long made it difficult to manumit slaves. In 1769, for instance, the Legislature required masters to post a 200-pound bond if they wanted to emancipate a slave, a prohibitive amount. It also passed harsh slave codes that rivaled the laws found in the South. New Jersey denied blacks the right to a trial by jury, permitted forced separations of slave families, and allowed draconian punishments of misbehaving slaves, including the burning of black arsonists at the stake. Not until 1804 did New Jersey finally pass "An Act for the Gradual Abolition of Slavery"—the last northern state to make slavery illegal.[36]

In its tardiness, the legislature was bowing to the importance of slavery to the state's economy and its relative popularity among its constituents. Slavery, small as it was in New Jersey compared with the plantation South, was ensconced in the state's economy, especially in what used to be East Jersey. Out of a statewide population of 139,000 in 1780, 7 percent (or 10,400) of New Jerseyans were black—and more than 8,000 of them were enslaved. This meant that New Jersey had the second-largest slave population north of the Mason-Dixon Line. In a society woefully short of labor, the value of slaves to the economy transcended their small numbers. Such was the case in Morris County and Hanover Township, where family farms predominated. Slaves were one strand in the economic fabric, supplementing the labor of family members by working as household servants and as laborers in farm fields and artisanal shops. Women spun wool, churned butter, cared for children, baked bread, cleaned houses. Men hoed fields, threshed grain, brewed beer, built cabinets, butchered hogs. From 1756 (the earliest year for which records are extant) to 1790, Hanover residents owned 19 percent of the slaves in Morris County, and 21 percent of the county's slaveholders resided in Hanover (table 3). (In the 1756–1850 period, Hanover owned 16 percent of the county's slaves.) Because farms were small and grain-based, owners had no use for large workforces: the township's holdings in this period averaged 1.3 slaves per owner. Indeed, in an 1840 letter to his son, Ashbel Green noted that "cultivators of the soil generally owned but small plantations; so that a farmer seldom needed more than from two to five or six slaves."[37]

Table 3   Slaveholding by township, 1751–1850

| Township | Slaves | Percentage held |
| --- | --- | --- |
| Pequannock | 127 | 32% |
| Morris | 79 | 20% |
| Hanover | 66 | 16% |
| Roxbury | 52 | 13% |
| Chester | 29 | 7% |
| Chatham | 25 | 6% |
| Mendham | 11 | 3% |
| Washington | 9 | 2% |
| Randolph | 4 | 1% |

SOURCE: *Slave Records of Morris County, New Jersey: 1756–1841*, edited by David Mitros, p. 119. Figures are derived from extant estate inventories.

Like Livingston and Cooper, Jacob Green stood little chance of effecting real change outside of his Hanover congregation. His crusade, however, did attract plenty of attention—much of it negative. In 1779, defenders of slavery accosted Green at the Hanover parsonage and harangued him for his views. Green calmly tried to reason with them, asking his uninvited visitors in for a mug of hard cider, but, according to Ashbel, "they were too angry to consent" and left.[38]

Slavery's supporters also turned to the newspapers to attack Green's views. One of the loudest voices was "Eliobo," who published two essays in the *New-Jersey Journal* in late 1780. Eliobo's main point was that emancipation would harm everyone, white and black alike. Bondage, he argued, helped the slaves and allowed them to live in happiness. Freeing them would produce the opposite effect—"making them free only lays out [the] means to make them wretched." The reason was a time-honored one: slaves were incapable of caring for themselves. Once free, "they could not support their families, from the establishment that they were naturally lazy and pitiless, profuse and vicious." Unable and unwilling to work, Eliobo darkly warned, the freed slave would face starvation. And that would present a vexing dilemma for whites: should they let them starve? "No—humanity obliges us to support them," but that duty would fall on the towns, an expensive proposition. Thus, emancipation would differ little from slavery: whites would still have to take care of blacks.[39]

Eliobo denied that the former slaves could be educated and turned into productive citizens; their natural habits were too ingrained to be eradicated. "It is to be expected," he explained, "that they will wish to act not according to our judgment and direction, but from principles and inclinations of their own; and that they will prefer their natural indolence." Eliobo also feared their sheer numbers—he estimated blacks totaled five hundred thousand in 1780, out of a nationwide population of three million, and that their numbers would grow once they were emancipated. The freedmen could not be controlled, he warned, and it would be impossible to bring them under the laws of white society. The prospect was real that the freed slaves would ally with Indian tribes to murder and rape whites: "In short it is transparently clear to me that setting them free would enkindle a universal propensity and disposition to mischief."[40]

Eliobo's arguments summed up every fear and racist statement uttered by slaveholders in years past and in the years to come. It also was a model of inconsistency—blacks should not be freed because they were too lazy to work and too dumb to learn new skills; yet, if freed, they would have the drive and the brains to join forces with the Indians to terrorize whites. Green did not let Eliobo's essays pass without comment, although he did not respect these "marvellous disquisitions" (as he sarcastically called Eliobo's arguments) or take them seriously. Instead of dignifying the remarks by directly refuting them, Green ridiculed Eliobo's fears of racial warfare by copying Eliobo word for word—except he substituted "slaveholders" for "negro." Green's larger point was that slave owners, not slaves, posed the real threat to society. It was a devastating line of attack, with Green positing such gems as "It is demonstrable that those slaveholders are as stupid as the————[word purposely omitted here], and that they have been brought up in ignorance." These slaveholders, Green noted, "are certainly enemies of what the Congress say in their Declaration of Independence, viz., *We hold these truths to be self-evident, that all men are created equal."* Green sarcastically went on to call them "Tories of the worst sort" who will ally with the British so they both can impose slavery on blacks and whites alike.[41]

"Marcus Aurelius" came to Eliobo's defense. Taking Eumenes's rebuttal at face value, this essayist denied that slaveholders would join the British, maintaining that there was no inconsistency in fighting a war for liberty while denying liberty to others. In fact, Aurelius wrote, the existence of slavery made slaveholders even more attached to liberty because they have seen firsthand what the loss of freedom can mean. To buttress his claim, he cited Edmund Burke's observation "that of all men on earth none are more tenacious of their own liberty than those who possess servants in a land where servitude is allowed." Aurelius also pointed to ancient Greece and Rome—two places that loved liberty but condoned slavery. Last, he noted that the Continental Congress could have outlawed slavery but did not. Aurelius also agreed with Eliobo that blacks were better off remaining in servitude: "Servants who are born in that state, by being from their earliest infancy acquainted with no other condition, can possibly have no idea . . . of a greater degree of happiness here than that of a kind and indulgent master. It is natural for them, like a child, to look up with gratitude and reverence to the hand that feeds and clothes them, all other wants being extraneous." Free them, and blacks "would very soon be a grievous nuisance to us, and a sore burden to themselves." He closed his two letters with an appeal for unity, criticizing Eumenes for calling slaveholders Tories: "It is our highest interest to join arm to arm, and shoulder to shoulder."[42]

Because Marcus Aurelius so badly missed Green's point, Green felt he needed to write a response in the *New-Jersey Journal*—and he then followed that up with a second, longer letter a week later. Patiently, Green explained that he wanted to expose Eliobo's "absurdities and improbabilities with something as absurd and improbable. . . . The falsehood and absurdity of representing the Negroes [as] naturally stupid and incapable of instruction, is contrasted with that which is equally absurd to suppose in slaveholders." Green was surprised that a few readers took his essay at face value and was amused that Marcus Aurelius was one of them: "'Tis really enough to make a body laugh, to see Marcus Aurelius set himself seriously, if not gravely, to prove that the slaveholders could not be what Eumenes, in a satirical or ironical light, exhibits them." Green reported that he "conversed with numbers" and found virtually no one who "thought Eumenes to be in earnest."

Eumenes used the rest of the letter to call for the revolutionaries to stand firm, to not yield to British arms and tyranny: "I detest the aims and conduct of our British enemies. I would risk everything and try to excite others to risk everything in defense of our liberties and not yield to Britain." Green hoped the war would soon end, but he repeated his contention that "the continuance of it is owing to the misconduct, and vices among ourselves. If our ways pleased the great all-wise disposer of all events, he would cause our enemies to be at peace with us." And that, Green stressed, was something that slaveholders should think about.[43]

The vitriol sent his way did not intimidate Green; in fact, in 1781, he banned slaveholders from membership at the Hanover Presbyterian Church. It was not an especially controversial decision. During Green's pastorate, only one slave was listed on the membership rolls—"Caesar, negro man of Sam Parrot." Caesar was baptized on April 30, 1775. Two years earlier, on August 15, Green baptized "Hagar, a negro child belonging to William Parrot." The congregation backed Green's decision on slaveholding by approving "the articles of agreement" using language that echoed Green's fast-day sermon: "All human creatures have a natural right to freedom . . . we cannot but look on their being held in slavery as an unnatural evil and one of the greatest injuries to mankind; therefore, we will not use this slavery ourselves and will prudently endeavor to prevent it in others."[44]

It was a historic vote nevertheless. The Hanover congregation became the first and only Presbyterian church in America during the Revolution to bar membership to those who participated in slavery. The vote followed a decision by the Synod of New York and Philadelphia a year earlier to do nothing on the slavery issue. Only Green and a few Presbyterian laymen—notably William Livingston, Benjamin Rush, and George Bryan—were speaking out against slavery. Green and Livingston did not get very far in New Jersey, but Rush and especially Bryan played a pivotal role in the successful fight in Pennsylvania in 1780 to make slavery illegal. Overall, the Presbyterian Church was relatively quiet in the slavery debate during the Revolutionary period. It did allow blacks to join white congregations, although the former sat in separate galleries. But that was about as much reform as the church was willing to undertake during the Revolution.[45]

Thus Green was a relatively lonely voice on the slavery issue; few Presbyterians outside of Hanover were ready to join him. And such was the case in another fight that he began simultaneously, when he took on a powerful—and surprising—foe in 1779.

## *The Loyalist Down the Road:*
### *Thomas Bradbury Chandler, Reformer*

Chandler's days were busy, but his causes were few. Two preoccupied him, as they had when he was minister to St. John's in Elizabeth Town. He doggedly resumed his quest for the church to send a bishop to America despite American opposition and the distractions of war. Certainly the administrative rationale for such a request remained in force—the presence of a bishop would improve the managerial efficiency of the American branch of the Church of England. Yet the broader philosophical reasons for installing a prelate had vanished—an American bishop could do nothing to strengthen church and state while the former colonies were in open rebellion against the king. Chandler, though, was unperturbed. As his correspondence during his exile demonstrates, he cared deeply about the American church and wanted to do all he could to aid it. Being in London presented him with unique opportunities to help the church. He was able to take his causes to the highest councils of state.

In early 1776, Chandler discussed the bishop's issue with the archbishop of York and the bishop of London, and he received a sympathetic hearing. Yet Chandler was chasing a ghost—they talked about things that happened twelve years ago, during a time when the colonies were professing their loyalty to the king and the state church had an important role to play in a colonial British society. At their meeting, the archbishop informed Chandler "that in the Year 1764, Dr. Wishart, one of the principal Clergy in Edinburgh, assured his Grace, that he could see no reasonable objections against the American Episcopate proposed, and that he did not believe any of the Scottish Clergy of any Eminence would disapprove of such an Appointment."

A year later, in January 1777, Chandler met with the bishop of Bangor "to request his Lordship that, at the Meeting of the Society [for the Propagation of the Gospel] on Friday next, he will move that a Committee be appointed to prepare an Account of the Attempts that have been formerly made by that Body to obtain an American Episcopate, and of the Reasons of the Failure, as also of the exact State of the Episcopal Funds. This was proposed as preparatory to the grand Question." In May, the society accepted Chandler's proposal to appoint "a Committee to examine into the Steps heretofore taken by the Society for obtaining an American Episcopate &c." Thirteen members were chosen, including six bishops. This was about as far as Chandler got—forming the committee led to talk, and more talk. A resolution of the bishop's issue stood no chance until the contest between the king and his American subjects was settled on the battlefield.

Chandler's second cause involved advocating on behalf of destitute American clergy who were "suffering for their Loyalty" to the Crown. Chandler's motives here were multifaceted. Compassion and the needs of the church were foremost in his attempt to obtain money for Anglican ministers. Yet he also was acting partly out of guilt: he left America for the safety of London; his fellow ministers stayed, to face the wrath of the American radicals. In addition, aiding the American clergy was a way for Chandler to deal with the deep psychic pain of having abandoned his family, as a 1777 letter to Samuel Seabury indicated: "It is the greatest Alleviation of my uneasiness at this cruel Absence from my Family, that it affords me an Opportunity of doing Something to mitigate the Difficulties of my Brethren and Sisters, and perhaps of promoting the general Interest of the American Church."

Chandler was able to meet with the bishop of London and others "about a proper Method of assisting the American clergy in their present Distresses." Unlike in the case of the bishop's cause, Chandler got immediate results. The English bishops "agreed to remit from the Society the Salaries of such Missionaries, as appear to have no Opportunity to draw [their pay]." The archbishop also agreed "that a Subscription shall be opened for their farther Relief." By April, the society had successfully raised some 2,000 pounds and left it up to Chandler to determine how to distribute the funds.

In trying to help his church, Chandler puzzled over some of the dilemmas posed by the rebellion. What should the American clergy do about the liturgy and the requirement that church members pray to the king? When the colonies declared independence, most Anglican clerics suspended services to avoid being charged with treason by American authorities. In 1779, Chandler wrote, "I hope they will act with the strictest Harmony and *Uniformity*, and either *all* proceed, or *all* keep back. It is taken for granted that it is no Question among them, whether they may pray *for the Congress* &c., as well as omit praying for the King. The former would actually be joining in the Rebellion; whereas the latter, all Circumstances considered, is no more than forbearing to exercise an agreeable Part of their office, in compliance with urgent Necessity."

As his exile (and the war) dragged on, Chandler remained in close touch with his brethren across the Atlantic. He wrote regularly to Charles Inglis and Samuel Seabury, as well as his family, keeping them abreast of developments in England and forwarding pamphlets and other items of interest. The correspondence was so heavy, in fact, that Chandler complained of the burden. When Seabury scolded him for not writing more and sooner, Chandler responded defensively: "The truth is, I have a number of *constant* correspondents, and so many occasional ones, that I have been obliged to make it a rule to write no letters but *in answer* to theirs . . . ; for by the time I have got through this task, I am so tired and surfeited of writing, that I have but little inclination to strike out as a *volunteer*."

By the early 1780s, Chandler was tired—of the incessant letter writing, of British peace efforts, and of London itself.[46]

# 10

*Dissenter*

The American Revolution, despite its many travails and frustrations, had taught Green something important by 1779: tyranny had to be confronted wherever it was found, even in the hallowed halls of the Lord's church. The American Presbyterian Church and its top-down mode of government, he believed, were oppressive, even tyrannical. Greater power, he felt, should rest with the congregation and the laymen who ran it. Democratic rights, he reasoned, should extend beyond the temporal to the sacred. Thus, amid his fight to reform the currency and abolish slavery, Green came to a fateful decision in late 1779.

He would withdraw from the Presbytery of New York and the Synod of New York and Philadelphia.

Fittingly, Green penned a declaration of independence in October explaining his decision and sent it to the New York Presbytery. Then, two years later, he took his act of political defiance to a broader stage when he published a sixty-one-page pamphlet detailing what he had done and why. Green's decision to secede from the Presbytery and Synod was no act of petulance but the coolly rational decision of an aging, fifty-seven-year-old minister and reformer who took the ideals of American Revolution with utmost seriousness. Just as Green in 1776 came to see Parliament as venal and overbearing, Green in 1779 came to see the Presbyterian Synod as selfish and dictatorial. He reached this conclusion after years of pondering the nature of authority; and a wide range of sources—his congregational upbringing, the Bible, Lockean political treatises, the American Revolution itself—influenced his thinking. The Revolution was especially critical to Green. Although the references to Calvinism and allusions to predestination remained, his writings of this period drew liberally on the revolutionary rhetoric and political language of the times, with Green defending his right to stand up to "spiritual tyranny" and to establish "that mode of worship & chh Government which I think most agreeable to the word of God."[1]

Green's unhappiness with the Presbyterian Church had been building for years, well before American rebels took up arms against their king. "I have [a] long time been uneasy with many things in the Synod," he told the New York Presbytery in his October 18 declaration, "& have for a Number of years absented myself, out of principle, & not because I was careless & inattentive to the affairs of the chh." His main objection to the Synod was that it "affirm[ed] a power that does not belong to them." The Synod, Green complained, repeatedly passed laws and backed them up with threats of censure and "Reprehension." Green pointed out "that the nature of a law is an order, command, Rule, or Direction attended with a sanction. . . . And tis easy to shew that the Synod have made many such laws." Synodal rulings and their imperious tone bothered Green greatly; in fact, in ranking the Synod's shortcomings, he placed this complaint first: "They use the Authoritative enacting stile in their Minutes ordering[,] appointing[,] & requiring instead of recommending & desiring." The Synod passed laws and issued commands with no authority from the entity that mattered most—God. Green believed that the Synod had no basis in the Bible or in the teachings of Jesus Christ: "They assume a legislative power, & make laws to bind men in matters of conscience; which is contrary to the great Protestant principle that 'Christ has not left a legislative power in his chh.'"[2]

In opposing the top-down structure of Presbyterianism, Green wanted to replace it with something akin to the Congregationalism of his New England youth. "We hold that each particular chh or congregation," he wrote to the Presbytery in his October letter, "has a Right to do or manage all their ecclesiastical Business within themselves." Power should rest with individual congregations, he believed, and not with a centralized body of pastors possessing coercive authority. Green, however, was not advocating a total break with Presbyterianism; nor was he suggesting that the independence of each congregation should be absolute. Instead, he wanted a middle ground—he wanted the Presbyterian Church's government to operate along the lines of the Articles of Confederation (although he never used that analogy). The Synod would meet as a legislative body, but in an advisory capacity only. It would, in other words, have approximately the same powers as the Continental Congress—it could instruct and cajole its member congregations, but it could not compel. The Synod would merely be a forum for ministers to gather "once a year or oftener," according to Green, where they could exchange notes and "may profitably hear several Sermons on ministerial duties." The Synod would also have the right to "converse & consult on proper methods to promote Religion, may encourage & excite one another," he explained. "But such Synods or presby have no power over chhs or ministers any further than matters are referred or left to them for advice or determination."[3]

In its stead, Green proposed creating an associated presbytery whose member congregations would join of their own free accord: such "a free plan suits best with a Land [at] a time & a Religion of Freedom." The voluntary nature of the associated presbytery was stressed in the rules outlined in the 1781 pamphlet that Green, with contributions from other members, wrote called *A View of a Christian Church*. The presbytery would meet "ordinarily" twice a year "to consult and agree upon the most expedient measures to promote religion, and to give the churches opportunity to apply to us for the advice and assistance that it is proper for an associated presbytery to afford them." Further, "we agree that this presbytery, as a body, shall never assume, or claim, any jurisdiction over the churches, or authoritatively intermeddle with their affairs." Its "rules" would not be binding. Secession by member congregations was permitted, even encouraged: "If any one, or a number of ministers, or an associated presbytery, should choose to withdraw from a synod with which they have been associated, they have liberty to do it, and not be thought schismatical or disorderly, if it be done in a quiet and peaceable manner." Even the name reinforced its limited powers—Green at first planned to call it the Presbytery of Morris County but added "associated," apparently so that the new body would not be on the same par as a full presbytery.[4]

In devising an associated presbytery, Green likely drew on two models. One, of course, was the New England Congregationalism of his youth: in Puritan New England, authority rested with the congregation and, ultimately, on the covenant, which drew together like-minded believers of laymen who ruled their church together. Yet even in the Puritan world the congregation's independence was never absolute, for associations began overseeing individual churches in the late seventeenth century. These "consociational" groups consisted of ministers and (sometimes) laity who met periodically to adjudicate disputes among the congregations, to advise them on religious matters, and to screen ministerial candidates. And the consociations of the founding period drew on a Reformed heritage that saw English Puritans, in their effort to weaken the authority of episcopal bishops, push for a decentralized church beginning in the reign of Elizabeth I. This effort, in turn, led to early reformers developing a congregational system in England where elected consistories of pastors and elders were put in charge of the discipline of individual churches. As one historian of these consistories noted, "Underlying this scheme was an implicit ethic of voluntarism. Thus hierarchical influence was dependent upon the willingness of 'particular churches' to 'communicate among themselves' and 'to yield mutual help one to another.'" These consociations became a common feature on the New England landscape, and Green was almost certainly familiar with them.[5]

A second possible model was the unity government attempted over a ten-year period by Connecticut Congregationalists and Presbyterians from the middle colonies. Beginning in 1766, delegates from these two groups met annually "to promote and defend the common cause of religion against the attacks of its various enemies," in the words of the Presbyterian Synod of New York and Philadelphia. The constitution establishing a general convention gave it no coercive powers; delegates could advise only and "unite our endeavors and counsels for spreading the Gospel," tasks nearly identical to Green's associated presbytery. Although Green attended only one meeting—the convention held at Elizabeth Town on October 5, 1768—he was familiar with its activities and its voluntary structure. At the session he did attend, delegates debated admission standards for the convention and approved a letter to a "dissenting committee in England" restating the convention's purpose. In spirit, the general convention resembled the associated presbytery Green envisioned for a recast Presbyterian Church.[6]

Green enlisted three allies in his crusade against the Presbyterian Church—two Presbyterian ministers from Morris County and one from New York—who agreed to join his Associated Presbytery of Morris County. Green's ties to these three ministers were ones of geography and temperament. All (with one exception) pastored to churches bordering his Hanover church. All were originally from New England and were sympathetic to the congregational system. All were young and likely saw Green as a father figure—one quite literally. Ebenezer Bradford had married Green's daughter Elizabeth in 1776 and was Jacob's son-in-law. A native of Canterbury, Connecticut, Bradford attended the College of New Jersey, graduating in 1773. A few years later, he became pastor of the Presbyterian congregation in south Hanover Township, serving at the church that became known as Bottle Hill in Madison. Joseph Grover was a Dartmouth graduate and another native New Englander who had been pastor in neighboring Parsippany since 1774. Amzi Lewis was the outsider—he served in Warwick, New York, and agreed to join Green's presbytery in Morris County. As the author of *The Covenant Interest of the Children of Believers Illustrated and Proved . . .* , Lewis was sympathetic to Green's mission to create a purer church and to give more authority to the congregation. Like the others who signed on, Lewis was a product of New England Puritan culture, having been born in Canterbury, Connecticut, in 1746 and graduating from Yale in 1768.[7]

Grover told the New York Presbytery in a letter that he agreed with Green's complaints that the Presbytery and Synod were overreaching, and he informed its members that "I now quietly withdraw as Mr. Green has done. And [I] shall view myself at Liberty freely to join with any valuable Ministers of Christs Chh as a council or Associate Body." On May 3, 1780, these four New Englanders made their secession official when they announced the formation of their presbytery.[8]

Green was careful to cultivate support for his plans and did everything he could to keep the secession as civil as possible. In his earlier letter to the Presbyterian leadership, Green made clear that he wanted to avoid the ugliness of the Great Awakening, when the New Side attacked the Old Side as unregenerate and split the Presbyterian Church into warring camps. Thus Green reassured the Synod that he remained a Presbyterian, even going so far as to declare that he and his supporters "are highly calvinistic in our sentiments" and hold the Westminster's "shorter Catechisms" in high esteem. "Nor are we unmindful of the danger of enthusiasm," he noted in a second letter. "I have, according to your desire, paid attention to the separations, errors, and extravagancies that were in New-England and other parts, about forty years ago." Green vowed that his reform movement would avoid the excessive emotionalism of the 1730s and 1740s. Most of all, his new presbytery would not attack other ministers personally. The "errors" made during the Awakening resulted because people of reason did not properly regulate "the exhorters and zealous persons," Green explained. "Their zeal and fervour was like a torrent which, if dammed up and opposed, will overflow and do damage." He insisted that his purpose in leaving the Presbytery and Synod was to create a stronger church. "I withdraw from the Synod with all Christian charity," he concluded in the October letter. "[I] desire not to make any Breach or Schism [and] would maintain the unity of the Spirit in the bond of peace."[9]

Surprisingly, the Synod had little formally to say about their rebellion, merely noting in its minutes "that Messrs. Green, Lewis, Grover, and Bradford have withdrawn from that [New York] Presbytery." Informally, its members were not happy and let Green know it—so much so that the Appendix to *View of a Christian Church* felt the need to defend the four ministers' actions: "We are sensible we have been represented in an unfavourable light, and, we think we may say we have, in some respects been misrepresented. We are willing and desirous to appear, in a true light, in our proper character." The Synod had long been upset that these four ministers and others were neglecting to come to the annual meeting. Green attended his first Synod on May 20, 1747, and his second a year later on May 18—and he almost never went again because of his philosophical differences with the Synod. In 1778, the Synod labeled such absences "a criminal neglect . . . a forgetfulness of their ordination obligation, and a want of that public spirit and benevolent care of the church with which ministers of the gospel ought to be filled."[10]

Green and his fellow rebels should not have been surprised about the negative reaction, for despite their professions of Christian love and unity their withdrawal represented an attack on the Synod's legitimacy. In *A View of a Christian Church*, the four pastors derided the Synod as an "imaginary body, for which we can find no warrant, or foundation, in Scripture." Their opinion of the Presbytery was little better. The word was from Greek, Green explained, and it had little basis in the Bible. "It is used thrice only in the New Testament" and "properly signifies the *eldership*, or a number of elders acting in concert." During the early days of the Christian church, elders served their congregation and formed a presbytery of neighboring churches. "Such a number of elders may associate, and agree to meet from time to time to . . . assist, and quicken one another; consult and agree upon measures to promote religion." The presbytery, however, "as a body has no power over the churches any other way than their advice." That was as far as Green and the other ministers would go. "A synod," he insisted repeatedly, "has no foundation in Scripture."[11]

To buttress his case, Green quoted at length from Johann Lorenz Mosheim, "a most approved historian, and no enemy to synods, [who] says,

'The churches, in those early times, were entirely independent . . . each one governed by its own rulers and its own laws.'" Only in the second century did Greek churches begin holding councils, a practice that spread to the rest of the Christian world. As he did in his October 1779 declaration to the Presbytery of New York, Green conceded that presbyteries could meet periodically in a synod. But a synod has "no warrant or right to intermeddle, in any authoritative way, with the affairs of particular churches."[12]

Despite his careful tone and vows to avoid a schism, Green made no apologies about secession; he defended it as the God-given right of a patriot in a revolutionary age, for "every man has a right to choose his religion, and to worship God according to the dictates of his own conscience." In numerous documents—from his 1776 tract advocating independence to his wartime letters on liberty—Green vigorously asserted the right of citizens to protest, and he did it again in his rebellion against the Presbyterian Church. He told the New York Presbytery in his October letter that "I have an undoubted right" to withdraw and that failing to assert this right would be "very sinful in me"; moreover, those who tried to deny him this right would be guilty of "spiritual tyranny." In *A View of a Christian Church*, Green expounded on what he meant: "To be denied [the right of protest and secession] would be of dangerous consequence; to be denied this, would cut off all attempts for reformation; and would, in time to come, prevent the increase of light and purity in the christian church." Green, in other words, saw dissent as healthy. It led to a stronger church, because the seceders would be free to correct the errors of the offending body. Forming the Associated Presbytery of Morris County was all about claiming "a right to worship and manage church affairs for ourselves, in a method that appears to us agreeable to scripture." The associated presbytery would run things its own way.[13]

It was a radical argument, even in a revolutionary era, for two reasons. Green was taking on a church detested in loyalist and British circles as a fomenter of rebellion. The Presbyterian Church in America was one of the strongest backers of independence, and Chandler for one hated it because of this. Thus Green's challenge was replete with irony. He was saying that Presbyterianism was not radical enough, that the synodal system could be as oppressive as a British parliamentary system headed by a venal king. Others may have seen the Presbyterians as a bunch of rebels, but Jacob Green did not.

Second, in this British colonial world with its strong social stratifications, deference had long held sway. Inferiors were not to question their superiors. The "better sort" were to lead, and the rest were to follow. Of course, the

American Revolution was dealing a severe blow to this deferential milieu; nevertheless, a hierarchical society remained in the late 1770s, and dissent was still seen as unhealthy, even wrong, especially when the former colonists were engaged in a life-and-death struggle against one of the world's strongest militaries: questioning the Continental Congress and fellow rebels could make one suspect, and the gentry expected people to bow to the wisdom of the elite. In both Europe and America, Christianity reinforced this great chain of being: social distinctions were essential and necessary if the community's well-being was to be maintained. For centuries, conventional Western thought had posited that God created government and that Christians' duty was to obey God and his earthly rulers. The foundation of this belief— a favorite passage of Anglican ministers such as Chandler—was Romans 13:1–2: "Let every soul be subject to the governing authorities. For there is no authority except from God, and the authorities that exist are appointed by God. Therefore whoever resists the authority resists the ordinance of God." Certainly this obeisance to authority was an article of faith in the High Church Anglicanism that Chandler loved and worshipped—the passage neatly, and succinctly, confirmed the core Anglican belief on the union of church and king. Rulers ruled with God's blessing, received their commissions from him, and had their authority buttressed by the majesty and power of the church. As Chandler put it in an address to Americans, "The principles of submission and obedience to lawful authority are as inseparable from a sound, genuine member of the Church of England as any religious principle whatsoever. . . . [Church] members are instructed in their duty to government by Three Homilies on Obedience, and six against rebellion." But even John Calvin and other Protestant reformers preached obedience. William Tyndale wrote in the early sixteenth century, "God hath made the king in every realm judge over all, and over him there is no judge. He that judgeth the king judgeth God, and he that layeth hand on the king layeth hand on God."[14]

Thus Green was taking on centuries of entrenched belief when he argued that ordinary people could question their government and their betters. Not surprisingly, his secession from, and criticisms of, the Synod encountered plenty of resistance among Presbyterian leaders. As the war for independence from King George III continued, they defended leadership of the few, forcefully arguing that church members *were* to obey the Synod's rulings. Moreover, they believed that Presbyterianism's synodal system was biblically sound and divinely ordained. Last but not least, they believed it was democratic and fair, because laymen were represented in each level of government—from the congregation's session on up to the Synod.

Green and the Synod's differences went deeper than an argument over how to construct a government. Presbyterianism's defenders saw themselves as members of the Church Universal—Christ's church did not reside in individual congregations, as Green and New England Congregationalists believed, but in the one true body of Christ. Congregationalists, including Green, viewed the laity as constituting the real church—the moral authority of the congregation rested on individual believers. On the elect, in other words. When one was saved, he or she was on an equal footing with the church's ministers. Such equality gave the laity a great say in the running of their church. It also afforded them the liberty to criticize their betters—who, of course, were not really their betters but their peers. The Congregationalists' great faith in the laity went too far for the Synod and its defenders. In Presbyterianism's federalist system, the laity did not exercise authority directly in the church but through their representatives: the elders and the clergy. No congregation stood alone in the Presbyterian cosmos; each was part of a whole, where authority ultimately rested with the Synod. In Scotland, the power of the church was even greater, for Presbyterianism was the established national church, and it possessed as much civil and spiritual power as the Anglican Church enjoyed in England. Green's associated presbyteries, if they spread beyond New Jersey and New York, would stick a dagger in the heart of Presbyterianism. The minister from Hanover and his allies wanted to take power from the Synod and place it with the congregation and its laymen, a reordering of authority that would upset Presbyterianism's carefully constructed tripartite balance of power among the Synod, presbytery, and session. Moreover, it would upset the carefully prescribed roles that Presbyterianism proclaimed for its clergy and its followers.[15]

Green's radicalism by 1779 was striking for this and other reasons—he had little to say during this period about membership requirements and the purity of the church, two topics that dominated his earlier publications and powered his reform agenda. Instead, he was now focusing on rights and liberties. The "corroborating" reason for withdrawing from the Synod, Green and his fellow ministers explained in their public declaration, was freedom; they relegated the membership issue to a footnote, where the ministers merely acknowledged that "we cannot agree with those who (upon Mr. Stoddard's principles) admit persons to sacraments without a profession of that which implies true grace."[16]

Despite Green's efforts here to skirt the whole issue of discipline and purity, the dilemma remained: how do you reconcile the liberties he was demanding during the American Revolution (where individuals have a wide range of choice) with his bedrock Calvinism (where God controls all and preordains what will happen)? For Green, the answer was very carefully—he walked a tightrope as he pressed his case for associated presbyteries while still insisting he was a committed Calvinist. In essence, what he argued was this: freedom, yes, but a *controlled* freedom where Christian love and moral behavior would predominate. Discipline would balance freedom.

Freedom of religion was something Green felt passionately about. He and his allies emphasized that the Revolution presented the perfect chance "to settle the externals of religion, upon a free and liberal plan. This is a time in which civil and religious liberty is attended to, is contended for. . . . It is a time in which a spirit of liberty prevails." Their presbytery was thus "a plan for liberty," and they hoped that others would follow their example and "revise their ecclesiastical principles, and see if they do not want something to make them fully consistent with christian liberty."[17]

The other side of the equation meant softening the blow of secession. Recoiling from discord and wanting to avoid an ugly fight with the church leadership, Green told the Synod that the withdrawing ministers would "guard against a party spirit" in their presbytery and that Christian love would predominate among members. Green also stressed that "we have no worldly interest in view; we have no secular schemes to promote." It was all about building a better church, based on sound biblical precepts.[18]

To build a stronger church and make it more democratic, Green also wanted to revamp the education and ordination procedures for ministerial candidates. The Presbyterian Church emerged from the war in a wounded condition. As a leading supporter of the Revolution (indeed, it was a truism on the British side that Presbyterian radicals had instigated the rebellion), the American church had seen its buildings and membership targeted by British troops. Five churches alone were burned in New Jersey and another three in New York. The economic turmoil of the 1780s badly hurt the church's finances, as its congregations struggled to pay their pastors and to come up with the money to rebuild their war-damaged buildings. An equally serious challenge was finding a way to serve an expanding frontier during a period when the Presbyterian Church faced a shortage of money and ministers. Victory over the British opened up western lands to American settlers, and the

Methodists and Baptists began moving aggressively to meet the needs of these sojourners. Leading Presbyterians, including Jacob Green, wanted their church to do so, too.[19]

The question was how. Green argued that the American church could expand to the frontier and elsewhere only by becoming more nimble and less centralized; pivotal to his vision of a revitalized Presbyterian Church was his plan to develop a larger ministry that could compete with the evangelical sects on the frontier by loosening the Presbyterians' rigid educational requirements for pastors so that the church could get more, and better, candidates into the field faster. In *A View of a Christian Church*, Green noted that "it is not necessary that every . . . [candidate] should be endowed with the highest degree of learning." The longtime Presbyterian requirements that ministers be college graduates who had mastered both theology and classical languages were too demanding and were unnecessary, he believed. The important thing was that candidates were evangelicals and effective teachers who possessed the ability to minister to the needs of settlers starved for Christian fellowship.[20]

Once again, Green was prescient in his views. He recognized the growing challenge of the frontier, as well as the shortcomings in the Presbyterian educational system, years before he formed the associated presbytery. In a 1775 letter to Joseph Bellamy, a New Divinity disciple of Jonathan Edwards and a renowned teacher of theological students, Green lamented "the great want of Gospel ministers in our Land. . . . From a little above Albany to Georgia we want near three hundred preachers." The shortage was growing acute on the frontier, he told Bellamy, and Presbyterian rivals were moving to fill the void: "We that are Ministers of Jesus Christ aught to exert ourselves for the good of his Chh. at a time when the harvest is so large, the Labourers so few, & the dangers from errors so great." But the Presbyterian insistence on college education was holding the church back. "The world," Green complained, "has long time been strangely disposed to waste time in learning dead languages, which are in reality no Qualification of a Gospel Minister, nor properly any part of science." For Green, the Presbyterians' stiff educational requirements were not only impractical but unbiblical. In Christianity's earliest days, "they . . . took the most suitable persons they could find & introduced them into the Ministry." The Presbyterian Church, by contrast, "has been first to make men gentlemen, & then make them preachers." When ready to finally take the field, these college-educated dandies shied away from the hardships of the frontier. In Green's mind, "those new parts of our land want men for Teachers that will live with a small salary; men of self denial, men that will take every prudent method to subsist in the world."[21]

In his 1770 *Vision of Hell*, Green had had harsh things to say about the ministry in general—the profession attracted too many men who were more interested in the good life than in leading lives of Christian discipline. Early in the tract, the devils agreed that to accomplish their nefarious designs, they needed "to induce bad men to enter into the ministry." And they could accomplish that by attracting men who were more interested in affairs of the world than in affairs of the church. As the devil Mammon put it, "To promote our design, I think we ought to lead all Clergymen, whether good or bad, to expect (by their calling) great things in this world, riches, honor, ease, and a state above the common level of mankind." This barb was aimed partly at those ministers who preferred a comfortable parish in the settled east over the frontier in the interior. Green felt strongly that the ministry was attracting too many well-educated, worldly candidates. In concurring with Mammon, Apollion noted, "Above all men in the world, I dread and abhor a minister that goes into his office with an humble mind, expecting much opposition and self-denial, and determined to follow the example of his master Jesus." Such humble, self-sacrificing men made the best preachers on the frontier and elsewhere.[22]

Yet, in another sense, Green was revisiting an old battleground. During the Great Awakening, the New Side had attacked the church's educational requirements as too rigid and the Old Side had vigorously defended them as necessary during a period of social upheaval. Old Side devotees viewed education as a way to stabilize society and to professionalize the ministry. They insisted that candidates had to master not only theology but also natural and moral philosophy as well as the ancient languages. The New Side agreed that Presbyterian ministers should be learned, but they wanted their pastors to be men who understood the heart as well as the head. They especially wanted to shorten the licensing process, which could take as long as three years. To implement its vision, the New Side founded two colleges—the famed Log College and the College of New Jersey.[23]

Green was well aware of this history. He was at Harvard in the 1740s during the Great Awakening's most fervent period, and he served as a trustee at Princeton from late 1748 until June 1764 (and was the college's interim president from November 23, 1758, until September 26, 1759). Both experiences allowed him to see the strengths and shortcomings of the educational system up close. Aaron Burr and Jonathan Dickinson of the New York Presbytery, two mentors of Jacob Green, were the driving forces behind the college's founding. They wanted the College of New Jersey to produce ministers who were educated *and* evangelical.[24]

But Green the radical felt these New Side innovations did not go far enough. To get "the right sort of men" into the ministry, he proposed creating seminaries that would feature a focused and shortened course of theological study. Overseeing the schools would be "an associate Body"—his associated presbytery in New Jersey and a congregational association in Connecticut— that would agree on "a method to educate, & licence men for the gospel Ministry." The seminaries' purpose, of course, would be to train talented preachers for "our back settlements," men who "would preach the precious truths of the Gospel, promote vital Religion, & maintain chh. Discipline." In their class work, students would hone the skills needed to preach; instead of wasting time on dead languages, candidates would focus on mastering English and "useful ideas." Green's proposal to create a seminary was years ahead of its time—it was not until 1807, when Calvinists from Harvard founded Andover Seminary, that schools were created solely to train ministers. His effort also predated that of New Divinity ministers in the Second Great Awakening, who in the early nineteenth century began forming local education societies to train men from modest and poor backgrounds. And his effort was an inspiration to his son Ashbel, who decades later was able to implement much of his father's vision on the education front.[25]

Green's second, and closely related, concern was to make ordination fairer and more democratic. It was something he had been long thinking about. In one unpublished notebook among his papers at Princeton University, Green wrote "that every assembly or congregation of christians [should] have power to manage & determine all their ecclesiastical affairs . . . and if every distinct chh or assembly has sole power within itself, I think the only rational dispute is concerning ordination. Who is to ordain a minister for a particular congregation when it wants one?" Such a question raised a more basic one for him: "What is ordination? . . . Is it in the power of all the men in the world to make a man a Gospel minister? How does a man become invested with the office of the Gospel ministry?" Green noted that Congregationalists and independents had much to say on the topic but that the Bible did not.[26]

He decided that a ministerial candidate had to first meet a few essential conditions, the most important being that "God calls him to the work"—in other words, that a Calvinistic God has chosen him to serve. When the candidate has shown he possesses an inclination for preaching, the individual congregation must then decide whether to ordain him. In rendering its decision, the congregation must "follow the light of nature and dictates of Reason with the best light we can gather from Scripture." But, Green continued, "leaving the arguments for lay ordination, & granting that according to Scripture, ordination must be by teaching elders: I yet maintain that the whole power of chh government so far as it reflects them lies in each particular congregation or chh." Thus his views of ordination closely tracked his views on church government. Power should reside with the congregation and not with a higher body; democracy should extend to the selection of ministers.[27]

It was a vision 180 degrees from Chandler's, whose views of ordination rested on *his* conception of church government. For Chandler, the Bible was quite clear on the matter. Bishops derived their power directly from Jesus Christ, and only bishops possessed the right to ordain ministerial candidates. It was utterly impossible for a bishop to confer this power to people beneath him, be it elders or laymen or other ministers. That's because, in Chandler's view, rulers ruled and followers followed. Or as he put it, "The Power or Right of *Government* is necessarily included in the Superiority of their Office. For in every Society, where there is a Subordination of Offices, that which constitutes the highest Office is the legal Possession of the highest Power." Power, in other words, is the sinew of government; the whole edifice, including the authority of bishops, would collapse were power to be diffused.[28]

Other Presbyterians recognized that the American church had to make changes if it was to thrive in the new nation, but they did not like Green's solutions. And because he had withdrawn from both the Presbytery of New York and the Synod in 1779, Green was in no position to win the church over to his point of view. First to lose out were Green's ideas to revamp ordination procedures for pastors: at the 1783 and 1785 synods, the ministers and elders in attendance voted down efforts to relax the educational requirements for ministerial candidates. As in the prewar years, those men wanting to become pastors still needed to study theology for two years and to be proficient in Latin, Hebrew, and Greek. In 1789, the new church constitution gave the presbyteries, and not the congregation, the authority to license and ordain ministers. Conservative factions, moreover, ensured that the church maintained its traditional, high standards on other fronts; for example, the

Synod castigated the New Brunswick Presbytery for allowing a candidate to deliver a part of his trial in English instead of Latin.[29]

Next, Green lost the even larger war with the American Presbyterian Church over centralization, when, in 1789, the organization began using a constitution that established a federal system of government overseen by a newly created General Assembly. Championing centralization was the powerful Presbyterian divine John Witherspoon, president of the College of New Jersey, who wrote the introduction to the church constitution and served as the General Assembly's first moderator (the equivalent of a president). Witherspoon was an ardent nationalist who wanted the U.S. Congress to possess the power to tax and to oversee the commercial regulations of the states. He wanted the Presbyterian Church's government to be equally strong. The resulting church constitution mirrored the federal one of 1787— power radiated downward from a national government (the General Assembly) to a state government (the synods) to a local body (the congregation). The church's top-down structure surely must have displeased Green. Yet, like the federal constitution, it did have checks and balances, and it did provide for religious liberty—democratic tendencies that allowed it to win the support of a Presbyterian majority. Representation in the General Assembly was proportional, based on the size of the presbytery. And the constitution left it up to local congregations to determine how to elect elders and deacons, thus giving laymen a significant say in the running of their church. Moreover, in an effort to improve church governance and allow Presbyterianism to better meet the needs of the expanding West, the constitution overhauled the creaky synodal/presbytery structure that permeated the colonial church. The reconstituted church consisted of four regional synods—New York/New Jersey, Philadelphia, Virginia, and the Carolinas—that in turn oversaw three to five presbyteries.[30]

Green was silent on the constitution's passage, but his actions during this period said volumes about what he thought of all this: the reforms did not go far enough. While Witherspoon and the Synod were maneuvering for a new constitution, Green concentrated on his associated presbytery and a second creation of his—the Morris County Society for the Promotion of Learning and Religion. If the church was going to stubbornly stick to its old ways, he would try to fill the void himself by developing a society that would educate missionaries and send them into the field. So the society, which was incorporated by the New Jersey legislature on May 30, 1787, "for the promotion of learning and religion," worked with young men interested in the ministry and sent them on preaching tours. Overseen by nine trust-ees, including Green, the society raised money and (in the words of one pamphlet) used those funds to "assist poor and pious youth in obtaining an education, and support itinerant evangelists and other instructors, who might labor to promote learning and religion among the poor in the desti-tute parts of our land." The society thus implemented many of Green's beliefs on education—it located "pious" youth, quickly trained them in the gospel, and sent them to the frontier to evangelize.[31]

Its focus in the early years was Dutchess and Westchester Counties in New York, a nearby spiritual wasteland that lacked strong churches at the close of the Revolution yet possessed congenial settlers of congregational leanings. The effort was successful enough that ten newly established churches in Westchester, where Amzi Lewis lived, and three in Connecticut formed an associated presbytery in October 1791. Two years later, a third presbytery called the Northern Associated Presbytery in New York was formed in that state's northern and western frontier, as was a fourth in 1807.[32]

The ties between the associated presbyteries were close, as the career of Silas Constant shows. Constant was born in 1750 in Waterbury, Connecti-cut, the son of a French army officer who was lost at sea shortly after Con-stant was born. Constant worked as a farmer and mill owner until the late 1770s, when he studied theology under Jacob Green. Constant became one of the first men to train with Green's new presbytery; on May 29, 1783, the presbytery's pastors formally examined his fitness for the ministry. Constant passed, and he reported, "I received ordination [on that day] and was sol-emnly set apart by fasting and prayer and the laying on of hands to the work of an evangelist." Amzi Lewis preached from Timothy 2:5, and Green deliv-ered the prayer and "gave the charge." Constant's first pastorship was in Orange County; by 1785 he was settled at Yorktown, New York. Green's influence on Constant was extensive; he taught him theology and passed on his views of a proper church government, so much so that one contempo-rary described Constant as "a Presbyterian of the Congregational order." Constant was a member of the Morris County Presbytery for nine years and became a founder and leading figure in the Associated Presbytery of West-chester County. During that time, as his journal shows, Constant attended the twice-yearly presbytery meetings in Morris County, which were held in Parsippany at Grover's church and in Hanover at Green's. On several occasions Constant preached while he was there, and Green returned the favor, delivering sermons in New York. Thus Green's presbytery and society remained in close touch with the men whom they sent into the field. Green, Grover, and other founding members of the Morris County Presbytery did brief evangelizing tours in New York as well. Things went well enough in these early years that ministers affiliated with the new presbyteries reported in 1796 that these bodies "increased in number, reputation and influence."[33]

Green's revolt, as a result, gained a small following within the American Presbyterian Church. He also succeeded in keeping the whole thing fairly civil. The secession did not devolve into ugly partisan warfare among Presbyterians, as had occurred during the Great Awakening. But the civility was the sign of a critical problem: Green avoided factionalism primarily because his rebellion, despite the movement's early promise, remained small and isolated. Only four associated presbyteries were formed, and all were in Morris County and New York. All four disbanded by 1825. Green's son Ashbel conceded that "the Morris county presbytery did not produce all the good effects which its founders (honestly we doubt not) expected, and almost predicted. Its influence was never extensive, and it gradually dwindled, till it has become nearly, if not altogether extinct." Presbyterianism's centralizing trend proved to be too powerful for Green to overcome, and his tiny movement was, to the church's leaders, more irritant than feared foe.[34]

Even in Hanover, Green's rebellion had only lukewarm support. Because of their great respect for Green, congregation members at Hanover Neck supported their pastor in his battle with the Synod, but they remained loyal to the Presbyterian Church. When the New York Presbytery in the early 1780s pressed the congregation to clarify its status with the church, members voted at a parish meeting on January 22, 1783, to continue their association with the New York Presbytery while retaining Green as their pastor. The Presbytery agreed to this odd arrangement, but it couldn't resist adding, "It is our sincere Prayer that God would so inform Mr. Green's mind, that he might have clearness to withdraw his declinature and return again to walk with us as formerly in the order of the Gospel when we took sweet counsel together."[35]

It did not happen. Hence, a great irony: Green led a movement for laymen's rights without the support of Presbyterian laymen. There was a second irony as well: although Green may have been out of step with his Presbyterian brethren, he was attuned to wider developments within American Protestantism in the postwar years. Spurred on by the ideals of the Revolution, American Christianity was becoming more democratic and more populist at the close of the eighteenth century. Laymen *were* gaining a stronger voice in the running of their churches, especially in the evangelical sects. A new gen-

eration of church leaders was attacking tradition and questioning the hierarchical principles that had overlain the prewar Christian scene. Viewed from
this broader perspective, Green was part of a far larger movement within
American Christianity. Methodists, Baptists, and others shared his crusade
for laymen's rights. They, too, wanted stronger congregations and a more
open ordination process that would allow lesser-educated men to enter the
ministry.[36]

Green's differences with these democratizing laymen were many, however.
Jacob Green still believed in an educated ministry; lower standards for some
did not mean *no* standards for all. The evangelical surge along the frontier
frightened him—the need to counter the advances of the Baptists and Methodists was one reason he was so anxious to get more Presbyterian ministers
into the field. He opposed the excessive emotionalism of the Great Awakening and wanted to avoid such a thing in the postwar years. He remained
uncomfortable with conversions spawned at evangelical revivals and camp
meetings that were not accompanied by a commitment to discipline. Although
he wanted laymen to have a greater say in the church, he opposed a Christian
democracy that trashed learning and respect for authority.

In all these ways, the conservative side of Jacob Green reemerged. He
espoused a postwar radicalism, with limits.

## The Loyalist Down the Road:
### Thomas Bradbury Chandler in Postwar Limbo

During the final years of the war, Chandler's mood was as fickle as the London weather—brief bouts of sunshine, followed by long periods of gloom.
News of battlefield victories raised his spirits, as did changes in administration. Greater resolve, and more money, would turn the tide for the redcoats,
he continually believed. Yet the trend was ominous, and Chandler knew it.
When talk arose in London of pursuing peace with the rebels, he advised his
British friends to fight on.

December 1780 was one such time late in the war when his mood was
hopeful. In a letter to Samuel Seabury, he reported, "One of the best Things
I can inform You of is, that we have got a good Parliament, with a respectable, secure Majority in Favor of Administration, and resolved to support

the King in pursuing the most vigorous Measures for bringing the War to an honorable and proper Termination. All the supplies called for have been granted without a Division."

But then came Cornwallis's surrender at Yorktown on October 19, 1781, dashing the last, best chance of a British military victory, and in March 1782 Parliament empowered the king to negotiate peace with the Americans. Still, Chandler was not yet ready to concede defeat:

> The death of Lord Rockingham, about a month ago [in July], has produced another change, which I hope will be advantageous. . . . Lord Shelburn, a warm and avowed enemy to the independence of the Colonies, is the Minister being at the head of the Treasury. . . . It is thought that the Administration will soon undergo a second refinement, without which the strength of the nation cannot be properly exerted. In the meanwhile, I am well assured that it is the fixed purpose of Lord Shelburn not to lose the colonies. . . . The negotiations for peace are, for the present, at an end; and nothing remains but to fight it out.

Chandler was badly misinformed. On November 30, 1782, the two sides signed a preliminary peace treaty in Paris, and on February 4, 1783, Britain declared an end to hostilities. The rebels had won. Chandler's mood once again turned foul—he was livid about the British capitulation to the Americans, and he complained that Shelburne has "plunged the Nation into irretrievable ruin and everlasting infamy. We have been at a loss to account for such monstrous conduct." Feeling so betrayed, Chandler pinned his last hopes on Parliament. He was, of course, to again be disappointed—Parliament approved the peace terms. Chandler, who had long defended the Crown, the constitution, and the empire, turned his fury on the entire British nation: "When the terms of the Peace were known, we were in hopes that the Parliament would have so much wisdom and Spirit as to set it aside, and to renew the war with proper vigour. But it is over with England, her Stamina have failed; her Constitution is ruined; and her Disposition must follow."

His complaint that Britain's "Constitution is ruined" was telling. A decade in exile had only strengthened Chandler's belief that the health of the political nation rested on the union of church and state. While Jacob Green's views evolved during the Revolution and became more democratic, Chandler's remained unwavering. A strong monarchy and invigorated Church of England were essential—it was why he wanted an American bishop so badly. The loss of the colonies was thus devastating, and he had no confidence that a new American nation of dissenters, which kept church and state separate and rested on the people, could survive.

Still, Chandler could not resist turning his eyes to America and wondering what was going on there. "I am extremely impatient to hear in what manner the concessions of this country affect the minds of people in America, both of the Loyalists and of the now legalized, sanctified rebels," he wrote in a letter home on March 15, 1783. Chandler had famously predicted in 1775 that the Americans would never be able to get along; in this letter he was still worrying about the prospects of civil war. "I want much to know, whether the country is likely to become peaceable; or whether there is not a greater probability of a contest, previous to it, between the Republicans and Anti-Republicans, which must again bring on a deluge of blood."

In this early stage of peace, Chandler hoped the victorious Americans would be magnanimous to the loyalists and that the king's supporters could safely reside among the former rebels in the independent thirteen states. If that was not to be the case, Chandler warned that the loyalists would have to "remove into some part of what are now British dominions." As for himself, returning to New Jersey seemed implausible in March 1783. The two sides were too far apart; the damage was too great. "In what part of the world I shall fix myself is at present impossible to [say]," he told Seabury. "Canada appears, at this instance, to be most eligible." But that prospect did not excite him. And with the war lost, his health declining, and his prospects bleak, Chandler's mood again darkened.[37]

# *11*

## *Disciplinarian*

It was the last great reform effort of his life. After devoting several years to issues of national importance—finance, slavery, church government—Green in 1781 turned his gaze homeward. His health was problematic in the final decade of his life, but he remained energetic and focused. He wanted to make one last push for improving religious life by improving discipline among the devout. This time, though, there would be no best-selling tract, no sweeping critiques of American society as he had unleashed in 1770 in his *Vision of Hell*. Green would concentrate on the small church at Hanover Neck. More specifically, he would concentrate on the youths of his congregation. Change would begin at home.

The timing of this crusade was both telling and interesting. Green was alarmed over the toll that the war had taken on Hanover's religious life. Piety was waning, and discipline was faltering. More important, Green was worried about the dangers posed by the freedoms that he was creating as he launched his associated presbyteries and society for learning. The Calvinistic dilemma, in other words, was still bedeviling him, and his new crusade was an important attempt to solve it. Discipline, Green decided, would have to balance freedom. As he pushed for more freedom, he would redouble his efforts to improve discipline among the faithful.

The winter of 1780 had brought hardship to civilians and soldiers alike. General Washington and his Continental troops began arriving at Jockey Hollow, just south of Morristown, on December 1, 1779. It was a mountainous, forbidding place to encamp during a rugged winter. But Washington preferred the site because of its numerous advantages—a safe distance from the enemy, a generous supply of water and firewood, and close proximity to the villages of Morris County and their fertile farms. But after Christmas the snow and wind came. The troops' canvas tents collapsed under the weight of the heavy snow and the destructiveness of high winds. Ashbel's younger brother Calvin described 1780 in his diary as "a hard winter[,] the hardest winter we have had in many years. The snow was so deep that we could ride on the banks over the tops of fences with horses and sleighs. In some places the ice was so hard and thick some people went over to Staten Island with horses and sled." For the soldiers struggling to stay warm at Jockey Hollow, the deep snow meant the roads were impassable, and that food could not be delivered. For civilians, the troops' presence was another irritant in a long war full of them.[1]

At Hanover Neck, bad weather, the stresses of war, and a poor economy had taken their toll as well. Attendance fell at Pastor Green's church, and members became lax in their devotion to the Lord. In his fast-day sermon of 1778, Green condemned the "neglect and contempt of religion. . . . Not only the Sabbath, but religious people and religious exercises are treated with contempt." Green, of course, was deeply upset with this development, and he convened the congregation's session to discuss the situation. Attendees, according to the minutes, agreed with their pastor that the commencement of the "civil wars . . . put all things into confusion, and church discipline was not for a time much attended to." Prodded by Green, the members decided in the spring of 1781 that the church had to bring "offenders to a sense of duty." Thus, with the backing and aid of the congregation's elders and deacons, Green began trying to re-instill discipline in the children and adults of the church. He also worked to rekindle religious enthusiasm, an effort that culminated in Green's version of a revival (intense preaching, catechizing, religious study) in 1790—the first since 1774, when New Jersey was a colony and answered to King George III.[2]

Over a three-year period, Green drew up a series of agreements and presented them to the session for its approval. The most "conservative" of the documents was the Articles of Faith and Practice that the congregation adopted between November 1781 and April 1782. The statement, which was a recommitment by members to Calvinism and to their all-important mission of Christian charity and love, was the most conservative of the various documents because it most forcefully laid out Green's most cherished principles for a strong, pure church. The opening article reaffirmed, "As we believe the Scriptures of the Old & New Testaments to be the word of God and a sure guide, so we believe and hold that system of truths that are called Calvinistic." The congregation was again rejecting "Arminianism," deism, Unitarianism, and any other religious system of a liberal, revolutionary age. Let other places make liberalism their lodestar. In Hanover, Calvinism and the Bible would still reign. The congregation was also letting the world know that it remained committed to Presbyterianism despite Green's ongoing war with the Synod of New York and Philadelphia. The opening article explicitly affirmed, "We highly approve the doctrines contained in the Shorter catechism of the Assembly of divines at Westminster; we have very little or no exception to anything in that system."[3]

Most of all, the articles reaffirmed that the congregation was committed to Green's high admission standards of the prewar years: "We cannot take any into our body of fellowship, but such as will for substance agree with us in educating, disciplining, and regulating the children of the church, and in other church matters, otherways we should bring confusion, jars and discord into our church." The disciplining of children took especially high priority in the articles of faith: "The children of regular church members we view and consider as being holy and belonging to the Kingdom of heaven . . . and are such as God claims for his peculiar property; and they are to be watched over and treated as church members in full . . . and must attend all Christian duties, according to their knowledge and ability."[4]

The emphasis on good behavior by children (as well as by adults) stemmed, of course, from Green's lifelong concern with creating a purer church. Better to reach people when they were young, before bad habits had developed, he reasoned. But proper discipline for children was also Green's answer to Calvinism's critics, who argued that the doctrine of predestination removed any incentive for individuals to act morally. If God arbitrarily decided who was saved and who was damned, why should people behave? Green's response, which he worked out during his polemical wars with George Beckwith and Hugh Knox in the late 1760s and early 1770s, was that no individual knew whether he or she was of the elect; nor can another human truly know whether someone else has been saved. All a person can do was behave morally and demonstrate that he or she was worthy of election; bad behavior, conversely, revealed that one was not saved. For Green, the possibility of redemption was a powerful incentive for getting people to change their bad behaviors, and this basic belief underlay his commitment to raising disciplined, well-behaved children. Saintly behavior should begin at a young age, before adulthood.

Of course, Green's drive to improve the behavior of the young was not something he had just thought up in 1781; his effort had actually commenced before the war, in 1770, when he was winding up his polemical wars with Beckwith and Knox. The appendix to his June 29, 1770, tract, "An Humble Attempt Truly to State the Controversy," carefully laid out his thoughts on the disciplining of baptized children and why it was so important for the congregation do this.

"Discipline in its largest sense, comprehends the instruction & education of children," Green noted in that tract. "And doubtless the chh. ought to take care that children are properly educated & instructed." His expectations and standards were much higher for those children who were baptized as infants. "Those who are baptized into the sacred name of the Trinity, ought to know it, & what is implied in it; & that they are under peculiar obligation, to renounce the flesh, the world, & the devil," he explained. "They should have it inculcated upon them, that 'tis expected by the chh. & the world, that there will be a difference between them & others; that they are not to be allowed to live like the vicious profain part of mankind."[5]

But neither the church, nor ministers, nor the youths themselves were living up to this high standard, he lamented: "All will grant there is much need of a reformation in general; and surely 'tis needed among our youth as well as among others. . . . Gods people who have religion at heart are praying & waiting for a reformation." The neglect, Green continued, meant that the advantages of infant baptism were being lost. Baptism was designed to bring children into "a state of discipline" and to introduce them into "Gods family, putting them under the watch & care of the chh. & giving them the advantage of a pious education." The failure to teach and discipline them properly, Green said, gave credence to Anabaptist charges that infant baptism was meaningless and that only adults who understand what they were doing should partake.[6]

Thus for Green, discipline was a way to reclaim youths and to bring them into the church family, which would ensure that they were set on a Christian path: "Let us consider, that discipline is a means that God has often blessed. It has done much good. . . . It [has allowed the church] to reclaim them [offenders]; it has done good to others to warn . . . them." The end result, Green concluded, would be a stronger church that would command greater respect "in the eyes of the ungodly world. . . . Christ will approve those who keep their Garments clean in a corrupt time."[7]

In 1771, Green had the congregation adopt rules for disciplining children that laid out how he and the congregation were to handle the wayward. Discipline was to be a communal effort. "When a subject of discipline is guilty of Adultery, Fornication, Gross Drunkenness, or any gross sin," the statement of rules began, "the first step shall be for the minister, or . . . one of the elders, to go to said person and endeavor to convince [him or her] of the sin and the necessity of making public satisfaction. If the person complies 'tis well." But if the person either denied the charge or refused to change his behavior, he would have to go before the elders. If the elders were unable to persuade him to amend his ways, the elders and minister were to go public with the offense. In other words, the person was to be publicly humiliated; from the pulpit, Green would tell the world what the sinner had done and that he was refusing to repent. The person was then "considered as cut off from the chh."[8]

The prewar rules were harsh, and were meant to be. Green sought to not only punish the transgressor but also purify the church. The statement made that goal explicit. In publicly announcing the sin, Green and elders wanted "to free the chh from reproach and Blame on account of [said] persons offence." But they did soften this stance a bit by noting, "As all offences are not equally hainous and scandalous, some will be passed over with only a rebuke in private. . . . Others may be passed over with a confession and admonition before the Elders in private."[9]

With the war winding down in 1781, Green dusted off the 1771 code of conduct and got the congregation to recommit to it. First, the elders began aggressively enforcing the rules, hauling violators before them. Then, in 1782 and 1783, they passed yet more rules that spelled out what was expected of congregation members. The times had changed, however, and the tone of these documents (which, according to the session minutes, Green had drawn up) was markedly different from the prewar rules. The first document dealt with families. It was a covenantal document, stressing "that we ought to join together in christian affection to help and assist one another in our spiritual interests, and especially, in regulating our families." It also stressed how important children were and of the need "to do more than we have done in instructing, encouraging and regulating our children, whom we have devoted to God in a solemn Covenant."[10]

Striking, though, was the document's nod to the liberty of the times and its moderation compared to its 1771 predecessor: "Though some needful and useful restraints may be proper to be laid upon young people, yet we by no means propose to deprive them of proper opportunities of being in company . . . and conversing with one another. Human nature is formed for society." The rules had limits, in other words—the elders would go only so far in enforcing discipline. Yet the document carefully added that it was not giving free rein to licentiousness: "The right which young people have to society does by no means prove, that they have a boundless liberty to go into what company they please, or to go out at unseasonable hours. It is evident by Scripture and reason, that young people need guiding and directing, regulating and restraining."[11]

Compared with other contemporary evangelical groups, including pietists, the rules were not terribly onerous. Youths were not, for instance, barred from attending "frolicks" or from mingling with "bad" company. Instead the agreement mildly stated, "If disorderly persons . . . come to our houses in the evening, we will take prudent measures to discharge them by bed-time." The rules also did not bar children from chasing after the latest worldly fashions; it merely encouraged them "to avoid extravagancies in fashions and dress." The agreement did require "that our baptized children above twelve or fourteen years old, shall attend sacramental lectures; and desire that our pastor will suit part of his discourse at these times, to instruct, excite and bring forward your youth for the Lord's Table." Children also needed permission to "go abroad into company" and were barred from going out after bedtime.[12]

By contrast, the Moravians and many other evangelical groups required their members to sign pages-long Brotherly Agreements regulating behavior. In the Moravian agricultural settlements in backcountry North Carolina—open communities that resembled Hanover in important ways—members of all ages pledged to avoid worldly customs, such as horse racing, excessive drinking, shooting matches, and "frolicks" (spinning, cotton picking, cornhuskings). Members also promised not to lie or cheat, and the Brotherly Agreements strictly regulated intermixing between the sexes. Hanover's agreement did none of those things and was voluntary, and it stressed how important cooperation was to its success: "With proper liberty to think for ourselves, and to differ in some things, we do for substance agree in the foregoing articles, and think proper to show our agreement by signing our names hereunto; and agree that none shall be urged to sign, and those that do it shall do it of their own offer and choice." Twelve families signed on—the fathers put their names to the pact, the mothers did not—but their signature did not automatically bind their children to the rules. They, too, had to voluntarily agree. Sixteen children did, including Green's three youngest.[13]

The careful tone continued in the "catechumens" adopted by the congregation on July 3, 1783. This document again stressed the voluntary nature of discipline—if a member wanted to be a candidate for communion, it was his choice, but once he applied, he would have to submit to the rigorous examination process involved. As with the rules for regulating families, communion candidates had to voluntarily sign the catechumens. In signing, a candidate signaled that he was "willing and desirous to attend the exercises, the instructions and examinations appointed by the chh., or the minister, for the purpose of instructing and fitting candidates for church communion." Green or the elders would personally examine each candidate in the congregation; candidates were further required to attend "sacramental lectures." Most of all, they were to "cheerfully submit to the care and discipline of the church, thinking it a privilege to be watched over in that manner. And if we shall be scandalous and not make satisfaction for our offense . . . we think it right for us to be cut off from the number of candidates in a manner that may be a warning to others."[14]

The document was extraordinary, even clever, in its careful balancing of discipline and liberty. One was not forced to submit to discipline, but when a member voluntarily agreed to abide by a higher standard, he or she was subject to far stricter rules of conduct. Thus these documents reflected Green's approach to the postwar years and the great influence of the American Revolution on his thinking. He wanted to keep standards high, but he was operating in an environment that fostered liberty and individual rights—an environment that he himself was encouraging with his rebellion against the Presbyterian Synod and his push for democratic rights. By the early 1780s, voluntarism had become the byword and inclusiveness the guiding spirit. Such an ethos linked Green's efforts to improve discipline with his effort to create an associated presbytery. Both reforms rested on a key pillar—those who joined did so because they wanted to. Green in the early 1780s was thus moving further and further away from the prewar (and Chandlerian) ideal of an all-encompassing state church that linked the temporal and the spiritual.

Beginning in 1781, the session resumed meeting regularly, and disciplinary cases dominated its proceedings. On April 4, 1782, Green reported that

"Widow Elisabeth Cooper had . . . offered her confessions for her sin [of fornication] and . . . that she will appear to make her confession in publick as soon as she has opportunity." Unlike the widow Cooper, Sylvanus Hedge proved to be uncooperative, and the session felt "obliged to, and do as a body, cut him off and declare him no to be longer a member of this church." Cooper, however, did not follow through on her promise to confess, and she found herself in trouble again in mid-June, when the session reluctantly cast her out, adding that "we shall yet be glad to find in her a penentent disposition, and shall be free to restore her when she gives satisfaction which the gospel requires." Eventually she did, in July, when she apologized for breaking the Seventh Commandment.[15]

The session's intent was always to bring the lost sheep back into the forgiving fold of the church family, and that principle applied not only to adult members but also to those persons who were baptized as babies but then strayed from the congregation as they grew older. Under Green's prodding, the session approved a formula for restoring these youthful offenders to full membership—a formula that again mixed the voluntary and the punitive. Signers agreed that "you do now freely acknowledge that you have been a sinful straying creature, have dishonored God by many sins, and have not improved church privileges . . . but you now seriously declare your renunciation of your sins; and that you turn to God thro. Jesus Christ." In other words, the wayward were welcomed back—if they followed the rules and made "the word of God the rule of your conduct."[16]

Green's sermons in the early 1780s reflected the changed times as well: he still preached on the need for his followers to live disciplined lives if they were to be saved, but the tone of his sermons was different—more hopeful, more unabashed in their calls for Christian activism, more evangelical. This change was most noticeable in Green's selection of sermon texts. He had always built his weekly sermon around a short reading from the Old or New Testament, and these texts established the lessons that he wanted to impart to his listeners. The texts, as a result, serve as markers of Green's thinking and goals. In the 1760s, an astonishing 78 percent of his extant, unpublished sermons were built around a passage from John (the fourth gospel in the New Testament and Green's personal favorite), and only 11 percent were from Acts of the Apostles (see table 4). In the 1770s, as war drew near and then finally got under way, Green drew on Acts 30 percent of the time, nearly triple the rate from a decade earlier, while his use of John dropped to 61 percent. In the 1780s, with the war over and Green's goals changing, Acts became the majority text, at 52 percent, and John the minority, at 46 percent.

Table 4   Jacob Green's sermon texts by decade

| Book of Bible | 1760s | 1770s | 1780s |
| --- | --- | --- | --- |
| John | 78% | 61% | 46% |
| Acts | 11% | 30% | 52% |
| Other | 11% | 9% | 2% |

SOURCE: Texts compiled from Green's extant unpublished sermons found in CO257, Box 11, Folders 1–7, Ashbel Green Papers 3A, Princeton University (total: 188 sermons).

John was Green's favorite New Testament book for so many years because its lessons meshed so neatly with his vision—to spark a believing faith in his listeners. In its pages, John tells the story of the seven miracles and relates the seven "I am" statements of Christ, recording events that led to Jesus's resurrection and his claims to divinity. John's narrative, in other words, was a progressive glorification of Jesus, relying on vivid imagery comparing Christ to bread, light, a shepherd, and a vine. The gospel was a heartfelt book on faith that appealed to a heartfelt minister who preached on the importance of believing in Jesus. In 1765, for example, Green read from John 1:29: "The next day John saw Jesus coming toward him, and said, 'Behold! The Lamb of God who takes away the sin of the world!'" Green's sermon then explained the passage's meaning, how Christ's sacrifices atoned for humankind's sins. "Christ takes away sin by bearing it," he stressed. "Our sins were imputed to him, i.e., he took the guilt upon himself."[17]

During the dark years of the American Revolution, when New Jersey was suffering from the twin blows of British invasion and civil war, Green devoted more sermons to bucking up his war-weary congregants, and he relied on both John and Acts to accomplish this task. His message was relatively simple. In November 1776, when New Jersey faced invasion from General Howe's troops, Green took to the pulpit and read from Acts 26:18, in which Jesus tells his persecutors to follow him, "to open their eyes, in order to turn them from darkness to light, and from the power of Satan to God, that they may receive forgiveness of sins." And then in 1779, when no end to the war appeared to be in sight, Green read from Acts 18: "Do not be afraid, but speak, and do not keep silent; for I am with you, and no one will attack you to hurt you."[18]

From such texts Green segued into his wartime message that good Christians must persevere during trying times. These sermons, though, were never overtly political. Instead, they sometimes used martial imagery to reinforce longtime themes of redemption. In one intriguing sermon he delivered in 1778, Green discussed "the advantage of faith in the dismal times we have to encounter." He likened "our corruptions" to the enemy: faith is "absolutely necessary . . . [if] our corruptions are to be withstood." Those who do keep the faith, Green told his listeners, can "consider the greatness of happiness that awaits every conqueror." By contrast, those without faith can expect to receive "wounds to our souls." The sermon ended quite lyrically by Green's standards: "Let us think of the crowns of Glory[,] the palms of victory[,] the songs of triumph that we shall be admitted to as soon as we have passed thro the battle St. Paul encouraged." We will get through this war, Green was telling his congregants. We will emerge from this ordeal stronger, because our belief in God will be stronger, and we will have the chance to reform our ways.[19]

In 1779, he gave a sermon on the new birth, which he delivered several times in various places across Morris County, that used the political imagery of the times to describe the life-changing nature of conversion. Its metaphors were twofold—slavery/bondage and sin; and freedom/liberty and Christ. The text's imagery was explicit as well: "If the Son makes you free, you shall be free indeed" (John 8:36). "Freedom," Green said succinctly as he began his sermon, "is desired by all men. We think it a dreadful thing to be Slaves," but in the religious sphere it actually presented an opportunity for the sinner: "When persons are faithful subjects to the prince he rules over them. They serve him with delight. So with sinners; you are one faith in service to him [the devil], & you take pleasure & delight therein." But believing in Christ and in God represented a way out of bondage: "Freedom lies on the other side. . . . Freedom in prayer, freedom in meditation can let you out of prison and into [a] new land of liberty." Rejecting this path will leave sinners as "Slaves. You are still in bondage. [You] are held in the cords of your sins: a worse servitude, a 1,000 times [worse] than to be the meenest [*sic*] Slaves upon Earth."[20]

Belief in Christ will put the sinner in "a happy state," Green continued. "You shall enjoy a glorious freedom throughout eternity if Christ sets you free from the reigning power of sin. You shall live and reign with him forever & ever—if you will now come from under your slavery, you shall never more be the servants of sin." Failing to change will carry dire consequences: "If you are not set at liberty now you will be shut up in the prison of hell & the everlasting seal set upon the door & there will be no possibility of being set at liberty."[21]

This sermon was about as political as Green ever got; the overwhelming majority of his wartime sermons were not odes to patriotism, and he never ventured far from his lifelong mission of constructing a purified church in a society polluted by humanity's sins. Unlike other Whiggish ministers of this period, he did not deliver sermons calling an independent America a New Israel; nor did he turn millennialism into a political tool, where the ancient Hebrews became republicans or where the return of Christ meant the establishment of a kingdom resting on civil and religious liberties. Instead, most of his extant sermons in the 1770s still argued that individuals must change their sinful behavior in order to show they were of the elect. The tone, nevertheless, was distinctive from other periods, with these sermons relying more on martial imagery than did those discourses that came earlier and later.[22]

The greater reliance on Acts beginning in 1781 signified yet another shift in Green's mood—he became more optimistic in the postwar years and more determined to make people good and active Christians. Acts has long intrigued theologians; one modern minister praised it as "one of the most thrilling books of the Bible—you can't help but see what power was unleashed . . . power to overcome great hardship and persecution, power to heal and bless, power to minister and preach and proclaim." A recent historian of Christianity likened Acts to a historical novel because of the way it recounted the adventures of Paul and other early Christian advocates. Green's attraction to Acts was thus fairly obvious. Through its tales of Paul's and Saul's conversions, and through its accounts of Paul's missionary journeys, Acts demonstrates the important ways that Christianity is an activist faith.[23]

The key theme in Acts is the universality of Christianity. It preaches that Jesus's teachings were for all humanity, and it emphasizes the centrality of the resurrection. Indeed, another minister sermonizing in the twenty-first century called Acts 10 "the single most important chapter in the Bible. Without this chapter, without what Peter discovered about the good news of Jesus, we wouldn't have a Christian church today. It tells us how the message of Jesus grew from something of interest to just a small corner of the world's people—one tribe, really, one limited community—to a universal message to Creation." For Green, the activist element stressed in Acts was essential to what he was trying to accomplish after the Revolution: he believed in a church that must grow and prosper. With greater urgency in the 1780s, he began preaching that as freedoms (and temptations) increased, disciplined people must give up their sinful ways and turn to Christ.[24]

That was a simple, basic evangelical message (one that bypassed the Calvinistic debate over Jesus Christ's role in salvation),[25] but Green's hour-plus sermons used Acts to inculcate several things simultaneously. On one Sunday in 1786, he first read from Acts 10:42: "And He Commanded us to preach to the people, and to testify that it is He who was ordained to be Judge of the living and the dead." One important message was that everyone will face Judgment Day, and everyone must prepare for that day. "We must all stand before the Judgment Seat of Christ," Green explained, and this meant that a person would be remanded "according or proportioned to their Works." (As other sermons made clear, he did not literally mean that someone could "work" their way into heaven; he was saying that a person would be judged by her faith in Christ and by her character.) Green then cited Acts 17:31, which showed that "God hath appointed a Day in that which he will Judge the world in Righteousness by that Man whom he hath ordained. . . . And he commanded us to preach unto the People & to testify that is he, who was ordained." Thus Green's second message was that people had to get out and share their faith. This hopeful message of Jesus's saving grace leavened the earlier, more harsh one that everyone will face a day of reckoning, with hell a distinct possibility. It was further leavened by Green's portrayal of Jesus—Christ was the "compassionate Saviour," an "elder Brother" who loves all.[26]

Other sermons expounded on what constituted good behavior—and what did not. Using Acts 24:16, Green preached that one must always "strive to have a good conscience without offense toward God and man." In another sermon, he addressed a complaint of the congregation's youths, who felt a double standard was at work, that their pastor was singling them out in his drive for greater discipline and letting older members get away with sinful behavior. For these critics, Green had a message on this day: "Young people wonder why we say so much to them & no more to the old—for let me tell them the old [are] as bad or worse than they. You hurt Religion & your own. [You] neglect your families" and "tarry late at taverns." He expected older members to set an example and to lay down the law in their homes. The young could take some comfort from this scolding, but not too much. Green reiterated in the sermon that they also must work harder to avoid sin, concluding, "I apply myself to you who are in your youth & especially to such of you [who] are most rude airy wanton & ungovernable. . . . I have built my doctrine [so that] you might be convinced of your evil—& I desire now to reason and expostulate with you and persuade you to forego this practice. I persuade you for your own good. Your soul may be lost."[27]

As his primary teaching tool, Green used Acts constantly in the 1780s, but one period especially stood out: beginning on May 23, 1784, and concluding on September 26, 1784, he delivered thirteen sermons on Sunday that went through about one-fifth of the book in order, beginning with the first verse in the first chapter. When he finally did give his hearers a break from Acts, his texts did not deviate much from his basic message that people can and should change their ways, and that all (in the spirit of Acts) were to be activists in bringing about a reformation of behavior.[28]

Green wanted all congregation members to participate in the great task of policing behavior, and he turned to Proverbs 27:5 ("Open rebuke is better than love carefully concealed") to explain how. Rebukes should be done forthrightly, forcefully, and fairly, Green instructed: "An open rebuke is one that is given in a full frank & hearty manner; to a man's face in his hearing; in opposition to a mean clandestine method of divulging a person's failings behind his back, & spreading them among others to his great disadvantage without letting him know them himself." Green noted that, given man's great moral shortcomings, the justifications for interceding were numerous: "Our usefulness in the world very much depends upon our being Suitably free from failings, oddities & disagreeable conduct, so tis absolutely necessary that we should acquaint others with their failings."[29]

He was careful to stress that criticisms should be offered up in a loving, Christian manner. "Reproving others or acquainting them with their failings should be done in the most suitable time, in the most suitable manner & by the most suitable persons. . . . Let your friend or Neighbour see that tis not done from any personal pique, or as retaliation for an injury that you suppose you have received, but from a kind regard you have for him." The point, he continued, was to use rebukes as "a means of converting a Soul from Sin & Error [and for leading the person to] God & holiness."[30]

In most of his postwar sermons, Green used the hopefulness of his evangelical message to counterbalance his dark, Calvinistic views of human nature. A sermon on Jeremiah 4:21 captured this balancing act well. The text read simply, "How long will I see the standard, *and* hear the sound of the trumpet?" From this cryptic passage, Green built a sermon around the terrible mistakes that God's people, including Jews, have made through the ages. He did not mince words at the outset—he called this failing "an exceeding great Stupidity and Insensibility" in all of humankind, a stupidity that hurts both God and religion. Yet it did not have to be that way, Green said. People have it in their capacity to change, to live moral lives of Christian rectitude, for balancing the "great Stupidity" inherent in human nature was man's reason. "Mankind have Reason & Understanding & Light & Evidence sufficient to discern or discover the importance of these things," he maintained. "The Fall has not destroyed man's reason & Understanding but mankind are capable by these to know & discover the Faith respecting God & his Perfections as is clear from Roman 1:20–21"—a passage that stresses that humans have "clearly seen" God's virtues since he created the world.[31]

Green's prewar sermons similarly noted that "God in great goodness honoured man with a nature far superior to [a beast's]. He has endowed man with rational & spiritual substances." Yet many of these sermons portrayed God as far more angry and vengeful to those who neglected him than did his Acts-inspired sermons of the 1780s. For Green, Acts 5:31 shows God's love, for he made Jesus our "Prince and Savior, to give repentance to Israel and forgiveness of sins." He used Acts 9:4 to demonstrate that "we learn great love & compassion from Christ to his chh. He was god. [He was] highly exalted." The postwar sermons thus were more evangelical, more focused on the good things that can happen to those who turn to Jesus and reform their ways. A sermon that Green gave on the new birth in 1789 exemplified this spirit. He used Psalm 55:22 to inspire: "Cast your burden on the Lord, and he shall sustain you." The God in this sermon was a kind one; he "freely receives and helps without exception. . . . It is for his Glory to forgive sins—to help in outward troubles. Others will be encouraged to put trust in him." The Calvinist in him was never far away, though—a new birth rested in God's hands, Green stressed, and not the sinner's; the ability of someone to become a new creature "depends wholly upon the good will and pleasure of God," Green said. The result was an entirely new creature who "has a new tongue, new ears, new hands, new feet, new companions."[32]

Green's twin drive in the 1780s to improve discipline and to spark piety enjoyed some success. Membership on Hanover Neck grew steadily, albeit slowly, during the decade from 102 members in 1780 to 138 in 1789, when it jumped in 1790 by more than 45. That year, the congregation experienced "a glorious revival of religion—a work silent, deep, and effectual," according to Ashbel Green. It was the congregation's first revival since 1774, and it led (by Ashbel's reckoning) to the conversions of more than thirty souls. Ashbel attributed the revival's success to his father's hard work; as he put it, "The people of this congregation had been thoroughly indoctrinated" by his father who catechized and "conversed" with the youths weekly. He also attributed it to the "special outpouring of the Holy Spirit"—a polite way of saying that the congregation felt the spirit, partly because of Green's evangelizing sermons.[33]

Still, during a forty-four-year pastorate, such "revivals" were few and far between. (Green, an evangelical minister, held only four, and they really had as much to do with catechizing and study as with Bible-thumping sermons.) Their infrequency was especially noteworthy considering what was happening elsewhere in the evangelical world—in the prewar years, the first Great Awakening continued to rumble into the 1760s with revivals being held periodically in the middle colonies; in the postwar years, revivals gripped New England from 1780 to 1782 and became a major force in other places, especially in the South, after 1785. Why Green held so few is attributable partly to his personality. He was not an emotional man. He espoused a controlled evangelicalism that downplayed emotion and played up reason. He avoided the histrionics of the successful revivalists, and he did not go on barnstorming tours (although he did preach in New York at the affiliated associated presbyteries). Not surprisingly, the 1790 revival attracted no attention beyond Hanover Neck despite the commencement of the Second Great Awakening—Ashbel reported that Hanover's "glorious work of grace had been so silently carried on, that a minister of gospel, only nine miles distant, told the present writer, that he had never heard there was a revival in the congregation." It was a quiet, unassuming revival befitting the quiet, unassuming personality of its pastor.[34]

To the end, his sermons read like the lectures of a Harvard professor. Green laid out his arguments and set out his points that he wanted to "prove." For all his deep faith, and for all his fears that man had been tainted since the Fall, Green still believed in the power of the mind and in man's ability to reason. In this important sense, he remained a creature of the Enlightenment, and of the revolutionary world he inhabited. Part of him believed in progress, and in the individual. People *can* change, and can improve. The Jacob Green of 1790 felt that when people were given a choice, they were capable of making the correct decision. As a pastor, the key was to lay out the terrible consequences that awaited those who made bad choices while experiencing the American freedoms—and the happy consequences that awaited those who made good ones. With great patience and persistence, Green expounded on this lesson year after year. Ashbel, the brilliant scholar son who knew his father as well as anyone, came up with the perfect epitaph that went on Jacob's gravestone: "He was a man of temper even, firm and resolute; of affections temperate, steady and benevolent; of genius solid, inquisitive, and penetrating. . . . As a preacher, he was instructive, plain, searching, practical."[35]

The American Revolution helped bring him to this point. He saw the war as a glorious, divine opportunity to achieve his dream of improving society. Into the 1780s, he retained his faith in the individual to make correct choices. Indeed, his democratic faith grew despite the turmoil of the decade, where many elites worried that revolts of unruly mobs posed a bigger threat to liberty than had the venality of the British Parliament. While fellow New Divinity devotee Samuel Hopkins was fretting that the gains of the American Revolution were temporary and that the chaos of the 1780s was becoming the norm, Green was unperturbed. And while others, including Chandler, were preaching on the need to create stronger churches and a more powerful central government to prevent anarchy and promote order, Green was pushing a holistic system of reform that emphasized voluntarism *and* good behavior. He evinced little concern about the rebellions along the Pennsylvania and Massachusetts frontiers or about the supposed weaknesses of the Articles of Confederation. He did not bother taking up his pen, as he had during the heady days of the American Revolution. Unlike legions of Federalists who were clamoring for a powerful national government, Green was serenely confident that the American nation would grow and prosper if it retained a proper balance between God and mammon, piety and hard work.

During this tumultuous period, Pastor Green kept his focus on his church and his associated presbytery. His final spate of reforms, which were all intended to lead to a purer church and society, drove him during the 1780s, and he put all his energies into making them a reality. Discipline was critical, and piety was essential. Some might see these causes as parochial. Jacob Green did not.

———◆◆◆———

## *The Loyalist Down the Road: Thomas Bradbury Chandler—* *Return of the Bishop's Cause*

Chandler was destined to spend two more years in London. This final chapter of his life contained a major surprise, and several ironies. With the war lost, Whitehall belatedly realized the role that episcopacy could play in keeping a colony loyal to the Crown. This reversal of policy was a vindication for Chandler, who had argued the importance of episcopacy for years. In Canada, the Crown would not repeat the mistakes it had made in the thirteen colonies to the south. Nova Scotia, where a loyalist community was forming in the 1780s, would get a bishop . . . and his name was Thomas Bradbury Chandler. The great reform cause of Chandler's life was at last close to being fulfilled, albeit in a remote outpost, and he himself would have the honor of holding the office.

But, in a cruel irony, it was too little, too late. The thirteen colonies were lost and Chandler was suffering from smallpox and a cancerous nose; indeed, his health was so poor that he did not think he could fulfill the demanding position of bishop. Instead, he badly wanted to go home to Elizabeth Town so he could see his family. In another cruel irony, however, his lifelong dream of securing an American bishop was complicating his efforts to return to New Jersey—to leave London for America, he needed the permission of the archbishop of Canterbury, John Moore, and his grace was reluctant to give it until the Nova Scotia question was settled. Chandler grew impatient with his delayed departure and took matters into his own hands. On April 19, 1785, he went ahead and "engaged a passage in the *Mentor*." On April 21, according to his diary, he met with Moore and "obtained the Archbishop's consent to cross the Atlantic on a visit to my family." A letter to his friend Samuel Seabury explained what happened during a whirlwind three days: "The *Mentor* was the last Ship of the season that was bound to New-York; in the full maturity of deliberation I resolved to take my passage in her. As soon as this resolution was formed, and before it was known to any one but Mr. Boucher, I waited on the Archbishop to inform [him] of it, and to resign my professions to the Nova-Scotia Episcopate. On talking the matter over, his Grace approved of the voyage."

But the archbishop would not release Chandler from "the above-mentioned claim" to the bishopric. The best deal that Chandler could get was that he would relocate to Elizabeth Town and there "hold myself in readiness to obey his Summon when he should be able to make it."

With the all-important meeting behind him, Chandler stepped up his preparations to depart. On April 29, he made a down payment of twenty-five pounds for passage on the *Mentor*. Then he began packing, an arduous task after ten years abroad that included filling more than twenty boxes of books. Into an "old large black trunk" went his clothes for the sea voyage and his ointments; into a "little flat hair trunk" went his breeches and understockings. On May 16, Chandler bade farewell to London and went to Gravesend, a river town about twenty-five miles from London, where the *Mentor* was docked. The next day, the ship set sail.

Reviled when he left ten years earlier, forced to flee a radical faction that wanted to string him up on the nearest liberty pole, Chandler arrived in Elizabeth Town after a voyage of fifty-five days to a far different scene. Elizabeth Town's Presbyterians must have still looked askance at their Anglican nemesis, but Chandler was jubilant to find a sympathetic, even adoring, crowd awaiting him. Indeed, he reported that the crush of visitors greeting him was so great, "I have not been able to command half an hour time together—such is the amazing crowd of visitors from all quarters . . . old and young, black and white, male and female, whig and tory, Churchman and Dissenters, not only from this but from all the neighboring towns, to congratulate me on my return to this country! When I tell you that I have not yet been able to open one of my 22 boxes of books, you will form some opinion of my want of time." Chandlerian excess, perhaps, but Thomas Bradbury Chandler was home.

Unresolved was what to do about Nova Scotia. When Chandler departed London, his superiors still wanted him to move to that chilly outpost and fill the proposed episcopal office there. His friends and allies wanted him to do so as well; other contenders for the post maneuvered cautiously as they tried to learn Chandler's intentions. One was Samuel Seabury, who had been elected bishop of Connecticut by the Anglican clergy in that state in March 1783. But it was a minor post, devoid of any real power, and it lacked official standing in London. A High Church Anglican who shared Chandler's dreams for episcopacy and monarchy in the colonies, Seabury wanted an appointment from the Church of England, and he wrote a letter to the home office informing it of that fact. "No competition with Dr. Chandler is intended," he began carefully, "but should he be set aside, there may be other contenders," and Seabury asked that his wishes be known. And, indeed, with Chandler's health declining, Archbishop Moore offered the position to Jonathan Boucher, but he would accept it only on Chandler's behalf, until the latter was well enough to don the episcopal robes. That offer was rejected as impractical, and Moore moved on to the next candidate—Charles Inglis, the Irish-born rector of Trinity Church in New York City who was a leader of the loyalist clergy during the war. Inglis, too, expected Chandler to become the first colonial bishop, but he wanted the post should his colleague be unable to accept. When that became obvious in 1786, Inglis agreed to serve, although it took a year for Moore's recommendation to receive official approval. By August 1787, a bishopric for Nova Scotia was a reality, and in these early years Bishop Inglis's realm would include Quebec, New Brunswick, and Newfoundland, until another bishop was appointed for them. The normally loquacious Chandler had little to say about this happy turn of events. But one can imagine a smile crossing his face when he heard the news that the colonies in America were, at last, getting a bishop.[36]

# *Epilogue*

In life, they lived parallel lives and pursued parallel reform causes; and so it was in death, with the two old warriors departing the earthly battlefield within a month of each other, in early 1790.

For Jacob Green, the Lord called first. It was an unexpected visit.

"In May, 1790, the influenza was epidemick and he was affected by it," Ashbel Green recalled. "The symptoms, however, did not seem threatening, and he did not consider himself as in a dangerous illness, till a very short time before his dissolution." With his condition worsening and his physician and his wife, Elizabeth, informing him that the end was near, Green grew silent and reflective. When, according to Ashbel, Elizabeth asked about his prospects for the afterlife, Green responded, " 'I have a hope'—and after a short interval added—'and some fear.' These, it is believed, were the last words that he uttered."

Green departed on May 24, 1790. He was sixty-eight.[1]

Thomas Bradbury Chandler would soon follow. His health had not been good for years. In 1760 or so, he contracted smallpox, and this distressingly common infliction of the early modern period (which killed an estimated four hundred thousand Europeans in the closing years of the eighteenth century alone) bothered him for the rest of his life. It worsened during his exile in sodden London, forcing him to spend one summer on the Isle of Wight, where he subsisted (according to a nineteenth-century biographer who interviewed Chandler's daughter) on goat's milk, "in the hope that he might thereby be benefited; but neither that nor any other expedient that medical skill could suggest, had any favourable effect."

As the "cancerous affection" worsened, Chandler's characteristic energy flagged, and he was too sick to serve as pastor of St. John's Church or to move to Nova Scotia. He spent his final years in quiet study, venturing outside only to officiate at an occasional funeral, "his head covered with a handkerchief." Chandler hung on for a few years, until the Lord commanded him to join him on June 17, 1790. Being the good loyalist that he was, Chandler complied. He was sixty-four.[2]

The simultaneous passing of Jacob Green and Thomas Bradbury Chandler in 1790 was fitting. The revolutionary era was ending, and the new republic, bolstered by George Washington's inauguration as president a year earlier after the adoption of the federal constitution, was beginning. In many ways, the religious terrain had shifted from the heady days of the 1760s and 1770s when Green was dueling with other ministers over the momentous questions of free will and predestination and Chandler was lashing out at Whig radicals as fanatics. Chandler's reform cause—bringing a bishop to the thirteen colonies—was no longer du jour; yet in some ways, neither was Green's. Keeping Calvinism relevant and untying the Gordian knots of predestinarian beliefs (two issues that so consumed Green during his lifetime) were also no longer relevant as the nineteenth century dawned. The nature of "radicalism" was changing in the new republic as well. Evangelism was becoming both more important and more mainstream as it gained acceptance—that is, bringing more people to the new birth was the all-consuming challenge for the Methodists, Baptists, Presbyterians, and others, not defending Calvinism in an enlightened age against the advances of science.[3]

Yet Green's reform legacy lived on in important ways. During the American Revolution, his far-reaching plans to change society could be boiled down to three essentials—establishing laymen's rights and a democratic educational system that would open the ministry to more people; pursuing a voluntarism that would reinvigorate the church and lead to the creation of reform societies; and instilling discipline in religious seekers. All three essentials were important components of the evangelism that was spreading across antebellum America. Led by Presbyterians, New Divinity adherents, and evangelicals, denominational reformers of the early nineteenth century sought to use evangelism as a weapon to transform society. Part of that mission involved spreading religion throughout the South and West by launching a Second Great Awakening: convert the individual, and ultimately convert society.[4]

A host of voluntary groups sprang up to support this new wave of revivalism and to undertake the arduous task of instilling Christian discipline among the wayward. Groups distributed Bible tracts, formed Sunday schools, and taught literacy so that people would possess the skills needed to understand the Good Book. To improve morals, they launched temperance societies and vigorously attacked the excesses of the age. Thus, among his Presbyterian and Congregational brethren, much of what Green fought for survived: his central vision of voluntaristic groups working to purify society remained a key tenet to mainstream reformers and, in modest ways, helped shape the direction that this reform took.[5]

Despite these developments, Jacob Green in the end was not a terribly effective reformer. His genius was in anticipating the direction that the nation was heading—a rising democracy resting on a Jeffersonian middle class; a society no longer dominated by the wellborn—but he was far less successful in shaping this direction. A shy man with modest speaking and organizational skills, Green shunned the nitty-gritty of working within a church bureaucracy to bring about change. This failing is especially evident when his career is contrasted with that of Ashbel Green, Jacob's talented son who died in 1848.

Ashbel Green was born on July 6, 1762, in Hanover, the second son of Jacob and Elizabeth Pierson Green, Jacob's second wife (see fig. 8). Excelling in the classroom, Ashbel persuaded his father to drop his initial plans of making him a farmer. Instead, after teaching school and serving in the Morris County militia during the Revolution, he enrolled at the College of New Jersey at Princeton in 1782 as a junior. A year later, he graduated as valedictorian, delivering an oration before a large assemblage that included George Washington and members of Congress. In 1785, Ashbel was named professor of mathematics and natural philosophy at his alma mater, despite struggling with geometry as an undergraduate and possessing no real love of mathematics. That year marked another milestone for him as well: he married Elizabeth Stockton, heiress of a politically prominent family that lived on an estate about half a mile from Nassau Hall.[6]

Despite holding the chair in mathematics and philosophy, Ashbel studied divinity under John Witherspoon, the college president, and received his

*Fig. 8*  Ashbel Green, the second son of Jacob and Elizabeth Pierson Green, became president of the College of New Jersey in 1812 and an important Presbyterian reformer in his own right. Princeton University, Gift of Mr. Stockton Green, PP386. Photo: Princeton University Art Museum / Art Resource, New York (Bruce M. White).

license to preach from the New Brunswick Presbytery in February 1786. Like his father forty years earlier, Ashbel was initially unsure whether he wanted to be a minister (the Stocktons urged him to become a lawyer), but he was unhappy teaching math and decided to accept an offer to serve as co-pastor at Philadelphia's Second Presbyterian Church. That decision launched

Ashbel's long and illustrious career in the American Presbyterian Church, where his ascent in the leadership ranks was swift. In 1790, he served as administrative secretary for the Presbyterian General Assembly (an ironic appointment, given his father's opposition to the Assembly's creation), and two years later became chaplain to the U.S. Congress as the Presbyterian representative. In 1812, he was elected president of the College of New Jersey, having earlier served as interim president.

Although Ashbel praised Witherspoon as the most important influence in his life, he pursued causes that so consumed his father decades earlier. Like Jacob, Ashbel believed that discipline and purity were essential to the functioning of church and society. Like Jacob, he favored voluntary associations over strong governing bodies; voluntarism, he believed, was the best way to renew society and to keep it strong. And Ashbel shared his father's views on education, carrying on Jacob's fight to open up ministerial learning to more people and to create more nimble schools for training pastors.[7]

In May 1805, with the ministerial shortage still bedeviling the American Presbyterian Church, Ashbel urged the General Assembly to reform how it selected and trained candidates for the pulpit. Like his father before him, he advised the church leadership to find the right balance between faith and learning. The presbyteries, he told the Assembly, should pick "youths of capacity as well as of piety." The shortage was severe in the 1770s when Jacob was recommending the creation of special schools of theology and in the 1780s when he formed his Morris County Society for the Promotion of Learning and Religion; it was equally severe when Ashbel took up the cause in the early nineteenth century. In 1802, the Presbyterians had more congregations needing pastors than it had congregations with ministers—242 of the former compared to 181 of the latter, by one reckoning. In addition to the problems Jacob had identified years earlier (overly rigid licensing requirements and excessive emphasis on classical training, among other things), the college at Princeton was no longer producing the ministerial candidates as it had during the late colonial period.[8]

One interim solution was to hire a theology professor at the College of New Jersey who would oversee the postgraduate training of candidates, a proposal the trustees supported. Their choice was Ashbel Green (he declined). The longer-term solution was to create a seminary devoted to training ministers. Ashbel had been discussing the idea with colleagues for years, and in 1806 he urged the General Assembly to act. When it agreed to put a seminary proposal on its agenda, Ashbel drafted a plan that would deliver more and better-educated ministers to the American Presbyterian Church. The Assembly, however, declined to approve the proposal, citing the lack of support from the presbyteries. Undeterred, Ashbel persuaded the Presbytery of Philadelphia, of which he was a member, to petition the Assembly to establish a seminary, and he continued lobbying individual Presbyterians on his own. His persistence paid off, with key help from Samuel Miller, the chairman of a committee that had been formed to poll the presbyteries on whether they would support the creation of a seminary. Although the balloting had been inconclusive, Miller got the committee to call for a centrally located seminary that would consist of three professors and would be under the Assembly's control. The committee then instructed Ashbel to draft a more detailed plan for the seminary and to report back. He complied, and the committee passed along his plan to the Assembly in 1811. The Assembly, at last, adopted the plan in nearly its entirety.[9]

Thanks to Ashbel's determined lobbying, Jacob's vision of 1775 was finally realized—the seminary opened on August 12, 1812, at Princeton, on two acres that Ashbel bought from the Stockton family. Ashbel, who led the efforts to raise money for the school and did so much to organize it, was elected president of the board. Unlike his father, Ashbel worked effectively inside the halls of Presbyterian power, serving on numerous committees and assuming leadership positions, including the presidency of the College of New Jersey, that enabled him to influence the course of events. Jacob, by contrast, refused to attend synodal meetings for years and then seceded from the Presbyterian Church in 1779, choosing instead to operate outside the leadership. This aloofness cost him dearly—he had no standing to push his educational reforms. It also cost him when he opposed the plans to create a General Assembly. He again lacked the standing to block such a change. Nor did his effort to create associated presbyteries get very far, because of his isolation within Presbyterianism. After publishing one tract explaining why he and several other pastors were seceding from the Presbyterian Church, Jacob did not publish anything else.[10]

Ashbel, by contrast, became editor of the *Presbyterian* in 1822 after he left the presidency at Princeton and renamed it the *Christian Advocate*, and this publication became an effective sounding board for his various causes. One longtime effort was missionary work: in 1802, Ashbel was elected chairman of the Standing Committee of the General Assembly until his appointment as college president in 1812; he returned to the missionary board in 1822 and immediately set to work raising money and restoring its energy and influence. Because of his efforts he was elected both president of the board and chairman of the executive committee. When the Synod of Pittsburgh founded a foreign missionary society, Ashbel was elected a member of that society as well.[11]

For Ashbel, missions and social reform went hand in hand. Revivalism would bring more people to Christ; a rise in religiosity, in turn, would improve personal behavior and provide the foundation for broader social changes, because the conversion experience required activist Christians to reject selfishness. Evangelical religion, in short, would be the engine driving change in the new nation, not science or economics or an empowered federal government. "The public institutions of religion are unspeakably beneficial—perhaps I should rather say they are absolutely essential, to civil society," Ashbel explained. "Abolish the observance of the Sabbath and its public worship, and you shall see men rapidly decline into barbarism, rapine, and every ferocious and abominable vice." While others at Princeton pinned their hopes on the mind and the power of reason, Ashbel placed his in God and the heart.[12]

Was Ashbel more radical or conservative than his father was? The answer is somewhat surprising: in many ways, Jacob was the radical one and Ashbel the conservative. Yet that answer says as much about the eras they lived in and the shifting meaning of radicalism as it does about their beliefs, for the two men's principles differed little, and neither man pushed his ideas to extremes. Neither, for example, challenged gender relations or tried to create utopian communities where the faithful lived apart from a sinful world. Millennial thoughts of the end times did not consume them. In the tumultuous landscape of nineteenth-century America, many *were* obsessed with the end times and how to shake up society. The experiences and beliefs of three utopian groups are illustrative of what "radicals" outside the evangelical mainstream were trying to accomplish in the nineteenth century: the Shakers, the Oneida Perfectionists, and the Mormons. The Shaker movement was founded in the late eighteenth century by Ann Lee, the wife of an English blacksmith, who argued that the source of all sin on earth was the sex act. Shakers thus practiced celibacy and rejected traditional family practices, communing in tightly regulated colonies where members attempted to live perfect, godly lives in preparation for the second coming of Jesus. Simplicity in all things—architecture, furniture, lifestyle—was their credo. The Oneida Perfectionists took an opposite tact from the Shakers: they pursued "complex marriage." Founded by John Humphrey Noyes in 1841, the Oneida community in Putney, Vermont, practiced a communism of property, where members shared everything—including their spouses. Each woman was the wife of every man, and every man was the husband of every woman. Noyes and his adherents saw this sharing as the opposite of sinful—in their minds, they were saints who were purified by religious experience. By living in godly perfection, Oneida's members believed they were hastening the day when the millennium would arrive.[13]

The Mormons shared with the Shakers and Oneida the desire to create a more perfect society. The movement's founder was Joseph Smith, a visionary who lived in the "burned-over district" in upstate New York. After being visited by an angel named Moroni, Smith unearthed golden plates in the Hill Cumorah that told the tale of the Nephites and Lamanites, descendants of the lost tribe of Israel. Smith's translation of these plates led to the publication in 1830 of *The Book of Mormon*, a holy tome that became the Mormons' bible and lodestar. A central tenet of Mormonism was that America was the promised land, a special place where the Mormons would restore the true church. Those who joined and followed its dictates could count on becoming gods and entering the celestial kingdom. Unlike Ann Lee (and other Christians for that matter), Smith rejected the idea of original sin; he saw Adam not as the source of human foibles but as a hero, the revered father of humankind who mated with nature. Early Mormonism embraced polygamy, believing the practice was a way to strengthen the church and allow more people to enter the celestial kingdom.[14]

Wildly divergent in practice, these radical groups shared a desire to achieve godly perfection. The reform drive of the two Greens—and, more broadly, evangelical America—was staid by comparison. Did this staidness make the Greens "conservative" reformers? Were they relics of a bygone era who were limited by their devotion to Calvinism? In one sense, the answer is yes: they did not challenge the basic tenets of society because of their commitment to an evangelical Calvinism. But probe deeper and a different picture emerges. Although Calvinism was a fading intellectual force in the new republic, its impact on reform among its adherents had not changed. It could still produce a reforming drive just as strong as that of Ann Lee, John Humphrey Noyes, and Joseph Smith. The Puritans of seventeenth-century New England were certainly not "conservative." They came to the New World in the 1630s because they feared that England and its state church were hopelessly corrupt; in the untamed forests of America, they would build their City upon a Hill and create a more perfect society. Their Congregationalist descen-

dants had lost much of this zeal by the 1790s, but they retained a deep thirst
for reform. Religious migrants from New England did as much as anyone to
create the famed burned-over district in the early nineteenth century where
Mormonism and other radical movements originated. The conversion experience necessary to produce a new birth, coupled with the inherent uncertainty of Calvinism's predestination doctrines, produced a wanderlust in
New Englanders and an intense desire in individuals to save themselves and
society. These former Puritans needed to prove to themselves—and to others—that they were of the elect. Once converted, they needed to demonstrate to the world—and to their fellow Congregationalists—that they were
living godly lives and truly deserving of the appellation "saint." In the end,
their desire for purity differed little from that of Mormon saints or Shaker
adherents.[15]

The reform impulse of Jacob and Ashbel Green drew from the same well
as these other evangelicals, and both men were aggressive reformers. Yet
Jacob *was* the more "radical" of the two Greens because of the era he lived
in. The heady times of the Revolution—so full of promise and disappointment—led him to walk right up to the line of true radicalism that many
religious reformers in the nineteenth century would cross. Recall Jacob's lev-
eling essays on liberty and finance, where he decried poverty and dreamed of
a communal society where wealth would be equal. And recall his views on
religious liberty. A full decade before the First Amendment to the federal
constitution was passed, Jacob was calling for freedom of conscience—a
very radical step for a supposedly stern Calvinist to take. And recall his
stance on slavery. Years before New Jersey finally outlawed slavery, Jacob was
advocating the institution's abolition. Ashbel, by contrast, stayed squarely
within the evangelical mainstream and was seen by many at Princeton as
"conservative" because of his devotion to traditional Calvinistic causes—discipline and piety. Ultimately, he lost the support of the trustees and the students due to this conservatism and resigned in 1822.

High Church Anglicanism was an even greater anomaly in the new
republic than was Calvinism. As the evangelical sects grew exponentially in
membership and influence, the Episcopal Church in America struggled with
declining numbers and internal dissension well into the nineteenth century
before it began a modest rebound after 1817. In the South, Episcopalians
pushed for a federated church that would be more in tune with the ideals
of the new nation, but in the North all eyes were on Canada, where the
Church of England was working to implement Chandler's prewar vision.

Charles Inglis had taken his place as bishop, and officials were strengthening the union of church and state there as a way to keep the Canadian colonies tethered to London and the Crown.[16]

This development was a discordant echo of an earlier time when Thomas Bradbury Chandler and his High Church allies were defending monarchy and hierarchy and denouncing Whiggish Americans, including members of Continental Congress, as tyrants. Reform, for Chandler, meant bringing a bishop to America. He lived long enough to see Inglis assume the episcopal office but not long enough to see the sweeping changes that were soon to come to the United States after 1790.

Green was also gone from the scene, but one suspects he would have approved of the democratization of American religion and society. Thomas Bradbury Chandler? Assuredly not. A Henrician union of church and state stood zero chance in the emerging United States, and the hierarchy that Chandler so loved was fading as well.

# Notes

## Preface

1. Emmanuel Le Roy Ladurie, *Montaillou: The Promised Land of Error*, anniv. ed. (New York: George Braziller, 2008); Carlos Ginsburg, *The Cheese and the Worms: The Cosmos of a Sixteenth-Century Miller* (Baltimore: Johns Hopkins University Press, 1992).

## Introduction

1. Good starting points for understanding the classical Whig aspects of the Revolution remain Gordon S. Wood, *The Creation of the American Republic, 1776–1787* (New York: W. W. Norton, 1972); and Bernard Bailyn, *The Ideological Origins of the American Revolution* (Cambridge: Harvard University Press, 1977). Recent works presenting the Revolution as a bottom-up insurgency include Gary B. Nash, *The Unknown American Revolution: The Unruly Birth of Democracy and the Struggle to Create America* (New York: Penguin, 2005); T. H. Breen, *American Insurgents, American Patriots: The Revolution of the People* (New York: Hill and Wang, 2010); and Jack Rakove, *Revolutionaries: A New History of the Invention of America* (New York: Houghton Mifflin Harcourt, 2010). Woody Holton takes the same tack in his examination of the constitutional movement. See Holton, *Unruly Americans and the Origins of the Constitution* (New York: Hill and Wang, 2008). For a broader look at radicalism in this period, see Seth Cotlar, *Tom Paine's America: The Rise and Fall of Transatlantic Radicalism in the Early Republic* (Charlottesville: University of Virginia Press, 2011).

2. Historians have long noted the affinity between political republicanism (the need for citizens to act virtuously if a republic is to survive) and the goals of evangelical reformers (who want sinners to act morally). For sophisticated looks at the links between religion and revolution, see Thomas S. Kidd, *God of Liberty: A Religious History of the American Revolution* (New York: Basic Books, 2010); James P. Byrd, *Sacred Scripture, Sacred War: The Bible and the American Revolution* (Oxford: Oxford University Press, 2013); Keith L. Griffin, *Revolution and Religion: American Revolutionary War and the Reformed Clergy* (New York: Paragon House, 1994); Mark A. Noll, *Christians in the American Revolution* (Washington: Christian University Press, 1977); J. C. D. Clark, *The Language of Liberty, 1660–1832: Political Discourse and Social Dynamics in the Anglo-American World* (Cambridge: Cambridge University Press, 1994); Daniel L. Dreisbach, Mark David Hall, and Jeffry H. Morrison, eds., *The Forgotten Founders on Religion and Public Life* (Notre Dame: University of Notre Dame Press, 2009); Thomas S. Engeman and Michael P. Zuckert, eds., *Protestantism and the American Founding* (Notre Dame: University of Notre Dame Press, 2004); and Nathan O. Hatch, *The Sacred Cause of Liberty: Republican Thought and the Millennium in Revolutionary New England* (New Haven: Yale University Press, 1977).

3. For this insight I am indebted to the work of Mark A. Noll, who has studied Green's career. See Noll, "Observations on the Reconciliation of Politics and Religion in Revolutionary New Jersey: The Case of Jacob Green," *Journal of Presbyterian History* 44 (1976): 217–23; Noll, "Jacob Green's Proposal for Seminaries," *Journal of Presbyterian History* 58 (1980): 210–22; and Noll, "Church Membership and the American Revolution: An Aspect of Religion and Society in New England from the Revival to the War for Independence" (Ph.D. diss., Vanderbilt University, 1975).

4. It should be noted that Calvinists argued among themselves over the details of their predestinarian beliefs, one point of contention being whether God decreed the preordaining before or after the Fall. Those who believed God decided on election before the Fall were supralapsarians, and they espoused "absolute" predestination; those who argued God did the decreeing after the Fall were sublapsarians. In related disputes, Calvinists argued over "perseverance"—whether the justified person can fall from grace if he or she sins—as well as Jesus Christ's role in salvation: did he die for the elect only? Or for everyone? For more on predestination, Arminianism, and the political implications of these beliefs, see Nicholas Tyacke, *Anti-Calvinists: The Rise of English Arminianism, c. 1590–1640* (Oxford: Oxford University Press, 1987). For more general treatments, see Dewey J. Hoitenga, Jr., *John Calvin and the Will* (Grand Rapids, Mich.: Baker Books, 1977); Martin Marty, *Martin Luther: A Life* (New York: Viking Penguin, 2004); and D. G. Hart, *Calvinism: A History* (New Haven: Yale University Press, 2013). And for more on Calvin, see F. Bruce Gordon, *Calvin* (New Haven: Yale University Press, 2011); T. H. L. Parker, *John Calvin: A Biography* (Louisville: Westminster John Knox Press, 2007); and Alister E. McGrath, *A Life of John Calvin: A Study in the Shaping of Western Culture* (Hoboken: Wiley Blackwell, 1993).

5. G. W. Bernard, *The King's Reformation: Henry VIII and the Remaking of the English Church* (New Haven: Yale University Press, 2005), 584–85.

6. Richard Hooker, *Of the Laws of Ecclesiastical Polity*, trans. Arthur Stephen McGrade (Cambridge: Cambridge University Press, 1989); Francis J. Bremer, *The Puritan Experiment* (New York: St. Martin's Press, 1976), 14–15.

7. Peter J. Thuesen, "Jonathan Edwards and the Transatlantic World of Books," *Jonathan Edwards Studies* 3 (February 2013), 43–54. For a recent overview of the Enlightenment in America and its complex relationship with religion, see Nathalie Caron and Naomi Wulf, "American Enlightenments: Continuity and Renewal," *Journal of American History* 99 (March 2013): 1072–91. Also see Henry F. May, *The Enlightenment in America* (Oxford: Oxford University Press, 1976): and Clark, *Language of Liberty*. For more on deism and the Enlightenment, see James Turner, *Without God, Without Creed: The Origins of Unbelief in America* (Baltimore: Johns Hopkins University Press, 1985); Christopher Grasso, "Deist Monster: On Religious Common Sense in the Wake of the American Revolution," *Journal of American History* 95 (June 2008): 43–68; and Kirsten Fischer, "'Religion Governed by Terror': A Deist Critique of Fearful Christianity in the Early American Republic," *Revue Française d'Études Américaines* 125 (Fall 2010): 13–26.

8. Bailyn, *Ideological Origins of the American Revolution*, 33–34; Nathan O. Hatch, *The Democratization of American Christianity* (New Haven: Yale University Press, 1989), 34. Besides the work of Mark Noll, historians who take an opposite tack and cite the importance of Calvinism include Alan Heimert, *Religion and the American Mind* (Cambridge: Harvard University Press, 1966); and Griffin, *Revolution and Religion*. The former is concerned with showing how Calvinism contributed to a "liberal" mind-set, and the latter with explaining how revolution was justified under reformed theology. But such works are not the norm, and Heimert's has been roundly criticized since its publication. Most historians of religion cite not Calvinism but the Great Awakening and the evangelical fervor of the 1740s as pivotal factors in helping spur the colonists to revolt in the 1770s; their point is that the Awakening prepared the way to revolution by encouraging ordinary people to question their betters. I want to stress that *Jacob Green's Revolution* is not out to "discredit" or "disprove" such studies; its intent, instead, is to show the ways that Calvinistic beliefs could lead to a reform regime during the revolutionary era.

9. Calvin quote is from Will Durant, *The Reformation* (New York: Simon & Schuster, 1957), 464; William Prynne, *The Church of England's Old Antithesis to New Arminianism* (London, 1629), quote is from chapter on "Booke of Common Prayer," 17.

10. "Two Sermons, hitherto unpublished, of Dr. Tobie Matthew . . . ," *Christian Observer* 47 (1847): 777–78; the catechism quote is from Tyacke, *Anti-Calvinists*, 2–3. Also see pp. 18–19 in Tyacke for more on this topic.

11. Isaac Watts, *The Rational Foundation of a Christian Church, and the Terms of Christian Communion* . . . (London, 1747), 1, 5.

12. One of the most cogent explanations of Edwards's views on the free will is George M. Marsden, *Jonathan Edwards: A Life* (New Haven: Yale University Press, 2003), esp. 436–46. Other excellent portrayals of Edwards's thought include Avihu Zakai, *Jonathan Edwards's Philosophy of History: The Reenchantment of the World in the Age of Enlightenment* (Princeton: Princeton University Press, 2003); Robert E. Brown, *Jonathan Edwards and the Bible* (Bloomington: Indiana University Press, 2002); and Amy Plantinga Pauw, *The Supreme Harmony of All: The Trinitarian Theology of Jonathan Edwards* (Grand Rapids, Mich.: Eerdmans Publishing, 2002).

13. Green's autobiography says he was a "zealous Calvinist" when he left Harvard but this was an exaggeration, as a May 4, 1744, letter from Green to Nathaniel Tucker, a classmate, shows. This letter is especially fascinating because it is the earliest extant letter from Green and because it was written at such a crucial time in his intellectual development, when he was finishing up college. It shows clearly the great intellectual turmoil that Green was experiencing over Calvinism's paradoxes. Green's will and inventory, despite listing every spoon he owned, cataloged only a fraction of his library, so it is impossible to know what exactly he read and what influenced him. We have to rely on Green's statements in his letters and autobiography; fortunately, he did mention the most influential things he read. The letter to Tucker is May 4, 1744, CO257, Box 11, Folder 1, Ashbel Green Papers 3A, Princeton University. Green's will and inventory is dated 1790 and is will No. 746, New Jersey State Archives, Trenton. Green's autobiography is reprinted in the *Christian Advocate* 9 (August–December 1831): 408–12, 465–68, 522–25, 578–81, 633–37; and 10 (January–May 1832): 11–13, 51–55, 99–102, 145–48, 194–99 (hereafter referred to as Green Autobiography). The "zealous Calvinist" quote can be found in 10:147.

14. The assertion of the importance of Green's tract is based on two facts: that after publication of *Observations on the Reconciliation of Great-Britain* in spring 1776, Green was elected to the Provincial Congress even though he did not want to serve; and that the Congress then selected him to head the committee appointed to write a constitution even though Green was not a lawyer and had zero experience as a politician and a constitutional thinker. I also find persuasive the conclusions of Larry R. Gerlach, the foremost authority on New Jersey revolutionary politics. Green in May 1776, Gerlach says, was as important and influential in New Jersey as John Witherspoon: "Especially significant [on the provincial congressional scene] was the appearance for the first time of John Witherspoon and Jacob Green. These two Presbyterian clergymen, perhaps the most outspoken and influential advocates of independence in the colony, personified the new temperament of the Congress." Quote is from Gerlach, *Prologue to Independence: New Jersey in the Coming of the American Revolution* (New Brunswick: Rutgers University Press, 1976), 331. Also see Gerlach's outstanding essay on the importance of Green's tract in his introduction to *Observations on the Reconciliation of Great-Britain* in a version published by the New Jersey Historical Commission in Trenton in 1976.

15. There are no full-scale biographies of Green until now. Other historians who have examined Green besides Noll include Clifford K. Shipton, "Jacob Green," *Sibley's Harvard Graduates* 11 (1960): 405–16, which gives a fine summary of his life, as well as Gerlach's excellent introduction to Green's *Observations*. An older essay of limited utility is Joseph F. Tuttle, "Rev. Jacob Green, of Hanover, N.J., as an Author, Statesman and Patriot," *Proceedings of the New Jersey Historical Society*, 2nd ser., 12, no. 4 (1893): 189–241. Green did leave behind an autobiography, edited by his son Ashbel, that covered part of his life. See note 13 above for details.

16. The key pamphlets include Jacob Green, *An Inquiry into the Constitution and Discipline of the Jewish Church* . . . (New York, 1768); Green, *A Reply to the Reverend Mr. George Beckwith's Answer* (New Haven, Conn., 1769); and Green, "An Humble Attempt Truly to State the Controversy Concerning Qualifications for Sacraments and to Inquire Where the Truth Lies," June 29, 1770, which was not published but can be found at Andover Newton Theological School, Newton

Centre, Massachusetts. Green's *A Vision of Hell, and a Discovery of some of the Consultations and Devices there, in the Year 1767* was first published in 1770 and went through numerous printings.

17. This, of course, was the Calvinist version of a conundrum that American constitutional thinkers such as James Madison would struggle with in the 1780s when creating a stronger central government—how to find the proper balance between liberty and order.

18. Quote is from Green, *Observations*, 29.

19. As with Green, there are no biographies of Chandler, although many a historian has described him when discussing the bishop's cause. Older works on Chandler include George Chandler, *The Chandler Family: The Descendants of William and Annis Chandler* (Worcester, Mass.: Press of Charles Hamilton, 1888); Albert Harrison Hoyt, *Sketch of the Life of the Rev. Thomas Bradbury Chandler, D.D.* (Boston: Press of David Clapp & Son, 1873); and Franklin Bowditch Dexter, *Biographical Sketches of the Graduates of Yale College, October, 1701–May, 1745* (New Haven: Yale University Press, 1885).

20. My forthcoming book, *An Unruly Kingdom: Religion and Revolution in the British Atlantic World*, will deal with the bishop's cause in depth. Older books on this topic include Carl Bridenbaugh, *Mitre and Sceptre: Transatlantic Faiths, Ideas, Personalities, and Politics, 1689–1775* (New York: Oxford University Press, 1962); and Arthur Lyon Cross, *The Anglican Episcopate and the American Colonies* (New York: Longmans, Green, and Co., 1902). Good recent studies of revolutionary Anglicanism that discuss the bishop's cause and Chandler include Nancy L. Rhoden, *Revolutionary Anglicanism: The Colonial Church of England Clergy during the American Revolution* (New York: New York University Press, 1999); Peter M. Doll, *Revolution, Religion, and National Identity: Imperial Anglicanism in British North America, 1745–1795* (Madison: Fairleigh Dickinson University Press, 2000); Janice Potter, *The Liberty We Seek: Loyalist Ideology in Colonial New York and Massachusetts* (Cambridge: Harvard University Press, 1983); James B. Bell, *A War of Religion: Dissenters, Anglicans, and the American Revolution* (New York: Palgrave Macmillan, 2008); and Patricia U. Bonomi, *Under the Cope of Heaven: Religion, Society, and Politics in Colonial America* (New York: Oxford University Press, 1986).

21. For good treatments of New Jersey during the Revolution, see Barbara J. Mitnick, ed., *New Jersey in the American Revolution* (New Brunswick: Rutgers University Press, 2005); Richard P. McCormick, *New Jersey from Colony to State, 1609–1789* (Newark: New Jersey Historical Society, 1981); Leonard Lundin, *Cockpit of the Revolution: The War for Independence in New Jersey* (Princeton: Princeton University Press, 1940); Arthur S. Lefkowitz, *The Long Retreat: The Calamitous American Defense of New Jersey, 1776* (New Brunswick: Rutgers University Press, 1998); David A. Bernstein, "New Jersey in the American Revolution: The Establishment of a Government amid Civil and Military Disorder, 1770–1783" (Ph.D. diss., Rutgers University, 1969); and Adrian C. Leiby, *The Revolutionary War in the Hackensack Valley: The Jersey Dutch and the Neutral Ground, 1775–1783* (New Brunswick: Rutgers University Press, 1962). For excellent general treatments of the military conflict, see John Ferling, *Almost a Miracle: The American Victory in the War of Independence* (Oxford: Oxford University Press, 2007); David Hackett Fischer, *Washington's Crossing* (Oxford: Oxford University Press, 2004); and Robert Middlekauff, *The Glorious Cause: The American Revolution, 1763–1789* (Oxford: Oxford University Press, 1982).

22. As my book will make clear, I agree with the main point of Heimert's thesis—Calvinism and Edwardseanism *were* ultimately radical—but he has run into such trouble because of the sweeping assertions he makes about "rationalists" (or "liberals" as he also calls them) and "Calvinists." *Religion and the American Mind* divides early America into two camps—the Calvinists who were supporters of the Great Awakening and Jonathan Edwards, a broad group that included New Lights, New Siders, and Baptists; the rationalists/liberals were opponents of the Great Awakening, and this group included Anglicans, Old Lights, and Old Siders. Heimert then goes on to argue that the rationalists either opposed the Revolution or were reluctant revolutionaries, while Calvinists were *the* driving force in the revolutionary movement. These asser-

tions go way too far. I argue in *Jacob Green's Revolution* that Edwardseanism was *one* source of radicalism but far from the *only* one. I also agree with the critics that Heimert's dichotomy between rationalist and Calvinist is far too simplistic. For a representative and enlightening review of Heimert's book, see the one by Edmund S. Morgan in *William and Mary Quarterly* 24 (July 1967): 454–59.

## Chapter 1

1. Clifford K. Shipton, *Sibley's Harvard Graduates* 11 (1960): 377, 486–87.
2. The February birth date is new style. Under the old calendar, Jacob was born on January 22; Green gives both dates in his autobiography. I am using the autobiography edited by his son Ashbel and printed in the *Christian Advocate* 9 (August–December 1831): 408–12, 465–68, 522–25, 578–81, 633–37; and 10 (January–May 1832): 11–13, 51–55, 99–102, 145–48, 194–99. Quotes are from 9:409.
3. The Green family history was reconstructed from the following sources: George Walter Chamberlain, ed., *Genealogical Records of Early Settlers in Malden, Commonwealth of Massachusetts, 1640–1800* (Malden, Mass.: Malden Historical Society, 1997); Samuel S. Green, *A Genealogical Sketch of the Descendants of Thomas Green[e] of Malden, Mass.* (Boston: General Books, 2010); William B. Stevens, *History of Stoneham, Massachusetts* (Stoneham, Mass.: F. L. and W. E. Whittier, 1891); *Vital Records of Stoneham, Massachusetts to the End of the Year 1849* (Salem, Mass.: Essex Institute, 1918); Deloraine Pendre Corey, *The History of Malden, Massachusetts, 1633–1785* (Malden, Mass.: Self-published, 1899); and Samuel Adams Drake, *History of Middlesex County, Massachusetts*, vol. 2 (Boston: Estes and Lauriat, 1880).
4. 1717 will of Henry Green of Malden, No. 9735, New England Historic Genealogical Society, Boston.
5. Chamberlain, *Genealogical Records of Early Settlers in Malden*, 471–72; *The Bi-centennial Book of Malden* (Boston: Geo. C. Rand & Co., 1850), 233–34.
6. Corey, *History of Malden*, 468, 632–33; Stevens, *History of Stoneham*, 27, 37, 42, 98.
7. Green Autobiography, 9:409.
8. Ibid.
9. Edmund S. Morgan, "The Puritan's Puritan: Michael Wigglesworth," in *American Heroes: Profiles of Men and Women Who Shaped Early America* (New York: W. W. Norton, 2009), 107.
10. Corey, *History of Malden*, 66; Stevens, *History of Stoneham*, 48–49.
11. Emerson quote is from Shipton, "Jacob Green," 170–75; also see Corey, *History of Malden*, 477–80.
12. *Records of the Governor and Company of the Massachusetts Bay in New England* (Boston, 1853), xvi, 29, 99; also see Corey, *History of Malden*, 632–33.
13. Morgan, "Puritan's Puritan," 105.
14. Michael Wigglesworth, *The Day of Doom; or, A Poetical Description of the Great and Last Judgment* (1662; repr., New York, 1867), stanza 38, p. 31; Morgan, "Puritan's Puritan," 105; Green Autobiography, 9:409.
15. Wigglesworth, *Day of Doom*, stanza 38.
16. Paul Leicester, ed., *The New-England Primer* (1789; repr., New York, 1899), no page number for "Adam's fall" quote. "Death's Arrest" quote is on p. 22.
17. Green Autobiography, 9:409.
18. Green quote is ibid.; "Come unto CHRIST" quote is from *New-England Primer*, n.p.
19. Green Autobiography, 9:410.
20. Ibid.
21. Ibid.

22. "About Admission into the College," reprinted in Benjamin Peirce, *A History of Harvard from Its Foundation in the Year 1636, to the Period of the American Revolution* (Cambridge: Harvard University Press, 1833), Appendix, p. 125; Samuel Eliot Morison, *Three Centuries of Harvard* (Cambridge: Harvard University Press, 1936), 26, 103–4.

23. Morison, *Three Centuries of Harvard*, 26–27, 103–10.

24. Ibid., 22; "Concerning the Scholars' Commons," reprinted in Peirce, *History of Harvard*, Appendix, p. 134, 137. For more on Thomas Hooker's migration to Connecticut, see S. Scott Rohrer, *Wandering Souls: Protestant Migrations in America, 1630–1865* (Chapel Hill: University of North Carolina Press, 2010).

25. "Concerning a Religious Virtuous Life," reprinted in Peirce, *History of Harvard*, Appendix, p. 126.

26. Figures are derived from Shipton, *Sibley's Harvard Graduates* 11 (1945), for the class of 1744; Green quote is from Green Autobiography, 9:523.

27. Morison, *History of Harvard*, 53–75.

28. Shipton, *Sibley's Harvard Graduates* 7: 554–55.

29. "Concerning Scholastical Exercises," reprinted in Peirce, *History of Harvard*, Appendix, p. 128.

30. Ibid.

31. Green Autobiography, 9:635.

32. Ibid., 9:635–37.

33. Ibid.

34. Richard Warch, *School of the Prophets: Yale College, 1701–1740* (New Haven: Yale University Press, 1973); historian's quote is from Harry S. Stout, *The New England Soul: Preaching and Religious Culture in Colonial New England* (Oxford: Oxford University Press, 1986), 213.

35. Warch, *School of the Prophets*, 224.

36. Josiah Quincy, *The History of Harvard University*, vol. 1 (Cambridge: Harvard University Press, 1840), 388.

37. Shipton, *Sibley's Harvard Graduates* 11: 339, 364, 365, 431, 441.

38. Green Autobiography, 9:523, 637; 10:13; Shipton *Sibley's Harvard Graduates* 11: 406; Jacob Green to Ashbel Green, June 22, 1782, CO257, Folder 36, Ashbel Green Papers 3A, Princeton University. For more on the difficulty of learning Hebrew, see Warch, *School of the Prophets*, 199.

39. Green Autobiography, 9:523.

40. George Whitefield, of course, has received a great deal of scholarly attention. In addition to Stout, *New England Soul*, 189–95, and Stout, *The Divine Dramatist: George Whitefield and the Rise of Modern Evangelism* (Grand Rapids, Mich.: Eerdmans Publishing, 1991), see Thomas S. Kidd, *The Great Awakening: The Roots of Evangelical Christianity in Colonial America* (New Haven: Yale University Press, 2007); Frank Lambert, *Inventing the "Great Awakening"* (Princeton: Princeton University Press, 1999), and Lambert, *"Pedlar in Divinity": George Whitefield and the Transatlantic Revivals, 1737–1770* (Princeton: Princeton University Press, 1994).

41. "Coming to Hear Whitefield," in *A Documentary History of Religion in America*, ed. Edwin S. Gaustad and Mark A. Noll (Grand Rapids, Mich.: Eerdmans Publishing, 2003), 163–65.

42. *George Whitefield's Journals* (London: The Banner of Truth Trust, 1960), September 24, 1740, 462.

43. Edward T. Dunn, ed., "The Diary of Henry Flynt of Harvard College, 1675–1760," vol. 2, pt. 2, pp. 1452–53, 1457 (Harvard University); for more on Whitefield's visit, see Morison, *Three Centuries of Harvard*, 84–86.

44. "The Testimony of the President, Professors, Tutors, and Hebrew Instructor of Harvard College, against George Whitefield," in *The Great Awakening: Documents Illustrating the Crisis and Its Consequences*, ed. Alan Heimert and Perry Miller (New York: Macmillan, 1967), 340–53. Also

see Flynt Diary, vol. 2, pt. 2, 1453; Stout, *New England Soul*, 220; and Perry Miller, *Errand into the Wilderness* (Cambridge: Harvard University Press, 1984), 154. It should be noted that Whitefield's relations with Harvard improved; for example, he helped raise money for books in the 1760s after a fire struck the college.

45. Green Autobiography, 9:523.

46. Shipton, *Sibley's Harvard Graduates* 7: 556. Rogers finally resigned his tutorship in March 1741.

47. *George Whitefield's Journals*, 463–75.

48. Green Autobiography, 9:523.

49. Ibid., 9:524.

50. Ibid.

51. Ibid., 9:411.

52. Ibid., 9:412.

53. Ibid., 9:465–68.

54. Ibid., 9:522–23.

55. Ibid.

56. Ibid., 9:580.

57. Ibid., 9:580–81; Jacob Green to Nathaniel Tucker, May 4, 1744, CO257, Box 11, Folder 1, Ashbel Green Papers 3A.

58. Green Autobiography, 9:634.

59. Ibid., 10:12–13.

60. Ibid.

61. For more on Dickinson and Burr, see Bryan F. Le Beau, *Jonathan Dickinson and the Formative Years of American Presbyterianism* (Lexington: University Press of Kentucky, 1997); and Leonard J. Trinterud, *The Forming of an American Tradition: A Re-examination of Colonial Presbyterianism* (New York: Books for Libraries Press, 1949).

62. Green Autobiography, 10:12–13.

63. Samuel Adams Clark, *The History of St. John's Church, Elizabeth Town, New Jersey* (Philadelphia, 1857); George Chandler, *The Chandler Family: The Descendants of William and Annis Chandler* (Worcester, Mass.: Press of Charles Hamilton, 1888); Albert Harrison Hoyt, *Sketch of the Life of the Rev. Thomas Bradbury Chandler, D.D.* (Boston: Press of David Clapp & Son, 1873); Franklin Bowditch Dexter, *Biographical Sketches of the Graduates of Yale College, October, 1701–May, 1745* (New Haven: Yale University Press, 1885).

*Chapter 2*

1. Description of Hanover's meetinghouse is gleaned from Parish Book 3, 1754–1839 (available on microfilm at Morris County Library, N.J.); Oliver W. Chapin, *A History of the First Presbyterian Church of Hanover, 1718–1968: 250 Years of Christian Service* (Hanover, N.J.: First Presbyterian Church, 1968), 12–14; and Elizabeth R. Myrone and Claire B. Kitchell, *Along the Whippanong: A History of Hanover Township, New Jersey* (Hanover, N.J.: Hanover Township Committee, 1966), 106. Green quote is from a brief church history he wrote; this history is reprinted in its entirety in Chapin, *History of the First Presbyterian Church of Hanover*, 6–7.

2. For an overview of Morris County's early years, see Theodore Thayer, *Colonial and Revolutionary Morris County* (Morristown, N.J.: Compton Press, 1975).

3. Leonard J. Trinterud, *The Forming of an American Tradition: A Re-examination of Colonial Presbyterianism* (New York: Books for Libraries Press, 1949), 120–28; *Minutes of the Synod of New York*, September 19, 1745, October 1, 1745, in *Records of the Presbyterian Church in the United States of America* (Philadelphia: Presbyterian Board of Publication, 1841).

4. For more on Dickinson and his importance to Presbyterianism, see Bryan F. Le Beau, *Jonathan Dickinson and the Formative Years of American Presbyterianism* (Lexington: University Press of Kentucky, 1997).

5. Green Autobiography, 10:13; Green church history, in Chapin, *History of the First Presbyterian Church of Hanover*, 6–7.

6. Green Autobiography, 10:101–2.

7. Jacob Green to Nathaniel Tucker, May 4, 1744, CO257, Box 11, Folder 1, Ashbel Green Papers 3A, Princeton University; "zealous Calvinist" quote in Green Autobiography, 10:147.

8. Green Autobiography, 10:147.

9. Green's first daybook covered November 6, 1754, to May 8, 1755; it can be found in CO257, Box, 10, Folder 35, Ashbel Green Papers 3A (hereafter referred to as Daybook 1). His second daybook covered December 18, 1754, to April 30, 1755; it can be found in Box 10, Folder 36 (hereafter referred to as Daybook 2). The literature on religion and the Enlightenment is large. Good starting points are Henry F. May, *The Enlightenment in America* (Oxford: Oxford University Press, 1976); and J. C. D. Clark, *The Language of Liberty, 1660–1832: Political Discourse and Social Dynamics in the Anglo-American World* (Cambridge: Cambridge University Press, 1994). Also see John Fea, *The Way of Improvement Leads Home: Philip Vickers Fithian and the Rural Enlightenment in Early America* (Philadelphia: University of Pennsylvania Press, 2008).

10. Daybook 1; quotes are from November 21 and November 28, 1754. Jacob's discussion of Arminianism and rationalism began in 1755.

11. Daybook 2, 59–60.

12. Ibid., 6, 60–66, 76.

13. Ibid.; Harry S. Stout, *The New England Soul: Preaching and Religious Culture in Colonial New England* (Oxford: Oxford University Press, 1986), 33.

14. Stout, *New England Soul*, 206; George M. Marsden, *Jonathan Edwards: A Life* (New Haven: Yale University Press, 2003), 54, 128, 220, 283. For more on Edwards, see Avihu Zakai, *Jonathan Edwards's Philosophy of History: The Reenchantment of the World in the Age of Enlightenment* (Princeton: Princeton University Press, 2003); Robert E. Brown, *Jonathan Edwards and the Bible* (Bloomington: Indiana University Press, 2002); Amy Plantinga Pauw, *The Supreme Harmony of All: The Trinitarian Theology of Jonathan Edwards* (Grand Rapids, Mich.: Eerdmans Publishing, 2002).

15. Daybook 2, 59–61.

16. Green Autobiography, 10:145–47; Green to Tucker, May 4, 1744.

17. Marsden, *Jonathan Edwards*, 444.

18. Green Autobiography, 10:148.

19. Jacob Green, "Sinners Faultiness, and Spiritual Inability, Considered in a Sermon" (New York, 1767).

20. Ibid., 15–16.

21. Ibid., 25–27; Marsden, *Jonathan Edwards*, 436–43.

22. Green Autobiography, 10:145–46; Isaac Watts, *The Rational Foundation of a Christian Church, and the Terms of Christian Communion . . .* (London, 1747), 5.

23. Watts, *Rational Foundation*, 14, 17–19.

24. The two tracts were Jacob Green, *An Inquiry into the Constitution and Discipline of the Jewish Church* (New York, 1768); and Green, "An Humble Attempt Truly to State the Controversy Concerning the Qualifications for Sacraments and to Inquire Where the Truth Lies," June 29, 1770, in Jonathan Edwards MSS, Parcel IV, p. 15, Andover Newton Theological Seminary, Newtown Centre, Massachusetts.

25. The literature on Puritanism is voluminous. Good starting points are David D. Hall, *Worlds of Wonder, Days of Judgment: Popular Religious Belief in Early New England* (New York: Alfred A. Knopf, 1989); Perry Miller, *Errand into the Wilderness* (Cambridge: Harvard University Press, 1956); Stout, *New England Soul*; and Marsden, *Jonathan Edwards*.

26. Jacob Green, "Christian Baptism: A Sermon Delivered at Hanover, in New-Jersey; November 4, 1764" (Woodbridge, N.J., 1766), 4–5. For excellent accounts of Green's purity drive and its larger importance to Protestantism and the revolutionary movement, see Mark A. Noll, "Jacob Green's Proposal for Seminaries," *Journal of Presbyterian History* 58 (1980): 210–22; and Noll, "Church Membership and the American Revolution: An Aspect of Religion and Society in New England from the Revival to the War for Independence" (Ph.D. diss., Vanderbilt University, 1975).

27. Green, "Christian Baptism," 6.

28. Green, "An Humble Attempt," 79–84, 87–94.

29. Ibid., 8–10.

30. Green, "Christian Baptism," 11–14; Green, "An Humble Attempt," 28–30.

31. Green, "An Humble Attempt," 30–31.

32. Green, "Christian Baptism," 5; also see Green, "An Humble Attempt," 76–78, for more details on his views.

33. Green, "Christian Baptism," 23–24; baptism figures are derived from listings in *Church Members, Marriages and Baptisms at Hanover, Morris Co., N.J., during the Pastorate of Rev. Jacob Green and to the Settlement of Rev. Aaron Condit, 1746–1796* (Morristown, N.J.: The Jerseyman, 1893).

34. In Green's telling, "I practiced on [Stoddard's] scheme, in the admission of church members. But my church were not generally in that opinion." Green Autobiography, 10:147. For a nice summary of Edwards's experience, see Marsden, *John Edwards*, 346–50.

35. Thayer, *Colonial and Revolutionary Morris County*, 95–97; Myrone and Kitchell, *Along the Whippanong*, 107.

36. This conclusion is based on readings of Green's autobiography, Hanover church records, and Green's writings.

37. It is unclear who selected the elders, but in the Presbyterian Church before the American Revolution the minister typically nominated the elders and the session approved them. Thus it is likely that Green nominated these five elders in consultation with the two deacons. Listings of the deacons and elders can be found in J. A. Ferguson, *A Historical Sketch of the Church of Hanover, N.J.* (Newark, N.J.: Amzi Pierson & Co., 1877), Appendix, pp. 86–88.

38. Myrone and Kitchell, *Along the Whippanong*, 31, 35, 37.

39. Conclusion is based on an examination of Parish Book 3, 1754–1839; and *Minutes of Church Meetings and Church Sessions, Discipline, and Other Matters of Record, 1769–1814*, Book 4. Both are on microfilm at the Morristown Public Library, New Jersey.

40. Minutes of November 26, 1754, April 28, 1758, April 12, 1765, April 17, 1767, April 26, 1769, October 20, 1769, Parish Book 3.

41. Ibid., April 26, 1769, October 20, 1769. For more on seating arrangements and the meetinghouse, see Stout, *New England Soul*, 193. Also see Dell Upton, *Holy Things and Profane: Anglican Parish Churches in Colonial Virginia* (New Haven: Yale University Press, 1997).

42. Green Autobiography, 10:101–2.

43. Ibid., 10:100.

44. Ibid., 10:53–54.

45. For a "typical" month, see Green's activities in January 1751, "Diary of Jacob Green," CO257, Box 10, Folder 37, Ashbel Green Papers 3A. Green's unpublished sermons are also in Ashbel Green Papers 3A at Princeton University, CO257, Box 11, Folders 1–7. For an excellent discussion of the sermon in New England and the differences between Harvard- and Yale-trained pastors, see Stout, *New England Soul*, esp. 220–22.

46. 1768 sermon, Morristown, New Jersey, in CO257, Box 11, Folder 1, Sermons 1744–69, Ashbel Green Papers 3A.

47. Daybook 2, 91–97.

48. Undated sermon delivered at Morristown, New Jersey, CO257, Box 11, Folder 4, Ashbel Green Papers 3A.

49. Sermon preached at Smithtown at Joseph Wood's, 1769, CO257, Box 11, Folder 4, Ashbel Green Papers 3A.
50. Sermon preached at David Tuttle's, 1779, CO257, Box 11, Folder 4, Ashbel Green Papers 3A.
51. Undated sermon, CO257, Box 11, Folder 5, Ashbel Green Papers 3A.
52. Samuel Adams Clark, *The History of St. John's Church, Elizabeth Town, New Jersey* (Philadelphia, 1857); George Chandler, *The Chandler Family: The Descendants of William and Annis Chandler* (Worcester, Mass.: Press of Charles Hamilton, 1888); Albert Harrison Hoyt, *Sketch of the Life of the Rev. Thomas Bradbury Chandler, D.D.* (Boston: Press of David Clapp & Son, 1873); Franklin Bowditch Dexter, *Biographical Sketches of the Graduates of Yale College, October, 1701–May, 1745* (New Haven: Yale University Press, 1885).

## Chapter 3

1. Jacob Green's Will & Inventory, Morris County, 1790, No. 746, New Jersey State Archives, Trenton; Theodore Thayer, *Colonial and Revolutionary Morris County* (Morristown, N.J.: Compton Press, 1975), 80–81.
2. Details about the parsonage and the Greens' farm were reconstructed from Oliver W. Chapin, *A History of the First Presbyterian Church of Hanover, 1718–1968: 250 Years of Christian Service* (Hanover, N.J.: First Presbyterian Church, 1968), 7, 12; Joseph H. Jones, ed., *The Life of Ashbel Green, V.D.M.* (New York: Robert Carter and Brothers, 1849), 86 (hereafter referred to as Ashbel Green Autobiography); "Calvin Green's 'Diary': The Life of Calvin Green," *New Jersey Historical Proceedings* 69 (April 1951): 115–36 (hereafter referred to as Life of Calvin Green). I also relied on an early-twentieth-century photo of the parsonage in *Church Members, Marriages and Baptisms at Hanover, Morris Co., N.J., during the Pastorate of Rev. Jacob Green and to the Settlement of Rev. Aaron Condit, 1746–1796* (Morristown, N.J.: The Jerseyman, 1893). It is unclear during what years Jacob Green's academy operated.
3. Preface to *Church Members, Marriages and Baptisms at Hanover*, and Jacob Green, "A Minister's Address to his Chh. & Congregation," December 1, 1768, CO257, Box 10, Folder 34, Ashbel Green Papers 3A, Princeton University (hereafter referred to as 1768 Address).
4. The deacon who lost five wives was Joseph Tuttle; see Thayer, *Colonial and Revolutionary Morris County*, 84.
5. The inscription on Anna Green's gravestone is reprinted in William Ogden Wheeler and Edmund D. Halsey, *Inscriptions on the Tomb Stone and Monuments in the Grave Yards at Whippany and Hanover, Morris County, N.J.* (Morris County, N.J., 1894), 49; quotes are from Green Autobiography, 10:51–53.
6. Richard Webster, *A History of the Presbyterian Church in America from Its Origin until the Year 1760* (Philadelphia: Joseph M. Wilson, 1857), 357–58; "Sketch of Ashbel Green," in Richard A. Harrison, *Princetonians, 1776–1783: A Biographical Dictionary* (Princeton: Princeton University Press, 1981), 404.
7. Ashbel Green Autobiography, 20.
8. Jacob Green, "A Sermon on Persons Possessing the Iniquities of Their Youth in After Life" (Chatham, N.J., 1780), 8–14.
9. Ashbel Green Autobiography, 20; Life of Calvin Green, 117.
10. James B. Finley, *Autobiography of Rev. James B. Finley; or, Pioneer Life in the West*, ed. W. P. Strickland (Cincinnati: Methodist Book Concern, 1854), 160–63.
11. Life of Calvin Green, 117; Ashbel Green Autobiography, 19.
12. Life of Calvin Green, 120; Ashbel Green Autobiography, 21.
13. Ashbel Green Autobiography, 22–23.

14. For more on inheritance practices, see Toby L. Ditz, *Property and Kinship: Inheritance in Early Connecticut, 1750–1820* (Princeton: Princeton University Press, 1986); Barry Levy, *Quakers and the American Family: British Settlement in the Delaware Valley* (Oxford: Oxford University Press, 1988); James T. Lemon, *The Best Poor Man's Country: A Geographical Study of Early Southeastern Pennsylvania* (New York: W. W. Norton, 1972); John Bossy, "Blood and Baptism: Kinship, Community and Christianity in Western Europe from the Fourteenth to the Seventeenth Centuries," in *Sanctity and Secularity: The Church and the World*, Studies in Church History 10, ed. Derek Baker (Oxford: Basil Blackwell, 1973), 129–43; and Jack Goody, Joan Thirsk, and E. P. Thompson, eds., *Family and Inheritance: Rural Society in Western Europe, 1200–1800* (Cambridge: Cambridge University Press, 1976).

15. Jacob Green's Will & Inventory, 1790.

16. Ibid.

17. Ashbel Green Autobiography, 22.

18. Life of Calvin Green, 118–20—quote is on p. 120; Jacob Green's Will & Inventory, 1790.

19. Ashbel Green Autobiography, 22–23; Life of Calvin Green, 116.

20. "Sketch of Mahlon Dickerson," in Ruth L. Woodward and Wesley Frank Craven, *Princetonians, 1784–1790: A Biographical Dictionary* (Princeton: Princeton University Press, 1991), 369–75, and "Sketch of Samuel Beach," 397–400.

21. Jacob Green's Will & Inventory, 1790; J. Green to Mr. A. Green, June 22, 1782, CO257, Box 9, Folder 36, Ashbel Green Papers 3A. The inventory of Green's estate inexplicably listed only a few titles in his library.

22. Helena M. Wall, *Fierce Communion: Family and Community in Early America* (Cambridge: Harvard University Press, 1990), esp. 130–31. For a nice overview of the Enlightenment, see Henry F. May, *The Enlightenment in America* (Oxford: Oxford University Press, 1976); and J. C. D. Clark, *The Language of Liberty, 1660–1832: Political Discourse and Social Dynamics in the Anglo-American World* (Cambridge: Cambridge University Press, 1994). The conclusion about Green's attitude toward membership for his children is based on Life of Calvin Green, 121–22, and an analysis of church membership lists.

23. Mather quote is from Wall, *Fierce Communion*, 8. For more on Puritan families and town life, see David D. Hall, *Worlds of Wonder, Days of Judgment: Popular Religious Belief in Early New England* (New York: Alfred A. Knopf, 1989); Robert A. Gross, *The Minutemen and Their World* (New York: Hill and Wang, 1976); and Kenneth A. Lockridge, *A New England Town: The First Hundred Years* (New York: W. W. Norton, 1970).

24. Life of Calvin Green, 121–22; the figures on female membership are derived from Hanover congregation membership lists, 1747–90; June 5, 1769, *Minutes of Church Meetings and Church Sessions, Discipline, and Other Matters of Record, 1769–1814*, Book 4.

25. Percentages derived from *Church Members, Marriages and Baptisms at Hanover*, 11–17.

26. For more on Scotch Irish Presbyterians, see Patrick Griffin, *The People with No Name: Ireland's Ulster Scots, America's Scots Irish, and the Creation of a British Atlantic World, 1689–1764* (Princeton: Princeton University Press, 2001); Ned C. Landsman, *Scotland and Its First American Colony, 1683–1765* (Princeton: Princeton University Press, 1985); Marilyn J. Westerkamp, *Triumph of the Laity: Scots-Irish Piety and the Great Awakening, 1625–1760* (New York: Oxford University Press, 1988); and S. Scott Rohrer, *Wandering Souls: Protestant Migrations in America, 1630–1865* (Chapel Hill: University of North Carolina Press, 2010).

27. Robert Witherspoon Memoir, 1734–80, in *Irish Immigrants in the Land of Canaan: Letters and Memoirs from Colonial and Revolutionary America*, ed. Kerby A. Miller, Arnold Schrier, Bruce D. Boling, and David N. Doyle (Oxford: Oxford University Press, 2003), 135–43.

28. Green Autobiography, 10:145; Leonard J. Trinterud, *The Forming of an American Tradition: A Re-examination of Colonial Presbyterianism* (New York: Books for Libraries Press, 1949), 38–52.

29. Samuel Adams Clark, *The History of St. John's Church, Elizabeth Town, New Jersey* (Philadelphia, 1857); George Chandler, *The Chandler Family: The Descendants of William and Annis Chandler* (Worcester, Mass.: Press of Charles Hamilton, 1888); Edwin F. Hatfield, *History of Elizabeth, New Jersey* (New York: Carlton & Lanahan, 1868).

## Chapter 4

1. Green's salary history is from 1768 Address.
2. Ibid.
3. Ibid.
4. The 1779 tax list for Morris County is listed in Theodore Thayer, *Colonial and Revolutionary Morris County* (Morristown, N.J.: Compton Press, 1975), 212–13; a copy is also available at the New Jersey State Archives in Trenton. Also see Peter O. Wacker, *Land and People: A Cultural Geography of Preindustrial New Jersey: Origins and Settlement Patterns* (New Brunswick: Rutgers University Press, 1975), 151.
5. Thayer, *Colonial and Revolutionary Morris County*, 186–87.
6. Elizabeth R. Myrone and Claire B. Kitchell, *Along the Whippanong: A History of Hanover Township, New Jersey* (Hanover, N.J.: Hanover Township Committee, 1976), 73–74.
7. 1779 tax list for Morris County; Thayer, *Colonial and Revolutionary Morris County*, 67–69; Dennis P. Ryan, "Six Towns: Continuity and Change in Revolutionary New Jersey, 1770–1792" (Ph.D. diss., New York University, 1974), 269.
8. 1768 Address.
9. In his 1768 Address, Green says in passing that he bought a Negro. Kelly's plantation is described in Thayer, *Colonial and Revolutionary Morris County*, 68. For more background on slavery in New Jersey, see Ryan, "Six Towns," 93–99; and James John Gigantino II, "Freedom and Unfreedom in the 'Garden of America': Slavery and Abolition in New Jersey, 1770–1857" (Ph.D. diss., University of Georgia, 2010).
10. Green Autobiography, 10:52–53; 1768 Address.
11. Ashbel Green Autobiography, 22, 86; Life of Calvin Green, 119.
12. Jacob Green's Will & Inventory, Morris County, 1790, No. 746, New Jersey State Archives; "brute" quote is from Ashbel Green Autobiography, 20; James T. Lemon, *The Best Poor Man's Country: A Geographical Study of Early Southeastern Pennsylvania* (New York: W. W. Norton, 1972), 164–66.
13. Jacob Green's Will & Inventory; Thayer, *Colonial and Revolutionary Morris County*, 66–71.
14. Jacob Green's Will & Inventory. No financial records of these businesses are extant, so it is impossible to construct how much income he derived from them.
15. 1768 Address.
16. Ibid. For Green's activities as a trustee and interim president for the College of New Jersey, see Board of Trustees Records, 1746–," available at Seeley G. Mudd Manuscript Library, Princeton University. He served from November 1748 until June 20, 1764. For an excellent look at early Princeton, see Mark A. Noll, *Princeton and the Republic, 1768–1822* (Vancouver: Regent College Publishing, 1989).
17. The congregation approved Green's request at an April 1762 meeting. See Parish Book 3, 1754–1839.
18. Green Autobiography, 10:52–53; Green's most forceful economic critique in the prerevolutionary years was in his 1770 tract *A Vision of Hell*.
19. Ashbel Green quote is from Green Autobiography, 10:52; also see David D. Hall, *Worlds of Wonder, Days of Judgment: Popular Religious Belief in Early New England* (New York: Alfred A. Knopf, 1989), 196–97, 241.

20. Jacob Green's Will & Inventory; quote is from Richard Brookes, *The General Practice of Physic*, vol. 1, 5th ed. (London, 1765), vi.

21. A summary of Lorenz Heister's career can be found in Frank J. Lutz, "Lorenz Heister," *St. Louis Medical Review* 75, no. 1 (1907): 1–4.

22. Fred B. Rogers and A. Reasoner Sayre, *The Healing Art: A History of the Medical Society of New Jersey* (Trenton: Medical Society of New Jersey, 1966), 6–10; Edmund S. Morgan, *The Gentle Puritan: A Life of Ezra Stiles, 1727–1795* (New York: W. W. Norton, 1962), 322.

23. Ashbel Green Autobiography, 24; Jacob Green's Will & Inventory. According to Calvin, Jacob gave up his practice in 1784 to a Dr. John Dorsey. See Life of Calvin Green, 119.

24. 1768 Address; 1779 tax list, New Jersey State Archives; Jacob Green's Will & Inventory; Thayer, *Colonial and Revolutionary Morris County*, 214.

25. 1768 Address.

26. Ibid.

27. Parish Book 3, 1754–1839, minutes of April 26, 1769, May 7, 1771, April 17, 1772.

28. Green, *Vision of Hell*, 3.

29. Ibid., 8–9.

30. Ibid., 8–10.

31. Ibid., 17–18.

32. Ibid., 6–7, 13.

33. Ibid., 19–20.

34. G. W. Bernard, *The King's Reformation: Henry VIII and the Remaking of the English Church* (New Haven: Yale University Press, 2005); J. J. Scarisbrick, *Henry VIII* (Berkeley: University of California Press, 1968); Richard Cust, *Charles I: A Political Life* (Edinburgh Gate, England: Pearson Longman, 2007); Carl Bridenbaugh, *Mitre and Sceptre: Transatlantic Faiths, Ideas, Personalities, and Politics, 1689–1775* (New York: Oxford University Press, 1962); Nancy L. Rhoden, *Revolutionary Anglicanism: The Colonial Church of England Clergy during the American Revolution* (New York: New York University Press, 1999); Peter M. Doll, *Revolution, Religion, and National Identity: Imperial Anglicanism in British North America, 1745–1795* (Madison: Fairleigh Dickinson University Press 2000).

## Chapter 5

1. Green's *An Inquiry into the Constitution and Discipline of the Jewish Church . . .* (New York, 1768) sparked the pamphlet war. George Beckwith attacked it in *Visible Saints Lawful Right to Communion in Christian Sacraments, Vindicated* (New London, 1769). Green answered Beckwith in "A Reply to the Reverend Mr. George Beckwith's Answer" (New Haven, Conn., 1769), and Hugh Knox joined the fray with *A Letter to the Rev. Mr. Jacob Green, of New Jersey, Pointing Out Some Difficulties in the Calvinistick Scheme of Divinity . . .* (London, 1772). Green then wrote a final tract summing up his views: "An Humble Attempt Truly to State the Controversy Concerning Qualifications for Sacraments and to Inquire Where the Truth Lies." Green apparently intended to publish this tract but it never made it into print. It should be noted that much of this debate among Beckwith, Knox, and Green reprised an earlier debate involving Jonathan Edwards, Joseph Bellamy, and Moses Mather. For more on the controversy and on Green's place within Presbyterianism and the New Divinity movement, see Clifford K. Shipton, "Jacob Green," *Sibley's Harvard Graduates* 11 (1960): 409–10; Mark A. Noll, "Observations on the Reconciliation of Politics and Religion in Revolutionary New Jersey: The Case of Jacob Green," *Journal of Presbyterian History* 44 (1976): 217–37; and Richard Webster, *A History of the Presbyterian Church in America from Its Origin until the Year 1760* (Philadelphia: Joseph M. Wilson, 1857), 658–61, which gives a summary of Hugh Knox's position in the controversy.

2. Green quote is from Green, *An Inquiry into the Constitution and Discipline of the Jewish Church*, 2. For more on New England and its warring camps, see William Breitenbach, "The Consistent Calvinism of the New Divinity Movement," *William and Mary Quarterly* 41 (April 1984): 241–64. Also see Mark Valeri, "The New Divinity and the American Revolution," *William and Mary Quarterly* 46 (October 1989): 741–69. For more on Jonathan Edwards's influence on Green, see Mark A. Noll, "Jacob Green's Proposal for Seminaries," *Journal of Presbyterian History* 58 (1980): 210–22; and Noll, "Observations on the Reconciliation of Politics and Religion."

3. Jacob Green, "Christian Baptism: A Sermon Delivered at Hanover, in New-Jersey; November 4, 1764" (Woodbridge, N.J., 1766); Green, "Sinners Faultiness, and Spiritual Inability, Considered in a Sermon" (New York, 1767).

4. Green, *An Inquiry into the Constitution and Discipline of the Jewish Church*, preface.

5. Ibid., 1–7.

6. Ibid., vi–ix.

7. Beckwith, *Visible Saints Lawful Right to Communion*, "Advertisement" and 6–18. For more on Beckwith, see Mark Allan Noll, "Church Membership and the American Revolution: An Aspect of Religion and Society in New England from the Revival to the War for Independence" (Ph.D. diss., Vanderbilt University, 1975), 294–99.

8. Beckwith, *Visible Saints Lawful Right to Communion*, 10–13.

9. Ibid., 58–61.

10. Green, "A Reply to the Reverend Mr. George Beckwith's Answer," preface and 4–5.

11. Ibid.

12. Ibid., 4, 12–12, 23; Green, *An Inquiry into the Constitution and Discipline of the Jewish Church*, vii; chapter titles are from chapters 3 and 4.

13. Knox, *A Letter to the Rev. Mr. Jacob Green*, 12–13.

14. George M. Marsden, *Jonathan Edwards: A Life* (New Haven: Yale University Press, 2003), 444.

15. Daybook 1; Green, "Christian Baptism"; Green, "Sinners Faultiness, and Spiritual Inability, Considered in a Sermon," 15–16.

16. Knox, *A Letter to the Rev. Mr. Jacob Green*, 39, 24.

17. Ibid., 42–43.

18. Ibid., 51, 66–67.

19. Ibid.

20. Ibid., 26, 96–97.

21. Ibid., 69.

22. Ibid., 33. Knox quoted Green's questions verbatim in a postscript to his tract. There were three total; see pp. 87–100.

23. Green, "Sinners Faultiness, and Spiritual Inability, Considered in a Sermon," 19–21; Marsden, *Jonathan Edwards*, 436–44.

24. Hugh Knox to Jacob Green, January 22, 1772, Gratz Collection, Case 9, Box 11, Historical Society of Pennsylvania, Philadelphia; Green, "An Humble Attempt."

25. Green, "An Humble Attempt"; amicable quote is on p. 100; self-love quote is on p. 11.

26. Ibid., 12; Green's discussion of the unregenerate covers pp. 12–26.

27. Ibid., 16.

28. Ibid., 25.

29. Ibid., 22.

30. Green, *An Inquiry into the Constitution and Discipline of the Jewish Church*, 57–58.

31. Green, "An Humble Attempt," 79–82.

32. Green, 1768 Address.

33. Green, "An Humble Attempt," 78; Jacob Green, *A Vision of Hell, and a Discovery of some of the Consultations and Devices there, in the Year 1767* (Boston, 1773); Shipton, *Sibley's Harvard Gradu-*

*ates* II: 410. For more on Paul Revere's role in creating the illustrations for the tract, see Barbara E. Lacey, *From Sacred to Secular: Visual Images in Early American Publications* (Newark, Del.: Rosemont Publishing and Printing, 2007), 64–65.

34. Noll, "Jacob Green's Proposal for Seminaries," 221; Green, *Vision of Hell*, 3.

35. Lacey, *From Sacred to Secular*, 65.

36. Green, *Vision of Hell*, 20.

37. For a listing of the editions for *Vision of Hell*, see Clifford K. Shipton, *National Index of American Imprints through 1800*, vol. 1 (Worcester, Mass.: American Antiquarian Society, 1969), 326.

38. Green unpublished sermon, in CO257, Folder 6, Box 11, Ashbel Green Papers 3A, Princeton University.

39. Green, *Vision of Hell*, 18–19.

40. Ibid., 17–18.

41. Thomas Bradbury Chandler, *An Appeal to the Public in Behalf of the Church of England in America* (New York, 1766); James B. Bell, *A War of Religion: Dissenters, Anglicans, and the American Revolution* (New York: Palgrave Macmillan, 2008); Carl Bridenbaugh, *Mitre and Sceptre: Transatlantic Faiths, Ideas, Personalities, and Politics, 1689–1775* (New York: Oxford University Press, 1962).

## Chapter 6

1. Gov. William Franklin to the New Jersey Assembly, January 13, 1775, in *Documents Relating to the Revolutionary History of the State of New Jersey*, 1st ser., vol. 18, ed. Frederick W. Ricord (Trenton: John L. Murphy Publishing, 1893), 479–81.

2. Ibid.

3. Thomas Bradbury Chandler, *What Think of Ye Congress Now; or, An Enquiry, How Far the Americans are Bound to Abide by, and Execute, the Decisions of the Late Congress?* (New York, 1775), 25.

4. Jacob Green, *Observations on the Reconciliation of Great-Britain, and the Colonies, in Which Are Exhibited Arguments For, and Against, That Measure* (Philadelphia, 1776). The tract was first published in New York City by John Holt in his *New-York Journal*. For an outstanding essay on the importance of Green's tract, see Larry R. Gerlach's introduction to *Observations* in a version published in Trenton in 1976, available at the Morris County Library, New Jersey. As Gerlach notes on pp. xxxi–xxxiii, historians have debated whether Green was truly the author since the essay was signed with a pen name. However, extant drafts in Green's handwriting at Princeton University prove conclusively that he was the author. The two extant drafts can be found in CO257, Box 11, Folder 6, Ashbel Green Papers 3A, Princeton University. The drafts are tucked away into folded sheets of paper that Green recycled because of the paper shortage during the war. Much of the sheets are in Weston's shorthand and contain miscellaneous jottings. Then, in the middle of these jibberings, are the drafts of *Observations* written in regular English.

5. Ashbel Green quote is from Green Autobiography, 10:196.

6. Paul H. Smith, "New Jersey Loyalist and the British 'Provincial Corps' in the War for Independence," *New Jersey Historical Society* 87 (1969): 76. However, Dennis P. Ryan questions these estimates in his dissertation "Six Towns: Continuity and Change in Revolutionary New Jersey, 1770–1792" (Ph.D. diss., New York University, 1974), 177n23. For more on this issue, see Joseph S. Tiedemann, Eugene R. Fingerhut, and Robert W. Venables, eds., *The Other Loyalists: Ordinary People, Royalism, and the Revolution in the Middle Colonies* (Albany: State University of New York Press, 2009), esp. 49.

7. May 22, 1775, pastoral letter from New York Synod, in *Records of the Presbyterian Church in the United States of America* (Philadelphia: Presbyterian Board of Publication, 1841); Leonard J. Trinterud, *The Forming of an American Tradition: A Re-examination of Colonial Presbyterianism* (New York: Books for Libraries Press, 1949), 246.

8. February 15, 1775, Hanover Committee of Observation Minutes, *Minutes of the Provincial Congress and the Council of Safety of the State of New Jersey* (Trenton: Naar, Day and Naar, 1879), 52–54; Theodore Thayer, *Colonial and Revolutionary Morris County* (Morristown, N.J.: Compton Press, 1975), 127, 132–33; Larry R. Gerlach, *Prologue to Independence: New Jersey in the Coming of the American Revolution* (New Brunswick: Rutgers University Press, 1976), 210.

9. Richard P. McCormick, *New Jersey from Colony to State, 1609–1789* (Newark: New Jersey Historical Society, 1981), 109–10. For an excellent overview of New Jersey in the revolutionary era, see Barbara J. Mitnick, ed., *New Jersey in the American Revolution* (New Brunswick: Rutgers University Press, 2005).

10. McCormick, *New Jersey from Colony to State*, 110.

11. Thayer, *Colonial and Revolutionary Morris County*, chap. 6.

12. David A. Bernstein, "New Jersey in the American Revolution: The Establishment of a Government amid Civil and Military Disorder, 1770–1783" (Ph.D. diss., Rutgers University, 1969), 65–73; Ryan, "Six Towns," 117.

13. Green was also following the custom of the day; most tracts were published anonymously. The "timid" quote is from an essay dated June 6, 1776, that ran in the *New-York Journal*, June 20, 1776.

14. Thomas Bradbury Chandler, *The Friendly Address to All* Reasonable *Americans on the Subject of Our Political Confusions* (New York, 1774), 2.

15. Green, *Observations*, 8.

16. Ibid., 13–14. For an analysis of where Green fits in with Calvinist revolutionaries, see Keith L. Griffin, *Revolution and Religion: American Revolutionary War and the Reformed Clergy* (New York: Paragon House, 1994), esp. 54–55.

17. Green, *Observations*, 7.

18. Ibid., 16.

19. Ibid., 20, 21.

20. Ibid., 26.

21. Ibid., 23, 28–29.

22. Thomas Paine, *Common Sense*, reprinted in Isaac Kramnick, ed. (New York: Penguin, 1986), 69, 81; Green, *Observations*, 24.

23. Gerlach, *Prologue to Independence*, 324.

24. Conclusion is based on an examination of the two extant drafts in CO257, Box 11, Folder 6, Ashbel Green Papers 3A.

25. Ibid. Green's "calmness" quote is from *Observations*, 6. For Green's views of good writing and preaching, see Daybook 2.

26. Extant drafts, CO257, Box 11, Folder 6, Ashbel Green Papers 3A.

27. Ads in *New-York Journal*, March 28, 1776, April 11, 1776; and ads in *Pennsylvania Evening Post*, April 16, 1776; *Pennsylvania Ledger*, May 4, 1776; and *Pennsylvania Packet*, May 13, 1776. Also see Gerlach, introduction to *Observations*; and Gerlach, *Prologue to Independence*, 302.

28. Green, *Observations*, 8.

29. Ibid., 19–20.

30. Jacob Green, Letter I on Liberty, *New-Jersey Journal*, May 3, 1780.

31. John Locke, "Second Treatise of Government," in *Modern Political Thought: Readings from Machiavelli to Nietzsche*, ed. David Wootton (Indianapolis: Hackett Publishing, 2008), 346.

32. Jonathan Edwards's *Freedom of the Will* is available online at http://edwards.yale.edu/research/major-works/freedom-of-the-will/ .

33. For an excellent discussion of Calvinists' views of liberty, see Alan Heimert, *Religion and the American Mind: From the Great Awakening to the Revolution* (Cambridge: Harvard University Press, 1966). Also see J. C. D. Clark, *The Language of Liberty: Political Discourse and Social Dynamics in the Anglo-American World* (Cambridge: Cambridge University Press, 1994).

34. Jacob Green, "A Sermon Delivered at Hanover, (in New-Jersey), April 22, 1778, Being the Day of Public Fasting and Prayer throughout the United States of America" (Chatham, N.J., 1779), 4 (hereafter referred to as Fast-Day Sermon).

35. Jacob Green, Letter II on Liberty, *New-Jersey Journal*, May 10, 1780.

36. Jeffry H. Morrison, *John Witherspoon and the Founding of the American Republic* (Notre Dame: University of Notre Dame Press, 2005), 78–83.

37. Witherspoon, "The Dominion of Providence over the Passions of Men," in *Political Sermons of the American Founding Era, 1730–1805*, ed. Ellis Sandoz (Indianapolis: Liberty Press, 1991), 529–58.

38. Ibid.

39. Morrison, *John Witherspoon and the Founding of the American Republic*, 78–83.

40. Moses Mather, "America's Appeal to the Impartial World," reprinted in *Political Sermons of the American Founding Era*, ed. Sandoz, 440–92.

41. Paine, *Common Sense*, 87.

42. Green, *Observations*, 19–20.

43. Gerlach, *Prologue to Independence*, 327–28.

44. Harriet Stryker-Rodda, ed., *Some Early Records of Morris County, New Jersey, 1740–1799* (New Orleans: Polyanthos, 1975), 124; Ashbel Green Autobiography, 60. Also see Joseph F. Tuttle, "Rev. Jacob Green, of Hanover, N.J., as an Author, Statesman and Patriot," *Proceedings of the New Jersey Historical Society*, 2nd ser., vol. 12, no. 4 (1893): 207–8; and Thayer, *Colonial and Revolutionary Morris County*, 80, 132, 135

45. Gerlach, *Prologue to Independence*, 331; Thayer, *Colonial and Revolutionary Morris County*, 144–45.

46. Thomas Bradbury Chandler, *An Appeal to the Public in Behalf of the Church of England in America* (New York, 1766); Chandler, *Friendly Address to All* Reasonable *Americans*; Green Autobiography, 10:145; *A View of a Christian Church, and Church Government; Containing Many Interesting Matters . . .* (Chatham, N.J., 1781), see esp. 11, 22, 25 (several pastors contributed to this tract but Green was the main author).

## Chapter 7

1. For more on New Jersey in the revolutionary era, see Barbara J. Mitnick, ed., *New Jersey in the American Revolution* (New Brunswick: Rutgers University Press, 2005); Richard P. McCormick, *New Jersey from Colony to State, 1609–1789* (Newark: New Jersey Historical Society, 1981); and David A. Bernstein, "New Jersey in the American Revolution: The Establishment of a Government amid Civil and Military Disorder, 1770–1783" (Ph.D. diss., Rutgers University, 1969).

2. Bernstein, "New Jersey in the American Revolution," 163–64; Charles R. Erdman, Jr., "The New Jersey Constitution of 1776" (Ph.D. diss., Princeton University, 1929), 41.

3. *Journal of the Votes and Proceedings of the Convention of New-Jersey Begun at Burlington the 10th of June 1776 . . . , July 6, 1776* (1776; repr., Trenton: Joseph Justice, 1831). Hereafter referred to as *Provincial Congress Journal*.

4. *Provincial Congress Journal*, June 14, 1776; *New-York Journal*, June 20, 1776.

5. *Provincial Congress Journal*, June 12 and June 19, 1776.

6. Ibid., June 22 and June 24.

7. Ashbel Green Autobiography, 22, 86, 43–44.

8. Jacob Green, *Observations on the Reconciliation of Great-Britain, and the Colonies, in Which Are Exhibited Arguments For, and Against, That Measure* (Philadelphia, 1776), 9–10.

9. Ibid.

10. Thomas Bradbury Chandler, *The American Querist; or, Some Questions Proposed Relative to the Present Disputes between Great Britain, and Her Colonies* (London, 1774), 43, 44.

11. Thomas Bradbury Chandler, *The Friendly Address to All* Reasonable *Americans on the Subject of Our Political Confusions* (New York, 1774), 9, 21; Green, *Observations*, 29. The Philadelphia edition of *Observations* contained "The Plan of an American Compact"—but Green didn't write it. For a detailed explanation of the issue, see Larry R. Gerlach, introduction to *Observations* (Trenton: New Jersey Historical Commission, 1976), lxiv, n. 69.

12. Green, *Observations*, 28.

13. Ibid., 23.

14. Ibid., 6.

15. Jacob Green, Letter II on Liberty, *New-Jersey Journal*, May 10, 1780.

16. The committee's makeup is derived from the *Provincial Congress Journal*.

17. Erdman, "New Jersey Constitution of 1776," 34, 37; Joseph F. Tuttle, "Rev. Jacob Green, of Hanover, N.J., as an Author, Statesman and Patriot," *Proceedings of the New Jersey Historical Society*, 2nd ser., vol. 12, no. 4 (1893): 214–15. For a recent example of a historian wondering if Green was the author, see Bernstein, "New Jersey in the American Revolution," 168.

18. Erdman, "New Jersey Constitution of 1776," 34–37; Julian P. Boyd, *Fundamental Laws and Constitutions of New Jersey, 1664–1964* (Princeton: Van Nostrand, 1964), 24–25.

19. Boyd, *Fundamental Laws and Constitutions of New Jersey*, 22–27; Erdman, "New Jersey Constitution of 1776," 34–37. For more on Sergeant, see James McLachlan, ed., *Princetonians: A Biographical Dictionary, 1748–1768* (Princeton: Princeton University Press, 1976), 407–9.

20. Erdman, "New Jersey Constitution of 1776," 40; Holt's *New-York Journal* put the constitution on p. 1 of its July 18, 1776, issue.

21. Preamble to New Jersey Constitution of 1776; I am relying on the version printed by Isaac Collins in Burlington, New Jersey, in 1776.

22. "The Interest of America, Letter II," *New-York Journal*, June 13, 1776.

23. New Jersey Constitution of 1776, Articles III and VI.

24. Ibid.; "The Interest of America, Letter II."

25. New Jersey Constitution of 1776, Article XIX.

26. Green, *Observations*, 29.

27. *Provincial Congress Journal*, July 3, 1776.

28. Ibid., July 2, 1776.

29. Ibid., July 3, 1776.

30. Ashbel Green Autobiography, 60.

31. Green Autobiography, 10:196.

32. *Provincial Congress Journal*, July 6, 1776.

33. William Livingston to Joseph Reed, July 3, 1776, 60–61, Livingston to Hugh Mercer, July 3, 1776, Azariah Dunham to Provincial Congress, July 4, 1776, 67n2, in *The Papers of William Livingston*, vol. 1, ed. Carl E. Prince (Trenton: New Jersey Historical Commission, 1979); Arthur S. Lefkowitz, *The Long Retreat: The Calamitous American Defense of New Jersey 1776* (New Brunswick: Rutgers University Press, 1999), 7–9.

34. *Provincial Congress Journal*, July 3, 1776.

35. Ashbel Green Autobiography, 55; Theodore Thayer, *Colonial and Revolutionary Morris County* (Morristown, N.J.: Compton Press, 1975), 135–37.

36. Thayer, *Colonial and Revolutionary Morris County*, 143–44.

37. Livingston to George Washington, July 4, 1776, and Washington to Livingston, July 5, 1776, *Livingston Papers*, vol. 1, 64–66.

38. Lefkowitz, *Long Retreat*, 18–19.

39. Ron Chernow, *Alexander Hamilton* (New York: Penguin, 2004), 76–77; Lefkowitz, *Long Retreat*, 6–7.

40. Chernow, *Alexander Hamilton*, 78–79; Lefkowitz, *Long Retreat*, 15–17.

41. Thomas Bradbury Chandler, *What Think Ye of the Congress Now? or, An Enquiry, How Far the Americans Are Bound to Abide by, and Execute the Decisions of, the Late Congress?* (New York, 1775); Chandler, "Memorandums, 1775–1786," Special Collections, Christoph Keller, Jr., Library, General Theological Seminary, New York; the Elizabethtown Association Resolutions are reprinted in *New Jersey in the American Revolution, 1763–1783: A Documentary History*, ed. Larry R. Gerlach (Trenton: New Jersey Historical Commission, 1975), 97–98 (helpful background information on Chandler can be found on p. 237).

## Chapter 8

1. Thomas B. Allen, *Tories: Fighting for the King in America's First Civil War* (New York: Harper, 2010), 184; also see Arthur S. Lefkowitz, *The Long Retreat: The Calamitous American Defense of New Jersey 1776* (New Brunswick: Rutgers University Press, 1999); and David McCullough, *1776* (New York: Simon & Schuster, 2005).

2. Lefkowitz, *Long Retreat*, 42–43; Ashbel Green Autobiography, 56–57.

3. Ashbel Green Autobiography, 56–57.

4. Ibid., 33–36; Charles Royster, *A Revolutionary People at War: The Continental Army and American Character, 1775–1783* (New York: W. W. Norton, 1979), 25, 97.

5. Ashbel Green Autobiography, 34; Brig. Gen. Alexander McDougall to George Washington, December 22, 1776, and George Washington to Gov. William Livingston, December 1, 1776, *The Papers of George Washington Digital Edition*, ed. Theodore J. Crackel (Charlottesville: University of Virginia Press, 2007).

6. I relied mostly on Lefkowitz, *The Long Retreat*, and McCullough, *1776*, for the details in this paragraph.

7. Thomas Paine, *The American Crisis* 2 (1776): 11.

8. Ibid.

9. December 2 and December 16, 1776, *New-York Gazette*; Theodore Thayer, *Colonial and Revolutionary Morris County* (Morristown, N.J.: Compton Press, 1975), 160; Allen, *Tories*, 193.

10. Ashbel Green Autobiography, 96.

11. Susannah Livingston to William Livingston, May 30, 1777, in *The Papers of William Livingston*, vol. 1, ed. Carl E. Prince (Trenton: New Jersey Historical Commission, 1979), 345; Thayer, *Colonial and Revolutionary Morris County*, 160–62.

12. Ashbel Green Autobiography, 82–90.

13. 1778 newspaper extracts, in *Documents Relating to the Revolutionary History of New Jersey*, 2nd ser., vol. 1, ed. William S. Stryker (Trenton, 1901), 76, 149–50; Ashbel Green Autobiography, 82; Thayer, *Colonial and Revolutionary Morris County*, 167–68.

14. For an excellent account of General Washington's position on inoculations, see Andrew M. Wehrman, "The People's Cure: A Reconsideration of General George Washington's Decision to Inoculate the Continental Army," a conference paper delivered on September 24, 2011, at Fort Ticonderoga, New York. I am grateful to the author for sharing this paper with me. It shows that Washington at first opposed inoculations and had to be talked into it by his staff.

15. Ashbel Green Autobiography, 88–89.

16. Ibid.; Joseph F. Tuttle, "Rev. Jacob Green, of Hanover, N.J., as an Author, Statesman and Patriot," *Proceedings of the New Jersey Historical Society*, 2nd ser., vol. 12, no. 4 (1893): 218–19.

17. Ashbel Green Autobiography, 81–84.

18. Ibid., 58.

19. William Livingston to George Clinton, January 15, 1777, *Papers of William Livingston*, vol. 1, 198.

20. Ashbel Green Autobiography, 33–36.

21. Ibid.

22. Ibid.

23. William Livingston to General Assembly, January 24, 1777, *Papers of William Livingston*, vol. 1, 202.

24. Ibid., February 3, 1777, 209; Green Autobiography, 10:197–98.

25. Green Autobiography, 10:198.

26. Ashbel Green Autobiography, 81–84.

27. Royster, *Revolutionary People at War*, 76–77; *New-Jersey Journal*, February 2, 1780.

28. Ashbel Green Autobiography, 89–92.

29. Ibid., 84, 89–92, 124.

30. Figures are compiled from data by Barbara Hoskins, *Men from Morris County, New Jersey, Who Served in the American Revolution* (Morristown, N.J.: Friends of the Joint Free Public Library of Morristown and Morris Township, 1979).

31. Ashbel Green Autobiography, 118.

32. Hoskins, *Men from Morris County Who Served in the American Revolution*, 80, 18. For details on Pierson's military service, see William S. Stryker, *Official Register of the Officers and Men of New Jersey in the Revolutionary War* (Trenton: Wm. T. Nicholson & Co., 1872), 51, 56, 202; also see "Calvin Green's 'Diary': The Life of Calvin Green," *New Jersey Historical Proceedings* 69 (April 1951): 117.

33. Allen, *Tories*, 189.

34. Ashbel Green Autobiography, 96–97.

35. Ibid., 98.

36. Ibid.

37. Ibid., 99–100.

38. Ibid., 102–4.

39. Ibid., 104–6.

40. Ibid.

41. Ibid.

42. Ibid., 106; Keith L. Griffin, *Revolution and Religion: American Revolutionary War and the Reformed Clergy* (New York: Paragon House, 1994), 18, 54–55.

43. Ashbel Green Autobiography, 106–7.

44. Fast-Day Sermon.

45. Ibid., 6, 8.

46. Ibid., 10.

47. Ibid., 10–12.

48. Ibid., 19.

49. Thomas Bradbury Chandler, "Memorandums, 1775–1786," and Chandler to Samuel Seabury, February 4, 1779, March 5, 1777, December 9, 1777, and June 7, 1778, Special Collections, Christoph Keller, Jr., Library, General Theological Seminary, New York.

### Chapter 9

1. Writing under the pen name "Eumenes," Green published five initial letters on the public currency. They appeared on the following dates in the *New-Jersey Journal*: Letter I, November 16, 1779; Letter II, November 16, 1779; Letter III, not extant but November 23, 1779; Letter IV, November 30, 1779; and Letter V, December 21, 1779. He followed that up with two letters on public debt for the *New-Jersey Journal* on April 5, 1780, and April 26, 1780; a final letter appeared on June 19, 1782.

2. Green Autobiography, 10:196; Ashbel Green Autobiography, 64–65, 70–73.

3. Postscript to Letter V, *New-Jersey Journal*, December 21, 1779.
4. Circular Letter to the States, January 13, 1779, *Journals of the Continental Congress*, vol. 13. All the journals are available online at http://memory.loc.gov/ammem/amlaw/lwjc.html. Also see Charles Rappleye, *Robert Morris: Financier of the American Revolution* (New York: Simon & Schuster, 2010), 107, 180–88; and Farley Grubb, "State Redemption of the Continental Dollar, 1779–90" *William and Mary Quarterly* 69 (January 2012): 147–80.
5. Circular Letter to the States, September 13, 1779, *Journals of the Continental Congress*, vol. 15; *Independent Ledger* of Massachusetts, February 21, 1780.
6. Jacob Green, Letter I, *New-Jersey Journal*, November 16, 1779.
7. Jacob Green, Letter II, *New-Jersey Journal*, November 16, 1779.
8. Letter III is not extant because the November 23, 1779, issue of the *New-Jersey Journal* has been lost, but its particulars can be gleaned from Green's other letters.
9. Jacob Green, Letter I upon Public Debts, *New-Jersey Journal*, April 5, 1780.
10. Ibid.
11. Green, Letter I on Liberty, May 3, 1780, and Letter II on Liberty, May 10, 1780, *New-Jersey Journal*.
12. Ibid.
13. December 14, 1779, *New-Jersey Journal*.
14. February 2, 1780, and March 29, 1780, *New-Jersey Journal*.
15. "A Farmer," in *Extracts from American Newspapers Relating to New Jersey*, 2nd ser., vol. 4, ed. William Nelson (Trenton: New Jersey Historical Commission, 1914), 72.
16. Postscript to Letter V, *New-Jersey Journal*, December 21, 1779; "Honestus," in *Extracts from American Newspapers Relating to New Jersey*, 2nd ser., vol. 4, ed. Nelson, 86.
17. Thomas Paine, *The Crisis Extraordinary: On the Subject of Taxation* (Philadelphia, 1780), 130–33.
18. "A True Patriot," in *Extracts from American Newspapers Relating to New Jersey*, 2nd ser., vol. 4, ed. Nelson, 282–84.
19. March 18, 1780, *Journals of the Continental Congress*, vol. 16; Rappleye, *Robert Morris*, 211–13.
20. Green Autobiography, 10:197; Ashbel Green Autobiography, 70–73; "Unshaken," in *Extracts from American Newspapers Relating to New Jersey*, 2nd ser., vol. 4, ed. Nelson, 258.
21. The three essays in the *New-Jersey Journal* were April 5, 1780, April 26, 1780, and June 19, 1782.
22. Eumenes, April 5 and 26, 1780, in *New-Jersey Journal*.
23. Mary R. Murrin, *To Save This State from Ruin: New Jersey and the Creation of the United States Constitution, 1776–1789* (Trenton: New Jersey Historical Commission, 1987), 30–33, 45–50.
24. June 19, 1782, *New-Jersey Journal*.
25. 1768 Address; Green Autobiography, 10:196. Pierson is listed on p. 6 in David Mitros, *Slave Records of Morris County, New Jersey, 1756–1841*, 2nd ed. (Morris County, N.J.: Morris County Heritage Commission, 2002); according to a 1771 estate inventory, he had "One Negro Boy" worth 10.7.6 pounds.
26. Jacob Green, *Observations on the Reconciliation of Great-Britain, and the Colonies, in Which Are Exhibited Arguments For, and Against, That Measure* (Philadelphia, 1776), 29.
27. Fast-Day Sermon, 12–13.
28. Ibid., 14–18.
29. Ibid.; George M. Marsden, *Jonathan Edwards: A Life* (New Haven: Yale University Press, 2003), 256–57. For more on the activities of the New Divinity, see Joseph A. Conforti, *Samuel Hopkins and the New Divinity Movement* (Grand Rapids: Christian University Press, 1981); Mark R. Valeri, *Law and Providence in Joseph Bellamy's New England: The Origins of the New Divinity in Revolutionary America* (New York: Oxford University Press, 1994); Valeri, "The New Divinity and the American Revolution," *William and Mary Quarterly* 46 (October 1989): 741–69; and William

Breitenbach, "The Consistent Calvinism of the New Divinity Movement," *William and Mary Quarterly* 41 (April 1984): 241–64.

30. Fast-Day Sermon, 16–17, 23.

31. Ibid., 16–17.

32. Ibid., 19–22.

33. Ibid., 12–17, 23.

34. John Cooper, *New-Jersey Gazette*, September 20, 1780. For more on Cooper, see Larry R. Gerlach, ed., *New Jersey in the American Revolution, 1763–1783: A Documentary History* (Trenton: New Jersey Historical Commission, 1975), 437–38. For more on the abolition movement in New Jersey, see Jonathan D. Sassi, "The Antislavery Challenge in New Jersey," a Society for Historians of the Early American Republic conference paper presented on July 17, 2011, in Philadelphia; and Arthur Zilversmit, *The First Emancipation: The Abolition of Slavery in the North* (Chicago: University of Chicago Press, 1967). For a recent treatment of the abolition movement in the young nation, see John Craig Hammond and Matthew Mason, eds., *Contesting Slavery: The Politics of Bondage and Freedom in the New Nation* (Charlottesville: University of Virginia Press, 2011).

35. *Journal of the Proceedings of the Legislative Council of the State of New Jersey, October 24, 1780–January 9, 1781* (Trenton, 1781), 57; *Votes and Proceedings, September 13–October 7, 1780* (Trenton, 1780), 262; November 4–10, 1780, 20–21; November 11–17, 1780, 27.

36. Mitros, *Slave Records of Morris County*, 1–2; William Livingston to Samuel Allinson, July 25, 1778, in *The Papers of William Livingston*, vol. 2, ed. Carl E. Prince and Dennis P. Ryan (Trenton: New Jersey Historical Commission, 1980), 403. For an example of a locality passing a statute disarming blacks, see minutes of the Shrewsbury Township Committee, reprinted in *New Jersey in the American Revolution*, ed. Gerlach, 149.

37. Green Autobiography, 10:197. Population figures in table 3 are from R. C. Simmons, *The American Colonies: From Settlement to Independence* (New York: W. W. Norton, 1981), 175; Theodore Thayer, *Colonial and Revolutionary Morris County* (Morristown, N.J.: Compton Press, 1975), 217. Slaveholding figures are derived from Mitros, *Slave Records of Morris County*, esp. Appendix B, p. 112; Ashbel Green Autobiography, 37–43.

38. Green Autobiography, 10:197.

39. December 27, 1780, *New-Jersey Journal*.

40. Ibid.

41. Eumenes, January 10, 1781, *New-Jersey Journal*.

42. Marcus Aurelius, January 17 and 24, 1781, *New-Jersey Journal*.

43. Eumenes, January 24 and 31, 1781, *New-Jersey Journal*.

44. *Church Members, Marriages and Baptisms at Hanover, Morris Co., N.J., during the Pastorate of Rev. Jacob Green and to the Settlement of Rev. Aaron Condit, 1746–1796* (Morristown, N.J.: The Jerseyman, 1893), 24, 25, 6. Quote is from Rules Adopted for the Regulation of Families, September 26, 1782, reprinted in Oliver W. Chapin, *A History of the First Presbyterian Church of Hanover, 1718–1968: 250 Years of Christian Service* (Hanover, N.J.: First Presbyterian Church, 1968), 82. Also see David Mitros, *Jacob Green and the Slavery Debate in Revolutionary Morris County, New Jersey* (Morris County, N.J.: Morris County Heritage Commission, 1993), 22–23.

45. Leonard J. Trinterud, *The Forming of an American Tradition: A Re-examination of Colonial Presbyterianism* (New York: Books for Libraries Press, 1949), 272–73, 207–8. Also see "Presbyterians and the American Revolution: A Documentary Account," *Journal of Presbyterian History* 52, no. 4 (1974).

46. Thomas Bradbury Chandler, "Memorandums, 1775–1786," and Chandler to Samuel Seabury, May 16, 1777, and August 5, 1782, Special Collections, Christoph Keller, Jr., Library, General Theological Seminary, New York.

*Chapter 10*

1. Jacob Green to New York Presbytery, October 18, 1779, CO257, Box 11, Folder 7, Ashbel Green Papers 3A, Princeton University; the pamphlet was titled *A View of a Christian Church, and Church Government; Containing Many Interesting Matters; with an Address to Our Congregations, and an Appendix, Representing the Case and Circumstances of the Associated Presbytery of Morris County* (Chatham, N.J., 1781), hereafter referred to as *View of a Christian Church*. It was published under the authorship of the Associated Presbytery of Morris County, but it is my firm belief that Green was the main author, as well as the inspiration behind the tract. Green founded the presbytery, and its ideals were his. The tract reflected his views and mimicked his writing style.

2. Green to New York Presbytery, October 18, 1779.

3. Ibid.

4. May 3, 1780, Statement, in *View of a Christian Church*, 49–56.

5. Robert F. Scholz, "Clerical Consociation in Massachusetts Bay: Reassessing the New England Way and its Origins," *William and Mary Quarterly* 29 (July 1972): 397. The literature on the New England Way is vast; studies of individual towns are good starting points, as is Harry S. Stout, *The New England Soul: Preaching and Religious Culture in Colonial New England* (Oxford: Oxford University Press, 1986).

6. *Minutes of the Convention of Delegates from the Synod of New York and Philadelphia, and from the Associations of Connecticut; Held Annually from 1766 to 1775, Inclusive* (Hartford, Conn.: E. Gleason, 1843), 6, 10, 20–23.

7. The letter announcing their withdrawal is in the Appendix of *View of a Christian Church*, 49–56. For more on the new presbytery, also see E. H. Gillett, *History of the Presbyterian Church in the United States of America*, vol. 1 (Philadelphia: Presbyterian Publication Committee, 1864), 210–12. The date of the Bradford-Green marriage was April 4, 1776, and is listed in *Church Members, Marriages and Baptisms at Hanover, Morris Co., N.J., during the Pastorate of Rev. Jacob Green and to the Settlement of Rev. Aaron Condit, 1746–1796* (Morristown, N.J.: The Jerseyman, 1893), 15. For more on Bradford, see Samuel L. Tuttle, *A History of the Presbyterian Church, Madison, N.J.* (New York: M. W. Dodd, 1855), 30–33. For more on Amzi Lewis, see William B. Sprague, *Annals of the American Pulpit; or, Commemorative Notices of Distinguished American Clergymen of Various Denominations*, vol. 4 (New York: Robert Carter & Brothers, 1858), 155; and E. M. Ruttenber and L. H. Clark, *History of Orange County, New York* (Philadelphia: Everts & Peck, 1881), 583–84. And for more on Joseph Grover, see James H. Hotchkin, *A History of the Purchase and Settlement of Western New York, and of the Rise, Progress, and Present State of the Presbyterian Church in That Section* (New York: M. W. Dodd, 1848), 33–34; and *A Brief History of the [Presbyterian] Church at Rockaway, New Jersey* (Newark, N.J.: Uzal J. Tuttle & Co., 1833), 5.

8. Grover's letter was mixed in with Green's October 18 letter to the New York Presbytery in CO257, Box 11, Folder 7, Ashbel Green Papers 3A.

9. Green to New York Presbytery, October 18, 1779; quotes from the second letter can be found in *View of a Christian Church*, 57–62.

10. *Minutes of the Convention of Delegates from the Synod of New York and Philadelphia*, 482, 490; *View of a Christian Church*, 47. Green's attendance record was derived from synodal minutes. The only years he attended were 1747, 1748, 1754, 1755, and 1759.

11. *View of a Christian Church*, 26–29.

12. Ibid.

13. Green to New York Presbytery, October 18, 1779; *View of a Christian Church*, 47–48.

14. Thomas Bradbury Chandler, *The Friendly Address to All Reasonable Americans on the Subject of Our Political Confusions* (New York, 1774), 51; Tyndale is quoted in Keith L. Griffin, *Revolution and Religion: American Revolutionary War and the Reformed Clergy* (New York: Paragon House,

1994), 3; Nancy L. Rhoden, *Revolutionary Anglicanism: The Colonial Church of England Clergy during the American Revolution* (New York: New York University Press, 1999), 64–70. Also see Gordon S. Wood, *The Radicalism of the American Revolution* (New York: Vintage Books, 1991).

15. Rhoden, *Revolutionary Anglicanism*, 68–69; Griffin, *Revolution and Religion*, 2–4; Leonard J. Trinterud, *The Forming of an American Tradition: A Re-examination of Colonial Presbyterianism* (New York: Books for Libraries Press, 1949), 16–20.

16. May 3, 1780, Statement, in *View of a Christian Church*, 50–51.

17. Ibid., 55–56.

18. Ibid.

19. For background on the Presbyterian Church's problems in the 1780s, see Trinterud, *Forming of an American Tradition*, 258–66. Also see Jon Butler, Grant Wacker, and Randall Balmer, *Religion in American Life: A Short History* (New York: Oxford University Press, 2011), 141.

20. *View of a Christian Church*, 61.

21. The 1775 letter is reprinted in Mark A. Noll, "Jacob Green's Proposal for Seminaries," *Journal of Presbyterian History*, 58 (1980): 218.

22. Jacob Green, *A Vision of Hell, and a Discovery of some of the Consultations and Devices there, in the Year 1767* (Boston, 1773), 6–7.

23. Howard Miller, *The Revolutionary College: American Presbyterian Higher Education, 1707–1837* (New York: New York University Press, 1976), 61–66.

24. Ibid., 66–67; also see Mark A. Noll, *Princeton and the Republic, 1768–1822* (Vancouver: Regent College Publishing, 1989).

25. 1775 letter in Noll, "Jacob Green's Proposal for Seminaries," 219; also see Joseph A. Conforti, *Samuel Hopkins and the New Divinity Movement* (Grand Rapids: Christian University Press, 1981), 186–87.

26. 1775 letter in Noll, "Jacob Green's Proposal for Seminaries," 219–20; Green notation is in an unpublished notebook, CO257, Box 11, Folder 5, Ashbel Green Papers. The notation is undated; the first few pages are missing and presumably contained a title page, but I suspect the document is from the 1750s during Green's study phase.

27. Green Notation, CO257, Box 11, Folder 5, Ashbel Green Papers 3A.

28. Thomas Bradbury Chandler, *An Appeal to the Public in Behalf of the Church of England in America* (New York, 1766), 8–17.

29. Trinterud, *Forming of an American Tradition*, 266–67.

30. Jeffry H. Morrison, *John Witherspoon and the Founding of the American Republic* (Notre Dame: University of Notre Dame Press, 2005), 5, 106–10; Trinterud, *Forming of an American Tradition*, 298–99; Noll, *Princeton and the Republic*, 89–90.

31. *A Brief Account of the Associated Presbyteries; and a General View of Their Sentiments Concerning Religion and Ecclesiastical Order: By a Convention of Said Prespyteries* [sic] (Catskill, N.Y., 1796), 11–15.

32. Ibid., 13–15.

33. Ibid.; Charles E. Knox, *Origin and Annals of the "Old Church on the Green": The First Presbyterian Church of Bloomfield* (Bloomfield, N.Y.: S. Morris Hulin, 1901), 25–27; Gillett, *History of the Presbyterian Church*, 213–17; Hotchkin, *History of the Purchase and Settlement of Western New York*, 33–34. Details on Green and Silas Constant are from Josiah Granville Leach, ed., *The Journal of the Reverend Silas Constant, Pastor of the Presbyterian Church at Yorktown, New York* (Philadelphia: J. B. Lippincott, 1903), xi–xiii, and entries of May 29 and 30, 1783; November 25, 1783; May 25–26, 1784; October 1, 1784; February 14, 1785; May 29 and 30, 1785; August 18, 1785; October 25, 1785; December 16, 1785; November 1, 1786; June 29, 1787; and June 5, 1788.

34. Green Autobiography, 10:196.

35. Parish Book 3, January 22, 1783. Quote from New York Presbytery can be found in Oliver W. Chapin, *A History of the First Presbyterian Church of Hanover, 1718–1968: 250 Years of Christian Service* (Hanover, N.J.: First Presbyterian Church, 1968), Appendix F, p. 83. Ashbel also disagreed with his father on this issue. In his account of the associated presbytery, Ashbel noted that "[I] differ on the subject of church government, from the opinions adopted by our venerated parent and his associates." Green Autobiography, 10:196.

36. Nathan O. Hatch, *The Democratization of American Christianity* (New Haven: Yale University Press, 1989), 3–11, 37–44.

37. Thomas Bradbury Chandler to Samuel Seabury, June 7, 1778, December 4, 1780, August 5, 1782, March 15, 1783, and July 28, 1785, and Chandler, "Memorandums, 1775–1786," Special Collections, Christoph Keller, Jr., Library, General Theological Seminary, New York.

## Chapter 11

1. "Calvin Green's 'Diary': The Life of Calvin Green," *New Jersey Historical Proceedings* 69 (April 1951): 117. For a nice description of this difficult winter of 1780, see chap. 12, "The 'Hard Winter,'" in Donald Wallace White, *A Village at War: Chatham, New Jersey, and the American Revolution* (Madison: Fairleigh Dickinson University Press, 1979).

2. Fast-Day Sermon. The session meeting was described in the minutes of a January 31, 1782, meeting in *Minutes of Church Meetings and Church Sessions, Discipline, and Other Matters of Record, 1769–1814*, Book 4; Green Autobiography, 10:53–54.

3. Oliver W. Chapin, *A History of the First Presbyterian Church of Hanover, 1718–1968: 250 Years of Christian Service* (Hanover, N.J.: First Presbyterian Church, 1968), Appendix G, p. 84.

4. Ibid.

5. Jacob Green, "An Humble Attempt Truly to State the Controversy Concerning Qualifications for Sacraments and to Inquire Where the Truth Lies," 103, 104.

6. Ibid., 105.

7. Ibid., 107.

8. The rules are reprinted in Chapin, *History of the First Presbyterian Church of Hanover*, Appendix C, p. 78.

9. Ibid.

10. Ibid., Appendix E, pp. 80–81.

11. Ibid.

12. Ibid.

13. Ibid., 80–82, for quote from Hanover agreement. For more on the Moravian Brotherly Agreements, see S. Scott Rohrer, *Hope's Promise: Religion and Acculturation in the Southern Backcountry* (Tuscaloosa: University of Alabama Press, 2005), chap. 2.

14. Catechumens, July 3, 1783, in Chapin, *History of the First Presbyterian Church of Hanover*, Appendix D, pp. 79–80.

15. Minutes of April 4, 1782, May 3, 1782, June 13 and 27, 1782, and July 25, 1782, in *Minutes of Church Meetings and Church Sessions, Discipline, and Other Matters of Record, 1769–1814*, Book 4.

16. Formula for the reception of members, 1782, in Chapin, *History of the First Presbyterian Church of Hanover*, Appendix H, pp. 85–86.

17. Sermon delivered in 1765, no specific day given; in CO257, Box 11, Folder 1, Ashbel Green Papers 3A.

18. CO257, Box 11, Folder 1, Ashbel Green Papers 3A.

19. The first page of the sermon is missing but apparently was delivered in 1778; CO257, Box 11, Folder 1, Ashbel Green Papers 3A. Green rarely used martial imagery in his sermons. An exception

was a sermon he delivered in 1768, when he stressed that congregation members must "put on the whole Armor of God." Those without faith, he said, are like soldiers without armor: "How would it look for a Company of Soldiers to go into the Field to engage an Enemy without [armor]—none [would be able to] ever stand against the wiles of the Devil." This sermon is also in Folder 1.

20. CO257, Box 11, Folder 6, Ashbel Green Papers 3A.

21. Ibid.

22. Sermon, July 10, 1768, Parsippany, New Jersey, CO257, Box 11, Folder 1, Ashbel Green Papers 3A. For a fascinating look at republican thought and millennialism in New England, see Nathan O. Hatch, *The Sacred Cause of Liberty: Republican Thought and the Millennium in Revolutionary New England* (New Haven: Yale University Press, 1977).

23. Sermon by the Reverend Judith Fulp-Eickstaedt, Trinity Presbyterian Church, Arlington, Virginia, May 27, 2012; Diarmaid MacCulloch, *Christianity: The First Three Thousand Years* (New York: Viking, 2009), 97–99.

24. Quote from modern sermon is from the Reverend Bill Davnie, "Breaking Up the Tribes," delivered to Trinity Presbyterian Church in Arlington, Virginia, January 30, 2011.

25. Yet another paradox of Calvinism that bedeviled its defenders was a series of tough questions: if God preordains who is saved, what role does Jesus play in salvation? If a reprobate turns to Christ, can she be saved? And, conversely, if God preordains that an individual is saved, but this person turns his back on Jesus, will he be damned? Critics pointed out that Calvinism seemed to be saying that Jesus performs his saving grace for only a select few. Calvinists in the early modern period did not agree on the answers to these difficult questions; some did, in fact, argue that the doctrine of predestination meant that Jesus played little or no role in salvation. Most hedged, though. Green himself did not directly deal with this conundrum in his writings, but his sermons all said that Jesus was essential to salvation, and that the seeker had to show she was a believer if she was to demonstrate she was of the elect.

26. Sermon delivered in 1786, no specific day given; in CO257, Box 11, Folder 1, Ashbel Green Papers 3A.

27. Undated sermon, but postwar, Folder 5; undated sermon, but postwar, Folder 6, both in CO257, Ashbel Green Papers 3A.

28. The series on Acts can be found in CO257, Box 11, Folder 3, Ashbel Green Papers 3A.

29. CO257, Box 11, Folder 4, Ashbel Green Papers 3A.

30. Ibid.

31. Ibid.

32. Ibid. Green gave this sermon four times—the first in 1765 at Campfields; he did give it once after the war, in 1788. He delivered the new birth sermon in five different places in 1789, including David Tuttle's in October and Moses Crane's in August. CO257, Box 11, Folder 3, Ashbel Green Papers 3A.

33. Green Autobiography, 10:52–53n; also see Ashbel Green Autobiography, 198. Membership figures are from *in Church Members, Marriages and Baptisms at Hanover, Morris Co., N.J., during the Pastorate of Rev. Jacob Green and to the Settlement of Rev. Aaron Condit, 1746–1796* (Morristown, N.J.: The Jerseyman, 1893), 5–9. The records show that a total of forty-six persons joined on June 20, July 4, and August 29, 1790.

34. Green Autobiography, 10:53; Thomas S. Kidd, *God of Liberty: A Religious History of the American Revolution* (New York: Basic Books, 2010), chap. 10.

35. Green Autobiography, 10:199.

36. Thomas Bradbury Chandler to Samuel Seabury, June 7, 1778, December 4, 1780, August 5, 1782, March 15, 1783, and July 28, 1785, and Chandler, "Memorandums, 1775–1786," Special Collections, Christoph Keller, Jr., Library, General Theological Seminary, New York; Peter M. Doll, *Revolution, Religion, and National Identity: Imperial Anglicanism in British North America, 1745–1795* (Madison: Fairleigh Dickinson University Press, 2000).

## Epilogue

1. Green Autobiography, 10:198–99; Ashbel Green Autobiography, 198–201.

2. William B. Sprague, *Annals of the American Pulpit; or, Commemorative Notices of Distinguished American Clergymen of Various Denominations*, vol. 5 (New York: Robert Carter & Brothers, 1861), 137–42.

3. For a good study that shows how evangelism became more mainstream as the nineteenth century progressed, see Christine Leigh Heyrman, *Southern Cross: The Beginnings of the Bible Belt* (New York: Alfred A. Knopf, 1997). Also see Stephen L. Longenecker, *Shenandoah Religion: Outsiders and the Mainstream, 1716–1865* (Waco: Baylor University Press, 2002); and Anne C. Loveland, *Southern Evangelicals and the Social Order, 1800–1860* (Baton Rouge: Louisiana State University Press, 1980).

4. For more on the activities of the New Divinity, see Joseph A. Conforti, *Samuel Hopkins and the New Divinity Movement* (Grand Rapids: Christian University Press, 1981); Mark R. Valeri, *Law and Providence in Joseph Bellamy's New England: The Origins of the New Divinity in Revolutionary America* (New York: Oxford University Press, 1994); Valeri, "The New Divinity and the American Revolution," *William and Mary Quarterly* 46 (October 1989): 741–69; and William Breitenbach, "The Consistent Calvinism of the New Divinity Movement," *William and Mary Quarterly* 41 (April 1984): 241–64.

5. Good accounts of Protestantism, evangelicalism, and reform in the antebellum period include Robert H. Abzug, *Cosmos Crumbling: American Reform and the Religious Imagination* (New York: Oxford University Press, 1994); Paul E. Johnson, *A Shopkeeper's Millennium: Society and Revivals in Rochester, New York, 1815–1837* (New York: Hill and Wang, 1978); John B. Boles, *The Great Revival: Beginnings of the Bible Belt* (Lexington: University Press of Kentucky, 1996); Timothy L. Smith, *Revivalism and Social Reform: American Protestantism on the Eve of the Civil War* (Baltimore: Johns Hopkins University Press, 1980); and Richard J. Carwardine, *Evangelicals and Politics in Antebellum America* (New Haven: Yale University Press, 1993).

6. The documentation on Ashbel Green's life is fairly extensive; his papers are kept at Princeton University. Good treatments of his life are Ashbel Green Autobiography; "Sketch of Ashbel Green," in Richard A. Harrison, *Princetonians: A Biographical Dictionary, 1776–1783* (Princeton: Princeton University Press, 1983), 404–20; and Mark A. Noll, *Princeton and the Republic, 1768–1822* (Vancouver: Regent College Publishing, 1989).

7. Ashbel summed up Witherspoon's influence by saying, "To Dr. Witherspoon, more than to any other human being, I am indebted for whatever of influence or success has attended me in life." Ashbel Green Autobiography, 146.

8. Noll, *Princeton and the Republic*, 258–70; "Sketch of Ashbel Green," in Harrison, *Princetonians*, 409–11.

9. Noll, *Princeton and the Republic*, 258–62.

10. Ashbel Green Autobiography, 322–28.

11. Ibid. For more on Presbyterianism, education, and voluntarism, see Howard Miller, *The Revolutionary College: American Presbyterian Higher Education, 1707–1837* (New York: New York University Press, 1976), 218–21; and Lois W. Banner, "Presbyterians and Voluntarism in the Early Republic," *Journal of Presbyterian History* 50 (1972): 187–205. For more on broader reform in this and later periods, see Michael Kazin, *American Dreamers: How the Left Changed a Nation* (New York: Alfred A. Knopf, 2011); and Craig Calhoun, *The Roots of Radicalism: Tradition, the Public Sphere, and Early Nineteenth-Century Social Movements* (Chicago: University of Chicago Press, 2012).

12. Ashbel Green, *A Discourse, Delivered at the Opening for Public Worship, of the Presbyterian Church, in the Northern Liberties of Philadelphia . . .* (Philadelphia, 1805), 19; also see Noll, *Princeton and the Republic*, 256.

13. Nice summaries of these groups can be found in Jon Butler, Grant Wacker, and Randall Balmer, *Religion in American Life: A Short History* (Oxford: Oxford University Press, 2011). For more on utopians, see Donald E. Pitzer, ed., *America's Communal Utopias* (Chapel Hill: University of North Carolina Press, 1997); Richard Lyman Bushman and Claudia Lauper Bushman, *Building the Kingdom: A History of Mormons in America* (New York: Oxford University Press, 2001); and Robert S. Fogarty, *All Things New: American Communes and Utopian Movements, 1860–1914* (Chicago: University of Chicago Press, 1990).

14. The literature on Mormonism is extensive; a good starting point for understanding the movement's beliefs is John L. Brooke, *The Refiner's Fire: The Making of Mormon Cosmology, 1644–1844* (Cambridge: Cambridge University Press, 1994).

15. For a look at ways that the conversion experience contributed to both migration and reform, see S. Scott Rohrer, *Wandering Souls: Protestant Migrations in America, 1630–1865* (Chapel Hill: University of North Carolina Press, 2010).

16. Probably the best account of the bishop's cause in the 1780s is Peter M. Doll, *Revolution, Religion, and National Identity: Imperial Anglicanism in British North America, 1745–1795* (Madison: Fairleigh Dickinson University Press, 2000). For an overview of the American Episcopal Church in the new republic, see Edwin Scott Gaustad and Philip L. Barlow, *New Historical Atlas of Religion in America* (New York: Oxford University Press, 2001).

# Index